Nuevos amigos

HBJ
Foreign Language Programs

SPANISH

- **Nuevos amigos**
  Level 1

- **Nosotros, los jóvenes**
  Level 2

- **Nuestro mundo**
  Level 3

Nuevos amigos

 HARCOURT BRACE JOVANOVICH, PUBLISHERS

Orlando   San Diego   Chicago   Dallas

Printed in the United States of America
ISBN 0-15-388300-6

PHOTO CREDITS   Key: (t) top, (b) bottom, (l) left, (r) right, (c) center
COVER: HBJ Photo/Peter Menzel
TABLE OF CONTENTS, page vi(t), HBJ Photo/Bob Daemmrich; vi(tc), HBJ Photo/David Phillips; vi(cl), HBJ Photo/Daniel Aubry; vi(c), HBJ Photo; vi(cr), HBJ Photo/David

Continued on page 392

Writers

José B. Fernández
University of Central Florida
Orlando, FL

Nancy Ann Humbach
Finneytown High School
Cincinnatti, OH

María J. Cazabon
Florida International University
Miami, FL

Douglas Morgenstern
Massachusetts Institute of Technology
Cambridge, MA

Editorial Advisors

Robert L. Baker
Middlebury College
Middlebury, VT

Pat Barr-Harrison
Prince George's County Public
  Schools
Landover, MD

Ann Beusch
Hood College
Frederick, MD

Nunzio D. Cazzetta
Smithtown High School West
Smithtown, NY

Charles R. Hancock
Ohio State University
Columbus, OH

William Jassey
Norwalk Board of Education
Norwalk, CT

Dora Kennedy
Prince George's County
  Schools
Landover, MD

Ilonka Schmidt Mackey
Université Laval
Québec, Canada

Jack Thayer
Rolling Hills High School
Rolling Hills Estates, CA

Eduardo Zayas-Bazán
East Tennessee State
  University
Johnson City, TN

Consultants and Reviewers

Gladys Acosta Toia
Edison High School
Fairfax, VA

Nicholas Aversa
Great Neck Middle School
  South
Great Neck, NY

Larraine Gandolfi
Lincoln Sudbury Regional
  High School
Sudbury, MA

Carola Lago
Robert E. Lee High School
Springfield, VA

Adriana M. Mills
Klein High School
Klein, TX

Henry Shatz
Smithtown High School East
St. James, NY

Fern Weiland
Rockville, MD

Henry P. Ziegler
Princeton High School
Cincinnati, OH

Field Test Teachers

Phoebe Ruiz-Badeer
Accompsett Intermediate
  School
Smithtown, NY

Lynn Belardo
Roton Middle School
Norwalk, CT

William Miles
Good Counsel High School
Wheaton, MD

Jo-Ann Sbrizzi
Brian McMahon High School
South Norwalk, CT

Lorna K. Shapiro
Bartram Motivation Center
Philadelphia, PA

Greg Schepanski
Smithtown High School East
St. James, NY

Clifford Taggart
The Gilman School, Inc.
Baltimore, MD

Bonnie Walters
Frederick High School
Frederick, MD

Matilde Yorkshire
Staten Island Academy
Staten Island, NY

v

ACKNOWLEDGMENTS

We wish to express our thanks to the students pictured in this textbook and to the parents who allowed us to photograph these young people in their homes and in other places. We also thank the teachers and the families who helped us find these young people; the school administrators who allowed us to photograph the students in their schools; and the merchants who permitted us to photograph the students in their stores and other places of business.

YOUNG PEOPLE

María Aguila, Elizabeth Alejo, Samuel Fontaner, Domingo García, Mabel Greve, Manuel Hernández, Faby Herrera, Carla Herrera, Nathan Hughes, José Limón, Ernesto López, Gustavo Martínez, Germán Mastrángelo, José Luis Mayo, Alicia Mitterer, Julio Morales, Robin Schmidt, Elaine Vazquez, Peter Villa, Claudia Villegas, Gerardo Zendejas, Mauricio Zendejas, Xochitl Zendejas

TEACHERS AND FAMILIES

Nilsa Acevedo, Consuelo Bonilla, María Evelyn Borrero, Clara Fontaner, Erika Hampton, Nancy Limón, María Morales, Juanita Velázquez, Norma Villegas, Marta y Javier Zendejas

CONTENTS

PRIMERA PARTE

COMMUNICATIVE FUNCTIONS	GRAMMAR	CULTURE
Socializing • Asking how someone is • Saying how you are • Saying hello and goodbye	Spanish equivalents for the word you (**tú, usted**)	Greeting and meeting people
Exchanging information • Asking and giving names • Asking and giving someone else's name	Gender of nouns and the definite article	Common Spanish first names Spanish nicknames
Exchanging information • Asking and saying where people are from	Subject pronouns and the verb **ser** Interrogative sentences	Map of the Spanish-speaking world Spanish-speaking population
Recombining communicative functions, vocabulary, and grammar		Writing postcards in Spanish to a pen pal
Reading for practice and pleasure		Places throughout the world where Spanish is spoken

COMMUNICATIVE FUNCTIONS	GRAMMAR	CULTURE
Exchanging information • Asking for and giving an explanation	The verb **venir** Two uses of **no**	How students get to school in Spanish-speaking countries
Expressing attitudes and points of view • Asking about classes and giving your opinion	Numbers from 0 to 20 The days of the week The verb **tener** Telling time	The school system in the Spanish-speaking countries Grading system in the Spanish-speaking world
Exchanging information • Asking how much something costs and giving the price	Forming plurals Definite and indefinite articles Numbers from 21 to 100	Classroom practices in the Spanish-speaking world
Recombining communicative functions, vocabulary, and grammar		A Spanish-speaking student's appointment book A report card from Venezuela
Reading for practice and pleasure		Textbooks in Spanish What young people like to read

COMMUNICATIVE FUNCTIONS	GRAMMAR	CULTURE
Expressing feelings and emotion • Talking about what you and others like and don't like	The verb **gustar**	Popular sports in Spanish-speaking countries
Exchanging information • Expressing what you need in order to do something	The present tense of **-ar** verbs The verb **jugar**	World Cup soccer championships
Exchanging information • Saying when and how often you play • Talking about the seasons and the weather	Word order The verb **hacer** in weather expressions	Seasons in the world's two hemispheres
Recombining communicative functions, vocabulary, and grammar		Students talk about their likes and dislikes concerning sports and pastimes
Reading for practice and pleasure		A Spanish television broadcast of a New York marathon
Reviewing communicative functions, vocabulary, and grammar		Leisure activities in Colombia

SEGUNDA PARTE

BASIC MATERIAL

COMMUNICATIVE FUNCTIONS	GRAMMAR	CULTURE
Exchanging information • Asking and saying where something is • Asking and giving directions	Possessive adjectives The verb **estar** The contraction **del**	Airports in Spanish-speaking countries
Exchanging information • Asking and saying where people are going **Socializing** • Answering the telephone, calling someone	The verb **ir** The contraction **al**	Notes on Spanish history Tourism in Spain Talking on the telephone
Exchanging information • Asking and saying the purpose of an action **Persuading** • Making suggestions	Verb endings in **-er** and **-ir**	Barajas Airport in Madrid The city of León
Recombining communicative functions, vocabulary, and grammar		A visit from Mexican friends
Reading for practice and pleasure		Six major cities in Spain

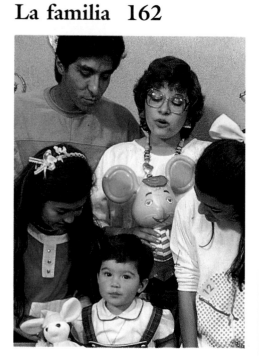

COMMUNICATIVE FUNCTIONS	GRAMMAR	CULTURE
Socializing • Making someone feel at home • Graciously accepting hospitality	The verb **querer**	Being a guest in a Spanish-speaking home Family life in Spanish-speaking homes
Exchanging information • Talking about age • Describing people and family relationships • Asking what someone or something is like **Expressing feelings and emotion** • Exclaiming	Descriptive adjectives: position and agreement	Spanish surnames The family in the Spanish-speaking world
Expressing attitudes and points of view • Asking for opinions and paying compliments	More possessive adjectives	Inside a Spanish-speaking home Houses in Spanish-speaking countries
Recombining communicative functions, vocabulary, and grammar		A family gathering in Mexico
Reading for practice and pleasure		Real estate ads in Spanish

	BASIC MATERIAL

COMMUNICATIVE FUNCTIONS	GRAMMAR	CULTURE
Socializing • Accepting and turning down invitations • Expressing regret **Expressing obligation** • Using **tener que**	The verb **poder** The verbs **salir** and **decir**	Where Spanish-speaking students go and what they do when going out
Expressing attitudes and points of view • Expressing intention • Expressing opinions **Persuading** • Making suggestions	Expressing future time Adjectives, adjective phrases, and deletion of nouns The verbs **pensar** and **empezar**	Going to the movies Film festival in Mar del Plata
Socializing • Getting someone's attention; interrupting politely • Asking information	The verb **saber** Direct objects and the personal **a** The verb **conocer**	Pop music concerts in Buenos Aires
Recombining communicative functions, vocabulary, and grammar		Writing an article for a Spanish magazine
Reading for practice and pleasure		Movie ads in a Spanish newspaper
Reviewing communicative functions, vocabulary, and grammar		A visitor from Costa Rica A letter from Costa Rica

TERCERA PARTE

BASIC MATERIAL

COMMUNICATIVE FUNCTIONS	GRAMMAR	CULTURE
Expressing attitudes and points of view • Saying what you like and don't like	The verb **gustar**	Eating at a restaurant Getting together at a cafe Different dishes served in Spanish-speaking countries
Expressing attitudes and points of view • Talking about food • Selecting what you like	The verb **hacer** Demonstrative adjectives	The metric system Two dishes with the same name
Expressing attitudes and points of view • Talking about whether people are hungry or thirsty • Expressing your enjoyment of food	The verb **poner**	The history of chocolate
Recombining communicative functions, vocabulary, and grammar		Where to go with your friends before the movies
Reading for practice and pleasure		A recipe for a Spanish dish

COMMUNICATIVE FUNCTIONS	GRAMMAR	CULTURE
Exchanging information •Saying what you usually do •Saying what you did at a specified time in the past •Expressing how long ago something happened	The preterit of regular **-ar** verbs	Spain's capital city Spain's second largest city
Exchanging information •Asking for information about something that happened in the past	The preterit of **hacer** The preterit of **ir**	Madrid's attractions
Exchanging information •Discussing whether or not something has already been done	Direct-object pronouns	A trip to Granada The Moorish legacy Two famous landmarks in Madrid
Recombining communicative functions, vocabulary, and grammar		Postcards from Madrid
Reading for practice and pleasure		A Spanish travel brochure

	BASIC MATERIAL

FOR REFERENCE

MAPS

GETTING TO KNOW YOUR TEXTBOOK

¡BIENVENIDOS!

Some of us are fortunate to be able to learn a new language by living in another country, but most of us are not. We begin learning the language and getting acquainted with a foreign culture in a classroom with the help of a teacher and a book. Your book can be a reliable guide if you know how to use it effectively. The following pages will help you get to know this book, **Nuevos amigos** (New Friends), and its various features.

INTRODUCTORY UNIT

Who speaks Spanish? Where is Spanish spoken? Where did the language come from? Why should I learn it? How can I learn it well? You'll find the answers to these questions in English, illustrated with colorful photographs, in the Introduction, which begins on page 1.

INTRODUCTION
Spanish and You

Welcome to the Spanish-speaking world! Today you are embarking on a new journey—the exploration and learning of Spanish. This trip will take you to many lands, where you will meet different people. The route you will take is the Spanish language; the destination is an understanding of how speakers of Spanish think, behave, and interact with others. You will discover their values, history, and traditions. Are you ready to start your trip?

Let's go!   ¡Vamos!

In this introduction you will learn:

1 where Spanish is spoken around the world

2 how Spanish and English are related

3 about Spanish-speaking areas in the United States

4 about Spanish and your leisure time activities—hobbies, sports, travel

5 about the knowledge of Spanish and your future career

6 suggestions for studying Spanish

1

PRIMERA PARTE

PART OPENER

There are twelve units in Nuevos amigos, which are grouped in three parts. Each part contains three units and a review unit based on them. At the beginning of each part, you'll see an illustrated table of contents like the one shown here. It will give you the number, title, and opening page of each unit (Unidad), as well as a brief preview in English of each unit's theme and content.

UNIDAD 3

Deportes y pasatiempos

UNIT OPENER

There are nine units that present new material in your textbook. Each of these units opens the same way. Before you begin a unit, examine its opening pages. First scan the photos—they'll give you an idea what the unit is about. Next read the introductory paragraph—it sets the theme and provides information about the life and customs of Spanish-speaking people. Finally, look at the outline of the unit. Read the objectives of each section carefully—they'll tell you how you'll use Spanish to communicate with others.

REVIEW UNIT OPENER

Review is essential to learning a second language. It's good to stop now and then to ask yourself what you've learned and, more importantly, to practice your new skills in different situations. That's just what each review unit (Unidad de repaso) will help you do. There's one at the end of each part—three in the book. In the review unit you'll be introduced to a new theme and setting, but you won't have to

Fútbol—called *soccer* in the United States—is the national passion in most Spanish-speaking countries. Children learn to kick a ball almost as soon as they can walk. Some of the world's great soccer players come from South America. Other popular sports include *tenis, golf, béisbol, polo, vólibol, básquetbol.* As you can see, many sports names are similar in Spanish and English.

Pastimes like dancing, singing, playing the guitar, taking pictures, and playing dominos add fun to life.

In this unit you will:

SECTION A	talk about sports and pastimes . . . say which you like and which you don't like
SECTION B	talk about the seasons in which you play certain sports, and the equipment you need
SECTION C	say when and how often you play . . . talk about the seasons and the weather
TRY YOUR SKILLS	use what you've learned
VAMOS A LEER	read for practice and pleasure

91

UNIDAD **4**

¡Playa, sol y deportes!

Repaso

learn any new vocabulary, grammar, or communicative functions (language uses). Just concentrate on using what you've already studied in new and interesting ways.

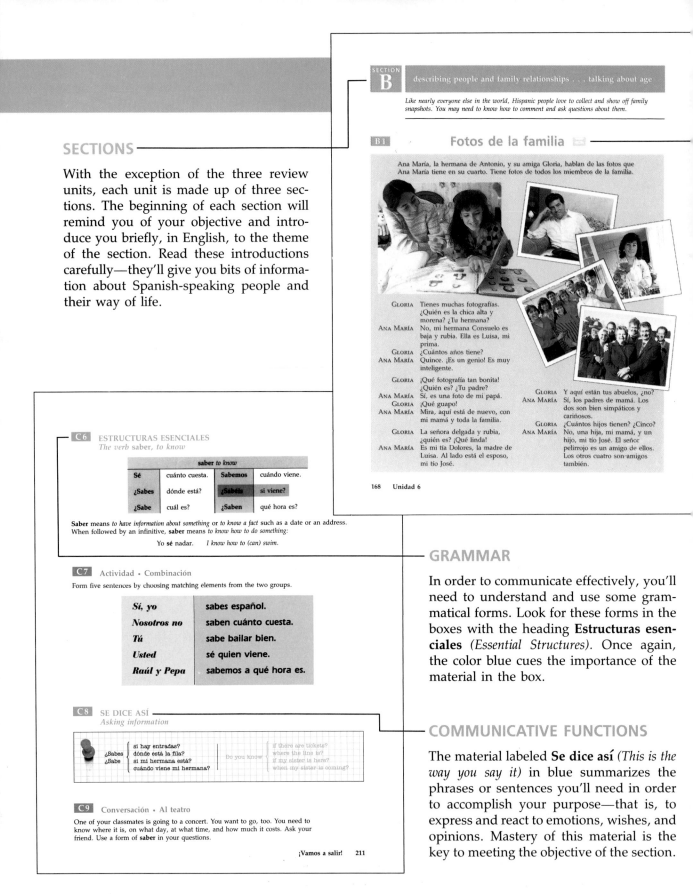

SECTIONS

With the exception of the three review units, each unit is made up of three sections. The beginning of each section will remind you of your objective and introduce you briefly, in English, to the theme of the section. Read these introductions carefully—they'll give you bits of information about Spanish-speaking people and their way of life.

SECTION B — describing people and family relationships . . . talking about age

Like nearly everyone else in the world, Hispanic people love to collect and show off family snapshots. You may need to know how to comment and ask questions about them.

B1   Fotos de la familia

Ana María, la hermana de Antonio, y su amiga Gloria, hablan de las fotos que Ana María tiene en su cuarto. Tiene fotos de todos los miembros de la familia.

GLORIA   Tienes muchas fotografías. ¿Quién es la chica alta y morena? ¿Tu hermana?
ANA MARÍA   No, mi hermana Consuelo es baja y rubia. Ella es Luisa, mi prima.
GLORIA   ¿Cuántos años tiene?
ANA MARÍA   Quince. ¡Es un genio! Es muy inteligente.

GLORIA   ¡Qué fotografía tan bonita! ¿Quién es? ¿Tu padre?
ANA MARÍA   Sí, es una foto de mi papá.
GLORIA   ¡Qué guapo!
ANA MARÍA   Mira, aquí está de nuevo, con mi mamá y toda la familia.

GLORIA   La señora delgada y rubia, ¿quién es? ¡Qué linda!
ANA MARÍA   Es mi tía Dolores, la madre de Luisa. Al lado está el esposo, mi tío José.

GLORIA   Y aquí están tus abuelos, ¿no?
ANA MARÍA   Sí, los padres de mamá. Los dos son bien simpáticos y cariñosos.
GLORIA   ¿Cuántos hijos tienen? ¿Cinco?
ANA MARÍA   No, una hija, mi mamá, y un hijo, mi tío José. El señor pelirrojo es un amigo de ellos. Los otros cuatro son amigos también.

168   Unidad 6

C6   ESTRUCTURAS ESENCIALES
The verb saber, to know

saber *to know*			
Sé	cuánto cuesta.	**Sabemos**	cuándo viene.
¿Sabes	dónde está?	**¿Sabéis**	si viene.
¿Sabe	cuál es?	**¿Saben**	qué hora es?

Saber means *to have information about something* or *to know a fact* such as a date or an address. When followed by an infinitive, **saber** means *to know how to do something:*

Yo **sé** nadar.   *I know how to (can) swim.*

C7   Actividad • Combinación

Form five sentences by choosing matching elements from the two groups.

Sí, yo	sabes español.
Nosotros no	saben cuánto cuesta.
Tú	sabe bailar bien.
Usted	sé quien viene.
Raúl y Pepa	sabemos a qué hora es.

C8   SE DICE ASÍ
Asking information

¿Sabes ¿Sabe	si hay entradas? dónde está la fila? si mi hermana está? cuándo viene mi hermana?	Do you know	if there are tickets? where the line is? if my sister is here? when my sister is coming?

C9   Conversación • Al teatro

One of your classmates is going to a concert. You want to go, too. You need to know where it is, on what day, at what time, and how much it costs. Ask your friend. Use a form of **saber** in your questions.

¡Vamos a salir!   211

GRAMMAR

In order to communicate effectively, you'll need to understand and use some grammatical forms. Look for these forms in the boxes with the heading **Estructuras esenciales** *(Essential Structures)*. Once again, the color blue cues the importance of the material in the box.

COMMUNICATIVE FUNCTIONS

The material labeled **Se dice así** *(This is the way you say it)* in blue summarizes the phrases or sentences you'll need in order to accomplish your purpose—that is, to express and react to emotions, wishes, and opinions. Mastery of this material is the key to meeting the objective of the section.

BASIC MATERIAL

The material in each section is numbered in sequence together with the letter of the section: A1, A2, A3, and so on. The first presentation is always new or basic material, signaled by a number and title in blue. In some sections new material may be introduced in two or three other places. Wherever you see the color blue, you'll know that there's something new to learn. The new material is a model of what to say in a situation. Its authentic language and pictures will help you appreciate the different attitudes and surroundings of Spanish-speaking people.

CULTURE NOTES

The heading **¿Sabes que . . . ?** *(Do you know that . . . ?)* in green invites you to find out more about the life of Spanish-speaking people. These culture notes in English provide additional information about the theme of the section to help you increase your cultural awareness.

ACTIVITIES

The headings of all the activities in the section begin with the word **Actividad** in orange. It's your signal to practice, either orally or in writing. Many of the activities are designed so that you may work together with your classmates in pairs or in small groups.

LISTENING

Listening is an essential skill that requires practice to develop. Whenever you see this cassette symbol ▤ after a heading, you'll know that the material is recorded, with pauses provided for your repetition or responses. A special listening comprehension exercise in each section is headed **Comprensión.** In order to respond, you will need to listen as your teacher plays the cassette or reads the Spanish to you.

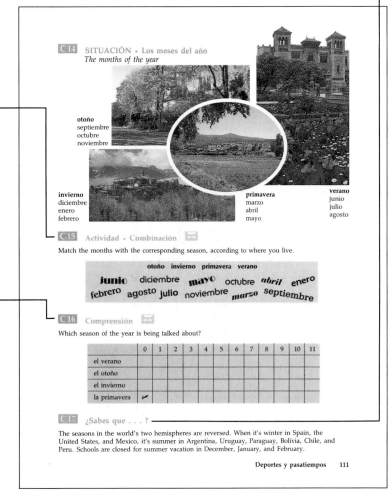

TRY YOUR SKILLS

This section will let you experiment with the skills and knowledge you've gathered in the previous sections of the unit. Its variety of activities will give you many opportunities to practice communicating with others.

You've learned how to greet people, give some information about yourself, and ask others about themselves. Here are some further opportunities to use your new skills!

1   Tarjetas postales

Some day you may want to have a pen pal in a Spanish-speaking country. For now, imagine that these postcards are for you.

¡Hola!
Me llamo Irene.
Soy de Buenos Aires,
la capital de
Argentina.
¿De dónde eres
tú?
Recuerdos,
Irene

Buenos Aires,
Argentina

Betty Mintz
3 Mount Vernon St
Boston, Mass.
03476
U.S.A.

¡Hola!
¡Qué tal! ¿Cómo
estás? Yo me llamo
Carlos Cajal. Soy
de Madrid. Es la
capital de España.
Adiós,
Carlos

Madrid,
España

Robert Reddy
1329 Stillman Ave.
Redlands, Ca.
92476
U.S.A.

2   Actividad • ¿Quién es la chica? ¿Quién es el chico?

Tell about your new pen pals. What are their names? Where are they from?

3   Actividad • ¡A escribir!

Write a postcard introducing yourself to a pen pal in a Spanish-speaking country. Use the postcards above as a model.

¡Hola, amigos!   49

¿LO SABES?

Let's review some important points you have learned in this unit.

SECTION A

When you are in a Spanish restaurant, can you order food at different ti[mes] of the day?
Order in Spanish something you might want for breakfast, something for lunch, and something for dinner.

Do you know how to talk about the foods you like and dislike?
Using **A mi me gusta(n)** and **A mí no me gusta(n)**, mention five types of food you like and five you don't.

Can you say what you would like to have for breakfast, lunch, and dinn[er] and what your friends and family would like (or don't like) to have for each meal if you were in a Spanish country?
First, make a list of the different types of food you have for each meal, th[en] say who likes them and who doesn't.

SECTION B

Can you talk to a friend who is organizing a picnic and find out information about it?
Write down five questions you might ask.

When organizing a picnic, can you say how you're going to contribute?
Make five sentences talking about what you are bringing and the steps that you'll follow to get it.

Can you choose items at the food store, fruit stand, or pastry shop?
Write down five of your selections, using forms of **este** or **ese**.

Are you able to tell the store clerk what you really want?
Answer these suggestions with **no**, and indicate what you want instead.

| ¿Esas peras? | ¿Esta piña? | ¿Esas uvas? |
| ¿Estos melocotones? | ¿Esta tarta? | ¿Ese bizcocho? |

SECTION C

When you are in a Spanish-speaking environment and you want a glass of water and something to eat, what would you say?
Make up four sentences.

Do you know how to ask in Spanish for something you need at the table?
Ask for:

| a cup | a knife | a napkin | a glass | a fork |
| a small plate | a dish | a spoon | a small spoon |

Can you complain in Spanish about the food or the service?
Write down five complaints you might have.

Do you know different ways to say how much you like the food?
You are having a meal with a Spanish-speaking family. What would you say about . . .

| la sopa | el arroz | el flan | la carne | las verduras | la tarta |

262   Unidad 9

SELF-CHECK

Each of the nine basic units ends with a one-page self-check called **¿Lo sabes?** *(Do you know it?).* It includes a series of questions in English that you should ask yourself. Following the questions are short activities that will check your knowledge and skills. The questions are grouped by section, so, if you can't answer yes to a question or if the exercise shows you need to review, you'll know which section to turn to.

VOCABULARIO

SECTION A
amable *kind*
bienvenido, -a *welcome*
la casa *house*
con permiso *excuse me*
la cosa *thing*
el cuarto *room*
es un placer . . . *it's a pleasure . . .*
estás en tu casa *make yourself at home*
igualmente *likewise*
un momento *just a moment*
norteamericano, -a *American*
pasa *come in*
pasar *to spend (time); come in*
el placer *pleasure*
querer (ie) *to want*
el refresco *soda*
la sala *living room*
la vacación *vacation*
ver *to see*
la visita *visit*

SECTION B
alto, -a *tall*
antipático, -a *not nice*
bajo, -a *short*
bien *very*
bonito, -a *pretty*
cariñoso, -a *affectionate*
casado, -a *married*
¿cómo es? *what's he, (she, it) like?*
¿Cuántos cuartos hay? *How many rooms are there?*
¿cuántos años tiene? *how old are you (is he/she?)*
de ellos *their*
de nuevo *again*
delgado, -a *thin*

los dos, las dos *the two*
egoísta *selfish*
el esposo *husband*
la esposa *wife*
estar casado, -a *to be married*
la familia *family*
feo, -a *ugly*
la foto *photo*
la fotografía *photograph*
generoso *generous*
gordo, -a *fat*
guapo, -a *handsome*
el hijo *son*
la hija *daughter*
los hijos *children, sons and daughters*
lindo, -a *pretty*
la madrastra *stepmother*
la madre *mother*
los miembros de la familia *family members (see p. 171)*
moreno, -a *dark (hair, complexion)*
murió *(he) died*
¿no? *right?*
el padrastro *stepfather*
el padre *father*
los padres *parents*
papá *dad*
pelirrojo, -a *redheaded*
¡qué cuarto tan bonito! *what a pretty room!*
¡qué guapo! *how handsome!*
rubio, -a *fair, blonde*
el señor *man*
la señora *woman*
simpático, -a *nice*
tan *so*
tener . . . años *to be . . . years old*
todo, -a, -os, -as *all*

tonto, -a *dumb*
la visita *visitor*

SECTION C
el apartamento *apartment*
la cocina *kitchen*
el comedor *dining room*
cómodo, -a *comfortable*
cuando *when*
de él *his*
de ella *her*
de ellas *their*
de usted *your*
de ustedes *your*
empezar (ie) *to start*
la entrada *entrance*
este, -a *this*
frente a *across from*
el garaje *garage*
grande *large*
importante *important*
el jardín *garden*
más *most*
mis *my (pl.)*
nuestro, -a, -os, -as *our*
el pasillo *hall*
pequeño, -a *small, little*
¡por supuesto! *of course!*
prohibido, -a *off limits*
la puerta *door, gate*
la sala de estar *family room*
sus *her, his, their (pl.)*
el tiempo *time*
el tiempo libre *free time*
tus *your (pl.)*
usar *to use*
¡vamos! *let's go!*
vivir *to live*
vuestro, -a, -os, -as *(fam. pl.)*
¡ya sé! *I know it!*

ESTUDIO DE PALABRAS

1. Write a list of the polite expressions you can use when you meet new friends and visit their home.

2. Make a list of the words you can use to describe a house or an apartment.

La familia

VOCABULARY

The Spanish-English vocabulary list, **Vocabulario,** after the self-check, contains the words and **phrases** you'll need to know. They're grouped according to the sections of the unit. A word-study exercise, **Estudio de palabras,** below the list, will focus your attention on the vocabulary and provide helpful ways to work with and learn the new words and phrases.

VAMOS A LEER°

Antes de leer *Before reading*

Before you begin to read in Spanish, here are a few suggestions. Read each new selection through for general meaning without looking up any words. Cognates—words that look alike in Spanish and English and have a similar meaning—will help you. Try to pronounce them the Spanish way, and write them down.

El mundo hispánico

España es un país° de Europa°, al suroeste° de Francia. Sus vecinos° son Francia y Portugal. La capital de España es Madrid. María Bernal es de Madrid.

Luisa Cano es de California y Pedro Gómez es de Texas. Los dos° son de los Estados Unidos. Ellos son mexicano americanos°.

vamos a leer *let's read*   **un país** *a country*   **de Europa** *of Europe*   **al suroeste** *to the southwest*
sus vecinos *its neighbors*   **los dos** *both*   **mexicano americanos** *Mexican Americans*

54   Unidad 1

READING

A reading section, **Vamos a leer** *(Let's read)* concludes the unit. Here you'll find one or more reading selections related to the unit's theme. They include postcards, movie ads, recipes, character sketches, and factual selections. In each reading section, you'll also find an episode of the adventure story, **El regalo** *(The gift).* Most reading selections are followed by questions and activities designed to help you practice and develop your reading skills.

PHOTO ESSAYS

Following each review unit in the book, you'll find a cultural photo essay called **Viñeta cultural.** The three essays will allow you to look into the life and surroundings of people who speak Spanish. The text in English provides interesting information on each theme. The photo captions are in Spanish.

Viñeta cultural 1

Pueblos y ciudades

In the large, bustling cities of the Spanish-speaking world, and the many small villages that dot the countryside, visitors can find great contrasts and a wide variety of cultures. In Spain, medieval castles, Gothic cathedrals, and ancient aqueducts are dramatic reminders of the past amidst the modern life of today.

❶ Iglesia de la Sagrada Familia en Barcelona, España
❷ Un café al aire libre en Barcelona, España
❸ El parque del Retiro en Madrid, España
❹ La hermosa ciudad de Ávila, España

Viñeta cultural 2

Paisajes

The Iberian Peninsula juts out into the Atlantic Ocean, separated from the rest of Europe by a chain of rugged mountains, **Los Pirineos.** Spain, which shares the Peninsula with Portugal, is a country of varied landscapes (*paisajes*)— mountains and plains, rocky coastlines, and sandy beaches. Its people have varying customs and divided loyalties, but the wonder and mystery of this ancient country remain eternal.

❶ Una r
Islas
❷ Gal
❸ U
E

Viñeta cultural 3

Festivales

Festivales . . . the word itself brings forth images of color, music, and dance. Spain seems to have festivals for every season and every reason. Many of the festivals celebrate religious holidays; others mark the end of winter and the beginning of spring. In Spain, and throughout the Spanish-speaking world, festivals are occasions when young and old alike rejoice in their heritage.

❶ Festival de los Mariscos en Galicia, España
❷ Festival de Santiago en Galicia, España
❸ La Muñeira, un baile popular de Galicia, España
❹ Festival de San Fermín en Pamplona, España

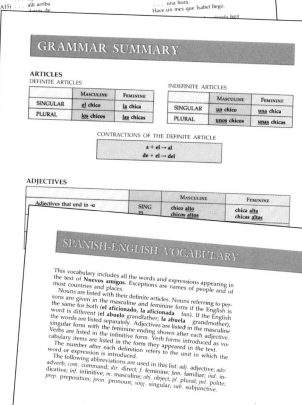

SUMMARY OF FUNCTIONS

The term *functions* can be defined as what you do with language—what your purpose is in speaking. Here is a list of all the functions with the expressions you have learned related to these functions. The number indicates the unit in which the expression is introduced, followed by the section letter and number in parentheses.

EXCHANGING INFORMATION

Asking and giving names
1 (B4) ¿Cómo te llamas tú?
Yo me llamo . . . .

Asking and giving someone else's name
1 (B8) ¿Cómo se llama él?
Él se llama . . . .
¿Cómo se llama ella?
Ella se llama . . . .

Asking someone's age, telling yours
6 (B5) ¿Cuántos años tienes?
Tengo (catorce) años

Asking and saying where people are from
1 (C6) ¿De dónde eres tú?
Soy de . . . .
¿De dónde son ellos?
Son de . . . .
¿Tú eres de . . . ?
Sí, soy de . . . .

Asking for directions
5 (A17) ¿Dónde está(n) . . . ?
¿Está(n) cerca de aquí?
¿Está(n) lejos?

Giving directions
5 (A17) Está abajo.
. . . . lejos
5 (A15) . . . . allí arriba

¿De dónde?
7 (C8) ¿Sabes si . . . ?
¿Sabes dónde . . . ?
¿Sabes cuándo . . . ?

Telling time
2 (B19) ¿Qué hora es?
¿A qué hora es . . . ?
Es la una.
Son las . . .
A la una.
A las . . . .

Discussing prices
2 (C8) ¿Cuánto cuesta(n)?
Cuesta(n) . . . .
11 (B7) ¿Cuánto vale?
Es muy caro.
Es demasiado caro.
No vale tanto.
No pago más de . . .
Es un regalo.
Es muy barato.
Es una ganga.

Saying what you usually do
10 (A9) Canto a menudo.
Casi siempre canto.

Expressing how long ago something happened
10 (A18) Isabel llegó hace
. . . . mucho tiempo.
. . . . quince días.
. . . . una hora.
Hace un mes que Isabel llegó.

GRAMMAR SUMMARY

ARTICLES

DEFINITE ARTICLES

	Masculine	Feminine
SINGULAR	el chico	la chica
PLURAL	los chicos	las chicas

INDEFINITE ARTICLES

	Masculine	Feminine
SINGULAR	un chico	una chica
PLURAL	unos chicos	unas chicas

CONTRACTIONS OF THE DEFINITE ARTICLE

a + el → al
de + el → del

ADJECTIVES

		Masculine	Feminine
Adjectives that end in -o	SING PL	chico alto / chicos altos	chica alta / chicas altas

SPANISH-ENGLISH VOCABULARY

This vocabulary includes all the words and expressions appearing in the text of **Nuevos amigos**. Exceptions are names of people and of most countries and places.

Nouns are listed with their definite articles. Nouns referring to persons are given in the masculine and feminine form if the English is the same for both (**el aficionado, la aficionada** fan). If the English word is different (**el abuelo** grandfather; **la abuela** grandmother), the words are listed separately. Adjectives are listed in the masculine singular form with the feminine ending shown after each adjective. Verbs are listed in the infinitive form. Verb forms introduced as vocabulary items are listed in the form they appeared in the text.

The number after each definition refers to the unit in which the word or expression is introduced.

The following abbreviations are used in this list: *adj.* adjective; *adv.* adverb; *com.* command; *dir.* direct; *f.* feminine; *fam.* familiar; *ind.* indicative; *inf.* infinitive; *m.* masculine; *obj.* object; *pl.* plural; *pol.* polite; *prep.* preposition; *pron.* pronoun; *sing.* singular; *sub.* subjunctive.

A

a at, to, 2
a casa (to) home, 5; a la derecha on the right, 5; a la izquierda on the left, 5; a la mesa to the table, 9; a la noche . . .
aceptar to accept, 7
acerca(n): se acerca(n) come close, near, 6
el ácido acid, 7
el agua (f.): el agua mineral min . . .

FOR REFERENCE

The reference section at the end of the textbook provides you with valuable aids. Here you may consult a Summary of Functions, Grammar Summary, Numbers, Verb Index, English Equivalents, Spanish-English and English-Spanish Vocabularies, and Grammar Index.

SUMMARY OF FUNCTIONS

The Summary of Functions sums up the communicative functions you have learned and practiced in a variety of situations throughout this textbook. If you want to ask for directions, invite someone to a party, pay a compliment, or respond to a friend's good fortune, for example, you will find the appropriate phrases and sentences listed here, as well as the unit in which the particular function was introduced.

GRAMMAR SUMMARY

The grammar points that have been presented in the book are organized in tables for easy reference and review in the Grammar Summary.

SPANISH-ENGLISH VOCABULARY

The Spanish-English Vocabulary contains all the words you will come across in this textbook. Besides the English meanings of the words, you can check on the gender of the nouns and identify the adjectives. The number you see after each entry tells you in which unit the word first appeared.

¡A COMENZAR!

There it is, a special textbook that will help you enlarge your view of the world and enable you to contribute to better understanding and communication among people. Now you're ready to begin an exciting, rewarding experience—learning another language and meeting new friends, **Nuevos amigos.**

INTRODUCTION

Spanish and You

Welcome to the Spanish-speaking world! Today you are embarking on a new journey—the exploration and learning of Spanish. This trip will take you to many lands, where you will meet different people. The route you will take is the Spanish language; the destination is an understanding of how speakers of Spanish think, behave, and interact with others. You will discover their values, history, and traditions. Are you ready to start your trip?

Let's go!   *¡Vamos!*

In this introduction you will learn:

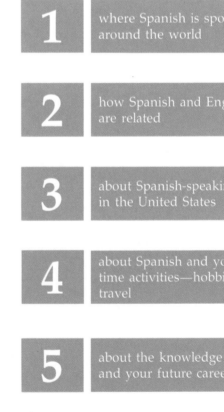

1 where Spanish is spoken around the world

2 how Spanish and English are related

3 about Spanish-speaking areas in the United States

4 about Spanish and your leisure time activities—hobbies, sports, travel

5 about the knowledge of Spanish and your future career

6 suggestions for studying Spanish

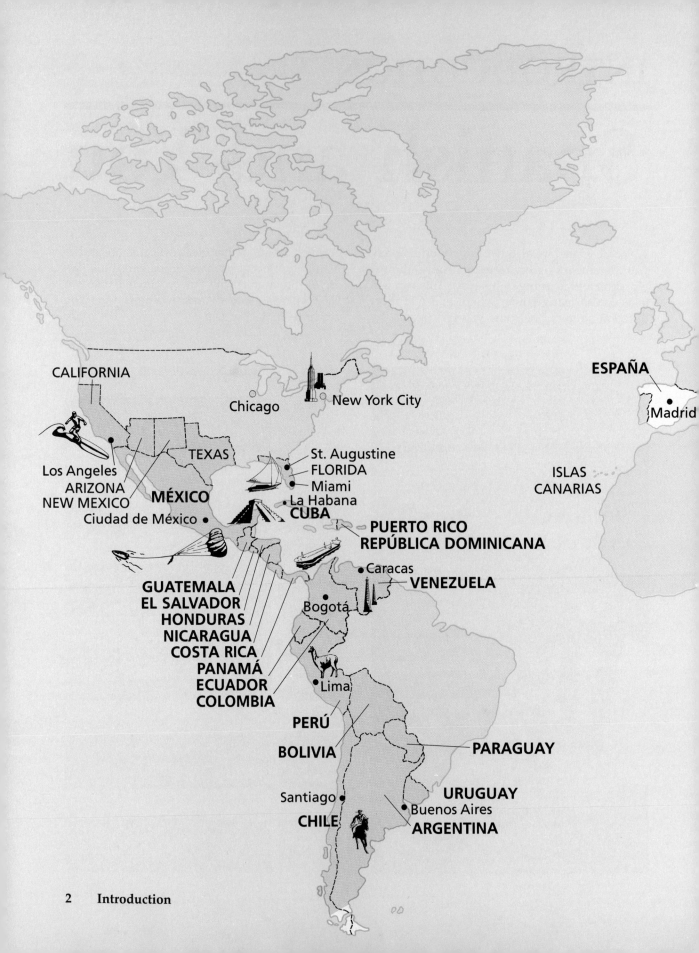

CALIFORNIA

Chicago

New York City

ESPAÑA

Madrid

Los Angeles
ARIZONA
NEW MEXICO

TEXAS

St. Augustine
FLORIDA
Miami
La Habana

ISLAS
CANARIAS

MÉXICO

Ciudad de México

CUBA

PUERTO RICO
REPÚBLICA DOMINICANA

Caracas

VENEZUELA

GUATEMALA
EL SALVADOR
HONDURAS
NICARAGUA
COSTA RICA
PANAMÁ
ECUADOR
COLOMBIA

Bogotá

Lima

PERÚ

BOLIVIA

PARAGUAY

Santiago

Buenos Aires

URUGUAY

CHILE

ARGENTINA

La Coruña
León
Bilbao
Pamplona
PIRINEOS
R. Ebro
Zaragoza
Barcelona
R. Duero
Segovia
Salamanca
Madrid
R. Tajo
Toledo
R. Júcar
R. Turia
Valencia
MENORCA
Palma
MALLORCA
IBIZA
R. Guadiana
ESPAÑA
ISLAS
BALEARES
R. Guadalquivir
R. Segura
Córdoba
Sevilla
Granada
Málaga
MAR MEDITERRÁNEO
Cádiz

Long ago Spanish explorers and settlers established themselves in many areas around the world. Mexico, Central and South America, and most of the islands of the Caribbean Sea were colonized by Spaniards. They also settled in vast territories that are now part of the United States. Spanish exploration even reached as far as Africa and some islands of the Pacific Ocean.

Come along now as we visit with some of the more than 300 million Spanish-speaking people around the world. Some of our ports of call will be familiar to you, but many will be full of surprises.

Spanish and You   3

First stop, first surprise! Did you know that the second largest Mexican city is right here in the United States? That's right, there are more Mexicans and Mexican Americans in Los Angeles, California, than in any other city in the world except Mexico City! And the sign you will see most often will probably be **Se habla español,** *Spanish is spoken here.* You will also be able to practice your Spanish in Miami, Florida, where about half of the residents are Cuban Americans, and in New York City, where there are hundreds of thousands of Puerto Rican Americans. In fact, just about anywhere you go in the United States you will have opportunities to speak the Spanish language, especially in our great Southwest!

Celebration at Calle Ocho in Miami, Florida

Old Spanish Mission in Santa Barbara, California

Color and music combine to create excitement in a Hispanic American Day Parade.

Portrait of a girl in Mexican costume

Spanish-American grocery store offering typical Spanish products

The Riverwalk in San Antonio offers a breathtaking view of its river.

Moving southward across the Rio Grande we come to Mexico, a land of surprising contrasts. Probably a country many of you will visit at least once, it is a breathtaking land of beautiful mountains and white, sandy beaches. Or you can climb the pyramids of the Sun and the Moon at Teotihuacán, parasail over Acapulco Bay, or bargain with artisans in the marketplaces of Toluca. Everywhere you will see the unique Mexican blend of Spanish and Indian cultures.

Steps leading to El Castillo in Chichén Itzá, one of the most important of the ancient Mayan cities

Vacation resort in Puerto Vallarta, Mexico, where romance and adventure go hand in hand

*In the **Plaza de las Tres Culturas** you can see examples of Aztec and Colonial architecture as well as modern high-rises.*

Mexico is one of the world's leading producers of silver. Pictured here is a silver shop in Taxco, Mexico.

The world-renowned **Ballet Folklórico** *on stage in Mexico City*

Parasailing in Acapulco, Mexico

A moment in time . . . fine food and good conversation in a restaurant in Mexico

Central America covers a smaller area than Texas, but its population is greater by more than three million. Each country of Central America has its own unique character. Guatemala and Honduras were inhabited by the Mayans, who could predict eclipses of the sun and moon with far greater accuracy than the Europeans of their time. El Salvador is a land of volcanoes, some still very active indeed. Nicaragua has the largest lake in the region, complete with fresh-water sharks! Costa Rica has no army, and has the most democratic form of government in Central America. And Panama, of course, is the home of the Panama Canal and the San Blas Indians, who live on artificial islands off the Atlantic coast.

Young Costa Rican

View of the Panama Canal, one of the world's most important waterways

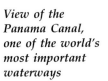

The Spanish conquerors were astonished by the splendors of the gold found in Peru.

Native Indian girl in costume, Guatemala

View of Lake Atitlán, with surrounding volcanoes, in Guatemala

Fishing in Lake Atitlán, Guatemala

Traces of Mayan civilization are everywhere in the mountainous land of Guatemala. Pictured here is a Mayan-Tikal site in Petán.

Mayan Ball Court in Copán, Honduras

Most South Americans speak the same Spanish that you will learn. Whether they are descendants of the Incas of Peru, or of the cowboys of the Argentine plains, the gauchos, they all speak the same language. In fact, the only countries of South America where Spanish is not spoken are Brazil, Guyana, French Guiana, and Surinam. And so, in Cuzco you can stroll among buildings constructed on ancient Incan foundations, catch the sun on a Caribbean beach in Venezuela, or dance the night away in a disco in Buenos Aires, all without having to buy additional phrasebooks!

Machu Picchu, the famous "lost city" of the Incas of Peru, located high in the Andes. It was not rediscovered until 1911.

The twin towers of the **Centro Simón Bolívar** *in Caracas, Venezuela, serve as a gateway to the downtown area of the city.*

View of church by the sea in
Cartagena, Colombia

Reed boats on Lake Titicaca,
Uros Island, Peru

Family barbecue in Buenos Aires,
Argentina

No description of the Spanish-speaking world would be complete without the country where it all started. Spain is the homeland, and although the Spanish-speaking countries around the world all have unique identities, they share the cultural bond of language and heritage. Spain is the land of great thinkers—the Muslim mathematicians and scientists of the Middle Ages and Maimonides, the great Jewish philosopher and judge. It is the country of warriors like Rodrigo Díaz de Vivar, a Spanish hero so respected by his enemies, the Moors, that they called him El Cid (a term of respect meaning *sir*), and of Don Quixote, hero of Cervantes' seventeenth-century novel. It was from Spain that Christopher Columbus sailed in search of Asia and found a new world. And now you can return to explore castles where medieval knights planned battles and crusades, and spoke *Castilian*, the language which later became modern-day Spanish. Or perhaps you would rather shout **olé** at the bullring in Madrid and later that evening applaud flamenco dancers!

A view of Poniente Beach, Costa Blanca, Spain

The Alhambra, a palace complex of ancient Moorish architecture surrounded by woodlands, gardens, fountains, and buildings.

The Pyrenees, a chain of mountains that spreads across France and Spain

A flamenco dancer
in Seville, Spain

The City of Ávila in Spain sits on a hill surrounded by massive walls.

Buying and selling at an outdoor market
in Barcelona, Spain

Young people in the gardens of a palace
in Málaga, Spain

Whatever your interests, the Spanish language will be your passport to excitement throughout the world!

Playing in the snow on the slopes of Cotopaxi, in Ecuador

View of a parish church in the town of San Miguel de Allende, Mexico

Three Spanish-American boys from San Antonio, Texas

View of the Peruvian altiplano, a high plateau in the Andes

Built by the Spaniards, El Morro overlooks the Atlantic Ocean in San Juan, Puerto Rico.

The Alcázar in Segovia, Spain, is one of the architectural treasures of the region.

View of Isla Grande on the Atlantic Coast of Panama

Group of teenaged tourists in the Aragón region of Spain

Children wearing traditional folk dance costumes in Tenerife, Canary Islands

¡SUPERIOR! ¡ESPECTACULAR! ¡MAGNÍFICO!

¡EXTRAORDINARIO! ¡ESTUPENDO! ¡FABULOSO!

¡MARAVILLOSO! ¡INCREÍBLE! ¡FANTÁSTICO!

All of the words above are adjectives that describe Spanish. Can you guess their meaning? Write your answers on a slip of paper and then check them with the help of your teacher. You will probably notice that the Spanish and English spellings are similar. In fact, some words are spelled exactly the same! These Spanish/English look-alikes will be of help to you as you learn Spanish. They are called *cognates*. But please beware! Some look-alikes may fool you; they are known as false cognates. Here is an example: the Spanish word **pan** means *bread* in English—not *pan*.

Why do Spanish and English have so many words which are similar? One reason is that Spanish is a *Romance* language, which means that it came from the language of the ancient Romans—Latin. In its early history Spain was called *Hispania*, and was part of the Roman Empire. Britain was part of that same empire, so the English language also shows the influence of Latin. Another reason is that many Spanish words have come into English because much of our country was first settled by Spaniards, and their descendants are now Americans.

Here are some Spanish words that are used in English. Do you recognize them?

alpaca	chile	taco	taxi
fiesta	piano	sombrero	mosquito

Some students who are studying Spanish like to use Spanish names. Most Spanish names and their English versions are cognates. If you want to be called by a Spanish name, you can choose one from the following list.

For girls		For boys	
Alma	*Alma*	Alberto	*Albert*
Alicia	*Alice*	Alfredo	*Alfred*
Ana	*Ann*	Andrés	*Andrew*
Bárbara	*Barbara*	Carlos	*Charles, Carl*
Beatriz	*Beatrice*	Eduardo	*Edward*
Carolina	*Caroline*	Jorge	*George*
Elena	*Ellen, Helen*	Enrique	*Henry*
Juana	*Jane, Jean*	Juan	*John*
Lucía	*Lucy*	José	*Joseph*
Margarita	*Margaret*	Pablo	*Paul*
María	*Mary, Marie*	Ricardo	*Richard*
Teresa	*Theresa*	Roberto	*Robert*

Activities

For a two-day period, keep a log on your contacts with Spanish. Include the following:

- Names of foods found in the supermarket
- References to Spanish-speaking countries on radio, TV, and in newspapers and magazines
- Spanish songs on radio or TV
- Call letters of local Spanish radio or TV stations
- Uses of borrowed Spanish words

Share your findings with your class. As a follow-up, teach a friend or family member two Spanish "borrowed" words.

As you recall, the ancient Romans called Spain *Hispania*. That is why the term *Hispanic* is used to refer to people from all of the Spanish-speaking countries, as well as to people of Spanish background within the United States.

The Hispanics who live in Central America and South America are also called *Spanish Americans*, or *Latin Americans* (because Spanish is a Romance language derived from Latin).

Activities

1. **A name game** See if you can match these names with their explanations or true meanings. Copy the two columns onto a sheet of paper and draw a line connecting each place and its meaning. Find additional Spanish place names and determine their original meanings. For example: Los Angeles/*the angels*. Are there any in your state? What do they mean?

Colorado	*High pole*
Florida	*Yellow*
Montana	*Mountain king*
Nevada	*Of mountains*
Amarillo	*Colored, reddish*
Palo Alto	*Snow-covered*
Monterey	*Full of flowers*

2. **Spanish place names** Look at the names of the cities in the box. Spanish names like these can be found throughout the United States. Find out the English meaning of these Spanish names.

Aurora (*Colorado*)	Las Vegas (*Nevada*)	Sacramento (*California*)	San Francisco (*California*)
Boca Grande (*Florida*)	Los Molinos (*California*)	Salinas (*California*)	Rio Grande (*Ohio*)
El Dorado (*Kansas*)	Mesa (*Arizona*)	San Antonio (*Texas*)	Valparaiso (*Indiana*)
El Paso (*Texas*)	Plano (*Texas*)	San Diego (*California*)	Ventana (*Arizona*)
Las Cruces (*New Mexico*)	Pueblo (*Colorado*)	Santa Fe (*New Mexico*)	Zapata (*Texas*)

A map of the United States showing the locations of the Spanish place names listed above. CANADA is labeled to the north and MEXICO to the south.

SPANISH FOR LEISURE

When people talk about studying Spanish, they usually mean learning and using it only in the classroom. But learning about the culture and language of Spanish-speaking countries can go beyond school into leisure activities that are interesting and fun. What are your hobbies and interests? Do you like sports? Most of the sports that are played in the United States are also found in Spanish America and Spain. See if you can guess the English equivalents of the names of these sports. Cover the answer key and then check your answers:

fútbol, tenis, golf, béisbol, polo, vólibol, básquetbol

> football/soccer, tennis, golf, baseball, polo, volleyball, basketball

Note that **fútbol** as played in Spain and Spanish America is called *soccer* here in the United States. American-style football is called **fútbol americano**.

Fútbol (soccer) is almost an obsession in Spanish America and in Europe. Thanks to satellite TV, you can follow international competitions in soccer and a number of other sports. If you are a soccer fan, you may even find yourself rooting for your favorite Spanish-speaking team and cheering in Spanish.

Béisbol is popular in Mexico, and the vocabulary in Spanish is easy—for example, **el filder, el cácher, el pícher,** and **el shorstop.**

Mountain-climbing as well as skiing are popular in the Andes Mountains. Because the seasons south of the equator are reversed, you would be skiing in July and August!

Spanish and You   19

Music is part of everyday life in Spain and Spanish America. Many famous singers and musicians come from Spanish-speaking countries. Latin music is also popular in the United States. You are probably already familiar with the "Latin beat" and with some of the popular Hispanic musical groups and singers. Because there are large Hispanic communities in the United States, cassettes and records are more readily available in Spanish than in other foreign languages. Make a list of your favorite Spanish songs, singers, groups, or records and cassettes and share it with the class or post it on the bulletin board.

Teenagers browsing in a Spanish-American record store

The Miami Sound Machine, a Spanish-American singing group that mixes a Latin rhythm with rock music

Menudo, a singing group from Puerto Rico

Again, because there are large Hispanic communities in the United States, newspapers, magazines, and books in Spanish are easy to get. There are even comic books in Spanish! Young people in Spain and Spanish America like to watch TV and go to the movies. If there is a Spanish television station in your area, you will be able to watch a soap opera or two in Spanish. The TV schedule will give you some idea of the programs that are available.

Don Quijote, *a classic tale of a man in search of the impossible dream*

Don Quijote is a classic of Spanish literature, which has been translated into many languages, including English. Millions of people have enjoyed the adventures of Don Quixote. The book has even been turned into a musical called *Man of La Mancha*. Here you can see a painting of Don Quixote and his servant, Sancho Panza, by Pablo Picasso.

Tourists arriving in Peru

Prince Phillip, heir to the throne of Spain, appears here on the cover of **Hola,** *a popular Spanish magazine.*

Although you may not be going to a Spanish-speaking country or area right away, eventually you might. You might even live there for a while with a family as an exchange student. In the meantime, reading books or watching travel films about these countries can be interesting and fun. So is having a pen pal from Spain, Mexico, or Peru with whom you can exchange letters or cassettes. Your teacher can tell you where to write to get the name of a pen pal. Having a pen pal is one way of keeping up on the latest records, sports news, TV programs, and board and video games—not to mention exchanging stamps and comparing notes on life in general in both your countries. You may start out by writing mostly in English, but you will find yourself gradually using more and more Spanish. Many Hispanic teenagers study English, so your pen pal will welcome the opportunity to practice English.

Learning Spanish requires study and concentration. But the most important thing about studying any foreign language is discovering how people live in other parts of the world—what they value, what they like, and what is important to them. Learning Spanish can become more than schoolwork—it can become a hobby.

Activity

Bring to class an item related to the Spanish language or Hispanic culture that you have found recently. It could be a recipe, a news item, information about travel to Spain or Latin America, a TV or radio program, or even a commercial. Share your findings with the class or with your learning group. Put the item in your Spanish notebook to start your collection. Be on the lookout for other items!

5 SPANISH AND YOUR FUTURE CAREER

Have you ever wondered what you will be doing ten . . . fifteen . . . or even twenty years from now? Where you will be working? What kind of job you will have? Because you are going to study Spanish, you may find it useful for the career that you will eventually choose. A career in almost any field that you name—from art to zoology—can be combined with a knowledge of Spanish.

For many jobs, knowing a foreign language is helpful, but for some it is essential. Teachers of Spanish must be fluent in the language and also know a great deal about the history, geography, and daily life of the countries or regions where Spanish is spoken. Teachers who can combine Spanish with science, mathematics, and social studies are needed to work with students who come to the United States from Spanish-speaking countries.

Translators and interpreters also must be very familiar with both Spanish and English. Most translators specialize in one field, such as medicine or commerce. Interpreters, who have to translate what people are saying in court or at meetings, must think very quickly in both Spanish and English. Interpreters also work in businesses and international organizations.

These interpreters translate a speech for the Spanish-speaking people at the United Nations.

This teacher is teaching people who need to know Spanish in their jobs.

Not only do American travelers go to Spain and to countries in Central and South America, but Spanish-speaking people from those countries come to the United States on business and vacation trips. Travel agents and tour guides therefore find Spanish very helpful in their work, as do flight attendants on airlines that serve Spanish America and Spain. Can you describe how a tour guide, travel agent, and flight attendant use Spanish in their jobs?

Spanish is an important international language, especially in agriculture, banking, business, and technology. Food importers travel regularly to Mexico and to countries in Central America, where they sample and buy fruits and vegetables. Spanish-American countries, such as Mexico and Venezuela, sell oil to the United States. Therefore, legal documents are printed in Spanish, and negotiations often are conducted in Spanish as well as English. In order to succeed, companies in the United States that sell their products to Spanish-speaking countries must have salespeople who are familiar with Hispanic culture and who know Spanish well.

People who work in international banking and trade find that speaking Spanish is extremely helpful. A bilingual secretary, for example, must be able to type and transcribe letters in both Spanish and English. An international corporate lawyer has to be fluent in Spanish as well as English and must know not only the laws in the United States but the laws of the countries with which he or she is dealing.

Would you like to live in a foreign country? Many companies have offices in Spanish-speaking countries and employ thousands of Americans. Jobs are available in manufacturing, engineering, banking, and many other areas.

This guide in a theme park helps visitors who come from Spanish-speaking countries.

Knowing Spanish will help this corporate lawyer with the research of laws in other countries.

An international banker consults with a Spanish-speaking client.

Because there are many Hispanic communities in the United States, opportunities to use Spanish in various types of jobs are increasing. In certain states, such as Texas, California, Florida, New York, and Colorado, salespeople in stores, personnel in hotels and restaurants, doctors and nurses in hospitals, as well as police, firefighters, librarians, school secretaries, and auto mechanics speak Spanish as well as English to serve the people in their communities. There are often Spanish newspapers in addition to radio and TV programs in Spanish. These states attract many visitors from Spanish America as well as from Spain and other parts of the United States.

It helps to speak the language of your customers when you are selling something! In the picture below, what kinds of questions might this visitor from Argentina be asking the salesperson and how might he answer? Fortunately, there is a sign in the store window that says **Se habla español** (*Spanish is spoken here*).

Police officers, firefighters, and paramedics in large cities like Chicago, New York, Los Angeles, San Antonio, or Miami need to know Spanish to help people in the Hispanic communities that they serve.

A police officer gives directions in Spanish to two visitors.

A doctor questions her patient in Spanish about her medical history.

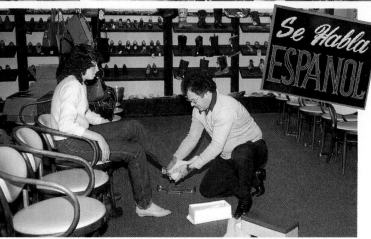

Spanish-speaking salespeople can be helpful to our foreign visitors.

Activities

Before you make a career choice, it is wise to talk with as many people as you can about their jobs—what they do and what they like and don't like about their jobs.

1. **Interviews** If you know somebody in your family, school, or neighborhood who uses Spanish in his or her work, interview this person. Ask the following (you may add questions to the list if you wish):

   - Please describe your job.
   - How do you use Spanish in your work?
   - What types of Spanish courses did you take?
   - What do you like best about your job?
   - What do you like least about your job?
   - Do you travel as part of your job? Where?

   Write the interview or record it on a cassette to share with the class or your learning group.

2. **Spanish in action** Look at the jobs listed below. Who are all these people and why are they speaking Spanish? Work in a group of two or three students. Try to think of as many reasons as possible why Spanish would be useful to these people. Take notes on your ideas and report to the class or write them to post on the bulletin board. If you really want to be creative, write an imaginary interview with one of these people. Follow the questions in activity 1 if you wish.

aerospace engineer	manager of gift shop	auto mechanic
museum director	computer programmer	
real estate agent	cosmetologist	singer	dentist
social worker	farmer	

LISTEN

Listening is particularly important in the beginning because you have to get used to a new set of sounds. You will have to listen carefully to what is being said so that you can answer in Spanish.

PRACTICE

Learning a foreign language is like learning to play a musical instrument. You have to practice a little every day. Daily short periods are more effective than one long, last-minute cramming session.

VISUALIZE

Remembering Spanish vocabulary is easy if you visualize what a sentence, phrase, or word means. For example, if you are practicing the sentence **Los chicos van a nadar** (*The boys are going swimming*), try to hold in your mind an image of children swimming in a lake while you say the sentence to yourself several times.

CONNECT

Make use of your English connections. When you read, find cognates (words which are very similar in different languages and have similar meanings) like these: **música,** *music;* **famoso,** *famous;* **ensalada,** *salad.* They will help you understand the meaning of the sentence or paragraph. Also, group Spanish words into word families—for example: **amigo,** *friend;* **amistad,** *friendship;* **amable,** *friendly.*

ORGANIZE

Look for ways to organize the material you are learning. Use memory devices. For example, make up a new word using the first letters of the words you are learning.

EXPAND

Use Spanish outside class. Speak Spanish with friends and classmates or find people who speak Spanish and practice with them. Talk into a cassette recorder in Spanish for practice; then after a few weeks listen to yourself. You will be surprised at your progress! Tune in to the Spanish-language radio and television stations in your area. You may not undestand much at first, but it will get easier as you learn more Spanish.

ENJOY

You may want to choose a new name in Spanish. Join the Spanish Club and make new friends. Above all—don't be afraid to make mistakes in Spanish. Concentrate on getting your message across and have fun doing it.

The Spanish alphabet

The Spanish alphabet has 30 letters. All words beginning with **k** and **w** are of foreign origin. There are no words in Spanish starting with **rr,** although **r** is pronounced as **erre** at the beginning of a word.

El alfabeto			
a	a	**n**	ene
b	be	**ñ**	eñe
c	ce	**o**	o
ch	che	**p**	pe
d	de	**q**	ku
e	e	**r**	ere
f	efe	**rr**	erre
g	ge	**s**	ese
h	hache	**t**	te
i	i	**u**	u
j	jota	**v**	ve
k	ka	**w**	doble ve
l	ele	**x**	equis
ll	elle	**y**	i griega
m	eme	**z**	zeta

Some classroom "survival" phrases

These are some of the expressions your teacher will be using in the classroom. Learn to *recognize* them when you hear them.

- Escuche(n), por favor. — *Listen, please.*
- Repita(n) después de mí. — *Repeat after me.*
- Díga(n)lo otra vez. — *Say it again.*
- Pónga(n)se de pie, por favor. — *Stand up, please.*
- Siénte(n)se, por favor. — *Sit down, please.*
- Silencio, por favor. — *Quiet, please.*
- Saque(n) una hoja de papel. — *Take out a sheet of paper.*
- Preste(n) atención. — *Pay attention.*
- ¡Está bien! ¡Es correcto! — *That's right!*
- No está bien. No es correcto. — *That's wrong.*

¡Buena suerte! *Good luck!*

UNIDAD 1

¡Hola, amigos!

Making new friends is exciting, especially if they speak another language. When you meet a Spanish-speaking person for the first time, you will want to say hello. The two of you will want to find out a little bit about each other.

In this unit you will:

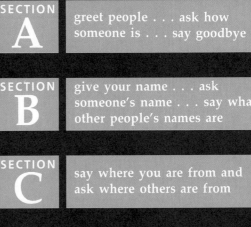

SECTION A	greet people . . . ask how someone is . . . say goodbye
SECTION B	give your name . . . ask someone's name . . . say what other people's names are
SECTION C	say where you are from and ask where others are from
TRY YOUR SKILLS	use what you've learned
VAMOS A LEER	read for practice and pleasure

Vacation is over, and it's back to school! Students greet one another and their teachers before classes begin.

A1

En el colegio

RAMÓN	¡Hola, Anita! ¿Cómo estás?
ANITA	Muy bien, Ramón. Gracias, ¿y tú?
RAMÓN	¿Yo? Regular. ¡Hasta luego!
ANITA	¡Chao!
RAMÓN	¡Adiós!

¿Qué tal?

¿Yo? ¡Muy mal!

¡Qué pena!

A2 Actividad *Activity* • Reacciones *Reactions*

Match each statement or question on the left with an appropriate response on the right.

¡Hola!	¡Hasta luego!
¿Cómo estás?	Regular.
Muy bien, ¿y tú?	Muy bien, gracias.
¡Adiós!	¡Muy mal!
¡Chao!	¡Hola!
¿Qué tal?	¡Adiós!

A3 · Actividad · Y ahora tú . . . *And now you . . .*

Choose a Spanish first name either from the list on page 17 or from another source. With a classmate, practice reading this dialog using your new names.

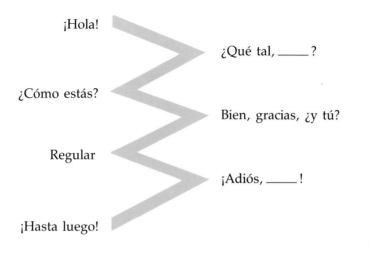

¡Hola!

¿Qué tal, _____?

¿Cómo estás?

Bien, gracias, ¿y tú?

Regular

¡Adiós, _____!

¡Hasta luego!

A4 · SE DICE ASÍ *This is how you say it*
Asking how someone is and saying how you are

PREGUNTA	QUESTION	RESPUESTA	ANSWER
¿Qué tal? ¿Cómo estás tú?	How are things? How are you?	Bien, gracias.	Fine, thanks.

A5 · Actividad · Charla *Small talk*

With your classmate, create your own dialog. Take turns asking how the other person is and then replying.

Muy bien

Bien

Regular

Mal

Muy mal

A6 Actividad • ¡A escribir! *Let's write!*

Unscramble the following conversation. Then write it out correctly.

—¡Hasta luego, Inés!　　　　　　　—Regular, ¿y tú?
—Muy bien, gracias.　　　　　　　—¡Hola, Pepe!
—¡Hola, Inés!　　　　　　　　　　—¡Adiós, Pepe!
—¿Cómo estás?

A7 Actividad • Para completar *To complete*

Luis—¡Hola, ____!　　　**Luis**—¿Cómo estás?　　　**Luis**— . . .
Elsa— . . .　　　　　　　**Elsa**— . . .　　　　　　　**Elsa**—¡Adiós!

A8 Actividad • Me llamo . . . *My name is . . .*

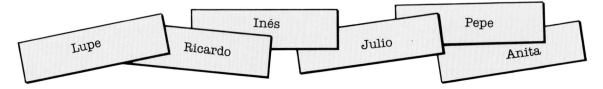

Lupe　Ricardo　Inés　Julio　Pepe　Anita

Choose a Spanish name either from the list in B3 (page 38) or from another
source. Make a name tag showing your new Spanish name. Wearing your tag,
turn to your right or left, greeting each of your classmates and saying goodbye.

A9 ¿Sabes que . . . ? *Do you know that . . . ?*

Spanish-speaking boys and girls often shake hands upon meeting. Girls usually kiss
each other on the cheek.

A10 SITUACIÓN • Saludos *Greetings* 📼

Carmen y el señor Colón　　　Jorge y la señorita López　　　Alicia y la señora Valdés

—Buenos días, señor.　　　　—Buenas tardes, señorita.　　　—Buenas noches, señora.
—Buenos días, Carmen.　　　—¡Adiós! Hasta mañana,　　　　—Buenas noches, Alicia.
　　　　　　　　　　　　　　　　Jorge.　　　　　　　　　　　　　¿Cómo estás tú?

A11 Actividad • Falta algo *Something's missing*

Supply the missing words.

1. Buenos _____ .
2. _____ tardes.
3. _____ mañana, señorita López.
4. ¿Cómo _____ tú, Jorge?

5. _____ noches.
6. Alicia y la _____ Valdés.
7. Buenas noches, _____ Colón.
8. Buenos días, _____ López.

A12 SE DICE ASÍ
Saying hello and goodbye

	Formal, respectful	Buenos días, señor. Good morning (Hello), sir.	Adiós, señorita. Goodbye, miss.
	Friendly, familiar	¡Hola, Anita! Hi, Anita!	¡Chao, Eduardo! 'Bye, Eduardo!

Buenos días is used until noon. **Buenas tardes** is used until nightfall. **Buenas noches** is used in the evening as both hello and goodbye.

When you say hello or goodbye to your teacher or any adult, it's polite to complete your hello or goodbye by adding **señor**, *sir, Mr.,* **señora**, *ma'am, Mrs.,* or **señorita**, *Miss.* The written abbreviations of these titles are **Sr., Sra.,** and **Srta.**

A13 Comprensión *Comprehension*

Greetings: Morning, afternoon, or night?

	0	1	2	3	4	5	6
11 A.M.							
3 P.M.	✔						
9 P.M.							

A14 Actividad • Y ahora tú . . .

Greet each of the people pictured below. Then say goodbye to each one.

Roberto

Lupe

Srta. López

Sr. González

Sra. Martínez

¡Hola, amigos! 35

A15 Actividad • ¿Buenos días, buenas tardes o buenas noches?

In your summer job as a bilingual receptionist, you must greet people in Spanish as they arrive for appointments. Here are some entries from your appointment book.

(9:00 P.M., Mr. Ruiz)   Buenas noches, señor Ruiz.

1. (4:00 P.M., Miss Ortiz)
2. (10:00 A.M., Mr. González)
3. (3:00 P.M., Mrs. Martínez)
4. (9:00 A.M., Mr. Soto)
5. (8:00 P.M., Miss Portillo)

6. (5:00 P.M., Mr. Rivera)
7. (11:00 A.M., Miss Alonso)
8. (9:00 P.M., Mrs. Henríquez)
9. (4:30 P.M., Mr. Silva)
10. (12:30 P.M., Mrs. Pérez)

A16 SITUACIÓN • María Luisa y la profesora

SRA. VALDÉS   Buenos días, María Luisa. ¿Cómo estás?
MARÍA LUISA   Muy bien, señora, gracias. ¿Y cómo está usted?
SRA. VALDÉS   Bien, gracias.

A17 ESTRUCTURAS ESENCIALES *Essential Structures*
Spanish equivalents for the word you

Spanish has several words that are equivalents for the English word *you*. These words are called pronouns. Use **tú** when you talk to a friend or relative. Use **usted** when you address an adult you don't know well. A different verb form goes with each pronoun. Until now, you have used them together in questions.

Informal	*Formal*
¿Question word + **estás** + **tú**?	¿Question word + **está** + **usted**?
¡Hola, Jorge! ¿Cómo estás tú?	Buenas noches, señora. ¿Cómo está usted?

Words like **¿Cómo?** (*How*) and **¿Qué?** (*What*) are question words. They indicate the type of information being requested.

A18 Actividad • ¡A escoger! *Let's choose*

Using A16 as a model, choose the proper completion for each sentence.

1. Buenos días, profesor Colón. ¿Cómo / estás? / está usted?
2. ¡Hola, Elena! ¿Cómo / estás? / está usted?
3. Buenos días, señora Martínez. ¿Cómo / estás? / está usted?
4. ¿Qué tal, Ramón? ¿Cómo / estás? / está usted?

Actividad • Combinación *Combination*

Pair up with a classmate. Make your own dialogs using items from this table.
Take the parts of different characters in each dialog and include the names in
your dialog lines.

Buenas noches	¿Cómo estás?	Muy bien	Hasta mañana
Hola		Mal	Chao
Buenos días	¿Qué tal?	Regular	¡Qué pena!
		Bien, gracias.	Adiós
Buenas tardes	¿Cómo está?	Muy mal	Hasta luego

A 20 Comprensión

Some people will speak to you in Spanish. Which of the following would you say in reply?

¡Hola!   ¡Buenos días, señor!   ¡Hasta luego!   ¡Chao!
¡Adiós!   ¡Muy bien, gracias!   ¡Adiós, señora!

A 21 Actividad • Situaciones *Situations*

What are these people saying to each other? Copy and complete each caption.

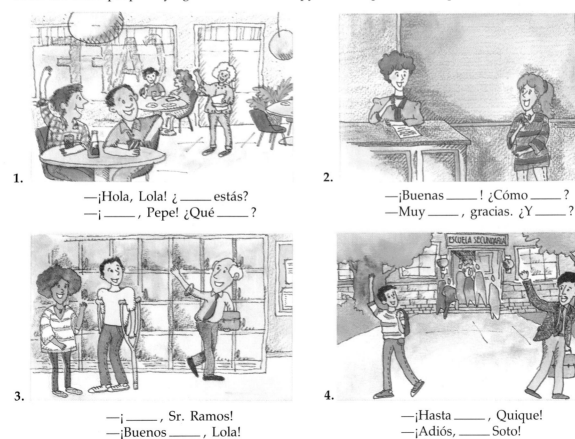

1.
—¡Hola, Lola! ¿ _____ estás?
—¡ _____, Pepe! ¿Qué _____?

2.
—¡Buenas _____! ¿Cómo _____?
—Muy _____, gracias. ¿Y _____?

3.
—¡ _____, Sr. Ramos!
—¡Buenos _____, Lola!

4.
—¡Hasta _____, Quique!
—¡Adiós, _____ Soto!

¡Hola, amigos!   37

Introducing yourself is the most direct way to make new friends. Sometimes another friend can help.

B1 # En la escuela. En la clase. 📼

RICARDO	¡Hola! Yo me llamo Ricardo. ¿Cómo te llamas tú?
LUPE	Me llamo Lupe. ¡Mucho gusto!
RICARDO	¡Mucho gusto! Bueno . . . hasta luego, Lupe.
LUPE	Hasta luego, Ricardo.

Él se llama Ricardo.

Ella se llama Lupe.

B2   Actividad • Para completar

Complete the sentences according to the dialog.

1. ¿Cómo te . . . ?
2. Yo me llamo . . .
3. Me . . . Lupe.

4. ¡Mucho . . . !
5. Hasta . . . , Ricardo.

B3   ¿Sabes que . . . ?

Many Spanish names are like English names: **Felipe** *Philip,* **Antonio,** *Anthony,* **Tomás,** *Thomas.* Other Spanish names are quite different: **Soledad, Javier, Pilar, Diego.** Here are some common Spanish first names. Do you know any others? Which ones?

Nombres de chicos y chicas							
CHICOS				**CHICAS**			
Alberto	Esteban	Juan	Pedro	Alicia	Dolores	Inés	Pilar
Alfonso	Fernando	Julio	Ramón	Amalia	Elena	Luisa	Rosario
Carlos	Francisco	Manuel	Raúl	Ana	Elsa	Margarita	Sofía
Diego	Gonzalo	Miguel	Santiago	Blanca	Eva	María	Soledad
Enrique	Guillermo	Pablo	Víctor	Cristina	Guadalupe	Olga	Victoria

	¿Cómo te llamas tú?	Yo me llamo . . .
	What's your name?	My name is . . .

B5   Actividad • Presentaciones   *Introductions*

Choose a Spanish name for yourself if you haven't done so before. Introduce
yourself to your friends and ask them what their names are. You introduce
yourself saying **Yo me llamo . . .   ¿Cómo te llamas tú?** The second student
answers: **Me llamo . . .   Mucho gusto,** and continues to introduce himself,
asking the next student's name.

B6   SITUACIÓN • Después de la clase   *After school*

En el patio de la escuela.

ANTONIO   ¡Ricardo!, ¡Ricardo!
RICARDO   ¿Sí?
ANTONIO   ¡Oye! Por favor, ¿cómo se llama la
chica nueva?
RICARDO   ¿Quién, la chica de Arizona?
ANTONIO   No, la chica de México.
RICARDO   Ella se llama Lupe.
ANTONIO   ¿Lupe? Gracias, Ricardo.
RICARDO   De nada, Antonio.

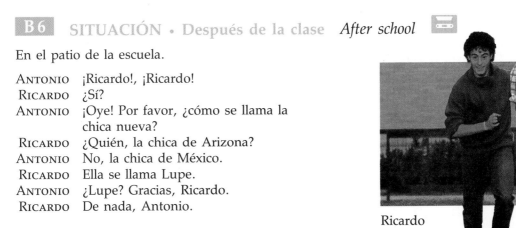

Ricardo
y Antonio

B7   Actividad • Para completar

Complete the sentences according to B6.

1. Por favor, ¿cómo . . . ?
2. ¿Quién, la . . . de Arizona?
3. No, la chica de . . .

4. Ella se . . . Lupe.
5. Gracias, . . .
6. De . . .

B8   SE DICE ASÍ
Asking and giving someone else's name

	¿Cómo se llama él?	Él se llama Ricardo.
	What's his name?	His name is Ricardo.
	¿Cómo se llama ella?	Ella se llama Lupe.
	What's her name?	Her name is Lupe.

B 9 Actividad • Nombres y más nombres   *Names and more names*

The new boy in class, Luis, is asking you the names of his classmates. Answer as indicated in parentheses.

—¿Cómo se llama la chica? (Ana)
—Ella se llama Ana.

1. ¿Cómo se llama el chico? (Paco)
2. ¿Cómo se llama ella? (Lupe)
3. ¿Cómo se llama el chico de California? (Pepe)
4. ¿Cómo se llama la chica de Nuevo México? (Ana)

5. ¿Cómo te llamas tú?
6. ¿Cómo se llama él? (Tomás)
7. ¿Cómo se llama el señor Ortega? (Esteban)
8. ¡Oye! ¿Cómo me llamo yo? (Luis)

B 10 Actividad • ¿Cómo se llama . . . ?

Ask a friend the Spanish names of other students in the classroom. Ask: **¿Cómo se llama el chico?** or **¿Cómo se llama la chica?**

B 11 Actividad • ¡A escribir!

Complete the answer to each question.

1. ¿Cómo te llamas?
   _____ Dolores.
2. ¿Cómo se llama el chico?
   _____ Diego.
3. ¿Se llama ella María?
   No, _____ Isabel.
4. ¿Se llama él Francisco?
   No, _____ Pablo.

5. ¿Cómo se llama la chica?
   _____ Susana.
6. ¿Te llamas tú José?
   No, _____ Enrique.
7. ¿Quién, la chica de Texas?
   No, la _____ de Arizona.
8. ¿Se llama Irene?
   No, se _____ Inés.

B 12 ¿Sabes que . . . ?

Persons named **José** are likely to have the nickname **Pepe.** Other common Spanish nicknames are:

Lupe for Guadalupe
Paco for Francisco
Lola for Dolores
Mongo for Ramón
Fina for Josefina
Tere for Teresa
Quique for Enrique
Ale for Alejandro or Alejandra

B 13 Actividad • ¡A escribir!

Antonio finally meets the new girl, Lupe. Write their conversation. Use dashes at the beginning of each line to indicate a change of speaker.

Actividad • Un juego *A game*

The class divides into two teams. Students take turns trying to recall the Spanish names of players on the opposing team, asking **¿Te llamas . . . ?** The student being questioned replies **Sí, me llamo . . .** or **No, me llamo . . .** Each correct guess is worth one point. After everybody has been questioned, volunteers may try to name all the students on the opposing team, saying **Él/ella se llama . . .**

B 15 ESTRUCTURAS ESENCIALES
Gender of nouns and the definite article

Definite article	Noun
el	chico
el	colegio
la	chica
la	escuela

1. A word that names a person **(chico, chica)** or a place or a thing **(colegio, escuela)** is called a *noun.* In Spanish, every noun has a gender: either masculine gender or feminine gender.

2. Most nouns ending in **-o** are masculine **(chico, colegio).** Most nouns ending in **-a** are feminine **(chica, escuela).**

3. The Spanish form of the definite article *(the)* depends on the gender of the noun it accompanies.
   el is used with a *masculine noun*   **el chico, el colegio**
   la is used with a *feminine noun*   **la chica, la escuela**

Note: Not all Spanish nouns end in **-o** or **-a**—for example, **señor** and **clase.** One good way to remember the gender of this type of noun is to learn the noun with its definite article: **el señor, la clase.**

B 16 Actividad • ¿El o la?

Say the following nouns with their definite articles.

escuela, clase, señorita, colegio, señora, chico, patio, señor

B 17 Actividad • ¿Qué crees? *What do you think?*

The Spanish words in the following list have *cognates* in English. They are similar in form and meaning to English words, though pronounced very differently. Can you figure out the gender of each word? On a piece of paper, write two headings: masculine and feminine. Now write each word from the list under the appropriate heading. Include the articles.

el director	el actor	la televisión	la imaginación	el fotógrafo
la fotografía	la idea	el café	el ingeniero	la hamburguesa
la rosa	el ángel	el tigre	la directora	la doctora

B 18 Comprensión

Boy or girl? That is the question.

	0	1	2	3	4	5	6	7	8	9	10	11	12
Chico													
Chica	✔												

B 19 SITUACIÓN • Una sorpresa *A surprise*

asking and telling where people are from

Spanish is spoken in many countries, including the United States. The Spanish-speaking young people in this section are from California, Texas, Puerto Rico, Mexico, Spain, and Argentina. You'll be meeting them again.

C1   ¿De dónde son?

Él se llama Pedro Gómez.
Pedro es de Texas,
Estados Unidos.

María Bernal
y Carlos Cajal.
Ellos son de
España.

Nosotras somos
de México. Yo me
llamo Elena Llansó.
Ella se llama Rosa.
¿De dónde son ustedes?

Yo me llamo
Pablo Matos.
Soy de Puerto
Rico. ¿De
dónde
eres tú?

C2   Actividad • ¿Cuál país?   *Which country?*

Look at the map on the following page. Find the countries where the young people in C1 are from.

¡Hola, amigos!   43

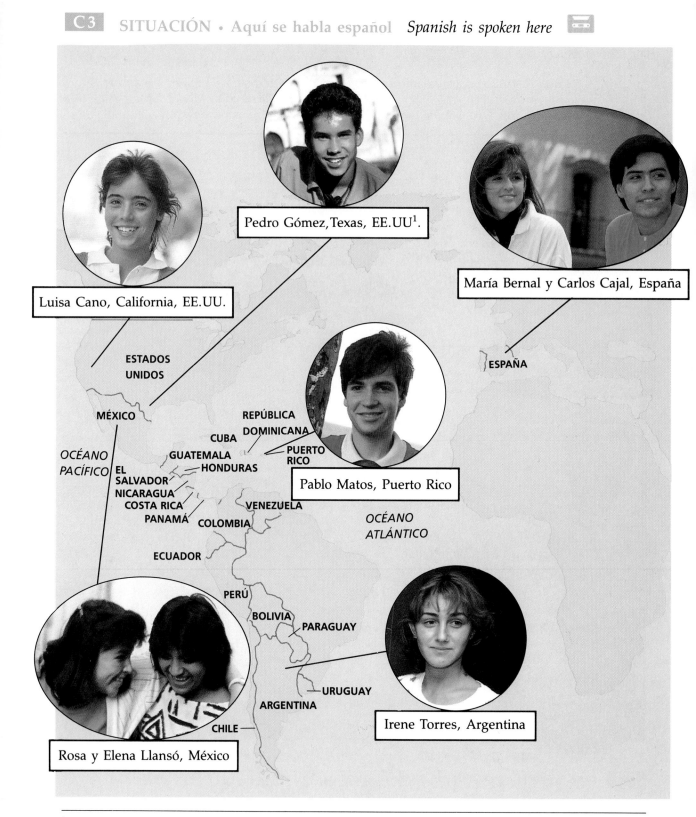

Pedro Gómez, Texas, EE.UU[1].

María Bernal y Carlos Cajal, España

Luisa Cano, California, EE.UU.

ESTADOS
UNIDOS

ESPAÑA

MÉXICO

REPÚBLICA
DOMINICANA

CUBA

PUERTO
RICO

GUATEMALA
HONDURAS

OCÉANO
PACÍFICO

EL
SALVADOR
NICARAGUA
COSTA RICA
PANAMÁ

Pablo Matos, Puerto Rico

VENEZUELA

COLOMBIA

OCÉANO
ATLÁNTICO

ECUADOR

PERÚ

BOLIVIA
PARAGUAY

URUGUAY
ARGENTINA

CHILE

Irene Torres, Argentina

Rosa y Elena Llansó, México

---

[1]**EE.UU.** is an abbreviation for **los Estados Unidos,** *The United States.*

C4 Actividad • ¿Cómo se llama . . . ?

Do you remember their names?

1. ¿el chico de Texas?
2. ¿la chica de España?
3. ¿el chico de Puerto Rico?

4. ¿el chico de España?
5. ¿la chica de México?
6. ¿la chica de California?

C5 Actividad • Combinación

To say where these people are from, choose an item from each column to form your answer. You will have to use some items more than once.

Irene es de Argentina.

Pablo Matos Nosotros	es de	**los Estados Unidos**
Rosa y Elena	somos de	**España** **México**
Irene María y Carlos	son de	**Puerto Rico**
		Argentina

C6 SE DICE ASÍ
Asking and saying where people are from

¿De dónde eres tú?	Soy de Los Ángeles.
¿De dónde son ellos?	Son de España.
¿De dónde es ella?	Es de Argentina.
¿Tú eres de México?	Sí, soy de México.

C7 Actividad • Charla

Ask your classmates where they are from and reply when they ask you.

—¿De dónde eres tú?
—Yo soy de Chicago. ¿Y tú?
—Yo soy de San Diego.

C8 Actividad • ¿De dónde es él? ¿De dónde es ella?

Look at the photos in C3. Identify each person
and say where he or she is from.

Ella es Luisa Cano.
Es de California.

C9 Actividad • ¿Sí o no?

Imagine that you are one of the people in C1. Your classmates will try to guess your identity by asking you questions. Reply **sí** or **no**. Here are some questions to try.

—¿Eres de España?   —¿Te llamas . . . ?

C10 ESTRUCTURAS ESENCIALES
Subject pronouns and the verb ser *(to be)*

| Singular | | Plural | |
Subject Pronoun	Verb Form	Subject Pronoun	Verb Form
yo	soy	nosotros(as)	somos
tú	eres	vosotros(as)	sois
usted (Ud.)		ustedes (Uds.)	
él	es	ellos	son
ella		ellas	

1. Do not capitalize the pronoun **yo** *(I)* except at the beginning of the sentence.

2. In Spanish America, **ustedes** (abbreviated **Uds.**) is used as the plural form of both **tú** and **usted** (abbreviated **Ud.**). In Spain, however, the plural form of **tú** is **vosotros.** In this textbook, only the form **ustedes** (**Uds.**) will be used.

3. The masculine plural forms **nosotros** and **ellos** are used to refer to any group of males or to any mixed group of males and females. The feminine forms **nosotras** and **ellas** are used to refer to a group that includes females only.

4. The name of the verb, for example **ser** *(to be)*, is called the infinitive. This is the form you will find in dictionaries and in vocabulary lists.

5. When you use a Spanish verb, you need to pick a form of the verb that agrees with the subject noun or pronoun: **yo soy** *I am;* **tú eres** *You are;* **Elena es** *Elena is.*

6. Most native speakers of Spanish use a verb without a subject pronoun because the verb form alone indicates who the subject is.
    ¿De dónde **es** Pedro? **Es** de Texas.   *Where is Pedro from? He's from Texas.*

7. The English verb *to be* has two Spanish equivalents, the verbs **ser** and **estar.** You will learn the verb **estar** in Unit 5. Use the verb **ser** to express *who* or *what the subject is,* and to indicate origin.
    Soy María Bernal.   *I am María Bernal.*
    Pablo Matos **es** de Puerto Rico.   *Pablo Matos is from Puerto Rico.*
    María y Pablo **son** estudiantes.   *María and Pablo are students.*

C11 Actividad • ¿Quién? ¿Yo? *Who, me?*

Sides are being chosen for a game. People are not sure who has been picked.
Answer affirmatively, using the correct subject pronoun.

—¿María y Carmen?   —Sí, ellas.   —¿Pablo y yo?   —Sí, ustedes.

1. ¿Enrique?
2. ¿Yo?
3. ¿Silvia y tú?
4. ¿Juan y Carlos?
5. ¿Ustedes?
6. ¿La chica y yo?
7. ¿Inés y Anita?
8. ¿La señora Valdés?
9. ¿Usted y Pablo?

Actividad • ¡A escribir!

Suppose you are one of the editors of your school's newspaper. You find that your star reporter repeats names too often. Rewrite her sentences, changing the underlined words to a subject pronoun.

> La chica es María López. María López es de Puerto Rico.
>
> La chica es María López. Ella es de Puerto Rico.
>
> Jorge y yo somos de California. Jorge y yo somos de los Estados Unidos.
>
> Jorge y yo somos de California. Nosotros somos de los Estados Unidos.

1. El chico es Roberto Mercado. Roberto Mercado es de Argentina.
2. ¿De dónde son Matilde y Carmen? Matilde y Carmen son de México.
3. La chica es Sofía. Sofía es de Madrid.
4. El chico es Miguel. Miguel es de Puerto Rico.
5. Dolores y yo somos de El Paso. Dolores y yo somos de Texas.
6. ¿De dónde son Marta y José? Marta y José son de Miami.
7. El señor Machado y Sara son de la Florida. Sí, el señor Machado y Sara son de Miami.
8. ¿De dónde es Lupe? Lupe es de Arizona.

C13 Actividad • Una entrevista   *An interview*

Soledad is being interviewed for the school magazine. Here are her answers to the reporter's questions. Write the questions.

1. Me llamo Soledad Muñoz.
2. Soy de San Agustín.
3. El chico se llama Salvador.
4. La chica se llama Rosario.
5. Ellos son de Texas.
6. Somos de los Estados Unidos.

C14 Actividad • Falta algo

Supply the correct form of **ser**.

1. Él _____ de California.
2. Nosotras _____ de México.
3. ¿_____ tú Miguel Soto?
4. Tú y yo _____ de los Estados Unidos.
5. ¿De dónde _____ ustedes?
6. Ellas _____ de España.
7. Lupe _____ de Panamá.
8. Yo _____ de Chile.

C15 Actividad • Combinación

Form at least five sentences in Spanish by choosing the appropriate items from each column. You will have to use some verb forms more than once.

> Yo soy de España.

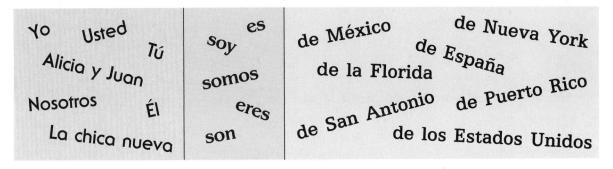

| Yo Usted Tú Alicia y Juan Nosotros Él La chica nueva | es soy somos eres son | de México de Nueva York de España de la Florida de San Antonio de Puerto Rico de los Estados Unidos |

More than 285 million people speak Spanish. Many live in the United States
(more than 20 million). Others live in Spain, Mexico, Central America, South
America, and the islands of the Caribbean.

C17 ESTRUCTURAS ESENCIALES
Interrogative sentences

The following four questions elicit a *yes/no* answer.

¿Tú eres de México?	Sí, soy de México.
¿Tú eres Miguel Soto?	Sí, soy Miguel Soto.
¿Es Carmen de Texas?	Sí, Carmen es de Texas.
¿Es Ud. el señor Colón?	Sí, soy el señor Colón.

Two ways of asking questions to elicit *yes/no* answers:

1	¿subject + verb + rest of sentence?
2	¿verb + subject + rest of sentence?

1. As you have seen, Spanish uses two question marks, an inverted one at the
   beginning of the sentence and a standard one at the end.

2. In both examples of interrogative sentences there is a change of intonation.
   The voice rises at the end of the sentence.

3. Notice that in the first two examples above, a regular sentence is made
   interrogative by only changing the intonation and adding the question marks.

4. In the last two examples, the verb is placed at the beginning of the sentence
   and the question marks are added.

C18 Actividad • Preguntas *Questions*

Your friend's questions are based on incorrect guesses. Ask the question again
using the correct information given in parentheses.

—¿Eres tú de España? (los Estados Unidos)
—¿Eres tú de los Estados Unidos?

1. ¿Son ellos de Argentina? (México)
2. ¿Son ustedes de Perú? (Venezuela)
3. ¿Es ella María López? (Blanca Nieves)
4. ¿Es él Pablo Matos? (Pedro Matos)

5. ¿Eres tú de Puerto Rico? (España)
6. ¿Son ellas María y Ana? (Teresa y Eva)
7. ¿Es ella de Nuevo México? (Nevada)
8. ¿Eres tú de Acapulco? (la Florida)

C19 Comprensión

Where are they from? Select an appropriate answer from the list.

A. Ella es de España.
B. Yo soy de Boston.
C. Somos de México.

D. Carlos es de España.
E. De Puerto Rico.
F. Irene es de Argentina.

G. No, es de California.
H. Son de San Antonio.

You've learned how to greet people, give some information about yourself, and ask others about themselves. Here are some further opportunities to use your new skills!

1   Tarjetas postales 📧

Some day you may want to have a pen pal in a Spanish-speaking country. For now, imagine that these postcards are for you.

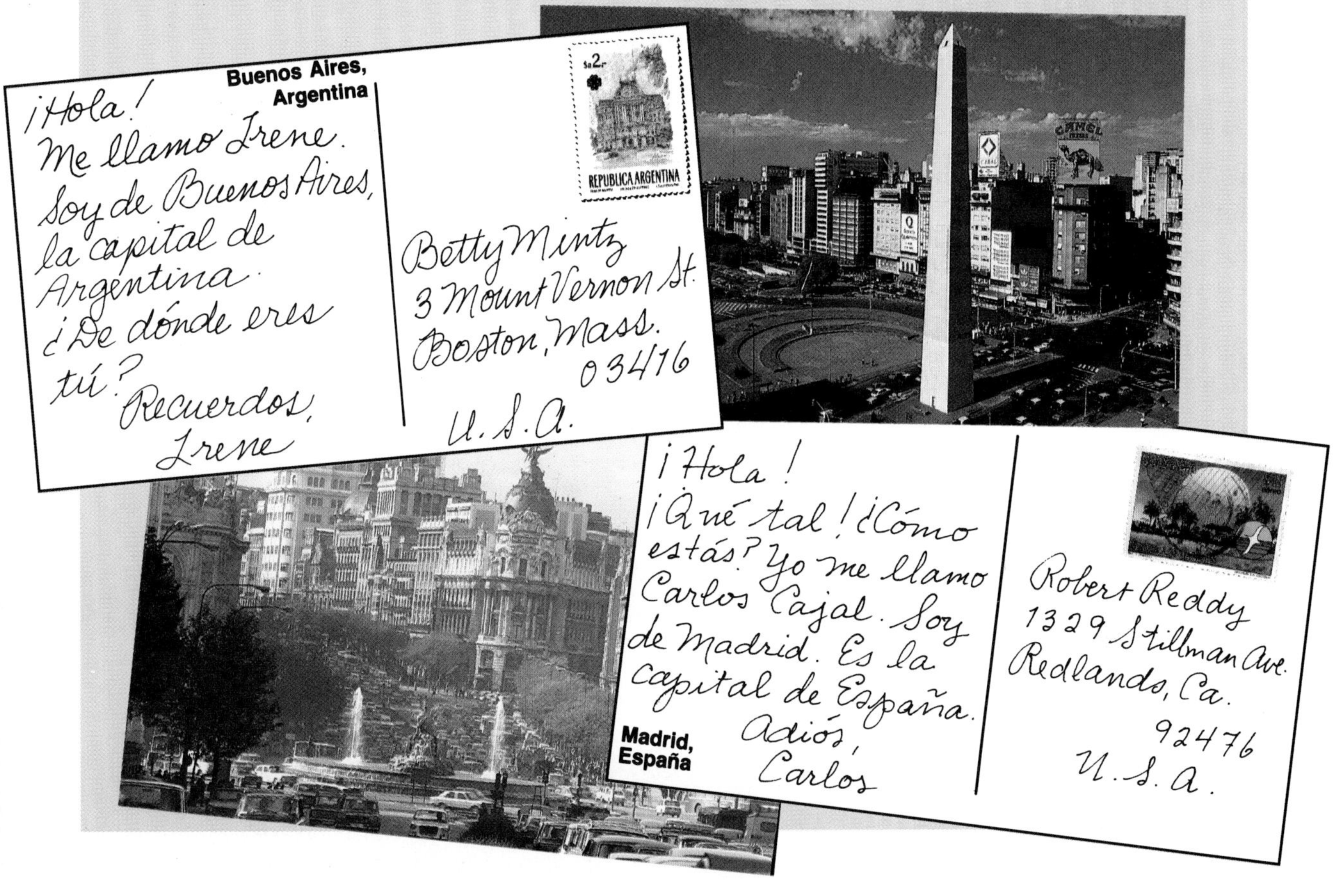

Buenos Aires, Argentina

¡Hola!
Me llamo Irene.
Soy de Buenos Aires,
la capital de
Argentina.
¿De dónde eres
tú?
Recuerdos,
Irene

REPÚBLICA ARGENTINA

Betty Mintz
3 Mount Vernon St.
Boston, Mass.
03416
U.S.A.

Madrid, España

¡Hola!
¡Qué tal! ¿Cómo
estás? Yo me llamo
Carlos Cajal. Soy
de Madrid. Es la
capital de España.
Adiós,
Carlos

Robert Reddy
1329 Stillman Ave.
Redlands, Ca.
92476
U.S.A.

2   Actividad • ¿Quién es la chica? ¿Quién es el chico?

Tell about your new pen pals. What are their names? Where are they from?

3   Actividad • ¡A escribir!

Write a postcard introducing yourself to a pen pal in a Spanish-speaking country.
Use the postcards above as a model.

¡Hola, amigos!   **49**

Actividad • ¿Qué falta? *What's missing?*

Read the dialogs, supplying the missing words. Then, write the lines.

1. EVA   ¿Cómo te ____ tú?
    ROSA   Me ____ Rosa.
    EVA   ¿Cómo ____ tú, Rosa?
    ROSA   Muy ____, gracias.

2. RICARDO   ¿De dónde ____ tú?
    ALBERTO   Yo ____ México.
    RICARDO   ¿Y Diego? ¿De ____ es él?
    ALBERTO   Diego ____ de Argentina.

5 Actividad • Diálogos *Dialogs*

Talk with a classmate. From each numbered group, use as many words and phrases as you can and add other words of your own.

1. Señor / señorita / ¿cómo . . . ? / muy / ¿de dónde . . . ? / Costa Rica
2. Buenos / llamas / Gabriel / Susana / gusto / adiós
3. ¿Qué tal? / llama / chico de México / Pablo / gracias

6 Actividad • ¡Buenas noches!

It's 8:00 P.M. You are at the door, handing out printed name tags at a Spanish festival. As people arrive, greet them and find out where they're from.

Señor Alonso, Carmen, Señora Méndez, Señorita Colón, Luz, Tomás, and Señor García arrive.

Señor Alonso
(arrives)

Buenas noches, señor.
¿Cómo se llama usted?
¿De dónde es usted?

Carmen
(arrives)

¡Hola!
¿Cómo te llamas tú?
¿De dónde eres tú?

7 Actividad • Reacciones

Give the correct reply to the following.

1. Buenos días.
2. ¿El chico se llama José?
3. Yo me llamo Gloria.
4. ¿Eres de España?
5. Adiós.
6. ¿Cómo estás?
7. Buenas tardes.
8. Hasta mañana.

8 Actividad • ¡Bienvenidos! *Welcome!*

You are at the airport to meet exchange students arriving from Spanish-speaking countries. What do you say? Write one possible conversation.

9 Actividad • ¡A escoger!

Choose the appropriate reply and say it.

¿Cómo estás?
• Soy de Argentina. • Bien, gracias. • José Gómez. • De nada.
You would say: *Bien, gracias.*

1. ¿De dónde eres?
• Muy bien, gracias. • Soy de Puerto Rico. • Se llama Fabio. • Buenas tardes.
2. ¿Cómo se llama ella?
• Buenas noches. • Javier González. • Mucho gusto. • Isabel Parra.
3. ¿Qué tal?
• Adiós. • Bien. ¿Y tú? • Ella es de Texas. • De Puerto Rico.
4. Me llamo Pilar.
• Muy bien. • No, soy de Argentina. • Hasta luego. • Mucho gusto.
5. ¿Es usted de México?
• Muy bien. • De nada. • No, soy de Nevada. • Hasta luego.
6. ¿Cómo está Lupe?
• Buenos días. • Muy bien, gracias. • Lupe López. • De España.
7. Adiós.
• ¡Hola! • Buenos días. • Hasta mañana. • Rosa Santos.
8. ¿Yo? ¡Muy mal!
• Bien, gracias. • ¡Qué pena! • Muy bien. • Hasta luego.
9. ¿Se llama Carlos?
• No, Pepe. • De México. • Regular. • ¿Y tú?

10 Pronunciación, lectura, dictado

1. Listen carefully and repeat what you hear.

2. The Spanish consonants **h** (always silent) and **ñ**. Listen, then read aloud.
hola   hasta   Sra. Henríquez   Honduras
señor   señorita   señora   España   español   mañana

3. Copy the following sentences to prepare yourself to write them from dictation.
¡Hola, Hilda!   ¡Hasta mañana, señor Núñez!   Horacio es de Honduras.

¿LO SABES?

Let's review some important points you have learned in this unit.

Do you know different ways to say hello and goodbye to young people and adults in Spanish?
Say hello and goodbye to the following people in Spanish, using different expressions.

1. Eva
2. Pablo
3. Mr. González
4. Mrs. González
5. Miss López
6. your teacher

Do you know how to introduce yourself, give your name, and say what other people's names are?
Say hello to your new classmates and give your name.

Find out what their names are. Start the questions using **¿Cómo . . .**

1. _____ tú?
2. _____ ella?
3. _____ él?
4. _____ la chica?

Say what their names are.

1. _____ Lupe.
2. Usted _____ Roberto.
3. _____ Diego.
4. Te _____ Carmen.

Can you ask and say where people are from?
Complete the following questions and answers about where someone is from.

1. ¿ _____ tú? _____ California.
2. ¿ _____ él? _____ Puerto Rico.
3. ¿ _____ ella? _____ Argentina.

Do you know the forms of the verb *ser?*
Write the correct form of **ser** that goes with each subject.

1. Ustedes
2. Yo
3. Juan y Eva
4. Usted
5. Nosotras
6. Ellas
7. El chico
8. Tú

VOCABULARIO

SECTION A

adiós *goodbye*
bien *well, good, fine*
buenas noches *good evening, good night, hello*
buenas tardes *good afternoon*
buenos días *good morning*
el **colegio** *school*
¿cómo? *how?*
¿cómo está? *how are you? (pol. sing.)*
¿cómo estás? *how are you? (fam. sing.)*
chao *so long, 'bye*
el **día** *day*
el *(m.) the*
en *in*
gracias *thank you*
hasta luego *see you later*
hasta mañana *see you tomorrow*
hola *hello*
la *(f.) the*
mal *bad*
muy *very*
muy mal *awful, terrible*
el **profesor** *teacher (m.)*
la **profesora** *teacher (f.)*
¡qué pena! *what a pity*
¿qué tal? *how are things?*

regular *so-so*
el **señor** (abbreviation **Sr.**) *Mr., sir*
la **señora** (abbreviation **Sra.**) *Mrs., ma'am*
la **señorita** (abbreviation **Srta.**) *Miss*
tú *you (fam.)*
usted *you (pol.)*
y *and*
yo *I*

SECTION B

bueno *well*
la **clase** *classroom*
¿cómo se llama él (ella)? *what's his (her) name?*
¿cómo te llamas tú? *what's your name?*
¿cómo se llaman? *what are their names?*
la **chica** *girl*
el **chico** *boy*
de *from*
de nada *you're welcome*
después de *after*
él *he*
ella *she*
la **escuela** *school*

me llamo . . . *my name is . . .*
México *Mexico*
mucho gusto *nice to meet you*
no *no*
nueva *new*
¡oye! *hey!*
el **patio** *inner courtyard*
por favor *please*
¿quién? *who?*
se llama . . . *his (her) name is . . .*
sí *yes*

SECTION C

¿de dónde? *from where?*
ellos *they (m.)*
ellas *they (f.)*
España *Spain*
los Estados Unidos (abbreviation **EE.UU.**) *United States (U.S.)*
nosotros, nosotras *we*
ser *to be*
Ud. (abbreviation of **usted**) *you*
ustedes (abbreviation **Uds.**) *you (pl.)*
vosotros, vosotras *you (fam. pl.)*

ESTUDIO DE PALABRAS

Look through the vocabulary list and pick out the nouns that identify persons, places, or things. Make two new lists, one for the masculine words and one for the feminine. Include the corresponding article.

VAMOS A LEER°

Antes de leer *Before reading*

Before you begin to read in Spanish, here are a few suggestions. Read each new selection through for general meaning without looking up any words. Cognates—words that look alike in Spanish and English and have a similar meaning—will help you. Try to pronounce them the Spanish way, and write them down.

El mundo hispánico

España es un país° de Europa°, al suroeste° de Francia. Sus vecinos° son Francia y Portugal. La capital de España es Madrid. María Bernal es de Madrid.

Luisa Cano es de California y Pedro Gómez es de Texas. Los dos° son de los Estados Unidos. Ellos son mexicano americanos°.

---

vamos a leer *let's read*   **un país** *a country*   **de Europa** *of Europe*   **al suroeste** *to the southwest*
sus vecinos *its neighbors*   **los dos** *both*   **mexicano americanos** *Mexican Americans*

Jorge Llansó es de México, un país al sur° de los Estados Unidos. La capital de México es la Ciudad° de México. Jorge es de la capital.

Pablo Matos es de San Juan, la capital de Puerto Rico. Puerto Rico es una° isla° en el Mar° Caribe. En Puerto Rico hablan° español.

¿De dónde es Irene Torres? Ella es de Argentina, un país de Suramérica°. Sus vecinos son: Uruguay al este°, Chile al oeste°, y Bolivia y Paraguay al norte°.

Actividad • ¡Faltan palabras!

Complete these statements, according to the reading **El mundo hispánico,** supplying the missing information.

1. Puerto Rico es una . . .
2. Madrid es . . . de España.
3. Luisa Cano y Pedro Gómez son de . . .
4. Uruguay es un país de . . .
5. México es un país . . . los Estados Unidos.
6. En España y en Suramérica hablan . . .
7. Chile es un . . .
8. Un país al norte de Argentina es . . .
9. San Juan es la capital de . . .

Actividad • Proyecto   *Project*

Make a postcard. On a piece of thin cardboard, tape a picture from a magazine showing one of the Spanish-speaking countries mentioned in the reading. On the other side of the card, write a message home in Spanish about the country.

---

al sur *to the south* **ciudad** *city* **una** *an* **isla** *island* **mar** *sea* **hablan** *they speak* **Suramérica** *South America*
al este *to the east* **al oeste** *to the west* **al norte** *to the north*

Un paseo por el parque°

Taking an afternoon walk is a cherished custom in Spanish-speaking countries.
Read what people say when they see each other in the park.

Actividad

Find replies for the greetings in the picture of the park, above. Then practice the
exchanges with a classmate.

Un paseo por el parque *A stroll in the park*   **a todo el mundo** *to everybody*   **más o menos** *so-so*   **¿Qué hay?** *What's
up?*   **nada** *nothing*   . . . **están ustedes?** *are you?* (plural)

El regalo°

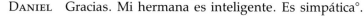

DANIEL Me llamo Daniel Arias. Soy de México. Vivo° con mi° familia en una colonia° de la capital.

ADRIANA Soy Adriana Arias. Daniel y yo somos hermanos°.

DANIEL Sí, ella y yo somos hermanos. ¡Qué tragedia!

ADRIANA Daniel es mi hermano menor°.

DANIEL "¡Menor!" Sólo un año° menor.

ADRIANA Mi hermano es inteligente. Es perfecto.

DANIEL Gracias. Mi hermana es inteligente. Es simpática°.

Tocan a la puerta°.

SEÑOR Buenas tardes. ¿Familia Arias?

ADRIANA Sí, ¿es para mi mamá°?

SEÑOR No. ¿Eres Adriana Arias? Y tú, ¿eres Daniel Arias?

DANIEL Sí.

SEÑOR Es un regalo para ustedes. Hasta luego.

DANIEL Adiós, señor. Adriana, ¿qué es?

ADRIANA Un regalo para nosotros, ¡tonto°!

DANIEL ¡Fantástico!

Actividad • Para completar

Complete the following sentences according to **El regalo**.

1. El chico se llama . . .
2. Él es de . . .
3. La chica se llama . . .
4. Daniel y Adriana son . . .
5. Ellos son de . . .
6. El regalo es para . . .

---

regalo *gift* **Vivo** *I live* **mi** *my* **colonia** *neighborhood* **hermanos** *brother and sister* **hermano menor** *younger brother* **Sólo un año** *Only one year* **simpática** *nice* **Tocan a la puerta.** *Someone knocks at the door.* **para mi mamá** *for my mom* **tonto** *fool*

UNIDAD 2
En la escuela

Schools in Spain and Latin America are not very different from your own. Many students attend private schools, usually called *colegios*. Others go to public schools, called *escuelas públicas*.

As in the United States, schools are often named after famous people. In this unit you will see one school named for Benito Juárez (1806–1872), president of Mexico around the time of Abraham Lincoln. Another school is named for Simón Bolívar, the Liberator (1783–1830), who was a hero of the Spanish American independence movement.

In this unit, you will:

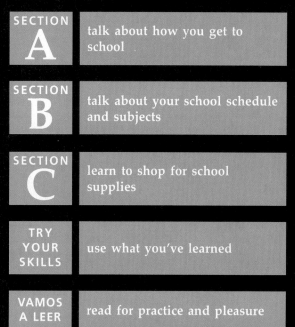

SECTION A	talk about how you get to school
SECTION B	talk about your school schedule and subjects
SECTION C	learn to shop for school supplies
TRY YOUR SKILLS	use what you've learned
VAMOS A LEER	read for practice and pleasure

59

talking about how to get to school

With a population of about 20 million, Mexico City may be the most densely populated city in the world. Students who live there travel through heavy traffic on their way to school. Some walk while others ride a bike, come by car, or take a bus or subway.

A1 # ¿Cómo vienes a la escuela? 📼

Los estudiantes de la Escuela Secundaria Benito Juárez vienen de muchas partes de la ciudad. Muchos vienen temprano, pero no todos. Algunos vienen tarde hoy. ¿Por qué? Porque el autobús escolar número ocho tiene un problema. Pero, ¡mira!, ahí viene el autobús.

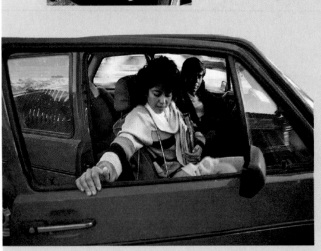

ISABEL	Andrés, ¿vienes tú en autobús con Carlos?
ANDRÉS	No, yo no vengo en autobús, vengo en auto.
ISABEL	Y ustedes, ¿cómo vienen?
RAÚL Y MARTA	Nosotros venimos en metro.
ISABEL	¿Y José? ¿Cuándo viene? ¿Viene él con Carlos?
MARTA	Yo no sé.
ANDRÉS	Mira, ahí viene José.
ISABEL	¿No viene en bicicleta?
RAÚL	No, hoy viene a pie.
ISABEL	¡Ah, por fin viene el autobús! ¡Carlos, mi libro de inglés, por favor!

Actividad • ¿Es cierto o no?

Say whether the following statements are correct (**Es cierto**) or not (**No es cierto**) according to the information in A1. Correct the statements that aren't true.

1. Los estudiantes vienen de muchas partes de la ciudad.
2. Todos vienen temprano.
3. El autobús número ocho viene temprano.
4. Andrés viene en bicicleta.
5. Raúl y Marta vienen a pie.

6. Raúl viene en metro con Carlos.
7. José viene a pie.
8. José viene hoy en autobús.
9. Carlos viene en bicicleta.
10. Isabel y Carlos vienen en auto.

A3   Actividad • ¿Qué es? *What is it?*

Es
un . . .

un . . .

una . . .

un . . .

A4   Comprensión

Are they all coming to school?

	0	1	2	3	4	5	6	7	8	9
Sí										
No	✔									

The verb venir

venir *to come*					
Yo	**vengo**	a pie.	Nosotros(as)	**venimos**	en bicicleta.
Tú	**vienes**	en auto.	Vosotros(as)	**venís**	en metro.
Usted, él, ella	**viene**	en metro	Ustedes, ellos(as)	**vienen**	en autobús.

1. The pronouns **usted, él,** and **ella** go with the same form, **viene.**
2. The pronouns **ustedes, ellos,** and **ellas** go with the same form, **vienen.**
3. Use **a pie** when somebody walks somewhere. With a means of transportation use the formula: **en** + means of transportation.

A6 Actividad • ¿Tarde o temprano? *Late or early?*

The school bus has had some trouble this morning. Report that the following people are coming to school late.

—¿Enrique?   —¿Yo?
—Enrique viene tarde.   —Yo vengo tarde.
                      vienen
1. ¿Carmen? viene   2. ¿Jorge y Antonio?   3. ¿La chica nueva? viene 4. ¿Usted? viene
5. ¿Nosotros? venimos   6. ¿Tú? vienes   7. ¿Ustedes? vienen   8. ¿Raúl y yo? venimos

A7 Actividad • A la escuela . . . ¡rápido!

Look at the drawings and say how you think these people come to school.

1.

2.

3.

4.

5.

A8 Actividad • ¡A escribir!

Write the correct form of **venir**.

1. El autobús _____ tarde.
2. Nosotros _____ en metro.
3. Yo _____ temprano.

4. Ellos no _____ temprano.
5. El profesor _____ en auto.
6. Ustedes _____ en bicicleta.

7. ¿Cómo _____ Isabel?
8. Ella _____ a pie.
9. Tú no _____ en autobús.

A9 ¿Sabes que . . . ?

In Spanish-speaking countries, the minimum age for obtaining a driver's license is 18. Few high school students drive cars or motorcycles. Bicycles are fairly common in large cities but to travel anywhere, most students use public transportation. Private schools sometimes have their own buses. Students who attend public schools usually use public buses.

A10 SE DICE ASÍ
Asking for and giving an explanation

¿Cómo vienen a la escuela?	Vienen en autobús.
How do they come to school?	They come by bus.
¿Por qué vienen tarde?	Porque el autobús tiene un problema.
Why are they late?	Because the bus has a problem.
	(Because there's a problem with the bus.)

To find out something, you can ask a question beginning with a question word:

| **¿Cómo?** | *How?* | **¿Quién?** | *Who?* | **¿Por qué?** | *Why?* |
| **¿Cuándo?** | *When?* | **¿De dónde?** | *From where?* | **¿Qué?** | *What?* |

When used to ask why, **¿por qué?** is written as two words. The **qué** has a written accent. When used to tell why, **porque** *(because)* is a single word without any accent.

A11 Actividad • Charla

With a classmate, talk about how you come to school. Here are some questions you might use.

¿Cómo vienes a la escuela? ¿Vienes temprano? ¿tarde? ¿Por qué?

A12 ESTRUCTURAS ESENCIALES
Two uses of no

To say *no* in Spanish, simply place the word **no** in front of the verb.

Yo **no** vengo en autobús.   *I do not come by bus.*

If the answer to a question is in the negative, the word **no** will appear twice, at the beginning of the sentence, as in English, and in front of the verb, meaning *not*.

—¿Carlos viene en bicicleta?   *Does Carlos come by bike?*
—**No,** Carlos **no** viene en bicicleta.   *No, he does not come by bike.*

Actividad • ¿Un autobús nuevo?

Perhaps we need a larger bus? The minibus we have now has to make two trips, so half the students come to school early and half come to school late. A classmate is asking who comes early. Answer as indicated.

    —¿Viene Ramón temprano? (No)
    —No, Ramón no viene temprano.

1. ¿Vienes temprano? (Sí)
2. ¿Vienen ellos temprano? (No)
3. ¿Viene Alicia temprano? (Sí)
4. ¿Vienen Carlos y María temprano? (Sí)
5. ¿Vengo temprano? (No)

A 14 Comprensión

Are you sure? Is that the answer?

	0	1	2	3	4	5	6	7	8
Sí									
No	✔								

A 15 Actividad • ¿Sí o no? ¿Por qué?

Ask these questions. Your classmate will answer **sí** or **no.** When you ask "How come?" your classmate will explain or say **¡No sé!** *(I don't know!)*

    —¿Vienes en autobús?   —¿Vienes en metro?
    —No.   —Sí.
    —¿Por qué?   —¿Por qué?
    —Vengo a pie.   —Porque vengo con Soledad.

1. ¿Vienes temprano?
2. ¿Vienes en bicicleta?
3. ¿Vienes de México?
4. ¿Vienes a pie?
5. ¿Viene tarde el autobús?
6. ¿Viene José con Carlos?
7. ¿Vienen Raúl y Marta en metro?
8. ¿No vienen Isabel y Andrés en bicicleta?

A 16 Actividad • ¡A escribir!

No es así. No, it's not so. Alfredo doesn't have his facts straight. Write answers to his remarks, telling him he's mistaken.

    —Ellos son de Texas.
    —No, ellos no son de Texas, Alfredo.

1. Tú te llamas Ramón.
2. Ella se llama Ramona.
3. Tú eres de España.
4. Ellos son de España.
5. Tú vienes en auto.
6. Ellos vienen en autobús.
7. Isabel viene tarde.
8. Ustedes vienen tarde.
9. Tú vienes tarde.
10. Tú estás muy mal.

Students in Spanish-speaking countries usually take ten or more subjects. Keeping them straight at the beginning of a new school year isn't easy.

B1

¿Qué materias tienes hoy?

En el recreo

ALBERTO ¡Hola, Enrique! ¿Tienes clase de matemáticas?
ENRIQUE No, tengo inglés.
ALBERTO ¿A qué hora?
ENRIQUE A las diez. ¿Y tú?, ¿qué tienes?
ALBERTO Hoy tengo clase de computadoras.
ENRIQUE ¿Hay muchos estudiantes?
ALBERTO Como veinte.
ENRIQUE Y, el profesor, ¿quién es?
ALBERTO Tenemos una profesora: la señora Suárez. ¿Cuántas materias tienes tú?

ENRIQUE Diez, once . . . no sé. ¿Qué hora es?
ALBERTO ¡Oh! Son casi las diez. ¡Adiós!
ENRIQUE ¡Chao!

B2 Actividad • ¿Es cierto o no?

Say whether the statements are correct **(Es cierto)** or not **(No es cierto)** according to B1. Correct the statements that aren't true.

1. Es el recreo.
2. Enrique tiene clase de matemáticas.
3. Enrique no tiene clase de inglés.
4. Hay como diez estudiantes en la clase de Alberto.
5. Enrique tiene clase de inglés a las diez.
6. El profesor de la clase de computadoras es Benito Martínez.
7. ¿Qué hora es? Son casi las once.
8. Enrique tiene veinte materias.

In many Spanish-speaking countries, the first six years of school are called **escuela primaria.** Three years of **secundaria** follow, which are equivalent to junior high school and the first two years of high school. Many students then enter the **bachillerato** for three more years of studies concentrating on the arts or sciences.

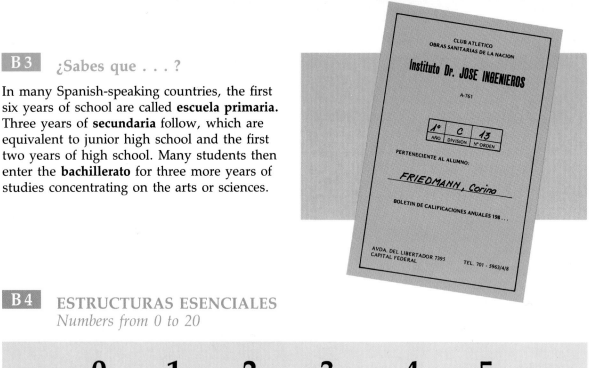

B4   ESTRUCTURAS ESENCIALES
Numbers from 0 to 20

0 cero	1 uno	2 dos	3 tres	4 cuatro	5 cinco
6 seis	7 siete	8 ocho	9 nueve	10 diez
11 once	12 doce	13 trece	14 catorce	15 quince
16 dieciséis	17 diecisiete	18 dieciocho	19 diecinueve	20 veinte

When talking about numbers **(números), uno** changes to **un** before a masculine noun and to **una** before a feminine noun.

B5   Actividad • La clase de matemáticas

• Read these numbers aloud in Spanish.

  18, 11, 2, 14   5, 19, 12, 13   2, 3, 4, 5, 6, 17, 15, 13, 7, 8, 10, 9

• Go through the numbers again, subtracting one from each.

• Now go through them adding one.

B6   Actividad • ¡A escribir!

Write the following as numerals.

  doce, tres, quince, siete, dieciséis, dieciocho, veinte, seis, trece, uno, cuatro, nueve

Actividad • Un juego

Draw a rectangle and divide it into twenty-one squares as shown. Number the squares from 0 to 20 in any order you choose. Use each number only once. Someone will call numbers from 0 to 20 in random order. The first to fill in a horizontal line is the winner.

8	2	5	13	14	11	16
7	1	6	4	15	0	12
9	10	3	19	17	18	20

B8   SITUACIÓN • El horario de Enrique   *Enrique's Schedule*

Enrique es estudiante de la Escuela Secundaria Benito Juárez. Tiene un horario fuerte. Hay diez materias, pero no hay clases el sábado.

Horario	LUNES	MARTES	MIÉRCOLES	JUEVES	VIERNES	SÁBADO	DOMINGO
9:00 AM	historia	ciencias naturales	historia	ciencias naturales	español		
10:00 AM	mat.	mat.	comput.	mat.	ed. física		
11:00 AM	comput.	ed. física	español	comput.	historia		
12:00 PM	ALMUERZO						
1:00 PM	español	español	ed. física	español	comput.	NO HAY CLASES	
2:00 PM	física	física	mat.	física	mat.		
Actividades Extra Curriculares	música	fútbol	fútbol	música	pintura		

As you walk past various classrooms, you hear a teacher or a student saying the following things. Try to guess what subject is being studied. You already saw some of the subjects in B8.

1. . . . un círculo, un triángulo y un rectángulo . . .
2. . . . los ácidos, en combinación con oxígeno y nitrógeno . . .
3. ¡Muy bien! Tienes mucho talento, los colores son muy artísticos . . .
4. . . . la repetición de la melodía del compositor clásico . . .
5. . . . y las partículas en el núcleo del átomo . . .
6. . . . el Océano Pacífico, el Atlántico, el Mar Mediterráneo . . .
7. . . . el "cursor" indica la posición del próximo carácter . . .
8. . . . las células nerviosas son entidades autónomas . . .
9. . . . anunciaron la independencia de la república . . .

B 10 ESTRUCTURAS ESENCIALES
Los días de la semana The days of the week

| lunes | martes | miércoles | jueves | viernes | sábado | domingo |

1. Notice that the days of the week are not capitalized in Spanish.

2. The days of the week are masculine in Spanish and take the definite article **el.** To say the plural form of a day, use the plural article **los.** Add **-s** to the day if it doesn't end in **-s** already **(sábado, domingo).**

 los lunes *Mondays* los sábados *Saturdays*

3. To express *on* (any given day or days), use **el** or **los.**

 Tengo inglés el lunes. *I have English on Monday (or next Monday).*
 Tengo inglés los lunes. *I have English on Mondays.*

4. When telling what day it is, omit the article.

 Hoy es jueves. *Today is Thursday.*

B 11 Actividad • El pobre Enrique *Poor Enrique*

Tell what courses Enrique has each day, according to his schedule in B8.

 El lunes Enrique tiene español, historia, física . . .

B 12 Actividad • ¿Qué tiene Enrique hoy?

Answer the following questions about Enrique's schedule (see B8).

 —¿Cuándo tiene Enrique música?
 —Tiene música los lunes y los jueves.

1. La actividad extra-curricular de hoy es pintura. ¿Qué día es hoy?
2. ¿Cuándo tiene Enrique educación física?
3. ¿Tiene él historia los viernes?
4. ¿Cuándo tiene ciencias naturales?
5. ¿Tiene él español los miércoles? ¿Y tú?

ESTRUCTURAS ESENCIALES
The verb tener

tener *to have*					
Yo	**tengo**	clase hoy.	Nosotros(as)	**tenemos**	música.
Tú	**tienes**	inglés.	Vosotros(as)	**tenéis**	química.
Usted, él, ella	**tiene**	dibujo.	Ustedes, ellos(as)	**tienen**	historia.

B 14 Actividad • ¿Tienes clase?

Supply the missing forms of **tener.**

1. ¿ _____ tú ciencias ahora?
2. No, yo no _____ ciencias los martes.
3. Nosotros _____ ciencias los martes.
4. ¿ _____ ustedes clase con el profesor Suárez?
5. No, ellos _____ química hoy.

6. ¿Qué día _____ nosotros clase de química?
7. Ustedes _____ clase los jueves, nosotros _____ clase los miércoles.
8. Yo _____ clase ahora.
9. ¿Qué clase _____ tú?

B 15 Actividad • Combinación

Form sentences by choosing items from each column.

nosotros ellas Alicia tú ustedes Felipe y José él ella yo Rosario	*tiene* *tienen* *tenemos* *tengo* *tienes*	ciencias naturales educación física computadoras deportes español pintura ciencias sociales	los lunes los martes los miércoles los jueves los viernes

B 16 Actividad • Un momento, por favor. *Just a moment, please.*

You have the class's schedule on file. Answer the supervisor's questions after first looking at your notes in parentheses.

—¿Tienes tú clases hoy? (No)
—No, hoy yo no tengo clases.

1. ¿Qué materias tienes tú hoy? (historia y física)
2. ¿Tienen los chicos español hoy? (Sí)
3. ¿Tenemos física hoy? (No)
4. ¿Tienen ellas música los martes? (viernes)

5. ¿Qué materias tiene Norma hoy? (inglés y ciencias)
6. ¿Tiene Marisa clase de computadoras hoy? (Sí)
7. ¿Tienes tú español hoy? (matemáticas)
8. ¿Tienen ustedes biología hoy? (No)

En la escuela 69

Actividad • ¡A escribir!

Haz tu horario. Make your own schedule. Write the names of the days of the week and fill in the subjects you're taking in school. **¡En español!** *In Spanish!*, of course.

B 18 Actividad • Los horarios

Compare schedules with a classmate, like this.

¿Tienes matemáticas hoy? ¿Qué tienes el martes a las dos? ¿Tienes inglés a las nueve?

B 19 ESTRUCTURAS ESENCIALES
Telling time

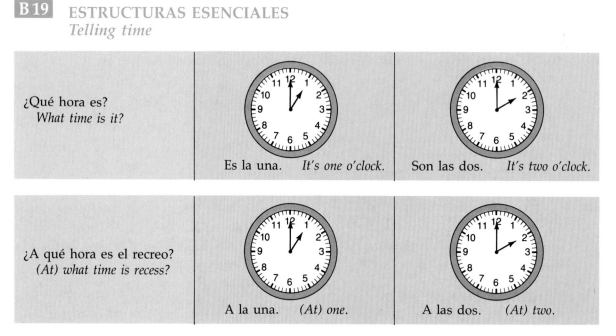

| ¿Qué hora es?
What time is it? | Es la una. *It's one o'clock.* | Son las dos. *It's two o'clock.* |
| ¿A qué hora es el recreo?
(At) what time is recess? | A la una. *(At) one.* | A las dos. *(At) two.* |

1. **Es** and **la** are used with **una**: (1:00) **Es la una.** For other hours use **las** and **son**: (2:00) **Son las dos**; (5:00) **Son las cinco.**

2. The equivalent of *past* or *after* is **y**: (10:05) **Son las diez y cinco.** Note that the hour is given before the minutes.

3. The equivalent of *to* or *till* is **menos**: (7:50) **Son las ocho menos diez.**

4. To ask or say at what time something happens use **a**: **¿A qué hora son las clases?** In your answer, use **media** for the half hours and **cuarto** as the equivalent for the quarter hours: (8:15) **A las ocho y cuarto.** (12:30) **A las doce y media.** (8:45) **A las nueve menos cuarto.**

B 20 Actividad • ¿Qué hora es?

Pair up with a classmate and say the time as indicated. Your classmate will say what class he or she has, or say **No tengo clase** if he/she has no class.

11:00   —Son las once.
          —Tengo geografía.

1. 10:00   **2.** 8:30   **3.** 9:45   **4.** 1:00   **5.** 4:15   **6.** 7:00   **7.** 3:00   **8.** 12:05

Comprensión 📼

Make sure the time is right.

0	1	2	3	4	5	6	7	8	9	10
2:00										

B 22 Actividad • ¿A qué hora?

Your classmate asks what time various classes are. Answer as indicated; then
switch roles.

> dibujo, viernes: 2:00
> —¿A qué hora tenemos dibujo el viernes?
> —A las dos.

1. inglés, lunes: 1:00
2. inglés, martes y miércoles: 9:00
3. física, lunes, miércoles y viernes: 11:30
4. matemáticas, miércoles: 10:45

5. ciencias naturales, martes: 11:20
6. música, jueves: 2:00
7. geografía, jueves: 1:10
8. educación física, viernes: 11:00

B 23 Actividad • ¿Qué hora es en la Ciudad de México?

Long-distance callers need to think what time it is at the other end of the line.
Team up with a classmate and test each
other on figuring out the time in the cities listed.

—Son las cuatro en Lima. ¿Qué hora es
en Madrid?
—Son las diez. ¿Qué hora es en Seattle?
—Es la una. ¿Qué . . . ?

Los Ángeles • Seattle	12:00
Denver • Albuquerque	1:00
San Antonio • México D.F.	2:00
Miami • Lima • Nueva York	3:00
Puerto Rico • Santiago de Chile	4:00
Buenos Aires • Montevideo	5:00
Madrid • Barcelona	9:00

B 24 Actividad • Charla

With a partner, talk about your classes and schedule.

¿Qué días tienes clase de . . . ?

El . . . (los . . .), ¿y tú?

¿A qué hora tienes clase de . . . ?

A la . . . (A las . . .), ¿y tú?

ANDRÉS ¿Qué tienes tú ahora?

CLARA Biología, ¿y tú?

ANDRÉS Historia. Con el Sr. Galván. Es mi materia preferida.

CLARA ¿Tu materia preferida? ¡Es muy aburrida! Es difícil. Hay mucha tarea.

ANDRÉS ¡Al contrario! Es fácil. Es muy interesante. Y tu materia favorita, ¿cuál es?

CLARA Química.

ANDRÉS Tienes bastante tarea y no es interesante, ¿verdad?

CLARA No, es muy interesante.

ANDRÉS ¿Cuántas materias tienes?

CLARA Tengo diez.

ANDRÉS ¿Diez? ¡Eres un genio!

B 26 Actividad • ¿Andrés o Clara?

Who might be saying each of the following lines, according to B25?

1. Mi materia preferida es química.
2. El señor Galván es el profesor de historia.
3. ¡La historia es difícil!
4. Tengo biología ahora.
5. La historia es muy interesante.
6. Tienes bastante tarea en química.

B 27 Actividad • ¡A escoger!

Choose the proper completion for each sentence according to B25. Then write them down.

1. Clara tiene ahora
   • química. • historia. • biología.
2. Andrés tiene ahora
   • biología. • historia. • química.
3. Andrés tiene clase con
   • Benito Juárez. • el señor Galván. • Clara.
4. La materia preferida de Andrés es
   • biología. • química. • historia.
5. Pero, Andrés, la historia es
   • muy difícil. • difícil. • muy interesante.
6. La materia preferida de Clara es
   • biología. • química. • historia.
7. Pero, Clara, la química no es
   • interesante. • bastante aburrida. • difícil.
8. Andrés y Clara tienen . . .
   • pocas materias. • <u>una diferencia de opiniones.</u> • inglés ahora.

SE DICE ASÍ
Asking about classes and giving your opinion

¿Cómo es la clase? ¿Es interesante? How's the class? Is it interesting?	No, es aburrida. No, it's boring.
¿Cuál es tu materia preferida? What's (Which is) your favorite subject?	Dibujo. Drawing.

B 29 Actividad • Charla

Talk about classes with a partner. Use **¿verdad?** if you want to ask, and **al contrario** if you don't agree. Here are some hints to help you get started.

—¿Qué materias tienes?
—¿Cuál es tu materia preferida?
—¿Cómo es la clase?
—¿Qué días tienes clases?

—¿A qué hora?
—¿Tienes mucha tarea?
—¿Tienes un diez?

B 30 Actividad • Encuesta *Survey*

You have to interview your classmates for an article that will appear in a Spanish newspaper. Ask them what they think of each class (**¿Cómo es la clase de inglés?**, etc.), find out which class is their favorite (**¿Cuál . . . ?**), and note their responses on a form like the one below. Report your results to the class.

Materia:	fácil	difícil	aburrida	interesante	preferida
inglés	3	6	5	4	5
español					
matemáticas					

B 31 Actividad • ¿Español? ¡Cinco estrellas! *Spanish? Five stars!*

You are trying to decide what classes to take next semester. Ask a classmate about a few classes—who the teacher is, and how many stars each class rates according to the following scale:

muy interesante

bastante interesante

aburrida

muy aburrida

A student gets a ten in math, and is called a genius? **Sí, ¡por supuesto!** *(Yes, of course!)* The grading system in many high schools in Spanish-speaking countries goes from 0 to 10. A 9 is **notable** *(excellent)*, and a 10 is very rare indeed. Some schools grade with a scale of 0–20, others use a 0–100 scale. There are other differences. Many schools are not coed. Also, instead of a general high school, teenagers must choose among technical schools that prepare them to be office workers or technicians, normal schools that prepare them to be teachers, and **colegios** that lead to the university.

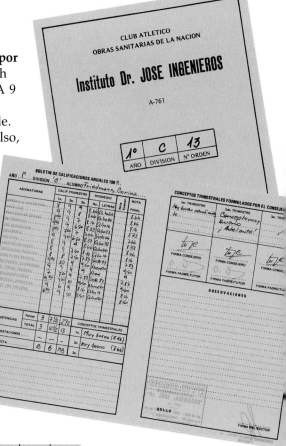

EVALUACIÓN

90 – 100	9–10	Sobresaliente
80 – 89	8	Notable
70 – 79	7	Aprovechado
60 – 69	6	Aprobado
0 – 59	0–5	Suspenso

Who's taking the same courses?

	0	1	2	3	4	5	6
Sí							
No	✔						

Supply the missing words.

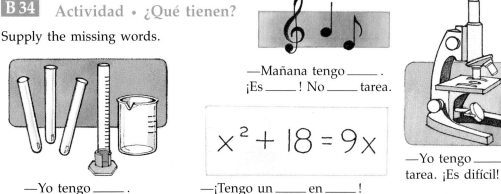

—Mañana tengo _____ .
¡Es _____ ! No _____ tarea.

$$x^2 + 18 = 9x$$

—Yo tengo _____ . Tengo _____ tarea. ¡Es difícil!

—Yo tengo _____ .
Tengo poca _____ .

—¡Tengo un _____ en _____ !
—¡Eres un genio!

Write three sentences about three of your own classes. Tell about your grades (0 to 10!), your homework, and how you feel about each class.

shopping for school supplies

Classes begin and it's time to buy school supplies. In Puerto Rico, everyone uses U.S. dollars, but they're called **pesos.**

C1 ¿Cuánto cuesta? 📼

En una tienda en San Juan, Puerto Rico.

ROSA Miguel, ¡una regla con calculadora!
MIGUEL ¿Sí? ¿Cuánto cuesta?
ROSA Catorce noventa y nueve.

MIGUEL Por favor, señor, ¿cuánto cuestan los bolígrafos? No tienen precio.
VENDEDOR Tres por dos pesos.
MIGUEL Gracias.

ROSA Perdón, ¿tiene usted carteras?
VENDEDORA Sí, cuestan quince pesos.
ROSA ¡Uy!, no tengo tanto. Gracias, señora.

MIGUEL ¿Qué más necesitas?
ROSA ¡Dinero, por supuesto!

C2 Actividad • No es así *It's not so*

Restate these sentences so that they are true according to the dialog.

—Rosa tiene quince pesos.
—No, no tiene quince pesos.
—El vendedor no tiene carteras.
—Sí, tiene carteras.

1. No hay regla con calculadora.
2. La regla cuesta veinte pesos.
3. No hay bolígrafos en la tienda.
4. Los bolígrafos tienen precio.

5. Dos bolígrafos cuestan tres pesos.
6. Las carteras cuestan diez pesos.
7. Rosa tiene dinero para una cartera.
8. Rosa no necesita más dinero.

ESTRUCTURAS ESENCIALES
Forming plurals

regla   reglas   libro   libros

If a noun ends in a vowel **(a, e, i, o,** or **u),** you form the plural by adding **-s.**

regla   reglas   libro   libros

señor   señores   autobús   autobuses

If a word ends in a consonant (any letter except **a, e, i, o,** or **u),**
you form the plural by adding **-es.**

señor   señores   autobús   autobuses

C4   Actividad • En la tienda

You work in a store after school. When customers ask if you have certain items,
reply *yes,* you have them.

—¿Una regla?
—Sí, tenemos reglas.

1. ¿Una calculadora?
2. ¿Un libro?
3. ¿Un bolígrafo?

4. ¿Una bicicleta?
5. ¿Una computadora?
6. ¿Una pintura?

7. ¿Un dibujo?
8. ¿Una cartera?

C5   Comprensión

One or more?

	0	1	2	3	4	5	6	7	8	9	10
one											
more than one	✔										

Actividad • ¡A escribir!

Using the words below, make two lists; one with the singular words and one with the plurals.

escuela clases bolígrafos chico autobús reglas profesores
bicicletas cartera señoras dólares libro chicas

C7   SITUACIÓN • Compras para la escuela

—Por favor, ¿cuánto cuesta . . .

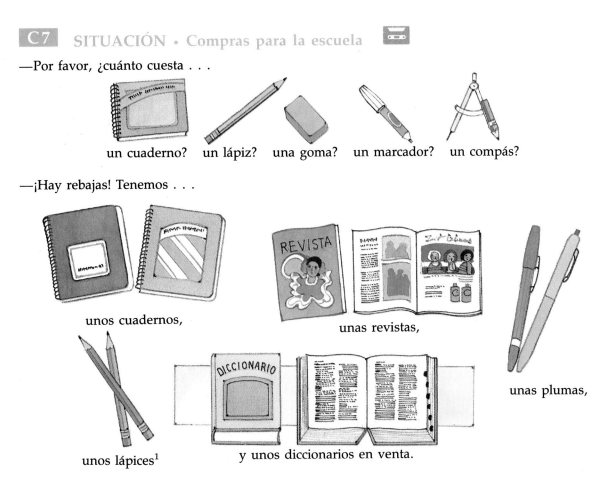

un cuaderno?   un lápiz?   una goma?   un marcador?   un compás?

—¡Hay rebajas! Tenemos . . .

unos cuadernos,   unas revistas,

                                                        unas plumas,

unos lápices[1]   y unos diccionarios en venta.

C8   SE DICE ASÍ
Asking how much something costs and giving the price

Singular	¿Cuánto cuesta?	Cuesta . . .	
	How much does it cost?	It costs . . . (It's . . .)	
Plural	¿Cuánto cuestan?	Cuestan . . .	
	How much do they cost?	They cost . . . (They are . . .)	

[1] The plural of **lápiz** *(pencil)* is **lápices** *(pencils)*. Words ending in **z** in the singular change to **c** in the plural.

C9 Actividad • ¿Cuánto cuestan?

Pair up with a classmate. Ask how much these items cost. Your classmate will answer as indicated. Then switch roles.

el bolígrafo, $3 | las reglas, $4
—¿Cuánto cuesta el bolígrafo? | —¿Cuánto cuestan las reglas?
—Cuesta tres dólares. | —Cuestan cuatro dólares.

1. las calculadoras, $8
2. las reglas, $2
3. los bolígrafos, 6 por $4
4. una regla con calculadora, $14
5. un libro de inglés, $13
6. los libros de historia, $9

C10 ESTRUCTURAS ESENCIALES
Definite and indefinite articles

Both Spanish and English have two kinds of articles, definite and indefinite. As you have already learned, the definite article *(the)* has four forms in Spanish:

	Singular	Plural
Masculine	**el**	**los**
Feminine	**la**	**las**

The form you use depends on the gender (masculine or feminine) and number (singular or plural) of the noun you want to say.

el chico; **el** cuaderno | **los** chicos; **los** cuadernos
the boy; the notebook | *the boys; the notebooks*

la chica; **la** escuela | **las** chicas; **las** escuelas
the girl; the school | *the girls; the schools*

The Spanish indefinite article, which is equivalent to English *a* and *an* in the singular and *some* in the plural, also has four forms.

	Singular	Plural
Masculine	**un**	**unos**
Feminine	**una**	**unas**

un chico; **un** cuaderno | **unos** chicos; **unos** cuadernos
a boy; a notebook | *some boys; some notebooks*

una chica; **una** escuela | **unas** chicas; **unas** escuelas
a girl; a school | *some girls; some schools*

C11 Actividad • ¿Cuál artículo?

Fill in the blanks with the appropriate definite or indefinite article.

Tengo ____ clases que tienen ____ profesores muy interesantes. ____ martes a ____ una hay biología. ____ biología es muy interesante. A ____ dos tengo español. ____ español es fácil. Tengo ____ profesor de Madrid.

Actividad • En venta *For sale*

Say you need the indicated items. Your classmate replies that they are for sale.

—¡Buenos días! Necesito un libro de inglés.
—¡No hay problema! Tenemos libros de inglés en venta.

1. cuaderno **3.** compás **5.** marcador **7.** revista
2. goma **4.** lápiz **6.** bolígrafo **8.** pluma

C13 ¿Sabes que . . . ?

Schools in the Spanish-speaking world usually don't provide lockers for students.
Students carry their books and supplies to school and take them back home every day.
In countries where the weather gets cold, students hang their coats in their classrooms.
Students in the same grade usually take the same courses and stay in the same classroom;
different teachers come to their classrooms to teach the different subjects.

C14 ESTRUCTURAS ESENCIALES
Numbers from 21 to 100

21 veintiuno	**22** veintidós	**23** veintitrés	**24** veinticuatro	**25** veinticinco
26 veintiséis	**27** veintisiete	**28** veintiocho	**29** veintinueve	**30** treinta
31 treinta y uno	**32** treinta y dos	**40** cuarenta	**41** cuarenta y uno	**50** cincuenta
60 sesenta	**70** setenta	**80** ochenta	**90** noventa	**100** cien

C15 Actividad • Los ganadores *The winners*

You've been chosen by a local store to read the student I.D. numbers
of 30 winners in a contest. Read the numbers aloud.

87	99	23	46	65	78	90	35	29	48	100	56	67	24	98
83	75	33	76	48	63	39	79	30	50	43	80	25	69	42

ESTRUCTURAS ESENCIALES
Use of numbers with nouns

Numbers are placed before the noun: **veintiocho chicas, treinta chicos.**
Uno changes its ending, depending on the noun's gender and number.

> **uno, veintiuno, treinta y uno**
> **un** chico, **una** chica
> **veintiún** chicos, **veintiuna** chicas
> **treinta y un** chicos, **treinta y una** chicas

Compound numbers beyond 29 are written separately and linked by a **y: treinta y ocho, cuarenta y dos.**

C17 Actividad • Hora de inventario *Inventory time*

Your job after school in the school-supplies store is getting complicated. Now your boss wants to take inventory. Say you have the quantities indicated as he calls out the item.

> gomas, 41
> —¡Gomas!
> —Cuarenta y una gomas.

1. cuadernos, 21   **3.** reglas, 79   **5.** diccionarios, 61   **7.** bolígrafos, 31
2. plumas, 38   **4.** compases, 84   **6.** revistas, 57   **8.** marcadores, 33

C18 Actividad • Varios precios *Different prices*

In a department store in San Juan, Puerto Rico, customers are asking the prices of many items. You, the salesperson, must answer their questions.

> —¿Cuánto cuesta? ($15)   —¿Cuánto cuestan? ($15.99)
> —Quince pesos.   —Quince noventa y nueve.

1. ¿Cuánto cuestan? ($23)
2. ¿Cuestan 10 pesos? (No, $9.95)
3. ¿Cuánto cuesta? ($100)
4. ¿Cuesta 80 pesos? (No, $75)

5. ¿Cuánto cuesta la calculadora? ($34.45)
6. ¿Cuestan 2 pesos? (No, $20)
7. ¿Cuánto cuesta el libro? ($14.65)
8. ¿Cuesta 59 pesos? (No, $60)

C19 Conversación • ¿Cuánto cuesta?

Pair up with a classmate. One of you is the customer, and the other one is the salesperson. Alternate roles. Choose six objects from C7. Ask about their prices. If the price seems high say, **¡Uy, no tengo tanto!** *(Wow! I don't have that much!)* If the price seems reasonable, buy the quantity you want.

> Tú   ¿Cuánto cuestan los cuadernos?
> VENDEDOR/A   Dos pesos.
> Tú   Bueno, dos por favor. ¿Y las reglas?
> VENDEDOR/A   Siete pesos.
> Tú   ¡Uy, no tengo tanto! Adiós.

Actividad • ¡A escribir!

Put down in writing all the prices used by the salesperson in C19.

($23) veintitrés pesos

C21 Actividad • Una confusión

Make sense out of the following conversation between two customers and the salesperson. Say the lines in their correct order and then write them.

—Cinco por diez dólares.
—Adiós.
—Por favor, ¿cuánto cuestan los cuadernos?
—Buenos días.
—¡Uy, no tengo tanto!

C22 Comprensión

Finding the corresponding price

	ESPAÑOL		CUADERNO			DICCIONARIO
A	$50.00	$10.00	$ 5.75	$ 1.00	$33.00	$ 6.05
B	$10.00	$99.00	$75.00	$ 2.01	$33.30	$ 5.06
C	$10.50	$99.10	$70.05	$12.00	$30.33	$56.00
D	$15.50	$10.99	$ 5.00	$ 1.02	$30.00	$65.00

C23 Actividad • Anuncios *Ads*

You work as an announcer for a Spanish television station. The local store has the following items on sale. Name the articles. Give their prices. Try to make your ads sound as attractive as possible.

—carteras ($40.00)
—calculadoras ($25.00)
—libros de español ($15.00)
—diccionarios ($13.00)
—reglas ($3.15)

En la escuela   81

TRY YOUR SKILLS

use what you've learned

1 Agenda

Take a look at Elena's appointment book for next week.

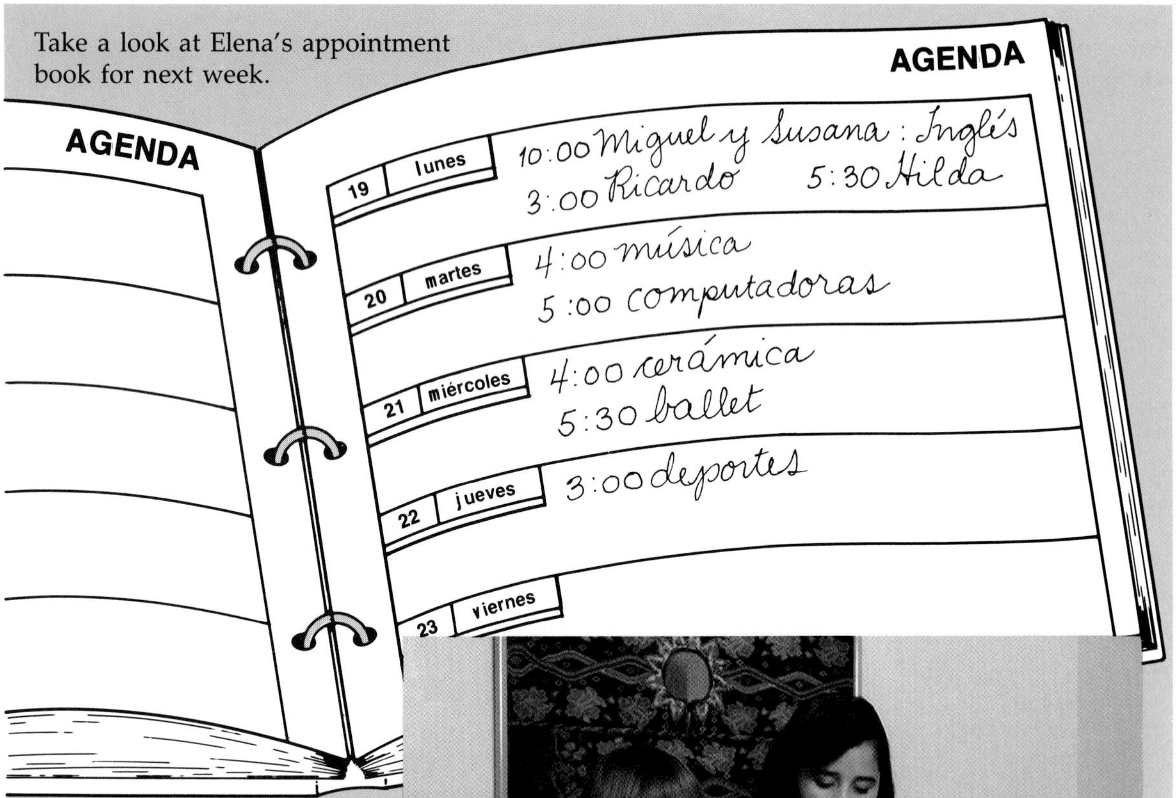

AGENDA
AGENDA
19 lunes
10:00 Miguel y Susana: Inglés
3:00 Ricardo 5:30 Hilda
20 martes
4:00 música
5:00 computadoras
21 miércoles
4:00 cerámica
5:30 ballet
22 jueves
3:00 deportes
23 viernes

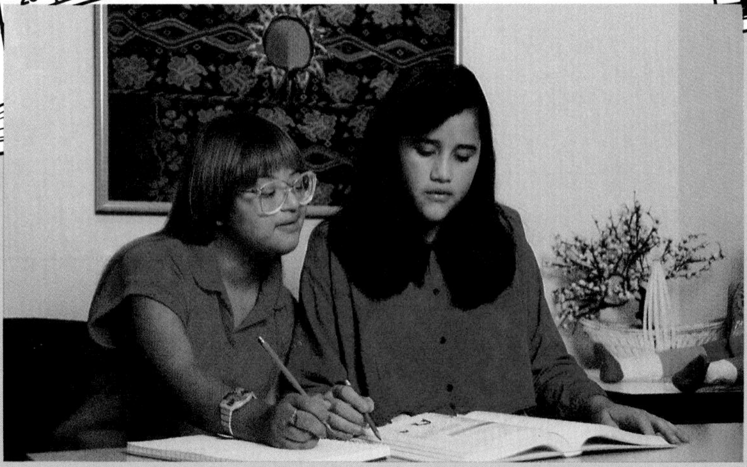

Make a weekly schedule of your own, using imaginary people and events or real ones. Be ready to read your appointments to the class.

2 Actividad • Dolor de cabeza *Headache*

You work for the photographer who's going to take every student's picture for the yearbook. Try to schedule everyone. Your classmates will look at their appointment books (1) to see if they can make it.

—¿Vienes el viernes a las tres?
—No, tengo deportes a las tres.

Actividad • No es así

Choose a partner. One of you will read an entry. Deny what you hear; then repeat the information with a number that is 10 lower or 10 higher. Take turns responding.

La calculadora cuesta $19.
—No, cuesta $9.
—No es así, cuesta $29.

1. Hay 28 estudiantes en la clase de historia.
2. Tenemos 40 dólares.
3. Luisa tiene diez clases hoy.
4. Hay 60 bicicletas aquí.
5. La profesora viene con treinta libros.
6. Hay dieciséis o diecisiete chicos en la clase.
7. El diccionario de español-inglés cuesta $15.99.
8. Ella tiene 18 dólares en la cartera.
9. Vienen quince estudiantes el martes.
10. Carlos viene a clase con doce plumas.

4 Actividad • El boletín de Patricia *Patricia's report card*

Here's Patricia's report card. She's a high school student in Caracas, Venezuela. How many subjects does she take? Does she take more or fewer subjects than you? Do both of you have any of the same subjects? What subjects does she take that you don't have? What about the grading system? What is the highest mark in this grading system? Is the same grading system used for all her subjects?

RENDIMIENTO ESCOLAR

MATERIAS	1er. Lapso Calificación	1er. Lapso Inasistencia	2o. Lapso Calificación	2o. Lapso Inasistencia	3er. Lapso Calificación	3er. Lapso Inasistencia	PREVIA	FINAL
Español	7	1	8	1	7	0	7	7
Matemáticas	8	1	8	1	8	0	8	8
Biología	9	2	9	0	8	0	8	8
Química	10	1	9	0	10	1	9	9
Física	9	1	9	0	10	0	9	9
Geografía	6	2	7	0	10	0	10	10
Historia	8	1	8	2	8	0	7	7
Inglés	7	2	8	0	8	1	8	8
Computadoras	10	3	10	1	10	1	6	7
Manualidades	9	1	10	0	9	0	9	9
Música	10	1	10	0	9	0	9	9
Educación Física	8	1	7	0	8	1	8	8

5 Actividad • ¿Y en los Estados Unidos?

An exchange student from Guadalajara, Mexico, is interviewing students in your area. She asks you the following questions. How would you answer?

1. ¿Cómo se llama la escuela?
2. ¿Cómo vienes a la escuela?
3. ¿Qué materias tienes?
4. ¿Qué días tienes clases de español?
5. ¿A qué hora?
6. ¿Tienes español hoy?
7. ¿Tienes mucha tarea?
8. ¿Es español una materia fácil o difícil? ¿Es interesante o aburrida?
9. ¿A qué hora tienes recreo?
10. ¿Vienes a la escuela los sábados?

6 Pronunciación, lectura, dictado

1. Listen carefully and repeat what you hear.

2. The sound of the Spanish consonants **ll** and **ch**. Listen, then read aloud.

llamo	llamas	llamamos	ellos	ellas
chicos	chao	muchos	ocho	Chávez

3. Copy the following sentences to prepare yourself to write them from dictation.
   Ella se llama Estrella Llorens.
   Guillermo es de Chicago.
   Chela es la chica de Chile.

¿LO SABES?

Let's review some important points you have learned in this unit.

SECTION A

Can you ask about the ways people get to school?
Use a form of **venir** each time.

—Lola, pie   ¿Viene Lola a pie?

1. Silvia, metro
2. Nosotros, autobús
3. Tú, pie
4. Magdalena, bicicleta
5. Alejandro, auto
6. Ustedes, autobús

SECTION B

Do you know the numbers from zero to twenty?
Complete these number sequences and write out the words. After you have finished writing, read them aloud.

2, 4, 6, _____ dos, cuatro, seis, ocho

1. 4, 3, 2, _____
2. 10, 13, 16, _____
3. 20, 18, 15, _____
4. 0, 6, 12, _____
5. 15, 11, 7, _____
6. 9, 10, 12, _____

Can you talk about your class schedule with a partner?
Talk about all your classes for each day of the week. Be sure to include the names of the days of the week.

Do you know the forms of the verb *tener*?
Write the correct form of **tener** that goes with each subject.

1. Él / dibujo.
2. Nosotros / español.
3. José y Marisa / álgebra.
4. Yo / química.
5. Usted / geografía.
6. Tú / música.

Do you know how to ask and tell what time it is?
Say what time it is: 1:00, 3:15, 10:00, 5:30, 8:50, 12:00.
Using your weekly schedule from skills 1 on page 82, say at what time you have each class.

Tengo inglés a las ocho.

Ask a classmate at what time his/her classes are.

SECTION C

When you go into a store, can you ask the price of different school items?
Ask how much these items cost.

1. la calculadora
2. el bolígrafo
3. las carteras
4. el diccionario

Can you say the price of each item?
Tell how much each item costs. Then tell how much two of them cost.

1. lápiz, $1
2. diccionario, $24
3. pluma, $45
4. libro de matemáticas, $14
5. calculadora, $3.95
6. cartera, $35
7. cuaderno, $2.95
8. goma, $2

VOCABULARIO

SECTION A

a *at, to*
a pie *on foot*
ahí *there*
algunos, -as *some*
el auto *car, automobile*
el autobús *bus*
el autobús escolar *school bus*
la bicicleta *bicycle*
la ciudad *city*
con *with*
¿cuándo? *when?*
de *of*
en *by*
la escuela secundaria
   secondary school
el estudiante *student (male)*
la estudiante *student (female)*
hoy *today*
el inglés *English (language)*
el libro *book*
los *the*
el metro *subway*
mi *my*
¡mira! *look!*
muchos, -as *many, a lot*
no *not*
el número *number*
pero *but*
por fin *finally*
¿por qué? *why?*
porque *because*
el problema *problem*
¿qué? *what?*
rápido *quickly*
tarde *late*
temprano *early*
tiene *it has*
todos *all*
un, una *a, an*
venir *to come*
yo no sé *I don't know*

SECTION B

a la una *at one o'clock*
¿a qué hora? *at what time?*
aburrido, -a *boring*
la actividad *activity*

ahora *now*
al (a + el) *to the, at the
   (contraction)*
al contrario *on the contrary*
el álgebra *algebra*
el almuerzo *lunch*
bastante *rather*
casi *almost*
la ciencia *science*
la clase *class*
como *about*
la computadora *computer*
¿cuál? *what? which?*
¿cuántos, -as? *how many?*
del (de + el) *of the, from
   the (contraction)*
los deportes *sports*
los días de la semana *days of
   the week (see p. 68)*
el dibujo *drawing*
difícil *difficult*
la educación física *physical
   education*
es la una *it's one o'clock*
el español *Spanish language*
fácil *easy*
la física *physics*
el francés *French language*
fuerte *heavy*
el genio *genius*
la geografía *geography*
la geometría *geometry*
hay *there is, there are*
la historia *history*
la hora *time, hour*
el horario *schedule*
interesante *interesting*
las *the (fem. pl.)*
las materias *subjects (see p. 67)*
mucha *a lot of*
o *or*
otras *other*
la pintura *painting*
poca *a little*
preferida *favorite*
¿qué hora es? *what time is it?*
la química *chemistry*
el recreo *recess*

la semana *week*
son las diez *it's ten o'clock*
la tarea *homework*
tener *to have*
tu *your*
¿verdad? *really?*

SECTION C

el bolígrafo *ballpoint pen*
bueno *well, all right*
la calculadora *calculator*
la cartera *schoolbag*
el compás *compass*
la compra *shopping*
el cuaderno *notebook*
¿cuánto cuesta? *how much
   does it cost?*
¿cuánto cuestan? *how much
   do they cost?*
cuesta *it costs*
cuestan *they cost*
el diccionario *dictionary*
el dinero *money*
en venta *for sale*
la goma *eraser*
el hombre *man*
el lápiz (pl. lápices) *pencil*
el marcador *felt-tip marker*
más *more; else*
los números *numbers (see p. 66
   and p. 79)*
el peso *peso*
perdón *excuse me*
la pluma *fountain pen*
por *for*
por favor *please*
el precio *price*
¿qué más necesitas? *what
   else do you need?*
la rebaja *discount*
la regla *ruler*
la revista *magazine*
tanto *so (as, that) much*
la tienda *store*
unos, unas *some*
el vendedor, la vendedora
   salesperson

ESTUDIO DE PALABRAS

Written accent marks
Some Spanish words have an accent mark written on the stressed vowel.
Accent marks tell the reader how to pronounce the words. Find all the words
in the vocabulary that have an accent mark, and write them in a new list.

VAMOS A LEER

Antes de leer

Spanish-speaking students use books like these for their classes. Can you guess by their titles what subjects they deal with? Are they similar to your own books? Which ones would you like to read?

Libros para la escuela

Y para los ratos libres° . . .

Tiras cómicas, ciencia ficción y aventuras.

Sin mirar   *Without looking*

How many of the book and magazine titles can you remember without looking at these pages?

Y para los ratos libres *And for your free time*

Socorro°

Read the selection once without consulting the vocabulary.
Then read it again, looking up the words you don't know.

Es lunes. Son las ocho de la mañana°. ¡Es tarde! Hoy es un día terrible. ¡Examen° de matemáticas! ¡A las nueve! No tengo el libro. No tengo los ejercicios°. Corro°. El autobús no viene ¡Viene un taxi! Lo tomo°. Cuesta diez dólares. ¡Es mucho! No tengo dinero.

Llego° a la escuela. Está desierta°, abandonada°. Entro a° la clase. La profesora espera°. El examen es muy difícil. Tiene cien preguntas. ¿Qué puedo hacer°? ¡SOCORRO!

Me despierto°. ¿Qué pasa?° ¡No hay° clases! No hay examen de matemáticas. No es lunes. Es domingo. ¡Qué suerte!°

Preguntas y respuestas

1. ¿Qué día es?
2. ¿Qué hora es?
3. ¿Viene el autobús?
4. ¿Cuánto cuesta el taxi?
5. ¿Cómo está la escuela?

6. ¿Es fácil el examen?
7. ¿Cuántas preguntas tiene?
8. ¿Es lunes?
9. ¿Hay clases?
10. ¿Hay examen de matemáticas?

Actividad • Combinación

Choose the correct ending from the right column to complete the sentence in the left column.

Son las ocho . . .   espera.
Hoy es un día . . .   de la mañana.
No tengo los . . .   terrible.
Llego a la . . .   difícil.
La profesora . . .   ejercicios.
El examen es muy . . .   escuela.

Socorro *Help!* **de la mañana** *in the morning* **examen** *exam, test* **ejercicios** *exercises* **corro** *I run* **lo tomo** *I take it* **llego** *I arrive* **desierta** *deserted* **abandonada** *abandoned* **entro a** *I go in (to)* **espera** *waits* **¿Qué puedo hacer?** *What can I do?* **me despierto** *I wake up* **¿Qué pasa?** *What's up?* **hay** *there is (are)* **¡Qué suerte!** *How lucky!*

El regalo

DANIEL   ¿De quién es el regalo? ¿De dónde viene? ¿Lo abrimos°?

ADRIANA   Un momento. Vamos a ver°. La etiqueta° dice°:

Daniel y Adriana Arias
Ciudad de México

Sí, es para nosotros, pero no tiene remitente°. Es un regalo anónimo.

DANIEL   ¿Anónimo? ¿Cómo anónimo?

ADRIANA   Es un misterio. Es un regalo misterioso.

DANIEL   Pero, si abrimos el paquete°, el misterio termina°, ¿no? Estoy seguro°
que hay una tarjeta° adentro° con el remitente.

Adriana abre° el paquete.

ADRIANA   No, no hay tarjeta. ¡Es un televisor° pequeño°!

DANIEL   ¡Bah! Ya° tenemos televisor.

ADRIANA   No, no tenemos. El televisor de casa° es de papá y mamá. Ahora
nosotros tenemos televisor. Éste° es para nosotros y para nadie más.°

Los chicos miran el televisor.

DANIEL   ¡Mira Adriana! No tiene cable. ¿Tiene pilas°? ¿Vienen las pilas en el paquete?

ADRIANA   No. Es un televisor portátil°, pero no tiene pilas. Sólo° tiene tres
canales°: 1, 17 y 99.

DANIEL   ¿Sólo tres canales? ¡Es muy poco! Seguro que no funciona°.

¿Lo abrimos? *Do we open it?*   **Vamos a ver** *Let's see*   **etiqueta** *label*   **dice** *it says*   **remitente** *sender*
paquete *parcel*   **termina** *it's over*   **Estoy seguro** *I'm sure*   **tarjeta** *card*   **adentro** *inside*   **abre** *opens*   **televisor** *TV
set*   **pequeño** *small*   **ya** *already*   **casa** *home*   **Éste** *This one*   **nadie más** *nobody else*   **pilas** *batteries*
portátil *portable*   **sólo** *only*   **canales** *channels*   **no funciona** *it doesn't work*

ADRIANA	¡Sí, funciona! ¡Funciona! Mira, el Canal Uno.
DANIEL	¿Funciona? ¿Funciona sin° pilas?
ADRIANA	Escucha°.
LOCUTOR°	Después de los anuncios°, las noticias° de las 6, de hoy, viernes.

ADRIANA	¿Cómo? Hoy es jueves, no es viernes. Hay un error.
DANIEL	Y son las cinco, ¿no? ¿Qué hora es, Adriana?
ADRIANA	Las cinco. Son las cinco, y hoy es jueves.
LOCUTOR	¡Superventa! Sí, señores, superventa en la Tienda Díaz. Sólo hasta el martes. Bolígrafos "Maravilla" Treinta pesos Calculadoras "Uno más uno" Ochenta y cinco pesos Y en la revista "Hoy" una entrevista° especial con el presidente de la República, el señor Martín Roldán.
DANIEL	¿Martín Roldán? El presidente no se llama Martín Roldán. ¿Es una broma°?

Adriana apaga° el televisor.

Preguntas y respuestas

Answer the following questions about **El regalo.**

1. ¿De quién es el regalo? ¿Cómo es?
2. ¿Tiene remitente el paquete?
3. ¿Tienen los chicos televisor?
4. ¿Cómo es el televisor nuevo?
5. ¿Cuántos canales tiene?
6. ¿Necesita pilas para funcionar?
7. ¿Qué hora y qué día es?
8. ¿Qué hora y qué día es en el Canal Uno?
9. ¿Qué hay en la Tienda Díaz?
10. ¿Se llama Martín Roldán el presidente?

Actividad • ¿Es cierto o no?

Say whether the statements are correct or not. Correct the statements that aren't true.

1. La etiqueta dice Pedro y Rosa Arias.
2. El paquete no tiene remitente.
3. El televisor es para papá y mamá.
4. La revista "Hoy" tiene una entrevista con el locutor.
5. El presidente no se llama Martín Roldán.
6. El televisor funciona sin pilas.
7. Los chicos miran las noticias en el canal 17.
8. En la Tienda Díaz hay bolígrafos a ochenta y cinco pesos.
9. El televisor necesita cable y pilas.
10. El televisor sólo tiene tres canales.

---

sin *without* **escucha** *listen!* **locutor** *announcer* **anuncios** *ads* **noticias** *news* **entrevista** *interview* **broma** *joke* **apaga** *turns off*

UNIDAD 3
Deportes y pasatiempos

Fútbol—called *soccer* in the United States—is the national passion in most Spanish-speaking countries. Children learn to kick a ball almost as soon as they can walk. Some of the world's great soccer players come from South America. Other popular sports include *tenis, golf, béisbol, polo, volibol, básquetbol.* As you can see, many sports names are similar in Spanish and English.

Pastimes like dancing, singing, playing the guitar, taking pictures, and playing dominos add fun to life.

In this unit you will:

SECTION A	talk about sports and pastimes . . . say which you like and which you don't like
SECTION B	talk about the seasons in which you play certain sports, and the equipment you need
SECTION C	say when and how often you play . . . talk about the seasons and the weather
TRY YOUR SKILLS	use what you've learned
VAMOS A LEER	read for practice and pleasure

talking about which sports and pastimes you like and which you don't like

In Spanish-speaking countries, nearly everybody you meet talks about sports and leisure-time activities. Join in the conversation.

A1 ¿Qué deporte te gusta? 📼

¿Qué deporte te gusta, Miguel?

Me gusta el béisbol.
¡No me gusta la gimnasia!

También me gusta mucho el tenis.
¡Y no me gusta correr!
Pero sí me gusta montar en bicicleta.

¿Qué deporte le gusta a Pedro?

¿Qué deporte le gusta a Olga?

A Pedro le gusta nadar.
Pero no le gusta el fútbol.

A Olga le gusta el volibol.
Pero no le gusta el básquetbol.

A2 Actividad • Para completar

Complete these sentences for Miguel.

1. Me gusta el . . .
2. También me gusta mucho . . .
3. Pero no me gusta la . . .
4. Y no me gusta . . .
5. Pero sí me gusta . . .
6. ¿Qué deporte te . . . ?

Complete these sentences about Pedro, Olga, and yourself.

7. A Pedro le gusta . . .

8. A Olga le gusta . . .

9. A Pedro no le gusta . . .

10. A Olga no le gusta . . .

11. Me gusta . . .

12. No me gusta . . .

 A3 Actividad • Y ahora, tú

Say what you like to practice and what you don't like.

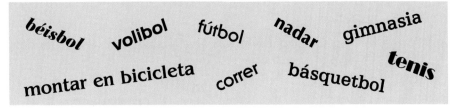

béisbol   volibol   fútbol   nadar   gimnasia

montar en bicicleta   correr   básquetbol   tenis

A4 ESTRUCTURAS ESENCIALES
The verb gustar

To say you like something, use the verb **gustar,** *to like.*

Me gusta el tenis.	*I like tennis.*	*(Tennis is pleasing to me.)*
Te gusta el béisbol.	*You* **(tú)** *like baseball.*	*(Baseball is pleasing to you.)*
Le gusta nadar.	*He/She likes* *You* **(usted)** *like* } *to swim.*	*(Swimming is pleasing to him/her/you.)*
No le gusta el volibol.	*He/She doesn't like* *You* **(usted)** *don't like* } *volleyball.*	*(Volleyball is not pleasing to him/her/you.)*

1. Use **me, te,** and **le** to say who does the liking.

> **Me** gusta el tenis.   *I like tennis.*
> **Te** gusta el béisbol.   *You* **(tú)** *like baseball.*
> **Le** gusta nadar.   *He/She/You* **(usted)** *like to swim.*

2. a. Put a definite article before any noun you use to mention what you like.

> Me gusta **el** béisbol.   Te gusta **el** volibol.   Le gusta **la** gimnasia.
> *I like baseball.*   *You like volleyball.*   *She likes gymnastics.*

   b. But don't use a definite article when you use an infinitive **(correr, nadar)** to express what you like.

> Me gusta **correr.**   ¿Te gusta **nadar?**
> *I like to run.*   *Do you like to swim?*

3. For clarification, you may want to name the person who does the liking by adding at the beginning of the sentence the preposition **a** + the name of the person.

> **A Olga** le gusta el volibol.   **A Pedro** le gusta nadar.

4. To say somebody doesn't like something, put **no** right before **me, te,** or **le.**

> **No** me gusta correr.   ¿**No** te gusta nadar?   A Pedro **no** le gusta el tenis.

Are you sure? Is that the answer?

	0	1	2	3	4	5	6	7	8	9	10
Sí											
No	✔										

A6 Actividad • Charla

¿Te gusta o no? With a partner, talk about which sports you like and which you don't like.

¿Te gusta . . . ?

• Sí, me gusta . . .
• No, no me gusta . . .
  pero sí . . .

volibol **nadar** gimnasia
correr
tenis montar en bicicleta
básquetbol fútbol béisbol

A7 ¿Sabes que . . . ?

Fútbol (*soccer* in the U.S.) is the most popular sport in Spain and most of Spanish America. Professional teams play before tremendous crowds in the stadiums while the rest of the nation watches on TV. The popularity of any one sport varies from country to country. Baseball is more important than soccer in Cuba, the Dominican Republic, Puerto Rico, and Venezuela. Many players from these countries as well as from Mexico and Central America have made their way to the major leagues in the United States and achieved stardom. Skiing attracts many to the mountains of Spain, Chile, and Argentina. Bicycle racing is especially important in Colombia. **La corrida,** *bullfighting,* attracts large audiences in Spain and Mexico. Many regard it as a form of art, not a sport.

¿Qué le gusta? Everyone has different likes and dislikes.
Complete the sentences and write them out.

Luisa / sí   A Luisa le gusta el tenis.
Carlos / no   A Carlos no le gusta.

1. Raúl / sí
    Olga / no

2. Antonia / sí
    Carlos / no

3. Roberto / no
    Pablo / sí

4. José / sí
    Cora / no

5. Marta / no
    Diego / sí

6. Pablo / no
    Anita / sí

7. Carmen / sí
    Pedro / sí

8. Lola / no
    María / sí

A9 SITUACIÓN • Pasatiempos

Luisa and Pedro, star reporters of the newspaper **El tiempo,** are comparing notes for a
feature article about favorite pastimes of teenagers.

—¿Qué pasatiempo le gusta a
   Alberto?

—¿A Ofelia le gusta estudiar
   música y cantar?

—Y a Pepe, ¿qué le gusta?

—A Alberto le gusta
   escuchar discos.
   Dice que es divertido.

—No, no le gusta.
   Dice que es muy aburrido.
   Le gusta patinar.

—A Pepe, le gusta tocar
   la guitarra y bailar.
—¿Por qué?
—Dice que es ¡estupendo!

—¿Y a Tato y a Lola?

—A Tato le gusta tomar
fotografías, pero a Lola
le gusta hablar por
teléfono.

—¿Qué te gusta, Luisa?

—Me gusta trabajar y jugar
con la computadora. ¡Es
fantástico! Y también me
gusta mirar televisión.

—Pedro, ¿te gusta mirar
televisión también?

—¡No! Odio mirar televisión.
—¿Por qué?
—¡Es horrible!

A 10 Actividad • ¡A escribir!

No es así. The editor's report is confused. Correct the statements that are not
based on information in A9.

1. A Alberto le gusta patinar.
2. A Ofelia le gusta mucho tocar música.
3. A Pepe le gusta escuchar discos.
4. A Tato no le gusta tomar fotografías.

5. A Luisa no le gusta trabajar con la
   computadora.
6. A Pedro no le gusta mirar televisión.

A 11 Actividad • Reacciones

Your partner asks what you think of various activities. You should answer with a
sentence that appropriately expresses your opinion. Then, switch roles.

—¿Patinar?   —¡Es estupendo!

¿Escuchar música?
¿Cantar? ¿Bailar?
¿Patinar?
¿Tocar la guitarra?
¿Estudiar?

¿Mirar televisión?
¿Hablar por teléfono?
¿Tomar fotografías?
¿Trabajar con la computadora?
¿Montar en bicicleta?

¡Es estupendo!
¡Es aburrido!
¡Es horrible!
¡Es fantástico!
¡Es divertido!

Talking about what you and others like and don't like to do

¿Qué te gusta? *What do you like?*	Me gusta patinar. *I like to skate.*
¿Qué no le gusta a Ofelia? *What doesn't Ofelia like?*	No le gusta tocar música. *She doesn't like to play music.*
¿Te gusta correr? *Do you like to jog?*	Sí, me gusta (mucho) correr. Es estupendo. *Yes, I like to jog (very much). It's great.* No, no me gusta. Odio correr. Es aburrido. *No, I don't like it. I hate to jog. It's boring.*

A 13   Conversación • ¿Qué te gusta? ¿Qué no te gusta?

With a partner, create a dialog about what you like or don't like to do. Perform it
for the class. This model may help.

ANA   ¿Te gusta mirar televisión?
PEDRO   No, no me gusta.
ANA   ¿Por qué?
PEDRO   ¡Es horrible!
ANA   ¿Qué te gusta?
PEDRO   ¡Me gusta tocar la guitarra!

¿Te gusta . . . ?

¡Me gusta mucho! ¿Por qué? ¡Es . . . divertido,
estupendo, fantástico! **No, no me gusta. ¿Por qué?**
Es . . . aburrido, horrible. **¡Odio!** . . .

A 14   Comprensión

¿Le gusta a Pepe . . . ?

	Sí	No		Sí	No
1. ¿escuchar discos?		✔	4. ¿bailar?		
2. ¿tomar fotografías?			5. ¿patinar?		
3. ¿tocar la guitarra?			6. ¿mirar televisión?		

A 15   Actividad • ¡A escribir!

Write comments about each picture. Use the expressions in A13.

1.   2.   3.

A 16 SITUACIÓN • El judo 📼

Me llamo Esteban Rodríguez. Mi pasatiempo
favorito es el judo. Me gusta practicar judo.
Soy cinturón azul. Después del azul vienen el
cinturón marrón y el cinturón negro. En el
judo hay un cinturón de color diferente para
cada categoría. El blanco es para los
principiantes y el negro para los más
avanzados. No hay cinturón rojo. Hay siete
colores en total:

blanco   amarillo   anaranjado
verde   azul   marrón   negro

A 17 Actividad • ¡A escoger!

Choose the option that best fits A16.

1. El pasatiempo favorito de Esteban es
   • practicar. • el judo. • los colores.
2. Esteban es
   • cinturón blanco. • cinturón azul. • cinturón negro.
3. Después del cinturón azul vienen
   • el blanco y el negro. • el marrón y el negro. • el azul y el negro.
4. En el judo hay un cinturón de color diferente para
   • cada estudiante. • cada principiante. • cada categoría.
5. El blanco es
   • para los más avanzados. • para los principiantes. • para Esteban.
6. El negro es
   • para los principiantes. • para Esteban. • para los más avanzados.

A 18 Actividad • Rompecabezas
Colores escondidos *Hidden colors*

The seven colors of judo belts are hidden in the squares.
Find them!

A	Ver	Blan	na
llo	co	zul	de
ja	ri	do	Ne
Ma	gro	rrón	ran

Are you a sports fanatic? Do you wait for winter and think about snow? Does spring mean baseball for you and not flowers? Spanish-speaking fans (aficionados) and athletes are among the most enthusiastic in the world.

B1 ¡Un fanfarrón!

Una entrevista imaginaria

Gracias por todo, amigos. Es un honor ser el atleta del año. Pero sí, ¡es verdad! Practico todos los deportes y juego en todas las estaciones. Como todo campeón, gano muchos premios.

Me gusta el invierno. ¡Soy estupendo en el hielo! Patino muy bien y . . . ¡esquiar es fantástico!

¡Ah, la primavera! ¡Soy campeón en la cancha de tenis! Ivan Lendl y yo somos amigos. Pero ahora no hablamos de Ivan.

En el verano, participo en los Juegos Olímpicos. Tengo medalla de oro en natación.

¿Preguntas, por favor? ¿Me gusta el fútbol? Sí, pero en el otoño. ¿Con quién practico? Diego Maradona y yo practicamos mucho.

¿Mi deporte favorito? ¡Ganar en todo momento! Y, ¡muchas gracias por el trofeo, amigos!

Otro fanfarrón. Match the activities on the left with the corresponding items in the box at the right.

Es un honor ser . . .
Practico . . .
Juego . . .
Gano . . .
Soy estupendo . . .
Patino . . .
Soy campeón . . .
Participo . . .
Tengo . . .
Muchas gracias . . .

muchos premios   una medalla de oro   muy bien

en todas las estaciones

en la cancha de tenis

por el trofeo

el atleta del año

todos los deportes

en los Juegos Olímpicos   en el hielo

B3   ESTRUCTURAS ESENCIALES
The present tense of -ar verbs

	hablar	*to talk*	ganar	*to win*
Yo	**hablo**	español.	**Gano**	premios.
Tú	**hablas**	español.	**Ganas**	premios.
Usted, él, ella	**habla**	español.	**Gana**	premios.
Nosotros(as)	**hablamos**	español.	**Ganamos**	premios.
Vosotros(as)	**habláis**	español.	**Ganáis**	premios.
Ustedes, ellos(as)	**hablan**	español.	**Ganan**	premios.

1. Spanish verbs are grouped according to their infinitive ending into three conjugations: **-ar, -er,** and **-ir.**

2. As you learned in Unit 1, the infinitive is the name of the verb, thus **hablar** *to talk,* and **ganar** *to win* are infinitives. Remove the **-ar** ending for these two infinitives and you have their stems: **habl-,** and **gan-.**

3. You can produce the present tense forms for **hablar** and **ganar** and most other regular **-ar** verbs by adding the following endings to the stem:

> **-o, -as, -a, -amos, -áis, -an**

The endings indicate who is doing the action. When you add **-o** to the stem **habl-,** you get **hablo,** *I speak.* When you add **-as** to the stem **habl-,** you get **hablas,** *you speak.* And so on.

4. Here are some other regular **-ar** verbs you have seen.

bailar	*to dance*	**montar**	*to ride*	**practicar**	*to practice*
cantar	*to sing*	**nadar**	*to swim*	**tocar**	*to play* (an instrument)
escuchar	*to listen to*	**necesitar**	*to need*	**trabajar**	*to work*
estudiar	*to study*	**patinar**	*to skate*		
mirar	*to look at*	**participar**	*to participate*		

You can produce the present-tense forms of these **-ar** verbs in the same way as the forms of **hablar** and **ganar** because these verbs are regular. That is, all their forms follow the basic pattern for **-ar** verbs.

B4 Comprensión

Is the reply appropriate?

0	1	2	3	4	5	6	7	8	9	10
✔										

B5 Actividad • Sí, me gusta bailar

Answer the following questions affirmatively.

—¿Escuchas música?
—Sí, me gusta escuchar música.

1. ¿Patina bien Eduardo?
2. ¿Nadas?
3. ¿Hablas español?

4. ¿Mira Alicia televisión?
5. ¿Toca él la guitarra?
6. ¿Bailas?

7. ¿Montas en bicicleta?
8. ¿Practicas béisbol?
9. ¿Canta bien?

B6 Actividad • Combinación

Choose elements from each group to form five complete sentences.

Yo	**patinamos**	*un premio*
Los chicos	**toco**	*televisión*
Felipe y yo	**montan**	*en el hielo*
Olga	**miras**	*en bicicleta*
Tú	**gana**	*la guitarra*

B7 Actividad • ¡A escribir!

Falta algo. Write the following sentences, providing the correct forms of the verb **practicar.**

1. Tú _____ volibol, ¿no?
2. ¿ _____ tú y yo?
3. No, yo _____ con ella.
4. Ella _____ tenis los sábados.

5. ¿ _____ ellas básquetbol?
6. No, _____ béisbol.
7. Nosotros _____ básquetbol.
8. ¿Cuándo _____ ustedes?

Actividad • Periodista   *Journalist*

Tell what is going on in each picture. Use the subject that is given.

1. Ellos

2. María y yo

3. El chico

4. Yo

5. Pepe y Ramón

6. Tú

B9   Actividad • Charla

Talk to your partner about the activities in B8. Do you
practice any of them? Do you like or dislike them? You
might want to use statements and questions like these:

—Yo (no) toco la guitarra.
—¿Tocas tú la guitarra?
—¿Te gusta tocar la guitarra?

B10   ¿Sabes que . . . ?

When Argentina defeated West Germany in the final game of
the 1986 **Campeonato mundial de fútbol** (*World Cup Soccer
Championships*), several billion people around the world
were watching on TV. No other sports event attracts as
much attention as these games, which are held every four
years. Since 1930, when Uruguay won the title in the first
Campeonato mundial de fútbol, half the championships
have been won by European teams and the rest by teams
from Latin America. The 1982 series was held in Spain;
Mexico hosted the series in 1970 and again in 1986. Italy
will be the host in 1990.

SITUACIÓN • ¿Qué necesitamos para jugar?

What equipment do we need to play various sports? **Para practicar un deporte necesitamos muchas cosas . . .**

Para practicar esquí necesitamos . . .

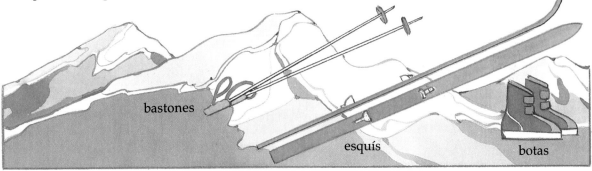

B 12 Actividad • ¡A escoger!

Choose the appropriate equipment for each of the sports mentioned.

1. Para jugar béisbol necesitamos . . .
   • unas botas • una pelota • una raqueta
2. Para jugar tenis necesitamos . . .
   • un guante • una red • una canasta

3. Para practicar esquí necesitamos . . .
   • un bate • unos zapatos • unas botas
4. Para jugar volibol necesitamos . . .
   • un cinturón • una red • una canasta

B 13 Actividad • No es así

The equipment is all wrong! Correct the statements below, using the name of the right equipment needed.

1. Me gusta el béisbol. Tengo *una red.*
2. ¿Practicamos tenis? ¿Necesitas *un bate?*
3. Venimos a jugar volibol, pero no tenemos *raqueta.*
4. En la cancha de tenis hay *una canasta.*
5. ¡No practico esquí! No tengo *guante.*

6. A él le gusta el tenis, pero no tiene *bastones.*
7. ¿Practicas béisbol? ¿Tienes *un esquí?*
8. ¿Vienen a jugar básquetbol? Necesitan *guantes.*

Saying what you need in order to do something

¿Qué necesitas para bailar?	Para bailar necesito música.

To express for which purpose you need something, use **para** plus a verb in the infinitive at the beginning or at the end of the sentence.

B 15   Actividad • Charla

With a partner, talk about what you need to practice different sports.

¿Qué necesitas para practicar . . .?

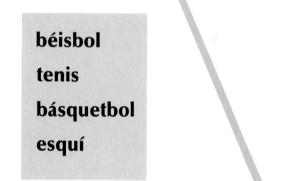

béisbol

tenis

básquetbol

esquí

raqueta
zapatos de tenis
canasta
esquís
bate
pelota
bastones
guantes
botas de esquí

Para practicar . . . necesito . . .

B 16   ESTRUCTURAS ESENCIALES
The verb jugar

In the present indicative tense, the verb **jugar** changes the stem-vowel **u** to **ue** in all forms except the first and second person plural. The endings are regular **-ar** endings.

jugar *to play*					
Yo	**juego**	fútbol.	Nosotros(as)	**jugamos**	básquetbol.
Tú	**juegas**	tenis.	Vosotros(as)	**jugáis**	tenis.
Usted, él, ella	**juega**	volibol.	Ustedes, ellos(as)	**juegan**	béisbol.

B 17   Actividad • ¿Juegan?

Who's playing? Answer as indicated, using a form of **jugar.**

    ¿Juega usted? (no)—No, yo no juego.
    ¿Alicia y usted? (sí)—Sí, nosotros jugamos.

Yo juego volibol, y ¿tú? (no); ¿Ustedes? (no); ¿Los chicos? (sí); ¿Pablo? (sí); ¿Pablo y yo? (sí); ¿Elvira? (sí); ¿Clara y tú? (no); ¿Yo? (sí); ¿Nora y Raúl? (sí); ¿El fanfarrón? (¡No, señor!).

B18 Actividad • Falta algo

Complete using the corresponding form of **jugar.**

—¿— ustedes tenis?
—¿Juegan ustedes tenis?

—¿— tú tenis? Sí, yo —. Alicia — y Pedro — también. Ellos — los sábados.
Nosotros — volibol en la escuela. ¿— ustedes en la escuela?
—Sí, pero nosotros — béisbol. Pedro y Carmen — básquetbol. ¿— ustedes
básquetbol?
—No, nosotros no —. Yo no —. ¿— tú?

B19 Actividad • ¡A actuar! *Let's act!*

With a partner, create your own dialog by changing the italicized words in the
following script. You can use the words from B15 to talk about your favorite
sport. Then act out your new dialog for the class.

A. Me gusta *el béisbol.*
B. ¿Tienes *un bate?*
A. No.
B. ¿Tienes *un guante?*

A. No. Necesito *un guante.*
B. ¿Tienes *una pelota?*
A. No. Necesito *una pelota* también.
B. ¡Pero tú necesitas todo!

B20 Actividad • ¿Y ustedes, amigos?

You want to find classmates with interests similar to yours. List your activities in
a chart, like the one below. Leave a space on the right where you can write the
names of classmates who enjoy the same activities, and those who don't. Ask
questions if necessary. **¿Patinas? ¿Cantas? ¿Bailas?** Once you've filled in your
chart, report who does what.

Yo	Amigos	
	Sí	No
Patino	María, Silvia	Olga
Canto	Jorge	Elena, Julia
Bailo	Olga	

Yo patino. María y Silvia patinan también. María, Silvia y yo patinamos,
pero Olga no patina.

B21 Actividad • ¡A adivinar! *Guess!*

A classmate will tell you what equipment he or she has and you have to guess
what sport is played. Then, switch roles.

—Tengo un bate y una pelota.
—Juegas béisbol.

saying when and how often you play . . . talking about the months, the seasons, and the weather

Why do you think so many major league baseball stars come from countries in the Caribbean? How often do you play sports? Does it depend on the weather? The seasons? Do you practice a lot?

C1 ## ¿Juegas siempre?

FELIPE	¿Te gusta jugar tenis, Sara?
SARA	Sí, a veces juego. No juego a menudo.
FELIPE	Yo juego siempre. Juego todos los días.
SARA	Necesito practicar más. ¿Jugamos un partido hoy por la tarde?
FELIPE	Por la tarde, no. ¿Por la noche?
SARA	No, nunca juego por la noche.
FELIPE	¿Y mañana por la mañana?
SARA	Bueno, ¡de acuerdo! ¡Hasta mañana!

C2 **Actividad • ¡A escoger!**

Select the option that best completes the sentence according to the dialog.

1. El diálogo se llama
   • ¿No juegas nunca? • ¿Juegas todos los días? • ¿Juegas siempre?
2. A Sara
   • no le gusta el tenis. • le gusta el tenis. • no le gusta jugar.
3. Sara juega
   • siempre. • a menudo. • a veces.
4. Felipe juega tenis
   • todos los días. • a veces. • nunca.

5. Sara necesita
- practicar por la mañana. • practicar más. • jugar por la noche.

6. Ella no juega
- por la noche. • nunca. • mañana.

7. Ellos no juegan
- nunca. • hoy. • mañana.

8. Felipe y Sara juegan
- hoy por la noche. • mañana por la tarde. • mañana por la mañana.

C3 Actividad • ¡No, al contrario! *No, on the contrary!*

Pair up with a classmate, and be difficult! No matter which phrase your classmate chooses, reply with the opposite. Exchange roles.

—¿Juegas béisbol hoy?
—No, mañana.

siempre sí
por la mañana
hoy
a menudo
a veces
mañana
no
nunca
por la noche

¡Soy perfecto! ¡Nunca necesito practicar!

C4 ESTRUCTURAS ESENCIALES
Word order

Siempre juego. Juego **siempre**.	*I always play.*
A veces juego. Juego **a veces**.	*Sometimes I play.*
Nunca juego. **No** juego **nunca**.	*I never play.*

You can place expressions that say *how often* either before or after your verb.
When you place **nunca** after a verb, put **no** before the verb.

Conversación • Los deportes y los pasatiempos

Work with a partner. Find out what sports and pastimes each of you enjoy, and when and how often you practice. Ask at least ten questions.

—¿Qué deportes practicas? ¿Qué pasatiempo te gusta?

¿Todos los días?   ¿Qué días?   ¿Cuándo?

¿Siempre,
a veces,
nunca?

¿los lunes,
martes,
miércoles, . . . ?

¿por la mañana,
por la tarde,
por la noche?

¿béisbol? ¿bailar? ¿básquetbol? ¿discos?
¿tenis? ¿volibol? ¿fútbol?
¿guitarra? ¿cantar? ¿patinar? ¿bicicleta? ¿televisión?

C6   Actividad • ¡A escribir!

Write sentences saying how often or when you do the following things, using C5 as a guide.

—¿Juegas tenis? —Sí, juego todos los días. Juego por la tarde.

1. ¿Miras televisión?
2. ¿Tocas la guitarra?
3. ¿Escuchas discos?
4. ¿Bailas?
5. ¿Cantas?
6. ¿Hablas mucho por teléfono?
7. ¿Nadas?
8. ¿Patinas?
9. ¿Montas en bicicleta?
10. ¿Trabajas con la computadora?
11. ¿Practicas deportes?

C7 Actividad • Una entrevista

Interview a classmate about his or her favorite sport or pastime. Ask the
questions below. Use **jugar** and **practicar** in your questions. Exchange roles.

1. ¿Qué deporte (pasatiempo) te gusta? **2.** ¿Cuándo . . . ? **3.** ¿Dónde . . . ? **4.** ¿A qué hora?
5. ¿Qué días? **6.** ¿Con quién? **7.** ¿Cómo . . . ?, ¿bien o mal? **8.** ¿Qué necesitas para practicar?

C8 Actividad • ¡A escribir!

Write the interview from exercise C7 in dialog form.

C9 SITUACIÓN • ¿Qué tiempo hace? *How's the weather?*

ANITA   ¡Otro día horrible! Hace mal
        tiempo. Llueve y hace mucho viento.
CONSUELO Ideal para mirar televisión
        y escuchar discos.

LUISA   ¡Hace frío!
CARMEN Sí, pero no nieva. ¡Estupendo
        para patinar en hielo!

FELIPE ¿Hace fresco?
JULIÁN No, hace sol y hace calor.
        ¡Es un día magnífico!
FELIPE Por fin hace buen tiempo
        para la playa.

C10 Actividad • Reacciones

Create three short dialogs by combining elements from the three groups. Be ready
to read them in class.

Hace sol y hace calor.	Estupendo para patinar en hielo.	¡Otro día horrible!
Hace frío.	Ideal para mirar televisión.	¡Es un día magnífico!
Llueve y hace viento.	Hace buen tiempo para la playa.	Pero no nieva.

Hace (muy) buen tiempo.	*It's (very) nice out.*
Hace (mucho) calor.	*It's (very) hot.*
Hace (mucho) sol.	*It's (very) sunny.*
Hace (muy) mal tiempo.	*The weather is (very) bad.*
Hace fresco.	*It's cool.*
Hace (mucho) frío.	*It's (very) cold.*
Hace (mucho) viento.	*It's (very) windy.*

1. To talk about the weather, you need to know several expressions with **hace. Hace** is a form of the verb **hacer,** *to make, to do.*

2. To express the idea *very.*
   a. Use **mucho,** an adjective, to describe a noun.
   > Hace **mucho** calor. *It's very hot.* (Literally, *it makes much heat.*)

   b. Use **muy,** an adverb, to describe an adjective.
   > Hace **muy** mal tiempo. *It's very bad out.*
   > (Literally, *it makes very bad weather.*)

3. **Hace** does not appear in every weather expression. Since **nieva,** *it's snowing,* and **llueve,** *it's raining,* are verbs, the verb **hacer** is not used.

C12 Actividad • ¡Al contrario!

The weather report is often dead wrong. React to the forecast by stating the opposite.

> —Hace buen tiempo.
> —Al contrario, hace mal tiempo.

1. Hace frío.
2. Hace buen tiempo para nadar.
3. Hace sol.
4. Hace mal tiempo.
5. Hace calor.
6. Llueve.

C13 Actividad • Charla

Work with a partner, talk about the weather using different expressions and activities.

¡Hace buen tiempo!

hace viento llueve
mal tiempo nieva
frío buen tiempo calor

¡magnífico!
¡horrible!
¡estupendo!
¡ideal!

¡Ideal para jugar béisbol!

SITUACIÓN • Los meses del año
The months of the year

otoño
septiembre
octubre
noviembre

invierno
diciembre
enero
febrero

primavera
marzo
abril
mayo

verano
junio
julio
agosto

C15 Actividad • Combinación

Match the months with the corresponding season, according to where you live.

otoño   invierno   primavera   verano

junio   diciembre   **mayo**   octubre   *abril*   enero
febrero   agosto   julio   noviembre   *marzo*   septiembre

C16 Comprensión

Which season of the year is being talked about?

	0	1	2	3	4	5	6	7	8	9	10	11
el verano												
el otoño												
el invierno												
la primavera	✔											

C17 ¿Sabes que . . . ?

The seasons in the world's two hemispheres are reversed. When it's winter in Spain, the United States, and Mexico, it's summer in Argentina, Uruguay, Paraguay, Bolivia, Chile, and Peru. Schools are closed for summer vacation in December, January, and February.

1 El equipo° 🔲

It's your job as coach to form a top-notch team to practice your favorite sport. You have to get a few good players together to form the nucleus of the team. The list below includes a brief description of the students who might be interested in playing the sport. Work with a partner. Study the list, decide on the sport you will coach, and pick the most promising players.

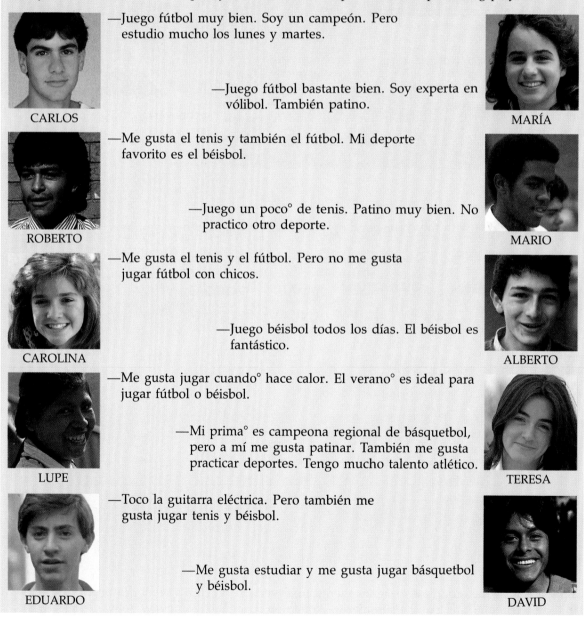

—Juego fútbol muy bien. Soy un campeón. Pero estudio mucho los lunes y martes.

CARLOS

—Juego fútbol bastante bien. Soy experta en vólibol. También patino.

MARÍA

—Me gusta el tenis y también el fútbol. Mi deporte favorito es el béisbol.

ROBERTO

—Juego un poco° de tenis. Patino muy bien. No practico otro deporte.

MARIO

—Me gusta el tenis y el fútbol. Pero no me gusta jugar fútbol con chicos.

CAROLINA

—Juego béisbol todos los días. El béisbol es fantástico.

ALBERTO

—Me gusta jugar cuando° hace calor. El verano° es ideal para jugar fútbol o béisbol.

—Mi prima° es campeona regional de básquetbol, pero a mí me gusta patinar. También me gusta practicar deportes. Tengo mucho talento atlético.

LUPE

TERESA

—Toco la guitarra eléctrica. Pero también me gusta jugar tenis y béisbol.

—Me gusta estudiar y me gusta jugar básquetbol y béisbol.

EDUARDO

DAVID

el equipo *team*   **un poco** *a little*   **cuando** *when*   **verano** *summer*   **prima** *cousin*

2 Actividad • ¡Que hable! ¡Que hable! *Speech! Speech!*

Prepare in Spanish a description of your favorite sport and read it in class. What equipment is needed to play? When is it played? In what season? In what kind of weather? How often? What days? Do you play it also? Be ready to answer questions from your classmates.

3 Actividad • Composición

Mi deporte (pasatiempo) favorito. Write in Spanish all you know about your favorite sport or hobby. Use Skills 2 above as a guideline.

4 Actividad • Una encuesta

Ask your classmates how often they practice a sport or pastime and in what season. Record their responses in a chart like the one below, using a similar code.

¿Deporte o pasatiempo?	¿Cuándo practicas?		¿En qué estación?	
béisbol	nunca	0	otoño	o
tenis				
mirar televisión	a veces	1	invierno	i
computadoras	a menudo	2	primavera	p
básquetbol . . .	todos los días	3	verano	v

For each sport or activity, add the numbers and note the season when it is usually practiced. Then report to the class which sports and pastimes are practiced the most, and in which season.

5 Pronunciación, lectura, dictado

1. Listen and repeat what you hear.

2. The sound of the Spanish vowels **a, e** and **o.** Listen, then read aloud.
   hay correr montar once voy hoy básquetbol Orlando

3. Copy the following sentences to prepare yourself to write them from dictation.
   La amiga de Marta nada.
   Nosotros tenemos clases a las tres.
   La profesora practica deportes todos los martes.
   Tú hablas mucho con Ana.

¿LO SABES?

Let's review some important points you have learned in this unit.

SECTION A

When talking about sports and pastimes in Spanish, can you name a few?
Name five. Add the definite article if necessary or use an infinitive.

Can you talk about your likes, dislikes, or preferences in sports?
Answer the following questions, expressing your preferences and say why you feel that way.

> ¿Qué deporte te gusta? ¿Por qué?
> ¿Cuál es tu pasatiempo favorito? ¿Por qué?
> ¿Qué deporte practican en tu escuela?
> ¿Te gusta? ¿Por qué?

SECTION B

Can you tell in which seasons you play different sports?
Make up four sentences.

> En (name of season) jugamos / practicamos (name of sport).

Do you know what equipment is needed for different sports?
Say what sport needs the following equipment. Start your sentences with
Necesitamos . . .

una raqueta	un bate	bastones
esquís	botas	unas pelotas
un balón	una canasta	un guante

SECTION C

Can you say how often you practice a sport or pastime, and whether you practice in the morning, in the afternoon, or at night?
Write four sentences. Say how often and when you practice two sports and two pastimes.

> Siempre juego tenis por la tarde.

Can you talk about the weather?
Answer these questions.

> ¿Qué tiempo hace hoy?
> ¿Llueve?
> ¿Nieva?
> ¿Para qué está bueno el tiempo?

VOCABULARIO

SECTION A
amarillo, -a *yellow*
anaranjado, -a *orange*
avanzado, -a *advanced*
azul *blue*
bailar *to dance*
blanco, -a *white*
cada *each*
cantar *to sing*
la **categoría** *category*
el **cinturón (pl. cinturones)** *belt*
el **color** *color*
correr *to run, to jog*
dice que . . . *he (she) says (that) . . .*
el **disco** *record*
divertido, -a *fun*
escuchar *to listen (to)*
estudiar *to study*
estupendo, -a *great*
fantástico, -a *fantastic*
el **fútbol** *soccer*
la **gimnasia** *gymnastics*
la **guitarra** *guitar*
gustar *to like, to be pleasing to*
me gusta *I like*
le gusta *you like, he/she likes*
te gusta *you like*
hablar *to speak, talk*
jugar (ue) *to play*
marrón *brown*
mirar *to look at, watch*
montar *to ride*
mucho *a lot*
nadar *to swim*
negro, -a *black*
odio *I hate*
el **pasatiempo** *pastime*
para *for*
patinar *to skate*
practicar *to practice, play*
el **principiante** *beginner (m.)*
la **principiante** *beginner (f.)*
rojo *red*
también *also, too*
el **teléfono** *telephone*
por teléfono *on the telephone*
el **tenis** *tennis*
tocar *to play (a musical instrument)*
tomar *to take*

tomar fotografías *to take photographs*
trabajar *to work*
verde *green*
el **volibol** *volleyball*

SECTION B
el **amigo, la amiga** *friend*
el **año** *year*
el **atleta** *athlete (m.)*
la **atleta** *athlete (f.)*
el **balón** *ball (basketball, volleyball, soccer ball)*
el **bastón (pl. bastones)** *ski pole*
el **bate** *bat*
la **bota** *ski boot*
el **campeón, la campeona** *champion*
la **canasta** *basketball hoop*
la **cancha de tenis** *tennis court*
como *as, like*
en todo momento *every time*
la **entrevista** *interview*
es verdad *it's true*
esquiar *to ski, skiing*
los **esquís** *skis*
la **estación** *season*
el **fanfarrón, la fanfarrona** *braggart*
favorito, -a *favorite*
ganar *to win*
el **guante** *glove, mitt*
el **hielo** *ice*
imaginario, -a *imaginary*
el **invierno** *winter*
el **juego** *game*
los **Juegos Olímpicos** *Olympic Games*
la **medalla de oro** *gold medal*
muchas gracias *thank you very much*
la **natación** *swimming*
necesitar *to need*
el **otoño** *fall, autumn*
para *to, in order to*
la **pelota** *ball (baseball, tennis ball)*
la **pregunta** *question*
el **premio** *prize*
la **primavera** *spring*
la **raqueta** *racquet*
la **red** *net*

todo *everything*
todo, -a, -os, -as *all, every*
el **trofeo** *trophy*
el **verano** *summer*
el **zapato** *shoe*
los **zapatos de tenis** *tennis shoes*

SECTION C
a menudo *often*
a veces *sometimes*
de acuerdo *all right*
hace (muy) buen tiempo *it's (very) nice out*
hace (mucho) calor *it's (very) hot out*
hace fresco *it's cool out*
hace (mucho) frío *it's (very) cold out*
hace (muy) mal tiempo *the weather is (very) bad*
hace (mucho) sol *it's (very) sunny*
hace (mucho) viento *it's (very) windy*
los demás *the rest*
llueve *it's raining*
magnífico, -a *excellent, very good*
mañana *tomorrow*
la **mañana** *morning*
por la mañana *in the morning*
el **mes** *month*
los **meses del año** *months of the year (see p. 111)*
nieva *it's snowing*
la **noche** *night*
por la noche *at night*
nunca *never*
otro, -a *other, another*
el **partido** *game, match*
patinar en hielo *to ice skate*
la **playa** *beach*
¿qué tiempo hace? *how's the weather?*
siempre *always*
la **tarde** *afternoon*
por la tarde *in the afternoon*
todos los días *every day*

ESTUDIO DE PALABRAS
Rearrange the vocabulary of the unit in broad thematic categories like the following: Names of sports/Sports equipment/Verbs that express sports actions/Names of pastimes/The seasons/Weather expressions. Group the rest of the words in a category called "Others".

VAMOS A LEER

Antes de leer

Before reading, look at the illustrations and the title. You should have an idea of what the selection is about. This will help you guess the meanings of new words without having to look them up.

Un maratón

A Spanish TV station is broadcasting a marathon from New York.

Por° las calles° de Nueva York.

LOCUTORA°   Los corredores° pasan por° las calles de Nueva York. ¡Todos° corren a la meta°, en el Parque Central! Pero . . . ¡sí! ¡Uno llega° a la meta! ¡Gana la competencia!

LOCUTORA   ¡Estupendo! ¿Cómo se llama usted?
GANADOR   Me llamo Ángel. Ángel Dos Pasos°.
LOCUTORA   ¡Dos Pasos! ¡Qué buen nombre° para el ganador°! ¿Y de dónde es usted?
GANADOR   Soy de Madrid, España.
LOCUTORA   ¡De Madrid! ¿Y cómo corre° en Nueva York?

---

por *along*   **las calles** *streets*   **locutora** *newscaster*   **corredores** *runners*   **pasar por** *to pass through*   **todos** *all,*
everybody   **la meta** *finish line*   **llegar** *to arrive*   **dos pasos** *two steps*   **nombre** *name*   **ganador** *winner*   **corre** *you*
(usted) run

GANADOR	Aquí° estoy. En la capital del mundo°. Con permiso°, un saludo a la familia y a los amigos en Madrid. ¡Juanita! ¿Me miras° en televisión? ¡Un saludo, chica!
LOCUTORA	¿Y quién es Juanita?
GANADOR	¡La novia°! Adiós, Juanita, ¡adiós!
LOCUTORA	Aquí, desde° el maratón de Nueva York. ¡Hasta luego!

Preguntas y respuestas

1. ¿Por dónde pasan los corredores?
2. ¿Adónde corren todos?
3. ¿Dónde está la meta?
4. ¿Cómo se llama el ganador?
5. ¿De dónde es él?
6. Para él, ¿qué es Nueva York?
7. ¿Quién es Juanita?
8. ¿Dónde está la locutora?

Actividad • ¿Es cierto o no?

Change the following statements so they agree with the reading.

1. Los corredores pasan por el maratón de Nueva York.
2. Todos corren a la capital.
3. Dos corredores llegan a la meta.
4. El locutor se llama Ángel.
5. Ángel Dos Pasos es de Nueva York.
6. Juanita está en el Parque Central.
7. El maratón es en España.

Actividad • Una entrevista

Imagine that you have to interview an athlete from your school. Using the marathon interview as a model, think how you would find out the information you need. When you've imagined your way through the interview and made some notes, write the interview.

---

aquí *here* **mundo** *world* **con permiso** *with your permission* **¿me miras?** *are you watching me?* **la novia** *girlfriend*
desde *from*

El regalo

Adriana y Daniel terminan° la tarea.
A Daniel le gusta la música; toca la guitarra
un poco, y después escucha el radio.

Hace sol. Adriana sale° y juega volibol con
unas amigas.

Pero los dos hermanos no dejan de pensar en° el regalo misterioso.

En su cuarto° Adriana prende° el televisor en el Canal 17.

Hay un partido de fútbol; juega el equipo° favorito de ellos. Los dos miran
como° hipnotizados. Hay un momento de confusión. Uno de los jugadores patea°
el balón, y el locutor grita° ''¡Gol!''

De pronto°, ¡Adriana y Daniel están° en el estadio de fútbol! Daniel mira a
Adriana.

---

terminan *finish* **sale** *goes out* **dejan de pensar en** *stop thinking of* **cuarto** *room* **prende** *turns on* **equipo** *team*
como *as if* **patea** *kicks* **grita** *shouts* **de pronto** *suddenly* **están** *they are*

DANIEL   ¡Estoy loco! ¡Es imposible!

ADRIANA   No, Daniel, no estás loco . . . Estamos° en el estadio, en el partido de
           fútbol del Canal 17.

(Hace frío y llueve. El público grita.)

ADRIANA   Vamos a casa° Daniel. Es tarde.

(Salen° del estadio y esperan° el autobús.)

ADRIANA   No me gusta el televisor, es muy
           peligroso°.
DANIEL   No es peligroso, pero debemos°
           controlarlo°.
ADRIANA   ¿Hablamos con papá y mamá?
DANIEL   No. El televisor es un secreto. El
           Canal 17 es fantástico. Mira, ahí
           viene el autobús.

Preguntas y respuestas

Answer the following questions about what you have just read.

1. ¿A Daniel le gusta tocar la guitarra? ¿Qué le gusta jugar a Adriana?
2. ¿Dónde tienen los chicos el televisor?
3. ¿Qué miran en el Canal 17?
4. ¿Qué equipo juega?
5. ¿Están Adriana y Daniel en el estadio?
6. ¿Qué tiempo hace?
7. ¿Le gusta a Adriana el televisor? ¿Por qué?

Actividad • Asociaciones

Give as many words, phrases, and sentences as you can that are associated with
these topics from the reading.

1. la música
2. "¡Gol!"
3. el estadio
4. el Canal 17
5. vamos a casa
6. llueve
7. el volibol

---

estamos *we are*   **vamos a casa** *let's go home*   **salen** *they leave*   **esperan** *they wait for*   **peligroso** *dangerous*
debemos *we ought to*   **controlarlo** *to control it*

¡Playa, sol y deportes!

Repaso

Cartagena is a resort city in Colombia. It's a port on the Caribbean Sea and has a tropical climate and fine beaches. The old fortifications, that were built by the Spaniards in the 17th century to protect the city from attacking pirates, are one of its tourist attractions.

CARTAGENA, PLAYA

¡Hola!
En Cartagena hace sol y muy buen tiempo.
Me gusta la playa
¡Hasta el jueves!
Tu amigo,
Enrique

Carlos Ramos
Calle Libertad 88
Bogotá

CARTAGENA, VISTA DE LA CIUDAD

¡Hola, Susana!
¿Qué tal? ¿Hace frío allí? En Cartagena hace calor, y me gusta la playa.
Chao,
Leticia

Susana Sánchez
Cantones 27-7° I
Quito
Ecuador

2   Actividad • ¡A escoger!

Choose the option that best agrees with Enrique's and Leticia's postcards.

1. **En Cartagena** • hace frío y llueve • hace muy buen tiempo • no hace sol
2. **A Enrique** • le gusta la playa • le gusta el tiempo • no le gusta el sol
3. **¡Hasta** • mañana! • el jueves! • luego!
4. **Enrique es amigo de** • Susana • Leticia • Carlos
5. **¿Hace frío en** • Bogotá? • Cartagena? • Quito?
6. **En Cartagena** • hace calor • hace frío • hace mal tiempo
7. **La tarjeta de Leticia es para** • Carlos • Enrique • Susana
8. **Las tarjetas vienen de** • Quito • Colombia • Bogotá

   Actividad • Para completar

You are spending a week in Cartagena with your family. You meet Enrique on the beach. Supply your part of the conversation.

ENRIQUE: ¡Hola! Me llamo Enrique. ¿Cómo te llamas tú?
Tú: _____
ENRIQUE: Yo soy de Bogotá. Y tú, ¿de dónde eres?
Tú: _____
ENRIQUE: ¿Por qué no juegas volibol con nosotros?
Tú: _____
ENRIQUE: Bueno. Me gusta la playa, pero me gusta más el tenis. ¿Juegas tú?
Tú: _____
ENRIQUE: ¿Por qué no jugamos mañana?
Tú: _____
ENRIQUE: ¿A las diez?
Tú: _____
ENRIQUE: Bueno, ¡hasta mañana!

4   Actividad • Charla

Pair off with a classmate. One of you is Enrique. You meet on the beach. Act out the conversation in Skills 3. Switch roles.

5   Actividad • Mi amigo Enrique

Write a short note to a friend. Tell your friend about Enrique, where he is from, what he likes, and what sport he likes to play.

6   Actividad • ¿Hablas español?

Enrique is very impressed with your Spanish. He wants to know about your Spanish classes, about school in general and the subjects you are taking. Make some notes of what you are planning to tell your new friend. Report it to the class.

7   Actividad • Charla

With a partner talk about your likes and dislikes in school, sports, and seasons. Tell why you like or dislike them. Listen to what your partner has to say; then report your partner's likes and dislikes to the class.

Actividad • Preguntas y respuestas

Answer in complete sentences according to **¿Quién juega tenis?**

1. ¿Qué día es?
2. ¿Por qué no juega Raúl?
3. ¿Qué clase tiene Anita? ¿A qué hora?
4. ¿Tiene Jorge raqueta?

5. ¿Vienen Luis y Pepe a jugar tenis?
6. ¿Cómo está Carmela?
7. ¿Juega ella los martes?
8. ¿Viene hoy el profesor de tenis? ¿Por qué?

10 Actividad • No es así

Change the following statements to make them agree with **¿Quién juega tenis?**

1. A Manuel no le gusta el tenis.
2. Raúl tiene clase de música mañana.
3. Raúl tiene poca tarea para mañana.
4. Anita tiene clase de química a las cinco.
5. Jorge tiene dos raquetas para jugar tenis.
6. Luis y Pepe vienen para practicar tenis.

7. Luis practica tenis con Pepe.
8. Carmen está muy bien.
9. Carmen siempre juega tenis los martes.
10. El profesor de tenis tiene clases hoy.
11. El profesor de física no viene hoy.
12. Los chicos juegan tenis con Manuel.

11 Actividad • Charla

Excusas. Pair off with a classmate. One of you is Manuel. The other one doesn't want to do what Manuel suggests. Think up good excuses based on what Raúl, Anita, Jorge, Luis, and Carmela say in the cartoon. Present your dialog to the class.

12 Actividad • ¿De dónde son?

Discover where all these people are from. The clue is that their names rhyme with the places where they live! Read your answers aloud to see if you are correct.

Fredo es de Laredo.

1. Olivia es de _____ .
2. Ramón es de _____ .
3. Alicia es de _____ .
4. Cristina es de _____ .
5. Federico es de _____ .
6. María es de _____ .
7. Manuela es de _____ .
8. Ramona es de _____ .

a. Puerto Rico
b. Venezuela
c. Bolivia
d. Pamplona
e. Andalucía
f. Aragón
g. Argentina
h. Galicia

13 Actividad • ¡A escribir!

Write a postcard to a friend from a place you have visited or that you'd like to visit. Tell your friend what you like and what you don't like about the place where you are. You can also write about new friends you've met and sports you practice there.

Viñeta cultural 1

Pueblos y ciudades

In the large, bustling cities of the Spanish-speaking world, and the many small villages that dot the countryside, visitors can find great contrasts and a wide variety of cultures. In Spain, medieval castles, Gothic cathedrals, and ancient aqueducts are dramatic reminders of the past amidst the modern life of today.

❶ Iglesia de la Sagrada Familia en Barcelona, España

❷ Un café al aire libre en Barcelona, España

❸ El parque del Retiro en Madrid, España

❹ La hermosa ciudad de Ávila, España

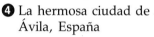

Spaniards carefully preserve their cultural heritage. **El Prado,** the museum in Madrid, houses a world-famous art collection begun long ago by the royal families of Spain. From the 1400s to the 1800s, the paintings were bought one by one by the Spanish monarchs, and what we see today are essentially the heirlooms of the royal families of Spain.

❶ La plaza España en Madrid, España
❷ El Palacio Real en Madrid, España
❸ Plaza de España en Sevilla, España
❹ La Fiesta Brava en Sevilla, España
❺ Museo del Prado en Madrid, España

In many cities and towns of the United States, the Hispanic presence can be seen and heard. Walk along any street and you can hear Spanish words that have become part of the English language—**mosquito, fiesta, taxi, patio.** Architectural styles reflect the Spanish influence with its red-tiled roofs, arched doorways, and brightly painted walls. Even in our food we enjoy a special Hispanic **sabor** *(flavor).*

❶ Un café cubano en Miami, Florida

❷ El Morro de Puerto Rico

❸ Los hermosos y coloridos murales hispanos en Sacramento, California

❹ La Misión de San Gabriel en San Gabriel, California

127

1. El centro de Guadalajara, México
2. El parque Chapultepec en la Ciudad de México
3. Tejedoras indias de Oaxaca, México
4. Una máscara antigua de jade hecha por los mayas en Palenque, México
5. Fiesta típica en Guanajuato, México
6. Mercado de frutas en Yucatán, México

In many parts of Mexico, especially in rural areas, traditional ways of life continue in the present. Even Mexico City, the capital, is a mixture of the ancient and the modern. There, tall skyscrapers stand beside buildings that are many centuries old. Indians dressed in traditional garb, woven by hand, walk by elegant shops offering the latest in European fashions.

1. Día de mercado en el pueblo de Chichicastenango, Guatemala
2. Las ruinas de Antigua, Guatemala
3. Una ciudad moderna de Guatemala
4. Un puesto de frutas en San José, Costa Rica

While the cities of Central America are the centers of economic and political life, the rural areas are characterized by farming. It is unfortunate that today the region is torn by unrest. One exception is Costa Rica. This small country, which boasts of not having an army, was honored in 1987 when its president, Oscar Arias, was presented with the Nobel Prize for Peace.

129

In addition to its many picturesque towns, such as Cuzco in Peru, South America has many large cities, among them Caracas, Bogotá, Lima, and Buenos Aires. Caracas is the birthplace of Simón Bolívar, the man most honored and loved in South America. Born of wealthy parents, he grew up determined to free his people of Spanish rule. In 1821, after ten years of war, he finally defeated the Spaniards. He brought independence to four South American countries and was given the title of **El Libertador.**

❶ La playa de Boca Grande en Cartagena, Colombia

❷ La Plaza de Bolívar en Tunja, Colombia

❸ El hermoso puerto de Caraballeda, Venezuela

1. La Catedral de Cuzco, Perú
2. La Plaza de Armas en Lima, Perú
3. Estatua de Francisco Pizarro en Lima, Perú
4. Paredes construidas por los incas en Cuzco, Perú

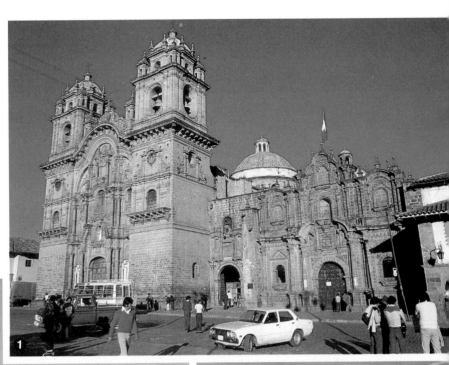

❶ El puerto de Valparaíso, Chile

❷ Un jardín hermoso en Viña del Mar, Chile

❸ El juego del pato en Buenos Aires, Argentina

❹ La Plaza de Mayo y la Casa Rosada en Buenos Aires, Argentina

Argentina and Chile are progressive countries with beautiful modern cities and extensive areas of open land. Both countries have thriving cattle industries, and agriculture plays an important role in their economies. In Chile, the fishing industry is a key source of income. Both countries also have famous resorts, where people from all over the continent come to enjoy vacations and watch traditional sports such as **"El pato"** and polo.

SEGUNDA PARTE

Every summer many American students go to Spain to study Spanish. Brian and Alice, with a group of students from Boston, arrive at Barajas Airport in Madrid. After picking up their luggage, they proceed through customs. When travelers arrive in a new place, they have to ask for directions to find out where everything is. Let's see how these American students go about it.

In the Spanish-speaking world, the family plays a vital role in the life of all its members. The family not only includes parents and children, but grandparents, aunts, uncles, cousins, godparents, and close friends as well. They often meet for meals and for family get-togethers, as well as for celebrating a holiday, a birthday, or some other occasion. Here you will meet the members of Antonio's family, who live in Mexico City.

Spanish-speaking teenagers, like teenagers everywhere, love to go out, especially to the movies and to concerts. In Buenos Aires, Argentina, teenagers have a wide selection of places to go and things to do. But first they have to plan, discussing their choices and preferences, and finally agreeing on where they will go and where they will meet.

Elena, a girl from Costa Rica, is going to New York to spend the summer with her relatives living there. By the end of her stay in New York, Elena has not only learned some English but also made many new friends.

UNIDAD 5
En el aeropuerto

The Hispanic world is immense. Madrid is 3,593 miles from New York and 6,050 miles from Buenos Aires; Buenos Aires is 6,170 miles from Los Angeles! Rugged mountain chains, enormous deserts, and tropical forests in some countries make long trips by land impractical. Travel by air is the solution!

Airports are busy places. People come and go, in a hurry to get to their destination, but how? Where's flight 321? our luggage? the customs office? How do you find where you are supposed to go? You ask!

In this unit you will:

SECTION A	ask where something or someone is, and learn how to give directions
SECTION B	discuss where you and others are going . . . make a telephone call
SECTION C	make suggestions . . . say what people are doing
TRY YOUR SKILLS	use what you've learned
VAMOS A LEER	read for practice and pleasure

135

Many American students go to Spain each summer to study Spanish. Most arrive at Barajas, the country's largest airport, just outside Madrid. International airports can seem a bit confusing at first. But once you find your luggage, show your passport, and go through customs, you're on your way to an exciting adventure.

A1

¿Dónde está? 📼

Un grupo de estudiantes llega a Madrid. Vienen en el vuelo 321 de Boston. Entran por la puerta 9. Están en Barajas, el aeropuerto internacional. Van primero a la sección de equipaje. Necesitan un carro para las maletas. Después, a la aduana. ¡Ya está todo! ¿Y ahora? ¡A cambiar de avión o a buscar un taxi!

ADUANA
CUSTOMS
DOUANE

BRIAN   ¡Oh! Mi maleta no está. ¿Dónde está mi maleta?
ALICE   ¿Tu maleta? Allí está.
BRIAN   ¡Qué suerte! ¿Tienes tu cámara?
ALICE   Sí, está en mi cartera. Pero, ¿dónde está mi diccionario de español? ¿Y mi mapa?
BRIAN   ¿Tu diccionario? No sé. ¿No está aquí?
ALICE   No. ¡Está con el mapa en el asiento del avión!

ADUANERO   Su pasaporte, por favor.
ALICE   Está en el bolsillo. Aquí tiene, señor.
ADUANERO   Muchas gracias.
ALICE   De nada.

A2   Actividad • ¿Es cierto o no?

Correct these sentences to make them agree with the dialog. Some of them are correct already.

1. Un grupo de profesores llega a Madrid.
2. Vienen en el vuelo 321 de San Francisco.
3. Están en Barajas, el aeropuerto de Madrid.
4. Van primero a la aduana.
5. Necesitan un taxi para las maletas.

6. Después, van a la sección de equipaje.
7. La maleta está allí. ¡Qué pena!
8. La cartera de Alice está en la cámara.
9. El diccionario está en el asiento del avión.
10. El pasaporte de Alice está en el avión.

Actividad · Combinación

Let's see how many sentences you can form in five minutes, using an element from each column.

La maleta de Brian La cámara El diccionario El pasaporte El mapa	*está* *no está*	aquí. en el bolsillo. en la cartera. en el asiento. allí.

A4 ESTRUCTURAS ESENCIALES
Possessive adjectives

Possessive adjectives (*my, your, his, her, its . . .*) always precede the nouns they introduce, and are never given vocal emphasis like in English. They agree in number with the noun they modify.

yo → mi	tú → tu	usted, él, ella → su
Mi maleta está aquí. *My suitcase is here.*	**Tu** maleta está aquí. *Your suitcase is here.*	**Su** maleta está aquí. *Your (His, Her) suitcase is here.*

Note that the possessive **tu** does not have a written accent like the subject pronoun **tú**. You will learn the plural forms of possessive adjectives in Unit 6.

A5 Actividad · Maletas, maletas . . .

Help the group leader find out how many suitcases the group has and where they are. Say that each person has one and that it's there.

    Eduardo   —Eduardo tiene una maleta.
                   Su maleta está allí.

    él Ana usted ella tú yo Brian

A6 SE DICE ASÍ
Asking and saying where something is

¿Dónde está mi pasaporte? Where's my passport?	Está en tu bolsillo. It's in your pocket.

You can't find anything that belongs to you! A friend helps you find what you're looking for. Prepare a list of the items you can't find. (Take turns with a partner.)

—¿Dónde está mi cartera?
—¿Tu cartera? Está aquí.

¿mi . . . ?
¿tu . . . ?

está . . .

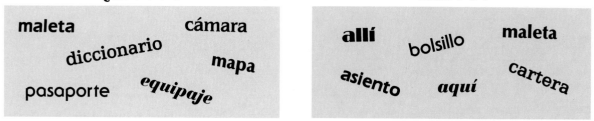

maleta   cámara
diccionario
mapa
pasaporte   equipaje

allí   bolsillo   maleta
asiento   aquí   cartera

A8   Actividad • ¡A escribir!

The group of students is at Barajas airport in Madrid, Spain. Ask them in writing where their belongings are. Follow the model.

Alicia / pasaporte
—¿Tiene Alicia el pasaporte?
—¿Dónde está su pasaporte?

1. usted / maleta
2. Brian / cámara
3. tú / mapa
4. el señor / equipaje

5. yo / diccionario
6. Alicia / cartera
7. Brian / carro
8. yo / revista

A9   ¿Sabes que . . . ?

After your plane has landed in a Spanish-speaking country, you first go to the **Control de pasaportes.** An officer checks your passport to see if everything is in order. Then you proceed to **la aduana,** *customs.* There you find your baggage and stand by it while a customs officer examines what you have. If you are bringing in new articles not for your own use, you may have to pay import duties.

ESTRUCTURAS ESENCIALES
The verb estar

Here are the present-tense forms of **estar,** a second Spanish equivalent for the English verb *to be.*
(You saw the present tense forms of **ser,** another equivalent, in Unit 1.)

estar		*to be*				
Yo	**estoy**	aquí.	Nosotros (as)	**estamos**	en el avión.
Tú	**estás**	en el aeropuerto.	Vosotros (as)	**estáis**	en Madrid.
Usted/él/ella	**está**	en España.	Ustedes/ellos (as)	**están**	en la tienda.

1. **Estar** is used to express location.

   Estoy en el aeropuerto.

2. **Estar** is also used to indicate how someone is feeling.

   —¿Cómo **estás?** —**Estoy** bien, gracias.

A 11 Comprensión

Which is the best description?

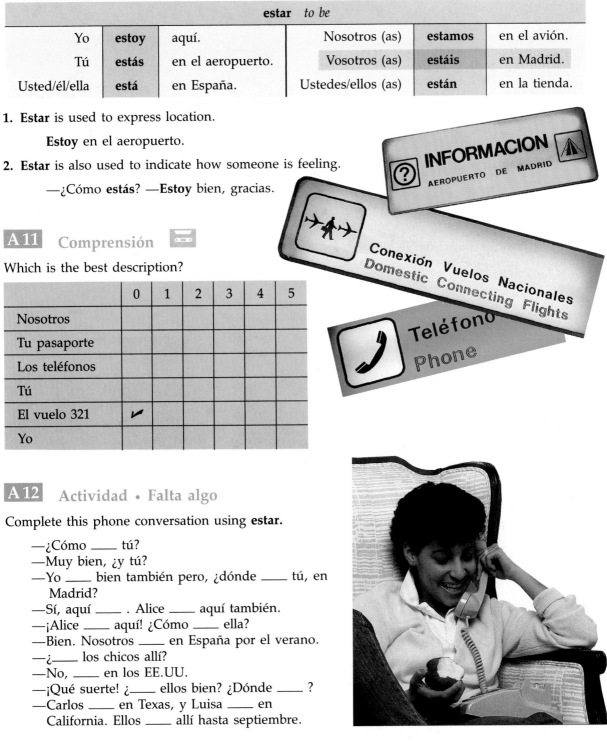

	0	1	2	3	4	5
Nosotros						
Tu pasaporte						
Los teléfonos						
Tú						
El vuelo 321	✔					
Yo						

A 12 Actividad • Falta algo

Complete this phone conversation using **estar.**

—¿Cómo ___ tú?
—Muy bien, ¿y tú?
—Yo ___ bien también pero, ¿dónde ___ tú, en Madrid?
—Sí, aquí ___ . Alice ___ aquí también.
—¡Alice ___ aquí! ¿Cómo ___ ella?
—Bien. Nosotros ___ en España por el verano.
—¿___ los chicos allí?
—No, ___ en los EE.UU.
—¡Qué suerte! ¿___ ellos bien? ¿Dónde ___ ?
—Carlos ___ en Texas, y Luisa ___ en California. Ellos ___ allí hasta septiembre.

En el aeropuerto   139

¿Dónde están? Ask a classmate where the persons, places, and things included in the box at the left are. Possible answers are listed in the box at the right. Then switch roles.

—¿Dónde está Madrid?
—Está en España.

la maleta	ella
tú	el equipaje
el aduanero	los chicos
el pasaporte	la aduana
yo	el avión
Madrid	nosotros
ustedes	

en mi cartera	en la aduana
aquí	en el taxi
en la puerta	en el aeropuerto
en España	en Madrid
en el avión	en los Estados Unidos
en el bolsillo	

 Actividad • ¡A escribir!

Make a phone call. The person you called wants to know where you and your friends are and how you are feeling. Write down three questions and your answers using a form of **estar** in all of them.

A15 SITUACIÓN • En información

Brian y Alice están en información. Tienen muchas preguntas.

aquí   allí

cerca (de)

entre

lejos (de)

detrás (de)

delante (de)

BRIAN   Señorita, por favor, ¿dónde está la cafetería?
EMPLEADA   La cafetería está allí arriba. ¿Tienen ustedes pesetas?
ALICE   No, señorita. Tenemos cheques de viajero.
EMPLEADA   La casa de cambio está detrás de ustedes, a la izquierda.

BRIAN   ¿Y el correo?
EMPLEADA   Abajo, al lado de los teléfonos y los baños.
ALICE   ¿Hay una tienda cerca de aquí?
EMPLEADA   Sí, señorita, la tienda del aeropuerto está a la derecha.
ALICE   Muchas gracias, señorita.

A16 Actividad • ¡A escoger!

Choose the best option to complete each sentence according to the information given in A15.

1. Brian y Alice están en
   • la sección de equipaje.   • la aduana.   • información.
2. Ellos tienen muchas
   • preguntas.   • pesetas.   • maletas.
3. La cafetería está
   • allí abajo.   • allí arriba.   • a la izquierda.
4. La casa de cambio está
   • a la derecha.   • a la izquierda.   • allí arriba.
5. El correo está
   • abajo.   • arriba.   • detrás.
6. El correo está
   • al lado de la tienda.   • al lado de la cafetería.   • al lado de los teléfonos.
7. ¿Hay una tienda
   • cerca de aquí?   • aquí detrás?   • al lado?
8. La tienda del aeropuerto está
   • a la izquierda.   • a la derecha.   • detrás de ustedes.

A17 SE DICE ASÍ
Asking and giving directions

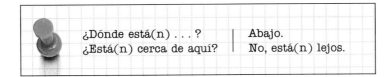

| ¿Dónde está(n) . . . ? | Abajo. |
| ¿Está(n) cerca de aquí? | No, está(n) lejos. |

You can use a form of **estar** and a location expression such as **lejos,** *far,* to ask or give directions.

A18 Actividad • ¡No, está allí!

Help these confused passengers find the places they are looking for. Things are just the opposite of what they thought. Work with a partner.

—La aduana, ¿está aquí?
—No, está allí.

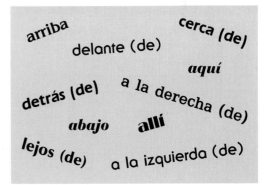

arriba   cerca (de)
delante (de)
aquí
detrás (de)   a la derecha (de)
abajo   allí
lejos (de)   a la izquierda (de)

1. La casa de cambio, ¿está arriba?
2. La tienda del aeropuerto, ¿está detrás?
3. El teléfono, ¿está allí?
4. La cafetería, ¿está a la izquierda?
5. El correo, ¿está cerca?
6. El baño, ¿está abajo?
7. La sección de equipaje, ¿está delante de la aduana?
8. Madrid, ¿está lejos?
9. Mi maleta, ¿está aquí?
10. La puerta 11, ¿está a la derecha?
11. Los carros, ¿están detrás de nosotros?
12. Los taxis, ¿están cerca?

When the preposition **de** is followed by the definite article **el,** the two contract to form the word **del.**

de	+	el	→	del
delante **de**	+	**el** teléfono	→	delante **del** teléfono *in front of the telephone*

1. De does not contract with the articles **la, los, las,** or with the pronoun **él.**

2. If **el** is part of a name, pronounce the contraction but don't write it.

Elena es **de El** Salvador.

A 20   Actividad • ¿Está aquí?

It's landing time. The passengers are gathering their belongings. Answer using the cues.

—¿Mi pasaporte?   Al lado / diccionario
—¿Mi pasaporte?—Está al lado del diccionario.

1. —¿La maleta?   en / asiento
2. —¿Mi cámara?   detrás / maleta
3. —¿Tu cartera?   a la derecha / cámara
4. —¿El diccionario?   al lado / pasaporte

5. —¿Las revistas?   al lado / mapa
6. —¿El mapa?   cerca de / revistas
7. —¿El equipaje?   lejos de / asiento
8. —¿Tu guitarra?   detrás / asiento

A 21   Actividad • ¡Información, por favor!

You work at the information booth of a Spanish airport. A passenger asks you for directions. Basing your answers on the floor plan, explain where everything is.

tienda   —Señor (Señorita), ¿la tienda, por favor?
          —La tienda está arriba, a la derecha, al lado de la cafetería.

*Spain, a country with 38 million citizens, received more than 38 million visitors in 1983—
tourists, students, business people, and others. Many travel in large groups. The group's
guide has to keep track of everyone, or the group won't ever be ready to proceed with its visit.*

B1

¿Adónde van? 📼

El profesor quiere saber adónde van los estudiantes.
¡Es muy difícil! Todos van a lugares diferentes.

B2 Preguntas y respuestas *Questions and answers*

1. ¿Dónde están el profesor y los estudiantes?
2. ¿Adónde va Alicia?
3. ¿Quién va a la casa de cambio?
4. ¿Quién va a la cafetería?

5. ¿Adónde van George y Mary?
6. ¿Adónde va Brian?
7. ¿Quién va al baño?
8. ¿Va el profesor con los estudiantes?

B3 ESTRUCTURAS ESENCIALES
The verb ir

This is one of the most useful verbs in Spanish. Its present-tense forms are irregular.

		ir *to go*			
Yo	**voy**	a la tienda.	Nosotros(as)	**vamos**	al aeropuerto.
Tú	**vas**	al correo.	Vosotros(as)	**váis**	a Barcelona.
Usted, él, ella	**va**	allí.	Ustedes, ellos(as)	**van**	a la aduana.

B4 Actividad • Para completar

Supply the missing forms of **ir**.

El profesor y los siete estudiantes no _____ a Madrid ahora. ¡No, señor! Están en el aeropuerto en Boston. El profesor _____ primero a la cafetería. Después _____ a la tienda a comprar algo. Brian _____ a la tienda también. Jennifer y yo _____ a la sección de equipaje.

—Tú _____ a la casa de cambio, ¿no?
—¿Ustedes _____ a la cafetería primero?
—¡Estupendo!
—Pero, ¿por qué no _____ ustedes a la casa de cambio después?

B5 Actividad • ¿Dónde estamos? ¿Adónde vamos?

Your classmate is impatient. Reply that the people mentioned will go there later.

¿Estamos en Madrid?
—No, vamos a Madrid después.

1. ¿Está el avión en España?
2. ¿Está Alice en la cafetería?
3. ¿Están Brian y Jennifer en la tienda?
4. ¿Está el aduanero en la aduana?

5. ¿Están ustedes en la sección de equipaje?
6. ¿Estás tú en el correo?
7. ¿Estamos en la casa de cambio?
8. ¿Están ellos allí?

The contraction al

The preposition **a** contracts with the definite article **el** to form the word **al**.

a	+	el	→	al	
a	+	el aeropuerto	→	al aeropuerto	*to the airport*

1. The preposition **a** does not contract with **la, las, los,** or with the pronoun **él.**

2. If the **el** is part of a name, pronounce the contraction but don't write it.

> Elena va **a El** Salvador.

 B7 Actividad • ¡No, no van allí!

Say that the people mentioned don't go to the places suggested but to the places indicated in parentheses.

> ¿Vas a la tienda? (baño)
> —No, voy al baño.

1. ¿Van los chicos a la escuela? (aeropuerto)
2. ¿Van primero a la casa de cambio? (cafetería)
3. ¿Va Gloria a la tienda? (baño)
4. ¿Va el profesor a la puerta 9? (puerta 7)

5. ¿Van ustedes al baño? (aduana)
6. ¿Va el profesor al avión? (sección de equipaje)
7. ¿Vas a la aduana? (casa de cambio)
8. ¿Vamos a México? (Madrid)

B8 Actividad • Charla

Ask a classmate where these people are going. Your classmate should respond as indicated.

> ustedes / cafetería
> —¿Adónde van?
> —Vamos a la cafetería.

> tú / tienda
> —¿Adónde vas?
> —Voy a la tienda.

1. Pedro / Madrid
2. nosotros / casa de cambio
3. los chicos / baño
4. taxi / aeropuerto

5. Alice y Brian / sección de equipaje
6. tú / cafetería
7. ustedes / avión
8. usted / puerta cinco

B9 Actividad • ¿Adónde vas?

Talk to your classmates about where you are going after class, tomorrow, and on Saturday . . .

B10 Actividad • ¡A escribir!

Write a brief paragraph about what you are going to do next Saturday.

SITUACIÓN · Conversación por teléfono

Brian llama por teléfono al señor González. ¡Hay un problema!

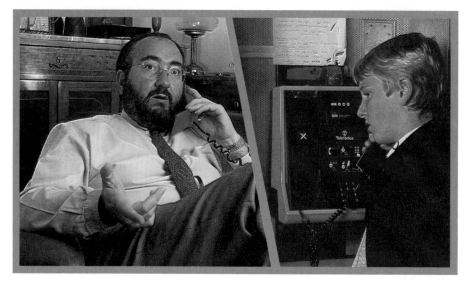

SR. GONZÁLEZ	¡Diga!		SR. GONZÁLEZ	¿Entonces llegas mañana?
BRIAN	Hola. ¿El señor González, por favor?		BRIAN	No, ya estoy en Madrid.
SR. GONZÁLEZ	Sí, soy yo. ¿Quién habla?		SR. GONZÁLEZ	¡Qué confusión! ¡Y son las once!
BRIAN	Brian Conally.		BRIAN	¿Debo tomar un taxi?
SR. GONZÁLEZ	¡Brian! ¿Dónde estás? Tu vuelo llega a las diez de la noche, ¿verdad?		SR. GONZÁLEZ	No, espera allí. Yo voy en mi coche al aeropuerto. Estoy allí dentro de una hora.
BRIAN	Bueno, sí y no. El vuelo llega a las diez, pero de la mañana, no de la noche.		BRIAN	Gracias, señor. Hasta luego.
			SR. GONZÁLEZ	Adiós, Brian.

B12 Preguntas y respuestas

Answer the questions according to **Conversación por teléfono.**

1. ¿Quién llama por teléfono?
2. ¿A quién llama él?
3. ¿A qué hora llega el vuelo?
4. ¿Llega Brian mañana?
5. ¿Qué hora es?
6. ¿Dónde está Brian?
7. ¿Debe Brian tomar un taxi? ¿Por qué?
8. ¿Cómo va el señor González al aeropuerto?

B13 Actividad · No es así

Correct the following statements to make them true according to B11.

1. Brian llega a Boston.
2. Brian llega mañana.
3. Brian está en la cafetería.
4. Él habla con Jennifer.
5. El vuelo llega a las diez de la noche.
6. El señor González no está en Madrid.
7. Son las doce.
8. El señor González va al aeropuerto dentro de dos horas.
9. El señor González va al aeropuerto en metro.
10. El señor González no tiene coche.

Actividad • Para completar

George is in Madrid, and he phones Gloria. Complete their conversation using B11 as a model.

GLORIA ¡Diga!
Buenas tardes. ¿La señorita González, _____ ?
GLORIA Sí, ella _____. ¿_____ es?
GEORGE George Ojeda, tu amigo de Boston.
GLORIA ¡George! ¿_____ estás? ¿En Madrid?
GEORGE Sí, estoy _____ aeropuerto. ¿Debo _____ el autobús para tu casa?
GLORIA No, voy _____ mi bicicleta. Estoy _____ en tres horas.
GEORGE ¿Tres horas? ¿Con tu _____ ?
GLORIA Sí. Es una bicicleta para dos. ¿Tienes muchas _____ ?
GEORGE Debo tomar el _____ 322 para Boston, Gloria. ¡Adiós!

B 15 ¿Sabes que . . . ?

Spain has a very long history. Cave paintings
in the north date from 25,000 B.C. The Romans
arrived in 218 B.C. and ruled for seven
centuries. In A.D. 409, Germanic tribes invaded
the country from the north and conquered
Spain from the Romans. In 711, Moslem invaders
from North Africa entered the south and
occupied almost all of Spain. Wars between
northern Catholic and southern Moslem
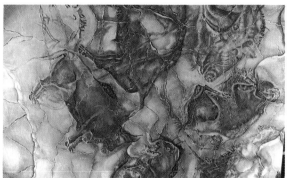
kingdoms continued off and on until 1492. In that year—the same year that Columbus
discovered the New World—the troops of King Ferdinand and Queen Isabella drove the last
Moslem forces from the Peninsula. The modern period of Spanish history had begun.

B 16 SITUACIÓN • ¡Hay problemas con el teléfono!

Actividad • Combinación

Join the elements in the two columns so that they make sense.

Hay problemas	se cortó.
La comunicación	con el teléfono.
¿El profesor	equivocado
Número	de matemáticas?
¡Hola, mamá! Habla	contestan.
Buenas tardes,	ocupado.
No	Paco.
Está	

B 18 Comprensión

Does the call go through?

0	1	2	3	4	5	6	7	8	9	10

B 19 SE DICE ASÍ
Answering the telephone, calling someone

The person answering says	¡Diga! ¡Hola! ¡Aló! Buenas tardes, familia González.
The person calling responds	Buenas tardes. ¿El señor González, por favor?

Many short phrases may be used to begin telephone conversations. **Adiós** or **chao** is often used to say goodbye. In Mexico, persons answering often say **¿Bueno?**

B 20 Actividad • Conversaciones por teléfono

You're talking to a friend on the phone. Use as many expressions as you can. Work with a partner.

1. You call your friend and ask for another friend's telephone number.
2. Your friend calls you from a pay phone. You want to know if he/she is near where you are or far away.
3. You call a friend after arriving in Madrid. You'll wait at the airport in the cafeteria that is to the left of customs.

¡Hola!
Buenas noches,
Buenos días,
¡Diga!
¡Aló!
Buenas tardes
¿Bueno?
¿Sí?

making suggestions . . . saying what people are doing

At the Barajas airport, in Madrid, Chicago's O'Hare airport, or any other international airport, if you're not rushing to catch a plane, chances are you're waiting for a connecting flight. Can you suggest something to do while you wait?

C1

En la sala de espera

Brian está en el aeropuerto de Barajas en Madrid. Alice y otros estudiantes del grupo esperan la llegada del vuelo para ir a León. Deben esperar una hora. ¿Qué deciden hacer?

BRIAN	¡Tengo mucha hambre! ¿Por qué no subimos a la cafetería a comer y beber algo?
ALICE	¡Estupendo! Pero primero, creo que debemos ir a la casa de cambio.
BRIAN	¿Para qué?
ALICE	Para cambiar un cheque de viajero. ¿Tú vienes, Jennifer?
JENNIFER	No, yo ya tengo pesetas.
MARK	¿Por qué no escribes a casa? Venden postales en la tienda y sellos en el correo.
JENNIFER	¿Una carta a mi familia? Ahora, no. Yo espero aquí. Tengo el periódico de hoy en español.
MARK	Yo no tengo el periódico. ¡Chao!

C2 Actividad • Combinación

Let's see how many sentences you can form by matching the items on the left with those on the right so that they make sense according to the dialog.

Los chicos esperan	un cheque de viajero.
Brian y Alice suben	una carta a su familia.
Primero deben ir	de hoy en español.
Deben cambiar	en el correo.
Jennifer ya	a la cafetería.
Venden sellos	la llegada del vuelo.
Jennifer no escribe	a la casa de cambio.
Ella tiene el periódico	tiene pesetas.

Actividad • ¡A escoger!

Choose the best option to complete each sentence according to the dialog in C1.

1. Brian, Alice y cuatro estudiantes más están en
   • la sala de espera.   • la cafetería.   • la tienda.
2. Los chicos esperan
   • un cheque de viajero.   • el vuelo para ir a León.   • postales de su familia.
3. Ellos deben esperar
   • a cuatro estudiantes más.   • una hora.   • el periódico de hoy.
4. Alice necesita cambiar
   • un cheque de viajero.   • sellos en el correo.   • pesetas.
5. Brian tiene
   • un cheque de viajero.   • sellos.   • mucha hambre.
6. Jennifer decide
   • esperar allí.   • subir a la cafetería.   • ir a la tienda.
7. Ella tiene
   • mucha hambre.   • el periódico.   • postales.
8. Mark no tiene
   • postales.   • sellos.   • el periódico en español.

C4   ¿Sabes que . . . ?

The city of León, founded by the Romans, is now an industrial and scientific center in northern Spain. Its gothic cathedral is one of the glories of European architecture. Besides its beautiful cities, churches, and museums, Spain has spectacular mountains, rich agricultural lands, and some of the finest beaches in Europe.

C5   SE DICE ASÍ
Asking and saying the purpose of an action

| ¿Vas a la tienda? ¿Para qué? | Para comprar algo. |
| You're going to the store? What for? | In order to buy something. |

When you want to ask the purpose of an action, use **¿Para qué?**
To answer, you can use **para** plus an infinitive.

C6 Actividad • Charla

Ask your partner where he or she is going and why he or she is going there. Switch roles.

¿Adónde vas? — Voy a . . . , al . . . , a la . . .

¿Para qué? — Para . . .

casa de cambio
cafetería
correo
sala de espera
tienda

C7 Actividad • ¡A escribir!

¿Adónde van? ¿Para qué? Choosing elements from each group of words, write ten sentences explaining why various people are going to different places.

Brian **Alice** **Jennifer** **Mark y George** **Los estudiantes**	***va*** ***van***	**a la cafetería** **al correo** **a la tienda** **a la casa de cambio** **a la sala de espera**	***para***	**comer** **comprar** **esperar** **beber** **cambiar**	**sellos** **algo** **postales** **cheques** **a su familia**

C8 ESTRUCTURAS ESENCIALES
Verbs ending in -er and -ir

Spanish verbs are classified according to the ending of their infinitives into three conjugations: **-ar, -er,** and **-ir.**

You learned the present-tense pattern for regular **-ar** verbs like **hablar** in Unit 3, B3. The patterns for regular **-er** and **-ir** verbs follow.

	comer *to eat*	**escribir** *to write*
yo	com**o**	escrib**o**
tú	com**es**	escrib**es**
usted, él, ella	com**e**	escrib**e**
nosotros(as)	com**emos***	escrib**imos***
vosotros(as)	com**éis***	escrib**ís***
ustedes, ellos(as)	com**en**	escrib**en**

In the present tense, the **-er** and **-ir** verb endings are identical except for the forms marked with an asterisk.

The regular **-er** verb **deber,** *should, ought to,* can be followed by the infinitive of another verb.

Yo debo **esperar.**   Ellos deben **llamar** por teléfono.

C9 Actividad • ¿Qué deciden hacer?

You're at a Spanish airport. Find out if the stores sell what you need. Ask questions using **vender.**

usted / revistas
—¿Vende usted revistas?

1. ustedes / postales
2. el señor / diccionarios
3. tú / sellos
4. ellos / cheques de viajero

5. la señora / periódicos
6. los chicos / mapas
7. ellos / cámaras
8. ustedes / casetes

C10 Actividad • ¿Venden o no?

Pair up with a partner. Ask each other the questions in C9. Alternate roles.
Answer four of the questions saying yes, you do; and four saying that you don't.

—¿Venden ellos cámaras?

—Sí, venden cámaras.
—No, no venden cámaras.

C11 Actividad • ¡A escribir!

Write the conversation you had with your partner in C10.

C12 Actividad • Combinación

Describe what the people in the left column are doing or thinking by using an element from the column on the right. (Make sure that they agree.)

Peter	deben cambiar un cheque.
Nosotros	escribe una postal.
Los chicos	come mucho.
Tú	venden postales, ¿no?
Yo	creo que el correo está a la izquierda.
Usted	bebo algo.
Ustedes	debemos llamar a Eduardo.
Ellos	vendemos sellos.
Cynthia	como en la cafetería.
El empleado	escribes a casa.
	deciden ir a la tienda.

C13 Actividad • ¡A escribir!

Write as many logical sentences as you can, combining the people and the activities in C12.

Actividad • Falta algo

These students are in the airport's cafeteria. Complete the sentences
with the appropriate verb from the list below in its correct form.
You may use a word more than once.

beber	creer	decidir	subir
comer	deber	escribir	vender

1. Nosotros ____ a la cafetería.
2. ¿____ tú algo?
3. ¿No ____ tú que tú y yo ____ comer algo?
4. Ellos ____ a las diez de la noche.
5. Los chicos ____ subir.
6. Ustedes ____ llamar a Enrique ahora.
7. Yo ____ a casa.
8. Alice ____ que es una buena idea.
9. Rafael ____ una postal.
10. Señor, por favor, ¿____ usted sellos?

SE DICE ASÍ
   Making suggestions

¿Por qué no comemos?	Why don't we eat?

One way to make a suggestion is to ask **¿Por qué no . . .** (verb in plural) *Why don't we . . . ?*

Conversación • ¿Por qué no . . . ?

Suggest that a classmate do the following things with you. Your classmate will
respond using the words given.

comer / hambre
—¿Por qué no comemos?
—Bueno. Yo tengo hambre. (*or:* Ahora no, yo no tengo hambre.)

1. subir a la tienda / necesitar postales
2. escribir a casa / tener sellos
3. esperar / ir sala de espera
4. cambiar un cheque / ir casa de cambio
5. llamar / tener número de teléfono
6. comer / ir cafetería

Comprensión

Is the reply appropriate?

0	1	2	3	4	5	6	7	8	9	10
✔										

En el aeropuerto   153

1   Pedro espera

¡Hoy es el día! Ramón y Rosario llegan de México. Pedro va al aeropuerto para esperar a los chicos. Primero va a información.

—Señor, por favor, ¿el vuelo No. 423 de México?
—Puerta No. 8. Llega a las siete.
—Gracias.

Son las seis. Pedro tiene una hora. Debe esperar, pero, ¿dónde? Va a la cafetería. Come y bebe algo. Veinte minutos después está en la tienda. Mira los periódicos, los libros, las revistas . . .

—¡Mmmmm! Hay unos casetes en venta . . . Cuestan mucho. ¡Oh! Tienen mapas . . . ¿Un mapa de la ciudad para Ramón y Rosario? No . . . , creo que ya tienen un mapa. ¿Y un diccionario en español? No, ellos hablan inglés y español. En la tienda venden postales también . . . postales . . . ¿para qué? Y . . . ¿qué hora es? ¡Es tarde! ¡El vuelo de los chicos!

Pedro corre a la puerta 8. Ramón y Rosario no están. ¿Dónde están los chicos? Pedro va a la sala de espera. ¡Qué suerte! ¡Ahí están Ramón y Rosario!
—¡Hola! ¡Hola! ¿Qué tal? ¡Aquí estoy!

2   Actividad • Charla

Pair off with a classmate. Ask each other questions about **Pedro espera** so that your answers retell the story.

—¿Quiénes vienen de México? ¿Adónde va Pedro? ¿Para qué?

3   Actividad • ¡A escribir!

Finish the conversation between Pedro and his friends at the airport. How do they greet each other? What do they say?

4 Actividad • Conversación telefónica

Pedro is calling home to let his family know their friends have arrived.
Play the role of Pedro. Work with a partner. Switch roles.

5 Actividad • En la aduana

You're going through customs—without your luggage! A customs officer will ask you a series of questions and will enter your answers into a computer. While you are waiting for your suitcase to show up, write answers to the questions on a separate piece of paper.

1. ¿Habla usted español?
2. ¿Cómo se llama usted?
3. ¿De dónde es usted?
4. ¿Tiene su pasaporte?
5. ¿Dónde está?
6. ¿Adónde va?
7. ¿Para qué va allí?
8. ¿Cómo va?
9. ¿Con quién va?
10. ¿A qué hora va?

6 Actividad • ¡Diga!

You're trying to reach Mr. González on the phone. No luck! What would you say in the following situations?

1. You asked for Mr. González but there was nobody there with that name.
2. You tried to reach Mr. González but you were cut off.
3. You dialed 5678 and you got 6578.
4. The line is busy.
5. Nobody answers.
6. Mr. González is out today—he's coming in tomorrow.
7. The telephone went dead after a minute or two.
8. The person who answered your call said **familia Fernández.**

7 Pronunciación, lectura, dictado

1. Listen carefully and repeat what you hear.

2. The sound of the Spanish vowels **u** and **i**. Listen and then read aloud.

> escuchar   Perú   gustar   mucho
> Allí está Isabel con mi equipaje.
> Necesito dinero para ir a Madrid.

3. Copy the following sentences to prepare yourself to write them from dictation.

> No tengo el número de teléfono de Humberto.
> Escribo unas postales a mis amigos americanos.
> El día está ideal para jugar tenis con Lucía.

¿LO SABES?

Let's review some important points you have learned in this unit.

SECTION A

Can you name in Spanish some of the things you need to take along when going on a trip?
Name six.

Do you know how to say where some of your things are and ask others about theirs?
Write five statements and ask five questions.

When somebody asks you for directions, how do you answer?
You're standing at the entrance to your school. Give directions to go to:

cafetería   baño   clase de música   teléfonos

SECTION B

When you want to know where somebody is going, how do you ask?

1. los chicos   **2.** tú   **3.** nosotros   **4.** Carlos   **5.** usted

Do you know how to say where someone is going?
Tell where the following people are going, using the second word as a clue.

1. la chica—comer   4. nosotros—sellos
2. yo—pesetas   5. Alice—postales
3. ellos—maleta   6. tú—avión

Are you able to answer the phone and to have a short conversation in Spanish?
The phone is ringing. You answer in Spanish. Use five different expressions.

You've tried to telephone Sr. González.
A woman answers. What do you say now?

You're trying to reach three different people on the phone. No luck!
Give three reasons why the calls can't go through.

SECTION C

Do you know how to say why you are doing something and to ask others for an explanation?
Explain why you are going to these places:

cafetería   correo   tienda   aeropuerto
sala de espera   puerta 8   sección de equipaje

Now ask three different people where they are going and why.

Are you able to suggest what to do or recommend a place to go?
You are at the airport with five friends. Respond to their statements or questions with helpful suggestions.

1. ¡Tengo hambre!   2. No tengo sellos.   3. ¿Esperamos aquí o arriba?
4. La familia González llega dentro de una hora.   5. ¡No tenemos pesetas!

VOCABULARIO

a la derecha *on the right*
a la izquierda *on the left*
abajo *below*
la **aduana** *customs*
el **aduanero** *customs agent*
el **aeropuerto** *airport*
al lado de *beside*
allí *there*
aquí *here*
arriba *up (there)*
el **asiento** *seat*
el **avión** *airplane*
el **baño** *bathroom*
el **bolsillo** *pocket*
buscar *to look for*
la **cafetería** *cafeteria*
la **cámara** *camera*
cambiar (de) *to change*
la **cartera** *purse*
el **carro** *cart*
la **casa de cambio** *money
    exchange office*
cerca (de) *near*
el **correo, correos** *post office*
el **cheque de viajero** *traveler's
    check*
delante (de) *in front (of)*
después *then*
detrás (de) *behind*
el **empleado, la empleada**
    employee
en *at, on*
entrar *to enter*
entre *between*
el **equipaje** *baggage*
estar *to be*
el **grupo** *group*
la **información** *information*

lejos (de) *far (from)*
llegar *to arrive*
la **maleta** *suitcase*
el **mapa** *map*
el **pasaporte** *passport*
la **peseta** *monetary unit of Spain*
por *through*
primero *first*
la **puerta** *gate*
¡qué suerte! *what luck!*
la **sección de equipaje** *baggage
    claim*
su *your, his, her, its*
van *they go*
el **vuelo** *flight*
ya está todo *everything's
    finished*

¿adónde? *(to) where?*
algo *something*
¡aló! *hello?*
¿bueno? *hello?*
el **coche** *car*
comprar *to buy*
contestar *to answer*
de la mañana *in the
    morning, A.M.*
de la noche *at night, P.M.*
¿debo . . . ? *should I . . . ?*
dentro de *in, within*
¡diga! *hello?*
entonces *then*
esperar *to wait (for)*
está ocupado *its' busy*
¡hola! *hello?*
ir *to go*
¡la comunicación se cortó!
    we were cut off!

el **lugar** *place*
llamar *to call*
la **mamá** *mom*
no contestan *there's no answer*
número equivocado *wrong
    number*
¡qué confusión! *what a mixup!*
quiere *he wants*
saber *to know*
¿verdad? *right?*
ya *already*

a casa *(to) home*
beber *to drink*
cambiar *to cash*
la **carta** *letter*
el **casete** *cassette*
comer *to eat*
creer *to think*
deber *should*
decidir *to decide*
escribir *to write*
la **familia** *family*
hacer *to do*
la **llegada** *arrival*
más *other*
¿para qué? *for what?*
el **periódico** *newspaper*
¿por qué no . . . ? *why
    don't we . . . ?*
la **postal** *postcard*
que *that*
la **sala de espera** *waiting area*
el **sello** *stamp*
subir *to go up*
tener (mucha) hambre *to be
    (very) hungry*
vender *to sell*
yo no *not me*

ESTUDIO DE PALABRAS

Most nouns that end in **-o** are masculine; in **-a**, feminine. Be alert to the gender of the nouns. Look through the word lists for this unit and find the nouns that don't end in **-o** or **-a**. Write them in one of two lists, *masculine* or *feminine*.

VAMOS A LEER

Antes de leer

If you're getting ready for a trip to a Spanish-speaking country, it will be useful to read some information about the place you're going to visit. You will notice that distances are expressed in meters and kilometers. One kilometer equals 5/8 of a mile. To convert kilometers into miles, divide by 1.6.

En España

¿Qué ciudad visitamos?

Once you are in Spain you might want to travel around the country. Here are some of the cities you might want to visit.

Toledo, una ciudad medieval a orillas° del río Tajo°, es famosa por su arte y arquitectura, testimonios de su gran° pasado° histórico.

San Sebastián, en el norte° de España, es una ciudad ideal para el turismo. Tiene playas muy bonitas°.

Segovia está cerca de Madrid, a 88 kilómetros de la capital. Su famoso acueducto° romano,° tiene más de dos mil° años.

---

norte *north*   **bonitas** *pretty*   **orilla** *shore*   **río Tajo** *Tagus River*   **gran** *great*   **pasado** *past*
famoso acueducto *famous aqueduct*   **romano** *Roman*   **dos mil** *two thousand*

Barcelona, la segunda° ciudad española después de Madrid, es uno de los puertos° más importantes del Mediterráneo.

Valencia, en la costa mediterránea, es un importante centro industrial y agrícola°. Es famosa por sus flores° y huertas°.

Sevilla es la cuarta° ciudad de España. Sus calles° estrechas° y los patios en el interior de sus casas° son muy pintorescos.

Actividad • Combinación

Match the items in the two columns to form sentences that agree with what you have just read.

En Segovia hay	en San Sebastián.
Barcelona es	un puerto muy importante.
Hay playas muy bonitas	un famoso acueducto.
San Sebastián es	está a orillas del río Tajo.
Valencia es	calles muy pintorescas.
Barcelona	ideal para el turismo.
Sevilla tiene	es la segunda ciudad de España.
Toledo	famosa por sus flores y huertas.

Actividades

1. Pair up with a classmate. Pick out one of the cities described above and make up questions in Spanish about it. Be ready to answer in return.
2. Go to the library and find out more about one of the cities described. Use reference, geography, and travel books. Prepare an illustrated travel brochure for your class.

---

segunda *second* **puertos** *ports* **agrícola** *agricultural* **flores** *flowers* **huertas** *orchards* **cuarta** *fourth*
calles *streets* **estrechas** *narrow* **casas** *homes*

El regalo

Es viernes. Otra vez° delante del televisor, Adriana y Daniel miran las noticias° en el Canal Uno.

LOCUTORA	Y ahora, una información urgente. Madrid: Hoy, sábado once . . .
DANIEL	¿Cómo? ¿Hoy sábado 11? Hoy es viernes diez.
ADRIANA	¡Ya sé, Daniel! ¡El Canal Uno trasmite° las noticias del futuro!
DANIEL	¿Del futuro? ¡No! ¡Imposible!
ADRIANA	Sí, también es imposible mirar un partido por televisión, y de pronto°, estar en el estadio.
DANIEL	Es verdad. Tienes razón°.
ADRIANA	Siempre tengo razón. Soy muy inteligente.
DANIEL	Sí, porque eres mi hermana.
ADRIANA	¡Mira, el aeropuerto de Barajas!
DANIEL	¿Y ese° avión? Es un avión enorme° . . .
LOCUTORA	El vuelo 28 detenido° en Barajas. Los 219 pasajeros° a bordo son rehenes°. Todo indica° que el piloto, el señor Héctor Ríos, es el responsable del secuestro°.
DANIEL	¿Llamamos a la policía?
ADRIANA	¡Pero, Daniel, por favor . . . ! La policía no va a creer que podemos ver° el futuro en el Canal Uno. Además°, el televisor es un secreto absoluto entre nosotros dos.
DANIEL	Está bien. Entonces, ¿por qué no llamamos al aeropuerto? Ellos deben tener la información. Hoy es viernes. Tenemos tiempo° hasta mañana.

---

otra vez *again*   **noticias** *news*   **trasmite** *broadcasts*   **de pronto** *suddenly*   **tienes razón** *you are right*   **ese** *that*
enorme *huge*   **detenido** *detained*   **pasajeros** *passengers*   **rehenes** *hostages*   **indica** *suggests*   **el secuestro** *hijacking*
podemos ver *we can see*   **además** *besides*   **tiempo** *time*

Los chicos llaman al aeropuerto por teléfono. Los sábados, el vuelo 28, con destino a Madrid, hace escala° en México de una a dos de la tarde. Los sábados el piloto es siempre Héctor Ramos. ¿Ríos, y no Ramos? ¿Hay un error?

DANIEL   ¡Escucha°, Adriana! Tengo una idea sensacional.
ADRIANA   ¿Tú, una idea sensacional? No creo. Bueno, ¿cuál es?
DANIEL   En Madrid, el piloto se llama Héctor Ríos, ¿no? En México, el piloto es
          Héctor Ramos. Mañana en México, entre la una y las dos, Héctor Ríos
          sube al° avión, y toma control del vuelo.
ADRIANA   ¡Eres un genio! Mañana, a la una, estamos en el aeropuerto, y
          esperamos la llegada del vuelo.
DANIEL   ¡Fantástico!

El sábado los chicos van al aeropuerto. El vuelo 28 llega a la puerta número 8.
Los chicos esperan. El vuelo llega. Primero, bajan° los pasajeros, después el piloto
y el copiloto. Un pasajero y una aeromoza° siguen° al piloto. El piloto entra en la
cafetería, detrás de él, el pasajero y la aeromoza. Daniel y Adriana deciden entrar
también.

Actividad • Asociaciones

Work with a partner. Ask as many questions as you can about this chapter of **El
regalo,** adding your own ideas to the clues below. You also have to answer your
partner's questions.

1. el Canal Uno
2. el viernes 10
3. el sábado 11
4. en Barajas
5. el responsable del secuestro
6. el vuelo 28
7. Héctor Ríos
8. a la policía
9. un secreto
10. Héctor Ramos
11. hace escala
12. la puerta 8
13. un pasajero y una aeromoza
14. la cafetería

---

hace escala *makes a stopover*   **¡Escucha!** *Listen!*   **sube al** *gets on*   **bajan** *get off*   **aeromoza** *stewardess*
siguen *follow*

UNIDAD **6**
La familia

For most speakers of Spanish, the family comes first. For example, before a family member makes a major decision, the issue is discussed by the entire family. To have a better understanding of Spanish-speaking people, you need to understand about family relationships and manners.

In this unit you will:

SECTION A	welcome people . . . extend invitations
SECTION B	describe people and family relationships . . . talk about age
SECTION C	ask someone's opinion . . . pay compliments
TRY YOUR SKILLS	use what you've learned
VAMOS A LEER	read for practice and pleasure

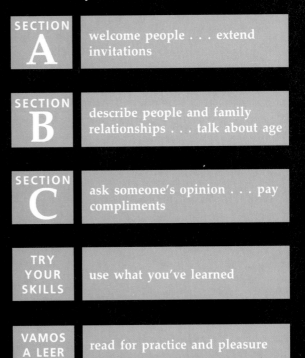

Living abroad with a Hispanic family is a thrilling experience. You are warmly greeted when you arrive, and you gain new insights about yourself and other people every day.

A1   ## La visita de Roberto 📼

Roberto, un estudiante norteamericano de Los Ángeles, llega a la casa de su amigo Antonio en la Ciudad de México. Va a pasar un mes de vacaciones con la familia de Antonio.

ANTONIO	¡Mamá! ¡Mamá! ¿Dónde estás?
MAMÁ	Aquí estoy, Antonio. En la sala. ¡Bienvenido, Roberto! Pasa, por favor. ¿Cómo estás? Mucho gusto.
ROBERTO	Igualmente, señora.
MAMÁ	Estás en tu casa, Roberto.
ROBERTO	Muchas gracias, señora. Usted es muy amable. ¡Es un placer estar aquí con ustedes!

ANTONIO	Con permiso, mamá. Queremos escuchar música. Vamos a mi cuarto.
MAMÁ	¡Un momento, Antonio! ¿Dónde están las cosas de Roberto? ¿Por qué no van a su cuarto primero? Y tú, Roberto, ¿no tienes hambre? ¿Quieres comer algo? ¿Quieres un refresco?
ROBERTO	No, señora, muchas gracias.
ANTONIO	¿Quieres ver tu cuarto, Roberto?

A2   Actividad • Para completar

What is Antonio's mother saying to Roberto? Complete the phrases.

—¡_____, Roberto! Pasa, _____. ¿Cómo _____? Mucho _____. Estás en _____.
¿No _____ hambre? ¿Quieres _____? ¿Quieres un _____?

Actividad • ¡No es así!

Correct these statements to make them true according to A1.

1. Roberto es de la Ciudad de México.
2. Antonio llega de Los Ángeles.
3. Antonio va a pasar un mes con la familia de Roberto.
4. La mamá de Antonio está en el cuarto de Roberto.
5. La señora: "Estás en mi casa, Roberto".
6. Roberto contesta: "Muchas gracias, señora. Tú eres muy amable".
7. Antonio y Roberto quieren mirar televisión.
8. La mamá pregunta dónde está la casa de Roberto.

A4 Actividad • ¡A escoger!

For each numbered sentence choose an ending that best fits **La visita de Roberto.**

1. Roberto llega a
   • Los Ángeles.   • la casa de un amigo.   • su cuarto.
2. Va a pasar un mes de vacaciones
   • con la familia.   • con su mamá.   • con los chicos.
3. La mamá de Antonio está en
   • Los Ángeles.   • su cuarto.   • la sala.
4. Es un placer estar
   • aquí.   • en Los Ángeles.   • en mi cuarto.
5. Antonio quiere
   • mirar televisión.   • comer algo.   • escuchar música.
6. Roberto no quiere
   • escuchar música.   • ver su cuarto.   • comer.

A5 ¿Sabes que . . . ?

Family life is very important in Spanish-speaking countries, and a great deal of socializing is done around the home. In many instances, grandparents live together with their married sons and daughters, and other relatives are frequent visitors, or live nearby. Even though much entertaining is done at home, only people within the family circle and close friends are invited. If you are a guest at a Spanish home, be sure to be polite and express your gratitude—you have been specially honored!

In Spanish, some verbs like **querer** have a change in the stem in the present tense. When the stem vowel **e** is stressed or emphasized, it changes to **ie**.

querer (ie) *to want*			
Quiero	comer ahora.	**Queremos**	un refresco.
¿Quieres	beber algo?	**¿Queréis**	ir?
¿Quiere	pasar?	**¿Quieren**	ver el cuarto?

Stem-changing verbs have regular endings like other **-ar, -er,** and **ir** verbs. They can be found in vocabulary lists with an indicator in parentheses such as: **querer (ie),** *to want.*

Querer can be followed by a noun or an infinitive.

Quiero un refresco.   *I want a soda.*
Quiero nadar.   *I want to swim.*

A7   Actividad • ¿Qué quieren hacer?   *What do they want to do?*

Complete the following sentences with the correct form of the verb **querer.**

1. ¿ _____ ustedes venir?
2. ¿Adónde _____ ir ustedes?
3. Nosotros _____ ir a la ciudad.
4. Yo, no. Yo _____ escuchar música.
5. Antonio _____ ir a su cuarto.
6. Los chicos _____ mirar televisión.
7. Y tú, Roberto, ¿ _____ venir?
8. No, yo _____ comer algo.

A8   Actividad • ¡A escribir!

Tienes invitados. You have guests—many of them—in your house. You ask what they want to do. Use the verb **querer.** Write down your questions.

    Roberto / ver mi cuarto
    —Roberto, ¿quieres ver mi cuarto?

1. Ana / ver la casa
2. Susana y Pablo / escuchar discos
3. señora López / comer algo
4. Antonio / subir a mi cuarto
5. ustedes / mirar televisión
6. chicos / jugar
7. Isabel / ir a la sala
8. usted / venir con nosotros

A9   Conversación • ¿Qué quieren?

Pair up with a classmate. You make many suggestions but they are not accepted. Everybody wants to do something else. Follow the clues and switch roles.

    tú / jugar tenis / mirar televisión
    —¿Quieres jugar tenis?
    —No, quiero mirar televisión.

1. ustedes / bailar / escuchar música
2. usted / comer / beber algo
3. los chicos / estudiar / jugar
4. tú / ver la computadora / ir a mi cuarto
5. ustedes / mirar televisión / hablar por teléfono
6. usted / hablar con mamá / ir a la sala
7. tú / pasar / montar en bicicleta
8. ustedes / estudiar / bailar

SE DICE ASÍ
Making somebody feel at home; graciously accepting hospitality

HOST, HOSTESS	GUEST
¡Bienvenido(a)! Welcome!	¡Gracias! ¡Es un placer estar aquí! Thanks! It's a pleasure to be here!
¡Pasa! Come in!	Sí, ¡gracias, señor(a)! Yes, thank you, sir (ma'am)!
¡Mucho gusto! Pleased to meet you!	¡Igualmente, señor(a)! Likewise, sir (ma'am)!
¡Estás en tu casa! Make yourself at home!	¡Usted es muy amable! You're very kind!

A 11 Actividad • Y ahora tú . . .

Welcome a classmate to your home. Use as many of the phrases in A10 as you can. Then switch roles.

A 12 Comprensión

Check the correct answer.

0	✔	Muchas gracias.
1		¡Usted es muy amable!
2		Igualmente.
3		¡Es un placer estar aquí!
4		¿Quieres pasar, por favor?
5		¡Estoy aquí!

A 13 Actividad • Charla

Make a guest feel at home. With a partner, create a dialog using as many expressions as you can from the box below.

Usted es muy amable   Pasa, por favor   ¿Un refresco?   Estás en tu casa
¡Bienvenido!   ¡Bienvenida!   ¿Quieres . . . ?   Es un placer estar aquí   Igualmente
Vamos a . . .   Con permiso   Mucho gusto

A 14 Actividad • ¡A escribir!

Write down the conversation you had with your classmate in A13 in dialog form.

Like nearly everyone else in the world, Hispanic people love to collect and show off family snapshots. You may need to know how to comment and ask questions about them.

B1   Fotos de la familia

Ana María, la hermana de Antonio, y su amiga Gloria, hablan de las fotos que Ana María tiene en su cuarto. Tiene fotos de todos los miembros de la familia.

GLORIA Tienes muchas fotografías. ¿Quién es la chica alta y morena? ¿Tu hermana?

ANA MARÍA No, mi hermana Consuelo es baja y rubia. Ella es Luisa, mi prima.

GLORIA ¿Cuántos años tiene?

ANA MARÍA Quince. ¡Es un genio! Es muy inteligente.

GLORIA ¡Qué fotografía tan bonita! ¿Quién es? ¿Tu padre?

ANA MARÍA Sí, es una foto de mi papá.

GLORIA ¡Qué guapo!

ANA MARÍA Mira, aquí está de nuevo, con mi mamá y toda la familia.

GLORIA La señora delgada y rubia, ¿quién es? ¡Qué linda!

ANA MARÍA Es mi tía Dolores, la madre de Luisa. Al lado está el esposo, mi tío José.

GLORIA Y aquí están tus abuelos, ¿no?

ANA MARÍA Sí, los padres de mamá. Los dos son bien simpáticos y cariñosos.

GLORIA ¿Cuántos hijos tienen? ¿Cinco?

ANA MARÍA No, una hija, mi mamá, y un hijo, mi tío José. El señor pelirrojo es un amigo de ellos. Los otros cuatro son amigos también.

Identify the people mentioned by Ana María according to B1, **Fotos de la familia**.

¿Quién es la chica baja?
—Es la hermana de Ana María.

1. ¿Quién es la chica alta y morena?
2. ¿Quién tiene quince años?
3. ¿Quién es un genio?
4. ¿Quién es el señor guapo?

5. ¿Quién es la señora delgada y rubia?
6. ¿Quiénes son simpáticos y cariñosos?
7. ¿Cuántos hijos tienen ellos, cinco?
8. ¿Quién es el señor pelirrojo?

B3 Actividad • Y ahora tú . . .

¿Cómo es tu familia?

1. ¿Tienes hermanos(as)? ¿Cuántos(as)?
2. ¿Cómo se llaman tus hermanos(as)?
3. ¿Son rubios(as) o morenos(as)?
4. ¿Son altos(as) o bajos(as)?

5. ¿Son inteligentes?
6. ¿Tienes tíos y tías? ¿Cómo se llaman?
7. ¿Tienes primos(as)? ¿Cuántos(as)?
8. ¿Cómo se llaman tus primos(as)?

B4 ¿Sabes que . . . ?

Spanish speakers usually have a first name (or a compound first name like **Ana María**) plus two surnames, their father's and their mother's. To find someone in the phone book, look under their paternal surname. Here is Ana María's family tree. Notice how the surnames **González** and **Rivas** descend to her.

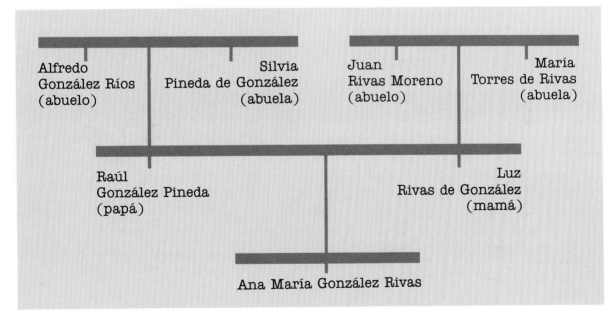

Alfredo
González Ríos
(abuelo)

Silvia
Pineda de González
(abuela)

Juan
Rivas Moreno
(abuelo)

María
Torres de Rivas
(abuela)

Raúl
González Pineda
(papá)

Luz
Rivas de González
(mamá)

Ana María González Rivas

When a woman marries, she usually drops her maternal surname and adds **de** plus her husband's paternal surname. Before her marriage, Ana María's mother was named **Luz Rivas Torres**. Now she is normally addressed as **Sra. Rivas de González**.

SE DICE ASÍ
Talking about age

| ¿Cuántos años tienes? | Tengo catorce años. |
| How old are you? | I am fourteen. |

To ask or answer how old someone is, use the verb **tener.**

B6 Actividad • Charla

Ask a classmate. Be ready to answer yourself.

¿Cuantos años tienes? ¿Tienes hermanos(as)? ¿Cuántos años tienen? ¿Tienes primos(as)? ¿Cuántos años tienen?

B7 Actividad • ¡A escribir!

Make a list of your brothers, sisters, cousins, and friends. (Use imaginary names if you'd prefer.) Then write their ages, like this:

   Mi hermano Andrés tiene 19 años.

B8 SITUACIÓN • Una foto más

GLORIA	¡Qué chico tan guapo! ¿Quién es?
ANA MARÍA	El hijo de una amiga de mi mamá. Se llama Anselmo.
GLORIA	Es muy rubio. Sus padres, ¿son los dos morenos?
ANA MARÍA	El señor de la foto no es su papá. Es su padrastro. Su papá murió. Ahora la mamá está casada de nuevo.

B9 Actividad • ¡A escoger!

For each numbered sentence choose an ending that best fits the conversation between Gloria and Ana María.

1. Anselmo es
   • el amigo de una hija de su mamá.   • el hijo de una amiga de su mamá.
   • el papá de un amigo de su mamá.
2. Anselmo es
   • un chico moreno.   • muy guapo.   • un genio.
3. Él es
   • rubio.   • moreno.   • pelirrojo.
4. El señor de la foto es
   • su papá.   • su abuelo.   • su padrastro.
5. El papá de Anselmo
   • está casado.   • murió.   • es guapo.

el **esposo** *husband*	la **esposa** *wife*	los **esposos** *husband and wife*
el **abuelo** *grandfather*	la **abuela** *grandmother*	los **abuelos** *grandparents*
el **padre** *father*	la **madre** *mother*	los **padres** *parents*
el **hermano** *brother*	la **hermana** *sister*	los **hermanos** *brothers and sisters*
el **hijo** *son*	la **hija** *daughter*	los **hijos** *children*
el **tío** *uncle*	la **tía** *aunt*	los **tíos** *uncles and aunts*
el **primo** *cousin*	la **prima** *cousin (female)*	los **primos** *cousins*
el **padrastro** *stepfather*	la **madrastra** *stepmother*	los **padrastros** *stepparents*

The masculine plural nouns are used to refer to any group that includes at least one male:

los esposos *husband and wife*
los esposos *husbands and wives*
los esposos *husbands*

The context usually clarifies which meaning is intended.

B 11   Actividad • Ana María habla de su familia

Ana María is talking about her relatives. Complete her remarks with the correct word from the list.

Mi tío José es el ____ de mi mamá.
Mi madre y tío José son los ____ de mis abuelos.
Mi tío José y mi mamá son ____ .
Mi tía Dolores es la ____ de mi tío José.
Luisa es la ____ de mis tíos José y Dolores.
Ella es mi ____ .
Mis ____ tienen tres hijos: mi hermano
Antonio, mi ____ Consuelo y yo.

hermano   hijos
hija   hermanos
prima   esposa
padres   hermana

La familia   171

La familia de Ana María

Juan ——— María

Raúl ——— Luz   José ——— Dolores

Consuelo   Antonio   Ana María   Luisa

B13 ESTRUCTURAS ESENCIALES
Descriptive adjectives: position and agreement

Words that you use to describe a noun are called **adjectives.** If you say *The tall woman is smart,*
tall and *smart* are both **adjectives.** Some typical **adjectives** are shown in the following chart.

Masculine			*Feminine*		
Article	*Noun*	*Adjective*	*Article*	*Noun*	*Adjective*
el	señor	alto	la	señora	alta
los	señores	altos	las	señoras	altas
un	chico	inteligente	una	chica	inteligente
unos	chicos	inteligentes	unas	chicas	inteligentes
el	libro	difícil	la	clase	difícil
los	libros	difíciles	las	clases	difíciles

1. Spanish adjectives are usually placed after the noun they describe.

2. You need to be sure that the ending of your adjective reflects the number and gender of the noun it accompanies.

3. Many adjectives that end in **-o** in the masculine, like **alto,** end in **-a** in the feminine.
   El señor **alto** es **aburrido.**   La señora **alta** es **aburrida.**

4. Adjectives that end in **-e,** like **inteligente,** stay the same with both masculine and feminine singular nouns. The same is true for many adjectives that end in a consonant, like **difícil.**

5. Adjectives form the plural the same way nouns do: words that end in a vowel add **-s** and words that end in a consonant add **-es.**

B 14   Actividad • ¿Quiénes son?

You invited your friend Consuelo to a family party. When she comes in, you tell her who the guests are. To complete the sentences, choose one of the adjectives in parentheses. Make changes to the ending of the adjective if necessary.

1. (rubio / alto) El chico _____ es mi hermano, la chica _____ es su amiga.
2. (pelirrojo / delgado) Los chicos _____ son los primos de la chica _____ .
3. (guapo / bajo) La señora _____ es la mamá del chico _____ .
4. (moreno / delgado) El señor _____ es el esposo de la señora _____ .

B 15   ¿Sabes que . . . ?

Some Spanish and Spanish American families seem large because grandparents, cousins, uncles and aunts, and in-laws take part in every family activity. Most of the relatives, and close family friends, are likely to attend every family party and celebration. Given a choice, family members live as close together in a town as they possibly can, often in the same building.

¿alto o baja?

¿gordo o delgada?

¿feo o guapa?

¿moreno, rubia o pelirroja?

¿Cómo son ustedes?

¿tontos o inteligentes?

¿antipáticas o simpáticas?

¿Y cómo eres tú, Roque?

¿generosos o egoístas?

B 17 SE DICE ASÍ
Asking what someone or something is like

¿Cómo es?	What's (he, she, it) like?
¿Cómo es tu cuarto?	What's your room like?
¿Cómo son tus padres?	What are your parents like?
¿Cómo son tus clases?	What are your classes like?

B 18 Conversación • La familia

Get together with a classmate and ask each other the following questions about your families.

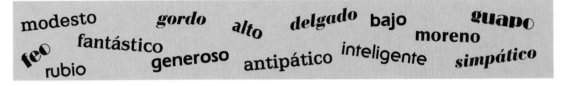

modesto   gordo   alto   delgado   bajo   guapo
feo   fantástico   moreno
rubio   generoso   antipático   inteligente   simpático

1. ¿Cómo es tu papá? ¿tu mamá? ¿tu profesor(a)?
2. ¿Cómo son tus hermanos(as)? ¿primos(as)?
3. ¿Cómo son los chicos y las chicas de tu clase?
4. ¿Cómo son tus amigos(as)?
5. ¿Y cómo eres tú?

B 19 Actividad • Y ahora tú . . .

Describe yourself. Then describe two imaginary characters: someone you like and someone you don't like.

B 20 Actividad • ¡A escribir!

Write a brief description of yourself. Describe your family also.

B 21 SE DICE ASÍ
Exclaiming

¿Tu hermana? ¡Qué linda!	Your sister? How pretty!
¿Tu hermano? ¡Qué guapo!	Your brother? How handsome!
¿Tu cuarto? ¡Qué bonito!	Your room? How pretty!
¡Qué chica tan linda!	What a pretty girl!
¡Qué chico tan guapo!	What a handsome boy!
¡Qué cuarto tan bonito!	What a pretty room!

The adjective in an exclamation agrees in gender and number with the noun stated or understood. The word **tan** in exclamations literally means *so*.

You and your friend are talking. One of you repeats a statement from the numbered list. The other expresses a reaction using an appropriate adjective from the box.

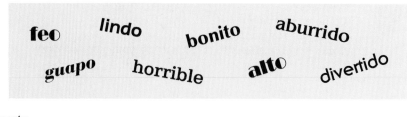

feo   lindo   bonito   aburrido

guapo   horrible   alto   divertido

—Es mi cuarto.
—¡Qué bonito!

1. Llueve y hace frío.
2. ¿Miramos fotos de mi familia?
3. Es una foto de mi tío Tomás.
4. Ella es mi prima Adela.

5. La sala de la casa.
6. Es mi primo. Juega básquetbol.
7. Le gusta practicar deportes.
8. ¿Por qué no escuchamos discos?

React with an exclamation, using the clues. Remember that the adjectives should agree. Make the necessary changes.

casa/bonito
¡Qué casa tan bonita!

1. foto / feo
2. familia / simpático
3. cuarto / grande
4. chicos / guapo
5. chicas / inteligente
6. señora / amable

7. chico / tonto
8. casa / lindo
9. amigos / simpático
10. chica / antipático
11. fotos / bonito
12. chicos / divertido

Which is the best description?

	0	1	2	3	4	5	6
Paying a compliment							
Welcoming someone							
Making someone's acquaintance	✔						
Extending an invitation							
Asking for an opinion							
Exclaiming							
Asking what something is like							

When you visit the home of a Spanish-speaking family, be sure to compliment your hosts about how nice things are. It will also be very helpful for you to know the Spanish names of the rooms in the house.

C1   La casa de Antonio

Antonio y Roberto están en la casa de Antonio.

el comedor

la sala

la cocina

ROBERTO   Me gusta mucho tu cuarto, Antonio. Es muy cómodo.

ANTONIO   ¿Quieres ver toda la casa?

ROBERTO   ¡Por supuesto!

ANTONIO   Bueno, ¡vamos! Empezamos por la sala de estar.

ROBERTO   ¡Qué linda!

ANTONIO   Aquí estamos en el comedor. Y, al lado por esta puerta, la cocina.

ROBERTO   ¿Y el baño?

ANTONIO   Tenemos tres baños. Uno a la derecha de la entrada, otro en el pasillo, y otro en el cuarto de mis padres.

ROBERTO   ¿Dónde estamos ahora?

ANTONIO   En la sala. No usamos mucho este cuarto. Es para cuando vienen visitas. Pasamos nuestro tiempo libre en la sala de estar. Es el cuarto más importante.

ROBERTO   ¿Entramos aquí?

ANTONIO   ¡No, está prohibido! Es el cuarto de mis hermanas.

ROBERTO   ¡Ya sé! Yo también tengo hermanas. Y vivimos en un apartamento pequeño. ¿Hay un garaje?

ANTONIO   Sí, en el jardín, detrás de la casa. ¿Qué te parece la casa, Roberto?

ROBERTO   Es grande y muy bonita. ¡Y mi cuarto es estupendo!

Actividad • ¡A escoger!

For each numbered sentence, choose the ending that best fits the conversation in C1.

1. Los chicos van primero
   - a la entrada y al pasillo.   • al comedor y a la cocina.   • al jardín y al garaje.
   - a la sala de estar.

2. La casa tiene
   - un baño en la cocina.   • tres baños: uno a la izquierda de la entrada, otro
   en el cuarto de las hermanas y otro más en la cocina.
   - un baño en el cuarto de los padres de Antonio, otro a la derecha de la
   entrada y otro más en el pasillo.   • dos baños.

3. La sala es para cuando
   - las hermanas están en la sala de estar.   • los padres de Antonio quieren
   hablar.   • vienen visitas.   • quieren comer y estar en el comedor está
   prohibido.

4. No entran en el cuarto de las hermanas de Antonio porque
   - el cuarto está frente al garaje.   • no usan mucho el cuarto.
   - está prohibido entrar.   • es para cuando vienen visitas.

5. El garaje está
   - detrás del jardín.   • frente a la entrada.   • frente a la casa.
   - detrás de la casa y en el jardín.

C3 Preguntas y respuestas

Answer the following questions according to **La casa de Antonio,** on p. 177.

1. ¿Le gusta a Roberto su cuarto? ¿Por qué?
2. ¿A qué cuartos van Roberto y Antonio?
3. ¿Le gusta a Roberto la sala de estar? ¿Por qué?
4. ¿Cuántos baños tiene la casa? ¿Dónde están?
5. ¿Usan mucho la sala en casa de Antonio? ¿Cuándo usan la sala?
6. ¿Dónde pasan el tiempo libre?
7. ¿Dónde está prohibido entrar?
8. ¿Vive Roberto en una casa grande?
9. ¿Dónde está el garaje en la casa de Antonio?
10. ¿Qué le parece la casa a Roberto?

C4 Actividad • ¿Y en tu casa? . . . ¿en tu apartamento?

Do you live in a house or an apartment? What is it like? Answer these questions.
You can base your answers on an imaginary home and family.

1. ¿Vives en una casa grande o en un apartamento pequeño?
2. ¿Te gusta tu cuarto? ¿Cómo es?
3. ¿En qué cuarto comen ustedes? ¿En el comedor? ¿En la cocina?
4. ¿Usan un cuarto para las visitas? ¿Cuál?
5. ¿Cuántos baños tiene tu casa? ¿Dónde están?
6. ¿Dónde pasan ustedes el tiempo libre?
7. ¿Cuántos teléfonos hay? ¿Dónde están?
8. ¿Cuál es el cuarto más importante de tu casa? ¿La sala? ¿La cocina? ¿Tu
   cuarto? ¿Por qué?
9. ¿Dónde está el televisor? ¿Tienes televisor en tu cuarto?
10. ¿Qué cuarto usas tú más? ¿La sala? ¿La cocina? ¿El comedor? ¿Tu cuarto? ¿Por qué?

Actividad • Adivinanza *Guessing game*

Look at the floor plan of Antonio's house. Imagine you are in one of its rooms.
Explain to a classmate where you are, without naming the room itself. Use
prepositions from the following list as needed.

a la derecha de	**cerca de**	**frente a**
a la izquierda de	**entre**	**lejos de**
al lado de		

Your classmate has to guess where you are.

—Estoy al lado de la cocina, frente a la sala de estar.
—Estás en el comedor.

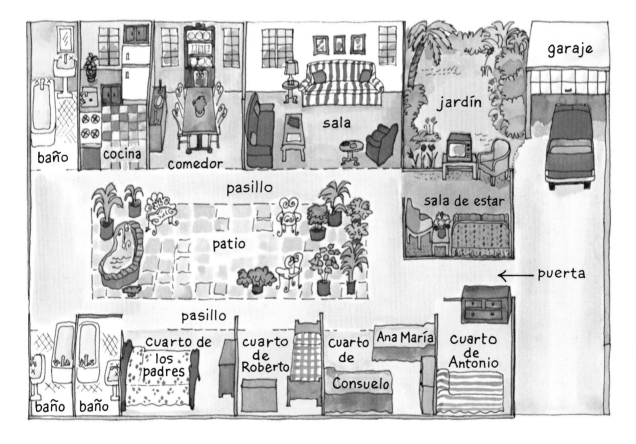

C6   Actividad • El plano de tu casa

Draw the floor plan of a house or apartment—either your own, or one you would like to
have. Make a copy of your plan for use in C7 before you write any words on it. Then
write the names of the rooms and spaces (garden, entrance, garage . . .) in Spanish.

C7   Actividad • Charla

Exchange unlabeled floor plans with a classmate. By asking each other questions in Spanish,
each of you should figure out what the different rooms are on the other's plan. Then label them.

Usually the **sala** of a Hispanic house is a living room used only when special guests are visiting. The **sala de estar** is the family room with the TV set where family members read, knit, watch TV, talk, and relax.

C9 Actividad • ¡A escribir!

Mi casa. Write all you can about your house, how many rooms it has, what's the most important room, where you spend your free time. You can follow the questions below as a guideline. Write about an imaginary house if you'd prefer.

¿Cuántos cuartos hay?   ¿Tiene tu casa comedor?
¿Cuál es el cuarto más importante?   ¿Dónde comes? ¿En la cocina? ¿En el comedor?
¿Cómo es?   ¿Dónde pasas más tiempo?
¿Dónde estudias?   ¿Dónde está tu cuarto? ¿Cómo es?

C10   **ESTRUCTURAS ESENCIALES**
More possessive adjectives

You have already learned three of the possessive adjectives: **mi,** *my,* **tu,** *your,* and **su,** *his, her, its; your.* The following chart shows them all.

	singular	*plural*	
(yo)	**mi**	**mis**	*my*
(tú)	**tu**	**tus**	*your* (informal)
(él) (ella) (Ud.)	**su**	**sus**	*his* *her* *its* *your* (formal)
(nosotros)	**nuestro** **nuestra**	**nuestros** **nuestras**	*our*
(vosotros)	**vuestro** **vuestra**	**vuestros** **vuestras**	*your*
(ellos) (ellas) (Uds.)	**su**	**sus**	*their* *your*

1. The possessive adjectives **su** and **sus** have several possible meanings. You may replace them with the following construction for clarification.

$$\text{article} + \text{noun} + \textbf{de} + \begin{cases} \textbf{él} \\ \textbf{ella} \text{ or} \\ \textbf{Ud.} \end{cases} \begin{cases} \textbf{ellos} \\ \textbf{ellas} \text{ or noun} \\ \textbf{Uds.} \end{cases}$$

   su cuarto → el cuarto **de ella**
   su casa → la casa **de Ud.**
   su familia → la familia **de Ana María**

2. Possessive adjectives show agreement with the noun that follows. **Nuestro** (-a, -os, -as) shows gender and number agreement. **Mi, tu,** and **su** show number agreement only.

Actividad • En la fiesta

There's a party at Antonio's home. All the guests are talking to their own relatives. Sum up the situations using an appropriate possessive adjective, depending on who is talking.

Pedro / la hermana
Pedro habla con *su* hermana.

1. Carmen / los abuelos
2. Tío Tomás / los hijos
3. Yo / el abuelo
4. Los chicos / el padre
5. El señor Colón / la hermana
6. Nosotros / los amigos
7. Tú / el primo
8. Mi prima / la madre

C12 Conversación • ¿Quiénes son?

There's a big family reunion. You don't know for sure who everyone is. Ask your classmate. Using appropriate possessive adjectives, your classmate will confirm that you are right. Then switch roles.

—¿Es él el amigo de ustedes?
—Sí, es nuestro amigo.
—¿La chica alta es la hermana de Luis?
—Sí, es su hermana.

1. ¿El señor es el padre de Carmen?
2. ¿Son los padres de Raúl?
3. ¿Son los hermanos de Gloria?
4. ¿Son mis primos?
5. ¿Es ella la hija de la señora?
6. ¿Es mi prima?
7. ¿La chica guapa es tu amiga?
8. ¿El chico alto es el amigo de ustedes?
9. ¿Los señores son tus abuelos?
10. ¿Son ellas las primas de ustedes?

C13 SE DICE ASÍ
Asking opinions and paying compliments

¿Qué te parece nuestra casa? What do you think of our house?	Tu casa es muy linda. Your house is very pretty. ¡Qué casa linda! What a pretty house!
¿Te gusta mi cuarto? Do you like my room?	Sí, tu cuarto es muy cómodo. Yes, your room is very comfortable.

Conversación · La visita

Pair up with a classmate. Imagine that you are visiting your classmate. He/she will ask your opinion on different subjects. Answer the questions using the adjective in parentheses and the correct possessive adjective. (Be careful to phrase your answer to fit the type of question your classmate asks.) Take turns.

la tía de Antonio (simpático)

A: ¿Te gusta la tía de Antonio?
¿Qué te parece la tía de Antonio?
¿Cómo es la tía de Antonio?

B: Sí, su tía es muy simpática.

Su tía es muy simpática.

1. tu cuarto (cómodo)
2. nuestra casa (grande)
3. nuestra cocina (lindo)
4. el amigo de mi hermana (alto)

5. la casa de mi tía (feo)
6. mi familia (simpático)
7. mi prima (divertido)
8. su amigo (guapo)

C15 Actividad · ¡A escribir!

Write the conversation you had with your classmate in C14. Include questions and answers.

C16 ¿Sabes que . . . ?

Many houses in Spanish cities are built in a row, with no space between each house and no front lawn, like town houses. The main door may open into a hall leading to a large courtyard which is surrounded by the various rooms of the house. The courtyard, or **patio,** is an uncovered open area usually paved with tile or flagstone and decorated with many varieties of colorful plants and flowers. It is a pleasure to sit in almost any room of a Spanish house, because you will have a wonderful view of the **patio.**

C17 Actividad · Combinación

Match the answers on the right with the appropriate questions on the left.

1. ¿Qué te parece mi cuarto?
2. ¿Te gusta tu cuarto?
3. ¿Es alta tu mamá?
4. ¿Cómo es tu hermana?
5. ¿Y tu hermano?
6. ¿Tienes tíos?
7. ¿Cómo son tus primos?
8. ¿Son amigas de ustedes?

No, es baja.
Muy simpática.
Son divertidos.
Sí, dos.
No, son sus amigas.
Muy alto.
Sí, es grande.
Es muy bonito.

using what you've learned

1   Fiesta de familia

While you are a guest at Lola's home, her parents, Jorge Ramírez Duarte and Delia Pentón de Ramírez give a party. As the family members arrive, Lola introduces you and tells you who they are.

LOLA   Mi tía Consuelo, la esposa del hermano de mi papá.
       Tío Guillermo, el esposo de tía Consuelo.
       Tía Adela, la hermana de mamá.
       Son mis abuelos, los padres de mi madre, don José y doña Elena.
       Es mi abuela Josefina, la madre de mi papá.
       Los hijos de tío Guillermo y tía Consuelo: Pedro y Pablo.
       La hermana de Pedro. Se llama Estrella.
       Tato, mi hermano.
       Don Mario Ramírez, el padre de mi papá.
       Mis primos, los hermanos de Pilar.
       Mis padres, Jorge y Delia.

Can you identify Consuelo and the other guests in the picture? Write a sentence about each person or couple that Lola mentioned.

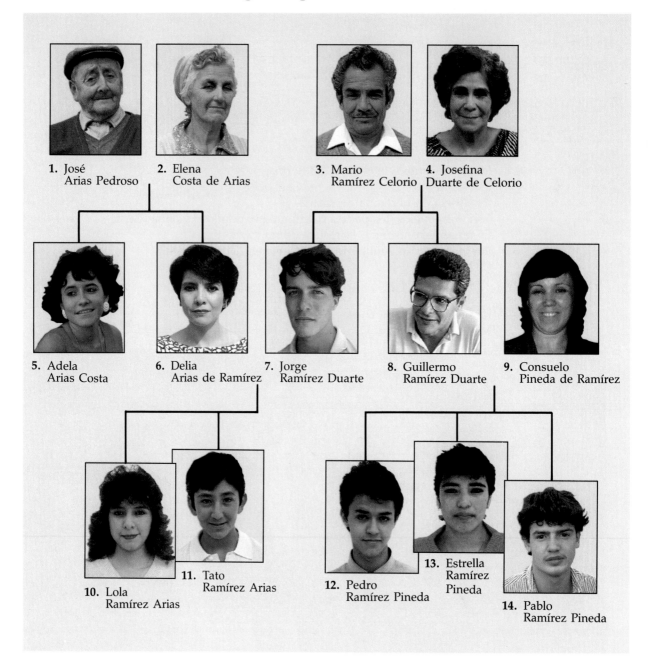

1. José
   Arias Pedroso

2. Elena
   Costa de Arias

3. Mario
   Ramírez Celorio

4. Josefina
   Duarte de Celorio

5. Adela
   Arias Costa

6. Delia
   Arias de Ramírez

7. Jorge
   Ramírez Duarte

8. Guillermo
   Ramírez Duarte

9. Consuelo
   Pineda de Ramírez

10. Lola
    Ramírez Arias

11. Tato
    Ramírez Arias

12. Pedro
    Ramírez Pineda

13. Estrella
    Ramírez
    Pineda

14. Pablo
    Ramírez Pineda

3 Actividad • ¿Quiénes son? ¿Cómo son?

Pair up with a classmate, who was also invited to Lola's party. It's three days
later. Discuss the members of Lola's family one by one and compare your
impressions—check the pictures in section 2 and your lists of names to refresh
your memory of the party. For each person, one of you should give a physical
description, and the other imagine what the person is like.

Consuelo —La tía Consuelo es la esposa del hermano del papá de Lola.
—Es alta y morena, ¿no?
—Sí. Me parece muy simpática.

1. Tato
2. Doña Elena
3. Don José
4. Doña Josefina
5. Pablo
6. La tía Adela
7. Delia
8. El abuelo Mario
9. El tío Guillermo
10. Estrella
11. Jorge
12. Lola
13. Pedro
14. La tía Consuelo

4 Actividad • Proyecto: Mi familia

Bring to class a few pictures of your family (or make up an imaginary family using pictures from magazines). Be prepared to tell the class who they all are and something about them. Be sure to make any adjectives you use agree in number and gender with the noun.

5 Actividad • Charla

Pair up with a classmate. Ask each other about the house where you live, use words from the box below.

sala cuarto televisor garaje baño
comedor cocina teléfono jardín

6 Actividad • Una entrevista

Work with a partner. Your father has asked AMISTAD S.A. to place a Spanish-speaking exchange student with your family. You have to tell the AMISTAD representative about your (real or imagined) family and house. Describe the house, tell how many rooms it has, and say what kind of student you would like to have as a guest. Switch roles.

7 Actividad • Una carta

You want to participate in a student-exchange program yourself. To be placed with a family in a Spanish-speaking country, you have to write a letter in Spanish. Describe yourself and your likes and dislikes. Give some information about the kind of family and type of house you would like.

8 Pronunciación, lectura, dictado

1. Listen carefully and repeat what you hear.

2. The sound of Spanish **c** before **a, o, u** and the sound of **qu** are the same. Listen and then read aloud.

    calculadora   cuál   como   con   aquí   quince   querer   raqueta

3. Copy the following sentences to prepare yourself to write them from dictation.

    Los discos cuestan quince dólares.
    Queremos esquiar con Carlos en Colorado.
    La hermana de Rebeca está casada con un chico de Cuba.

¿LO SABES?

Let's review some important points you have learned in this unit.

Do you know how to make a Spanish-speaking guest feel at home and how to show your appreciation when visiting a Spanish-speaking home?
Welcome a Spanish-speaking guest to your home.
Show your appreciation as a guest.

Can you suggest different activities to friends, using the verb *querer*?
Invite the following people to do the suggested activities:
   un amigo(a): escuchar música / ver mi cuarto
   la Sra. González: pasar / beber un refresco
   los chicos: mirar televisión / comer algo

Can you describe family members, other people, and things using:

alto   inteligente   grande   guapo
divertido   bonito   rubio   simpático

and changing their endings accordingly, describe:

un chico   una chica   tu casa   el colegio   tus hermanos
tus hermanas un señor   una señora   tus primos   tus primas

When a friend is showing you something, can you react with an appropriate exclamatory remark?
Use the correct form of the adjective in parentheses.
   1. Es mi cuarto. (lindo)   **3.** Es mi hermana. (guapo)
   2. Es nuestra casa. (bonito)   **4.** Son las fotografías de mi familia. (lindo)

Can you talk about family relationships?
Express as many relationships as you can for the people in the following family. Then talk about your own family.

   Esteban es el hijo de Tomás y María.
   Ana es la esposa de Esteban, ellos tienen tres hijos: Julia, Juan y José.

Can you name five different rooms in a house or an apartment?

Do you know how to express possession in Spanish?
For each item, compose a phrase with a possessive adjective.
   1. familia / (nosotros)   **2.** hermanos / (tú)   **3.** cuarto / (yo)
   4. hijo / (mi tío)   **5.** casa / (mis amigos) **6.** fotos / (Antonio)

Are you able to ask someone's impression about something or somebody?
Rephrase each sentence using **parecer**.
   1. ¿Te gusta la casa?   **3.** ¿Te gusta tu cuarto?
   2. ¿Te gusta mi primo?   **4.** ¿Te gusta la foto?

Compliment the following people on their possessions or relatives, as indicated. Use the correct form of an appropriate adjective.
   1. María: sus fotos.   **2.** Nosotros: nuestros discos.   **3.** Ellos: su hermana.

VOCABULARIO

(see p. 171)

SECTION A

amable *kind*
la **casa** *house*
con permiso *excuse me*
la **cosa** *thing*
el **cuarto** *room*
es un placer . . . *it's a pleasure . . .*
estás en tu casa *make yourself at home*
igualmente *likewise*
un momento *just a moment*
norteamericano, -a *American*
pasa *come in*
pasar *to spend (time); come in*
el **placer** *pleasure*
querer (ie) *to want*
el **refresco** *soda*
la **sala** *living room*
la **vacación** *vacation*
ver *to see*
la **visita** *visit*

SECTION B

alto, -a *tall*
antipático, -a *not nice*
bajo, -a *short*
bien *very*
bonito, -a *pretty*
cariñoso, -a *affectionate*
casado, -a *married*
¿cómo es? *what's he, (she, it) like?*
¿Cuántos cuartos hay? *How many rooms are there?*
¿cuántos años tiene? *how old are you (is he/she?)*
de ellos *their*
de nuevo *again*
delgado, -a *thin*

los **dos, las dos** *the two*
egoísta *selfish*
el **esposo** *husband*
la **esposa** *wife*
estar casado, -a *to be married*
la **familia** *family*
feo, -a *ugly*
la **foto** *photo*
la **fotografía** *photograph*
generoso *generous*
gordo, -a *fat*
guapo, -a *handsome*
el **hijo** *son*
la **hija** *daughter*
los **hijos** *children, sons and daughters*
lindo, -a *pretty*
la **madrastra** *stepmother*
la **madre** *mother*
los **miembros de la familia** *family members (see p. 171)*
moreno, -a *dark (hair, complexion)*
murió *(he) died*
¿no? *right?*
el **padrastro** *stepfather*
el **padre** *father*
los **padres** *parents*
papá *dad*
pelirrojo, -a *redheaded*
el **primo** *cousin*
la **prima** *cousin*
¡qué cuarto tan bonito! *what a pretty room!*
¡qué guapo! *how handsome!*
rubio, -a *fair, blonde*
el **señor** *man*
la **señora** *woman*
simpático, -a *nice*
tan *so*
tener . . . años *to be . . . years old*
todo, -a, -os, -as *all*

tonto, -a *dumb*
la **visita** *visitor*

SECTION C

el **apartamento** *apartment*
la **cocina** *kitchen*
el **comedor** *dining room*
cómodo, -a *comfortable*
cuando *when*
de él *his*
de ella *her*
de ellas *their*
de usted *your*
de ustedes *your*
empezar (ie) *to start*
la **entrada** *entrance*
este, -a *this*
frente a *across from*
el **garaje** *garage*
grande *large*
importante *important*
el **jardín** *garden*
más *most*
mis *my (pl.)*
nuestro, -a, -os, -as *our*
el **pasillo** *hall*
pequeño, -a *small, little*
¡por supuesto! *of course!*
prohibido, -a *forbidden*
la **puerta** *door, gate*
la **sala de estar** *family room*
sus *her, his, their (pl.)*
el **tiempo** *time*
el **tiempo libre** *free time*
tus *your (pl.)*
usar *to use*
¡vamos! *let's go!*
vivir *to live*
vuestro, -a, -os, -as *your (fam. pl.)*
¡ya sé! *I know it!*

ESTUDIO DE PALABRAS

1. Write a list of the polite expressions you can use when you meet new friends and visit their home.

2. Make a list of the words you can use to describe a house or an apartment.

VAMOS A LEER

Antes de leer

Don't be slowed down in your reading by looking up all unknown words. Let the context help you guess the meaning. For example, in the sentence **Usted X las preguntas,** can you guess that **X** must be the Spanish word for *answer* **(contesta).** Sometimes you must read further before the meaning becomes clear to you.

¡HOGAR, DULCE HOGAR!

Home sweet home! Will this real estate agency help you find the home of your dreams?

AGENCIA BRAVO | CASAS APARTAMENTOS CONDOMINIOS | Teléfono: 32.78.21 Av. Quinta

Contesta° estas preguntas. ¡Escríbenos°! ¡Tú puedes° conseguir° la casa de tus sueños!

¿Es una casa grande? ( )
¿Pequeña? ( )
¿Un apartamento? ( )
¿Qué tiene?
   Una sala grande ( )
   Baños (1) (2) (3) (4)
   Sala de estar ( )
   Cocina ( )
   Comedor ( )
   Dormitorios (1) (2) (3) (4) (?)
   Estudio ( )
   Jardín ( )
   Piscina ( )
¿Dónde está?
   En los suburbios ( )
   En el campo° ( )
   En la ciudad ( )

¡Tenemos la casa de tus sueños°!

¿Piscina, jardín, estudio?

Write a description of what you want in your dream house. Take a poll of your classmates. Ask them: **¿Qué quieres en la casa de tus sueños?** Make a list of their answers and share your findings with the class.

---

contesta *answer*   **escríbenos** *write us*   **puedes** *you can*   **conseguir** *to get*   **campo** *country*   **sueños** *dreams*

Actividad • Un agente de propiedades *A real estate agent*

You are a real estate agent. Below are descriptions of some of your customers as well as some ads for properties. Match the customers with the appropriate dwellings.

1. A young working woman is looking for an apartment to share.
2. A mother and her daughter need a house.
3. A young family is looking for a one-family house.
4. A professional man is looking for a room. He doesn't have a car.
5. A family whose elderly grandmother lives with them is seeking a house with a small apartment for her.

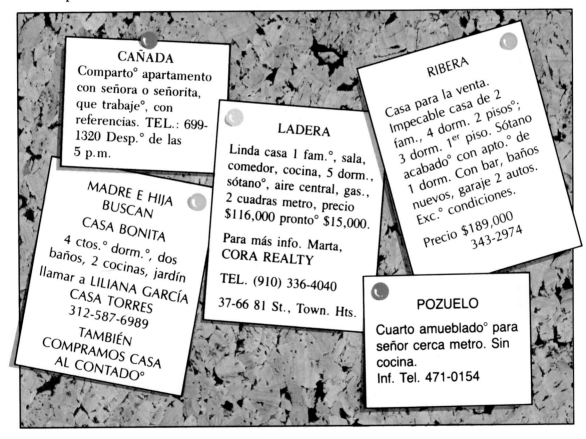

CAÑADA

Comparto° apartamento con señora o señorita, que trabaje°, con referencias. TEL.: 699-1320 Desp.° de las 5 p.m.

MADRE E HIJA BUSCAN CASA BONITA

4 ctos.° dorm.°, dos baños, 2 cocinas, jardín llamar a LILIANA GARCÍA CASA TORRES 312-587-6989 TAMBIÉN COMPRAMOS CASA AL CONTADO°

LADERA

Linda casa 1 fam.°, sala, comedor, cocina, 5 dorm., sótano°, aire central, gas., 2 cuadras metro, precio $116,000 pronto° $15,000.

Para más info. Marta, CORA REALTY

TEL. (910) 336-4040

37-66 81 St., Town. Hts.

RIBERA

Casa para la venta. Impecable casa de 2 fam., 4 dorm. 2 pisos°; 3 dorm. 1er piso. Sótano acabado° con apto.° de 1 dorm. Con bar, baños nuevos, garaje 2 autos. Exc.° condiciones.

Precio $189,000
343-2974

POZUELO

Cuarto amueblado° para señor cerca metro. Sin cocina.
Inf. Tel. 471-0154

Actividad

Pair up with a classmate. One is a real estate agent. The other plays the client. The client is looking for a house or an apartment. The agent has to offer what he or she has available. Make it sound attractive. Switch roles.

---

comparto *I share* **que trabaje** *who works* **desp.** *después* **ctos.** *cuartos* **dorm.** *dormitorio* **al contado** *cash* **fam.** *familia* **sótano** *basement* **pronto** *down payment* **pisos** *stories* **acabado** *finished* **apto.** *apartamento* **exc.** *excelentes* **amueblado** *furnished*

El regalo

Adriana y Daniel van a la cafetería del aeropuerto. Allí, sentado en° una de las mesas° con la aeromoza, está el piloto, Héctor Ramos. Beben refrescos y conversan. En otra mesa está el hombre rubio. Él y la aeromoza intercambian miradas°.

DANIEL	¡El refresco! . . . , la aeromoza echó° algo en el refresco.
	(Los chicos corren a la mesa del piloto.)
ADRIANA	¡Tío! ¡Tío Héctor! ¿Cómo estás? (El piloto no contesta.)
DANIEL	Tío Héctor, queremos hablar contigo°. ¡Es muy importante!
HÉCTOR	Yo me llamo Héctor pero . . . ¿quiénes son ustedes?
DANIEL	Tío Héctor, somos tus sobrinos°.
HÉCTOR	Mucho gusto. Pero, . . . ¿mis sobrinos? Yo tengo muchos sobrinos, pero no . . .
ADRIANA	Sí, nuestra mamá es tu hermana.
HÉCTOR	¿Mi hermana? Mi hermana no tiene hijos.
DANIEL	¿Cómo se llama ella?
HÉCTOR	Sara. Es baja, un poco gorda y tiene cuarenta años . . .
DANIEL	Sí, Sara Ramos, nuestra mamá, tu hermana. Es alta y baja, digo°, baja y gorda.
AEROMOZA	¿Qué quieren ustedes? ¡Váyanse°!, o . . .
ADRIANA	O, ¿qué? ¿Va a llamar a la policía, señorita?

---

sentado en *seated at*　**mesas** *tables*　**intercambian miradas** *(They) exchange glances*　**echó** *poured*　**contigo** *with you*
sobrinos *nephew and niece*　**digo** *I mean*　**váyanse** *go away*

La aeromoza no contesta. Héctor comienza a sentir° los efectos del refresco. El señor
rubio se levanta° de la mesa. Muchas personas se acercan°. El piloto se desmaya°.
En la confusión la aeromoza y el señor rubio desaparecen°. Daniel y Adriana
escapan. Ya en casa, ellos prenden° el televisor. La locutora entrevista° a una mujer
bonita. Es la aeromoza.

LOCUTORA	La policía busca a dos chicos que trataron de° asesinar° a Héctor Ramos, un piloto de Mexicana de Aviación. Aquí con nosotros la aeromoza del vuelo 28.
AEROMOZA	Creo que son hermanos. El chico es alto y moreno, y tiene 14 ó 15 años. La hermana es mayor°, es flaca° y fea.
DANIEL	¡Hablan de nosotros°!
ADRIANA	¿Yo? ¿Flaca? ¿Fea? ¡Imposible!

Actividad • ¿Quién habla?

Which of the characters from **El regalo** might say or think each of the following?

1. Bueno, tengo unos minutos. Voy a tomar un refresco con ella.
2. ¿Quiénes son estos chicos? ¿Por qué quieren hablar con Héctor?
3. ¿Por qué están esos chicos en la mesa de mi amiga y el piloto?
4. No es mi hermana Sara. Mi hermana Sara no tiene hijos.
5. Mi hermana es inteligente. Tenemos un plan muy bueno.
6. Yo soy delgada, no flaca. Y soy muy bonita.

---

comienza a sentir *starts to feel*   **se levanta** *gets up*   **se acercan** *(they) come close*   **se desmaya** *faints*
desaparecen *disappear*   **prenden** *(they) turn on*   **entrevista** *(she) interviews*   **que trataron de** *who tried to*   **asesinar** *to*
murder   **mayor** *older*   **flaca** *skinny*   **de nosotros** *about us*

UNIDAD 7

¡Vamos a salir!

Spanish-speaking teenagers generally like to go out together in mixed groups. They may go to a movie or a concert. More often, they just go for a walk. In small cities, they may walk to the main square, where they meet their friends and chat. In a modern metropolis like Buenos Aires, Argentina's capital, they may go to a club or a shopping mall. Like teenagers everywhere, they have to plan, discuss, and agree on where they are going to go for a walk or what kind of movie or concert they will attend.

In this unit you will:

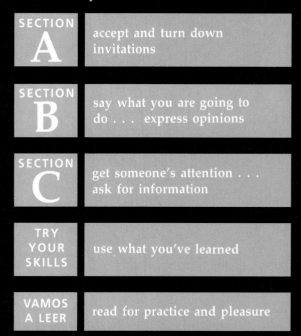

SECTION A	accept and turn down invitations
SECTION B	say what you are going to do . . . express opinions
SECTION C	get someone's attention . . . ask for information
TRY YOUR SKILLS	use what you've learned
VAMOS A LEER	read for practice and pleasure

193

What do Spanish-speaking students do when they go out? Where do they go? The answer depends partly on where you live. If they were living in Buenos Aires, they would have a lot of choices!

A1

¡A pasear! 📼

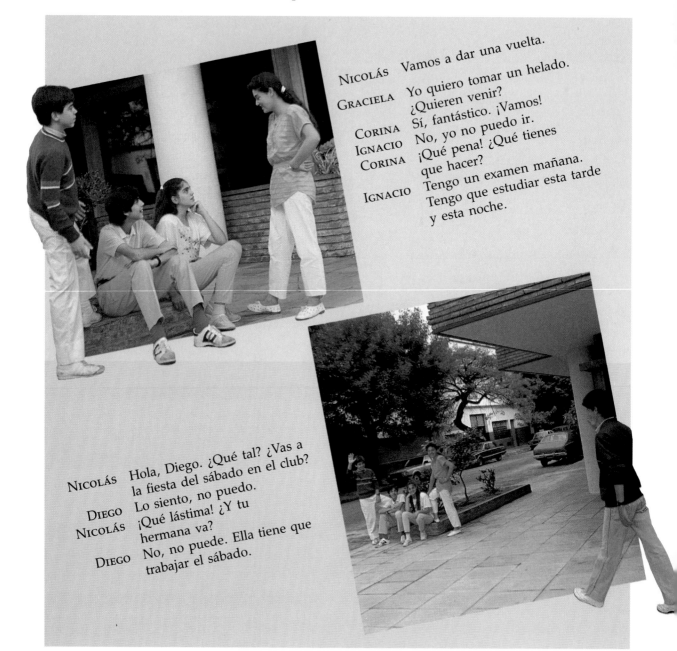

NICOLÁS   Vamos a dar una vuelta.

GRACIELA   Yo quiero tomar un helado.
            ¿Quieren venir?

CORINA   Sí, fantástico. ¡Vamos!

IGNACIO   No, yo no puedo ir.

CORINA   ¡Qué pena! ¿Qué tienes
          que hacer?

IGNACIO   Tengo un examen mañana.
           Tengo que estudiar esta tarde
           y esta noche.

NICOLÁS   Hola, Diego. ¿Qué tal? ¿Vas a
           la fiesta del sábado en el club?

DIEGO   Lo siento, no puedo.

NICOLÁS   ¡Qué lástima! ¿Y tu
           hermana va?

DIEGO   No, no puede. Ella tiene que
         trabajar el sábado.

Match the items in the two boxes to agree with the conversations in A1.

Vamos a	Tengo	puedo ir.	examen mañana.
Yo quiero	¿Qué tienes	fiesta del sábado?	tomar un helado.
Yo no	¿Vas a la	trabajar el sábado.	dar una vuelta.
Tengo un	Ella tiene que	que estudiar.	que hacer?

A3 ESTRUCTURAS ESENCIALES
The verb poder

poder (ue) *to be able, can*			
Puedo	ir a la fiesta.	**Podemos**	dar una vuelta.
¿Puedes	venir?	**Podéis**	estudiar.
Puede	esperar.	**Pueden**	tomar un helado.

You saw the stem-changing verb **querer** in Unit 6. **Poder** is also a stem-changing verb. In the four present-tense forms that are stressed on the stem, the stem vowel changes from **o** to **ue**. The stem of the **nosotros(as)** form does not change: **podemos**.

Poder has the same endings in the present tense as regular **-er** verbs. In sentences, **poder** is often followed by an infinitive.

No **puedo ir.** *I can't go.*
Diego y Luisa no **pueden ir** a la fiesta. *Diego and Luisa can't go to the party.*

A4 Actividad • ¡Nadie puede ir!

Complete the following using **poder.**

¡Vamos a la fiesta! ¿_____ ir tu hermana? No, no _____ . ¿Y los chicos, _____ ?
No, ellos no _____ . Ustedes, ¿_____? No, nosotros no _____ .
Y tú, ¿_____? No, yo no _____ . Pero, ¿quién _____ ir?

A5 Actividad • ¿Quieres ir?

Answer the following sentences using **querer** and **poder.**

—¿Quieres tú venir el sábado?
—Sí, quiero pero no puedo.

1. ¿Quieren ustedes dar una vuelta?
2. ¿Quiere usted venir?
3. ¿Quieres tú venir mañana?
4. ¿Quieren ustedes tomar un helado?
5. ¿Quieres tú esperar aquí?
6. ¿Quieren ir los chicos?

¿a la piscina?

¿a una discoteca?

¿al cine?

¿al parque?

¿a la playa?

A7 Actividad • Adivinanza

You have to guess where these people are according to what they're saying. Refer to the places mentioned in A6.

—¿Quieres bailar?
Están en la discoteca.

1. ¿Montamos en bicicleta?
2. Hace mucho calor.
3. Ella baila muy bien
4. ¿Puedes ver bien?
5. ¿Jugamos fútbol ahora?

6. Siempre corren aquí.
7. No quiero nadar, quiero comer.
8. ¿Corremos o montamos en bicicleta?
9. Hace frío para nadar.
10. Sí, me gusta mucho bailar.

A8 Conversación • ¿Puedes ir . . . ?

Pair-up with another student. Ask your partner the following questions. Exchange roles.

¿Quieres ir a . . .
¿Puedes ir hoy a . . .
¿Por qué?
¿Puedes ir el sábado a . . .
¿Por qué?

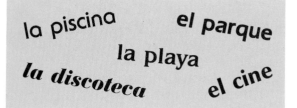

la piscina   el parque
la playa
la discoteca   el cine

SE DICE ASÍ
Accepting or turning down invitations

	¿Quieres venir? *Do you want to come?*	Sí, fantástico. ¡Vamos! *Yes, great! Let's go!*
	¿Puedes venir? *Can you come?*	Lo siento, no puedo. *I'm sorry, I can't.*

A10 Conversación • Vamos a . . .

Tell your partner where you and your friends are going and ask him or her to join in.

—Vamos a la playa,
¿puedes venir?

• Sí, fantástico, vamos.
• Lo siento, no puedo.

el parque la piscina el cine la discoteca
el club dar una vuelta la playa

A11 SE DICE ASÍ
Expressing obligation with tener que

Tengo que estudiar.	**Tenemos que** trabajar.
Tienes que venir a las ocho.	**Tenéis que** comer.
Tiene que esperar.	**Tienen que** decidir.

When you want to say that *you have to do something,* you can use a form of **tener** followed by **que** and the infinitive of the verb that tells what has to be done.

A12 Actividad • Instrucciones

Your musical group is playing for a party. The bandleader is giving instructions. Complete each instruction using the expression **tener que.**

1. Ustedes _____ venir temprano.
2. Todos _____ estar aquí a las nueve.
3. Tú _____ llamar a Ignacio.
4. Él también _____ venir. Él _____ cantar.
5. Su hermana _____ tocar la guitarra.
6. Nosotros _____ practicar.

A13 Conversación • ¿Qué tienes que hacer?

Ask your partner what he/she has to do. Exchange roles.

1. ¿Qué tienes que hacer hoy después de la escuela?
2. ¿Tienes que ir a tu casa?
3. ¿Qué tienes que hacer en tu casa?
4. ¿Qué tienes que hacer mañana a las 8 de la mañana?
5. ¿Y a las 3 de la tarde?
6. ¿Tienes algo que hacer el fin de semana?
7. ¿Y el sábado?
8. ¿Qué tenemos que hacer para la clase de . . . ?

A 14 SE DICE ASÍ
Giving an excuse, expressing regret

The excuse—a reason why you can't.	Regret that the invitation can't be accepted.
No puedo, tengo que estudiar.	¡Qué lástima! ¡Qué pena!

A 15 Actividad • Charla

Extend an invitation to your partner. Your partner turns it down, giving a reason why. You express regret.

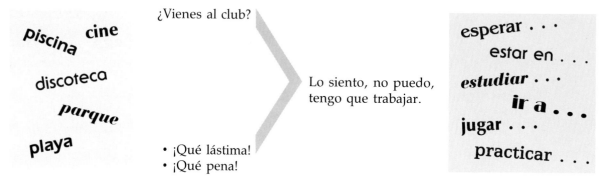

¿Vienes al club?

Piscina   cine

discoteca

parque

playa

Lo siento, no puedo, tengo que trabajar.

• ¡Qué lástima!
• ¡Qué pena!

esperar . . .
estar en . . .
estudiar . . .
ir a . . .
jugar . . .
practicar . . .

A 16 Actividad • ¡A escribir!

Write the conversation you had with your partner in A15.

A 17 SITUACIÓN • ¿Sales mucho?

La revista *Juventud de hoy* entrevista a cuatro estudiantes. Ellos contestan nuestras preguntas: ¿Sales mucho? ¿Cuántas veces por semana sales? ¿Qué te gusta hacer cuando sales?

Cristina

Yo salgo bastante, una o dos veces por semana. Voy al cine, a conciertos de rock o, sencillamente, a casa de mis amigos.

Roberto

Lo que más me gusta es bailar. Yo voy a bailes y discotecas todo el tiempo. ¡Bailar es fantástico!

Ricardo

Me gusta mucho salir a pasear con otros chicos. Salimos a menudo. Damos una vuelta, si tenemos ganas, vamos a un café, tomamos algo y hablamos mucho.

Marta

Yo salgo todos los domingos. También los sábados por la noche. Me gusta salir los fines de semana porque puedo volver a casa tarde. A veces voy al cine.

A 18 Actividad • No es así

Correct these sentences so they are true according to the interviews in A17.

1. Cristina va bastante a casa de sus tíos.
2. Ella sale tres o cuatro veces por semana.
3. Roberto va mucho a casa de sus amigos.

4. Ricardo siempre va a pasear con sus hermanas.
5. Si tienen ganas, ellos van a la discoteca.
6. Marta tiene que volver temprano los sábados.

A 19 Actividad • Preguntas y respuestas

Answer the following questions according to the interviews in A17.

1. ¿A quiénes entrevista *Juventud de hoy?*
2. ¿Qué preguntas contestan ellos?
3. ¿Adónde va Cristina?
4. ¿Le gusta a Roberto bailar? ¿Por qué?
5. ¿Adónde le gusta ir a él?

6. ¿Qué le gusta a Ricardo?
7. ¿Con quién sale él?
8. ¿Qué días sale Marta?
9. ¿Por qué le gusta a ella salir los sábados?
10. ¿Adónde va ella a veces?

A 20 Actividad • Entrevistas

Interview a classmate using A17 as a model.

A 21 ESTRUCTURAS ESENCIALES
The verbs salir *and* decir (e → i)

salir	*to go out*	decir	*to say*
salgo	salimos	digo	decimos
sales	salís	dices	decís
sale	salen	dice	dicen

1. The verbs **salir** and **decir** add a **-g-** in the **yo** form of the present tense.

2. In Spanish, some verbs like **decir** change the **e** to an **i** in the stem of all singular forms and the **ellos** plural form.

3. The endings of **salir** and **decir** are regular.

A 22 Actividad • ¡A escribir!

¿Cuándo salen? Write full sentences using **salir.**

los chicos / ahora   Los chicos salen ahora.

1. yo / por la tarde
2. nosotros / el sábado
3. ¿(tú) / mañana?
4. Marta y yo / esta noche
5. ¿(usted) / a menudo?
6. Ricardo / en dos minutos

A 23 Actividad • ¿Con quién salen?

Say who goes out with whom.

—Ella sale con su hermana.

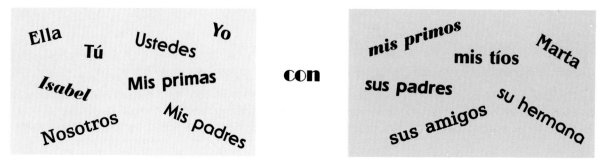

A 24 SE DICE ASÍ
Asking how often people go out

¿Cuántas veces por semana sales? { ¿Una vez? / ¿Dos veces? / ¿Tres o más? }

- Yo salgo tres veces por semana.
- Yo salgo una vez por semana.

A 25 Conversación • De paseo

Answer the following personal questions.

1. ¿Sales los fines de semana?
2. ¿Qué días sales? ¿Los sábados, los domingos?
3. ¿Qué te gusta hacer cuando sales?
4. ¿Con quién sales?
5. ¿Cómo vas? ¿En auto? ¿A pie?
6. ¿Cuántas veces por semana sales?

A 26 Conversación • ¿Sales mucho?

Once again explore the subject of going out, this time with a classmate.
Ask your partner:

1. ¿Dices que sales mucho?
2. ¿Cuántas veces por semana sales?
3. ¿Vas mucho al cine?
4. ¿Y a la discoteca?
5. Y tus amigos. ¿Van ellos al parque?
6. ¿A la playa?
7. ¿A discotecas?
8. ¿A bailes o a fiestas?

A 27 Actividad • ¿Qué preguntan?

State appropriate questions for each of the following answers.

> **Tengo un examen**
> **Por la tarde**
> **Sí, salgo bastante**
> **Los fines de semana**
> **Lo siento, no puedo**
> **Con otros chicos**
> **Al cine**
> **A las diez**
> **Tengo que estudiar**
> **Matemáticas**

> *A veces bailamos*
> *A casa de nuestros amigos*
> *Escuchar discos*
> *Dos veces por semana*
> *Con mi hermano*

A 28 Actividad • ¡A escribir!

Write your questions for A27, and their corresponding answers.

A 29 Comprensión

Are we all going?

	0	1	2	3	4	5	6	7	8
Sí	✔								
No									

A 30 Actividad • Una encuesta

Make a data sheet like the one shown below. Interview six of your classmates about how often they go out, on what days, and where they go. Write the answers on your sheet. Fill in all the spaces.

¿Quién?	¿Adónde?	¿Qué días?	¿Cuándo?	¿Cuántas veces por semana?
David	discoteca	sábados	por la noche	una
Paula	...	jueves y domingos	....	dos
....	cine	....	por la tarde	....

A 31 Actividad • Informe *Report*

Report the results of your interview to the class. Indicate what form of entertainment is most popular among the classmates you interviewed. Prepare a written version of your report.

Most Argentines love to go to the movies. The annual film festival in Mar del Plata is the country's most important showcase for new movies. To decide what movie to see, you need to be able to understand the ads in the newspaper.

B1

¿Qué vamos a ver?

Paula y Miguel están en el Café Suárez, en Buenos Aires. Dicen que piensan ir al cine, pero, ¿qué van a ver? Miguel mira el periódico.

MIGUEL Mmm . . . Aquí está el programa de mañana. Van a dar *Bodas de plata.* ¿Hoy? . . . Hoy dan *Basta de ruido.*

MIGUEL ¿Qué vamos a hacer? ¿Vamos al cine? ¿Qué clase de película quieres ver?

PAULA ¿Qué dan en el cine Belgrano?

MIGUEL *Detenidos en el tiempo.* ¡Premio de oro, Mar del Plata! Creo que es una película de ciencia-ficción.

PAULA ¿Y si vamos al Savoy? ¿Qué te parece? ¿Qué dan ahí?

PAULA ¿*Basta de ruido?* Me parece que es una musical. Mejor vamos al Belgrano.

MIGUEL Bueno, entonces, vamos a ver *Detenidos en el tiempo.* ¡Vamos! La película va a empezar. Son casi las seis.

Actividad • ¡A escoger!

Choose the option that better reflects the conversation in B1.

1. Paula y Miguel están en
   • el cine Savoy.   • Mar del Plata.   • el Café Suárez.
2. Miguel mira
   • a Paula.   • el periódico.   • la película *Basta de ruido.*
3. En el cine Belgrano dan
   • *Detenidos en el tiempo.*   • *Bodas de plata.*   • *Basta de ruido.*
4. Parece que *Basta de ruido* es
   • una película de ciencia-ficción.   • una musical.   • ¡Premio de oro!
5. En el cine Savoy van a dar *Bodas de plata*
   • hoy.   • mañana.   • el jueves.
6. Paula y Miguel van
   • al cine Belgrano.   • al Savoy.   • al Café Suárez.

B3   ESTRUCTURAS ESENCIALES
Expressing future time

To say what someone will do or is going to do, you can use:

1. A present-tense form of the verb.

   Paula **va** al cine.   *Paula goes to the movies.*

   Often other words, usually time expressions, are added to more clearly indicate the future time.

   ¿Qué película **dan mañana?**   *What movie is playing tomorrow?*
   ¿Qué película **dan a las nueve?**   *What movie is playing at nine?*

2. A present-tense form of **ir** + **a** + the infinitive of the main verb.

Voy a ver la película.	**Vamos a ir** al cine.
¿Qué **vas a hacer?**	**Vais a dar** una vuelta.
Va a mirar el periódico.	**Van a tomar** algo.

   To make a negative statement with **ir,** put **no** before the form of **ir.**

   Paula **no va a mirar** el periódico.   *Paula is not going to look at the paper.*
   ¿Tú **no vas a mirar** el periódico?   *Aren't you going to look at the paper?*

B4   Actividad • Combinación

¿Adónde van a ir? Match the three columns.

Cristina	vamos a ir	con mis padres.
Irene y yo	van a bailar	un helado.
Yo	va a escuchar	a dar una vuelta.
Tú	voy a salir	un concierto de rock.
Mario y ella	vas a tomar	a una discoteca.

Actividad • ¿Qué van a hacer?

Complete the answers using the verb in parentheses in an **ir** + **a** + infinitive construction.

1. (hacer) ¿Qué _____ tú?
2. (salir) Yo _____ .
3. (dar) ¿Y Paula? Ella _____ una vuelta.
4. (tomar) Nosotros _____ un helado.
5. (salir) ¿Y Raúl y Mario? Ellos _____ con sus padres.

6. (estudiar) ¿Y tú? Yo _____ .
7. (trabajar) ¿Y tu hermano? Él _____ con la computadora.
8. (salir) ¿Y ustedes _____ ?
9. (mirar) No, nosotros _____ televisión.
10. (ir) ¿Quién _____ al cine?

B6 Conversación • El fin de semana

Make plans with a classmate to go out on the weekend.

> ¿Qué día van a salir? ¿Adónde van a ir? ¿Con quién? ¿A qué hora? ¿Cómo van a ir? ¿En auto, tren, autobús? ¿Cuánto dinero van a necesitar?

B7 Actividad • ¡A escribir!

Write down the plans for the weekend that you made with your partner.

B8 SITUACIÓN • Mejor una policial

TERESA ¿Vamos a ver *Sueño de amor?*
RAQUEL No, hoy no tengo ganas de ver una película de amor.
TERESA ¿Y si vemos *El amigo de Frankenstein?*
RAQUEL ¿Una de terror? ¡No! Mejor vemos *Fantasía.*
TERESA *Fantasía* es de dibujos animados. En el Rex dan una del oeste. ¿Qué te parece?
RAQUEL Si quieres ver una de aventuras, aquí hay una: *Vuelo fantástico.*
TERESA ¿*Vuelo fantástico?* ¡No! Es de ciencia-ficción. Vamos a ver una cómica: *Líos locos.*

RAQUEL *Crimen en el hielo,* ¡la mejor policial del año!
TERESA ¿Una policial? ¡Fantástico! ¡Vamos!

B9 Actividad • Combinación

Match each movie title with its correct description.

> —*Sueño de amor* es una película de amor.

Sueño de amor	**cómica**
El amigo de Frankenstein	**policial**
Fantasía	**ciencia-ficción**
Vuelo fantástico	**dibujos animados**
Líos locos	**terror**
Crimen en el hielo	**amor**

Pair up with another student. Ask each other the questions. Take notes on what your partner answers and compare notes.

1. ¿Te gusta ir al cine? ¿Por qué?
2. ¿Vas al cine a menudo o ves películas por televisión?
3. ¿Qué clase de películas te gusta? ¿De amor, de aventuras . . . ?
4. ¿Vas a ir al cine hoy? ¿Y el fin de semana?
5. ¿Qué película tienes ganas de ver?
6. ¿Qué clase de película es?
7. ¿Tiene premios? ¿Cuáles?

B 11   ESTRUCTURAS ESENCIALES
Adjectives, adjective phrases, and the deletion of nouns

1. You can describe a noun with an adjective. You can also use an adjective phrase with **de**.

   adjective
   Vemos una película **policial**.   *We're seeing a detective movie.*

   adjective phrase
   Vemos una película **de terror**.   *We're seeing a horror movie.*

2. It is common, unless confusion would result, to delete a noun that is modified by an adjective or adjective phrase.

   No, mejor vemos una policial.   *No, better to see a detective one.*

3. **Un** becomes **uno** if the noun is deleted. (Notice that while in Spanish you just delete the noun, in English you sometimes have to replace it with the word *one* or *ones*.)

   Él tiene tres coches, uno rojo   *He has three cars, a red one*
   y dos azules.   *and two blue ones.*

B 12   Actividad · ¡Al cine!

Edit the following script for a movie commercial. The writers repeat nouns too often. Delete some of them.

   —¿Vamos a ver una película musical?
   —No, mejor vemos una policial.

1. ¿Quieres ir al cine Rex?
2. ¿Y si vamos al cine Metropolitan?
3. En el cine Metropolitan dan una película de terror.
4. ¡No!, no quiero ver una película de terror.
5. Mejor vemos una película de ciencia-ficción.
6. ¡Buena idea! Vamos al cine Plata.

Actividad • Charla

Read the following script aloud with a partner. Then create a script of your own, replacing the underlined words.

A —¿Vamos al cine Real?
B —¿Al Real? ¿Qué película dan?
A —Una de terror, *La hermana de Drácula*.
B —No, no quiero ver una de terror. Quiero ver una cómica.

A —¿Una cómica? Entonces, podemos ver *Líos locos*.
B —¿Y si vemos una musical?
A —¡Fantástico! Vamos al Rex a ver *Basta de ruido*.

B 14 Actividad • ¡A escribir!

Prepare a written version of the script you created with your partner in B13.

B 15 SE DICE ASÍ
Different ways of making suggestions

¿Tienes ganas de ir al cine?	No, mejor vamos al parque.
¿Vamos a ver *Premio de honor*?	¿Por qué no vemos *Detenidos en el tiempo*?
¿Quieres ver *Detenidos en el tiempo*?	¿Y si vemos *Premio de honor*?

When people make suggestions, you sometimes want to respond with a better idea. One way is to begin with **No, mejor . . .** (*No, it would be better to . . .*). Another way is just to suggest something else, in the form of a question.

B 16 Conversación • ¿Qué quieres ver?

You and your friends want to go out. Discuss with a classmate what movie house to go to, what movie to see, and at what time. Here are some possibilities.

Cines	Películas	Hora
Nuevo	policial	4 p.m.
Real	de ciencia-ficción	5 p.m.
Palace	de amor	6 p.m.
Plaza	cómica	7 p.m.

¿Vemos una película de misterio?

No, mejor una de ciencia-ficción.

B 17 Actividad • ¡A escribir!

Write a dialog based on the conversation you had in B16. Prepare to act out the dialog with your partner.

ESTRUCTURAS ESENCIALES
The verbs pensar *and* empezar (e → ie)

pensar	*to think*	empezar	*to begin*
pienso	pensamos	empiezo	empezamos
piensas	pensáis	empiezas	empezáis
piensa	piensan	empieza	empiezan

The verbs **pensar,** *to think, to plan,* and **empezar,** *to begin,* change the stressed **e** in the stem to **ie.** The **nosotros(as)** form does not change.

Actividad • ¿Qué piensan hacer?

Complete each of the following using the corresponding form of **pensar.**

¿Tú ____ ir al cine?   —¿Tú piensas ir al cine?

1. ¿Tú ____ salir el fin de semana?
2. ¿Qué ____ hacer tú?
3. ¿Vas al cine? Nosotros también ____ ir.
4. ¿Qué película ____ ustedes ver?
5. Nosotros ____ ver una cómica.
6. ¿A qué cine ____ ustedes ir?
7. Nosotros ____ ir al Rex.
8. ¡Fantástico! Yo ____ ir al Rex también.
9. ¿Y Julia? Julia ____ ir al teatro.
10. Yo ____ que ella no va a venir.

Actividad • ¿Piensan ir?

Substitute the underlined words with the appropriate form of **pensar.**

—Voy a salir temprano.   —Pienso salir temprano.

1. Voy a ir al cine con Alberto.
2. ¿Vas a venir con nosotros?
3. Nosotros vamos a ver una película policial.
4. ¿Qué quieres ver tú?
5. ¿Quieres ver una película cómica?
6. Nosotros vamos a ir temprano.

SE DICE ASÍ
Expressing opinions

¿Qué piensas?	Pienso que (no) cuesta mucho.
¿Qué crees?	Creo que (no) es interesante.
¿Qué te parece? Horrible, ¿no?	Me parece que sí (. . . que no).

To ask what somebody thinks or to give your own opinion, you can use a form of **pensar** or **creer.** You can also use a construction with **parece.**

B 22   Actividad • ¿Qué crees?

Discuss a movie you want to see with a partner.
The following questions will give you a guideline.
Fill in the blanks with the appropriate information.
Then answer these questions using **pienso, creo,**
and **me parece.**

1. ¿Cuánto ____ el cine? (costar)
2. ¿A qué hora ____ la película? (empezar)
3. ¿Cómo se ____ la película? (llamar)
4. ¿Dónde ____ el cine Metro? (estar)
5. ¿____ una película policial o cómica? (Ser)

B 23   Conversación • Opiniones

Talk to two classmates. Say each sentence. Your classmates will express their
opinions, each using one of the words given in parentheses. Switch roles.

> —Vamos a ver *Verano en la playa.*
>   (estupenda / horrible)
> • Creo que es estupenda.
> • Me parece que es horrible.

1. Quiero ver *Premio de honor.*
   (interesante / aburrida)
2. El cine cuesta 10 dólares.
   (mucho / poco)
3. Dan la película en el Real.
   (lejos / cerca)
4. La película empieza a las doce.
   (tarde / temprano)
5. Es una película policial.
   (amor / oeste)

B 24   Comprensión 📼

Which one is it?

Películas	Cines	Clases
1. Genio de las computadoras	1. Parque	1. del oeste
2. Genio de bolsillo	2. Real	2. musical
3. Música de bolsillo	3. Conde	3. cómica
4. La hora de las computadoras	4. Metro	4. de amor
5. Música en el parque	5. Genio	5. policial
6. Computadoras musicales	6. Plaza	6. de ciencia-ficción
7. Computadoras de bolsillo	7. Arte	7. de dibujos animados

Concerts of popular music in Buenos Aires often take place at Luna Park, a giant downtown auditorium. To hear a concert, you have to find out how to get there, arrange to meet your friends, find the line for tickets, and find out if any tickets are left.

C1   ¡Tito Ortega canta hoy! 🖭

En el autobús.

NICOLÁS   ¡Mira, Paula! Ahí está Diego. ¡Hola, Diego! ¿Qué tal? ¿Conoces a Paula?
DIEGO   No. ¡Hola! ¿Cómo estás? ¿Adónde van?
PAULA   Al teatro, a escuchar a Tito Ortega.
DIEGO   ¿Sí?, yo también.
NICOLÁS   ¡Fantástico! Oye, Diego, ¿sabes dónde tenemos que bajar?
DIEGO   Sí, en la próxima parada, en la calle Sarmiento.

Frente al Luna Park.

DIEGO   ¡Cuánta gente! ¡Permiso, por favor!
NICOLÁS   Perdón, señor. ¿Sabe si hay entradas?
SEÑOR   No, nosotros esperamos el autobús.
PAULA   Por favor, señora, ¿sabe cuál es la fila para comprar entradas?
SEÑORA   Hay entradas en la ventanilla, a la derecha, señorita.

Unos minutos más tarde.

PAULA   ¿Vienes con nosotros, Diego?
DIEGO   No, espero a mi hermana. Ella busca a su amiga Susana.
NICOLÁS   ¡Ahí están! Vamos, el concierto va a empezar.

Actividad • Para completar

Complete the sentences so they agree with C1.

1. Paula y Nicolás van al _____, a _____ a Tito Ortega.
2. Ellos van en _____. Tienen que _____ en la calle Sarmiento.
3. Diego, ¿ _____ tú a Paula?
4. ¡Cuánta _____! ¡_____, por favor!
5. ¿Cuál es la _____ para comprar entradas?
6. Hay _____ en la _____, a la derecha.
7. Diego espera a su _____. Ella busca a _____.
8. El concierto va a _____.

C3 **SE DICE ASÍ**
Getting someone's attention, interrupting politely

To get a friend's attention	¡Mira! ¡Oye!
To get a stranger's attention	¡Por favor, señora! (señorita, señor) ¡Perdón!
Interrupting politely or excusing an action you wish to take	¡Perdón! ¡Permiso, por favor!

C4 Actividad • Reacciones

For each statement or question, select an appropriate lead-in from the expressions in the box below.

　　—¡Aquí viene Roque!
　　—¡Mira! ¡Aquí viene Roque!

1. ¿Bajamos aquí?
2. Es mi parada.
3. ¿Puedo salir?

4. ¡Dan una película musical!
5. ¿Cuál es la fila para las entradas?
6. ¿Tienes dinero?

C5 Actividad • ¡A escribir!

Write down your reactions to the statements or questions in C4.

ESTRUCTURAS ESENCIALES
The verb saber, *to know*

saber *to know*			
Sé	cuánto cuesta.	**Sabemos**	cuándo viene.
¿Sabes	dónde está?	**¿Sabéis**	si viene?
¿Sabe	cuál es?	**¿Saben**	qué hora es?

Saber means *to have information about something* or *to know a fact* such as a date or an address. When followed by an infinitive, **saber** means *to know how to do something:*

Yo **sé** nadar.   *I know how to (can) swim.*

 C7   Actividad • Combinación

Form five sentences by choosing matching elements from the two groups.

Sí, yo	**sabes español.**
Nosotros no	**saben cuánto cuesta.**
Tú	**sabe bailar bien.**
Usted	**sé quien viene.**
Raúl y Pepa	**sabemos a qué hora es.**

C8   SE DICE ASÍ
Asking information

¿Sabes ¿Sabe	si hay entradas? dónde está la fila? si mi hermana está? cuándo viene mi hermana?	Do you know	if there are tickets? where the line is? if my sister is here? when my sister is coming?

C9   Conversación • Al teatro

One of your classmates is going to a concert. You want to go, too. You need to know where it is, on what day, at what time, and how much it costs. Ask your friend. Use a form of **saber** in your questions.

ESTRUCTURAS ESENCIALES
Direct objects and the personal a

| Ella espera **el autobús**. | Los chicos escuchan **un concierto**. |
| Mario espera **a su hermana**. | Los chicos escuchan **a Tito Ortega**. |

1. A *direct object* is the word or words you use to indicate who or what gets acted upon by the verb. In the example sentences, **autobús** and **hermana** tell us who or what gets waited for. **Concierto** and **Tito Ortega** tell us who or what gets listened to. They are direct objects.

2. You can identify the direct object as the word or words that answer the question *what* or *whom* about the subject.
   Ella espera **el autobús**. *(What is she waiting for?)*
   Mario espera **a su amiga**. *(Whom is Mario waiting for?)*

3. When a direct-object noun refers to a *person,* use the preposition **a** before the noun and its modifiers.
   Ella busca **a** su amiga Susana.   Diego espera **a** sus hermanas.

4. When the direct object is **quién** or some other pronoun that refers to a *person,* use the personal **a** before it.
   ¿A quién espera Diego?   Espera **a** su hermana.

5. Don't use the personal **a** after the verb **tener.**
   Paula **tiene** muchos hermanos.   Yo **tengo** muchos amigos.

6. Do not use the personal **a** when the direct object is not a person.
   Ella espera el autobús.

Actividad • ¿Qué dicen?

There's too much noise—you can't hear what these people are saying. Ask for clarification. Use **¿Qué . . . ?** or **¿A quién . . . ?** in your question.

   —¿Los chicos? Van a escuchar un concierto.
   —¿Qué van a escuchar?
   —¿Los chicos? Van a escuchar a Tito Ortega.
   —¿A quién van a escuchar?

1. ¿Nosotros? Esperamos el autobús.
2. ¿Ellos? Esperan a sus amigos.
3. ¿Nosotros? Vamos a escuchar a Tito Ortega.
4. ¿Diego? Compra las entradas.

5. ¿Yo? Busco el dinero.
6. ¿Susana? Busca a su hermana.
7. ¿Él? Mira el periódico.
8. ¿Ellos? Miran a Tito Ortega.

Actividad • ¡A escribir!

All your friend's guesses are wrong. Say no and give the correct information as suggested in parentheses.

   —¿Esperas el autobús? (mi mamá)
   —No, espero a mi mamá.

1. ¿Buscas entradas? (mis amigos)
2. ¿Esperas a Gloria? (su prima)
3. ¿Esperan ustedes a José? (sus amigos)

4. ¿Buscas a tus amigos? (entradas)
5. ¿Miran ustedes el periódico? (Tito Ortega)

ESTRUCTURAS ESENCIALES
The verb conocer

The meaning of the English verb *to know,* is divided between two Spanish verbs,
conocer and **saber.**

conocer *to know, to meet, to be familiar with*			
Conozco	a tu primo.	**Conocemos**	el lugar.
¿Conoces	a mi amiga?	**Conocéis**	Buenos Aires.
¿Conoce	mi casa?	**¿Conocen**	a Diego?

1. In the present tense, **conocer** is irregular in the **yo** form: **Conozco.** All other forms are regular.

2. Use **conocer** when you mean *to be acquainted with* or *to be familiar with a place or a person.*
   ¿Conoces a Paula?　　*Do you know Paula?*
   Conocemos Argentina.　*We have been to (know) Argentina.*
   Remember to use the personal **a** whenever the direct object is a person.

3. Earlier in this unit you learned the verb **saber.** Use **saber** when you mean *to know a fact or to have information about something.*
   Él **sabe** dónde está el teatro.　*He knows where the theater is.*
   Ellos **saben** cuánto cuestan las entradas.　*They know how much the tickets cost.*

Actividad • Una fiesta

Nicolás is having a party at home. He's introducing his friends to his family.
Complete the following using **conocer.** Use the personal **a** also.

　　¿Usted _____ mi primo Raúl?
　　¿Usted conoce a mi primo Raúl?

1. ¿_____ mi prima Corina?
2. Pablo, ¿tú _____ Corina?
3. No, yo no _____ tu prima.
4. ¿Y ustedes? Sí, nosotros _____ Corina,
   pero Miguel y Paula no _____ su
   hermana.
5. ¿Ustedes _____ mis padres? Yo, sí.
6. Yo no _____ tus padres.
7. Señora, ¿usted _____ mi tío Julián?—No,
   ¡mucho gusto!

Actividad • La familia de Tito Ortega

Complete the dialog using appropriate forms of **saber** and **conocer.**

LUZ　Quiero ir al concierto, pero no _____
　　　dónde está el teatro. ¿Tú _____ dónde
　　　está?
ALE　No, pero yo _____ a Tito Ortega.
LUZ　¿Tú _____ a Tito Ortega?

ALE　Sí, yo _____ a toda su familia.
LUZ　¿Tú _____ a sus padres?
ALE　Y _____ a sus hermanos también.
LUZ　¿Tú _____ cuántos hermanos tiene?
ALE　Sí, pero yo no _____ cómo ir al teatro.

1   Para una revista

You are a reporter for a Spanish magazine. You are preparing an article about what teenagers do when they go out. Prepare ten questions to ask your classmates about what they like to do when they go out, where, when, and how often they go out.

2   Actividad • Entrevistas

Write down your questions for 1. Interview your classmates, and report the results to the class.

3   Actividad • ¡A escribir!

Write the article for your magazine based on your interviews. Choose a title for your article. Add pictures and illustrations to your article if you want.

4 Actividad • ¿Adónde vamos?

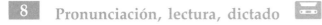

¿Adónde? ¿A qué hora? ¿Sabes? ¿En auto? ¿Con quién? ¿Cuándo? ¿Qué día? ¿Conoces? ¿Cómo?

Work with three or four classmates. You are going out together. Decide where you are going, what you are going to do there, and on what day and at what time you are meeting. Make sure that your arrangements are convenient for everybody in the group. Report your plans to the class and ask other classmates to join your group.

5 Actividad • ¿Qué o a quién?

Answer each question with one of the words in parentheses. Don't forget to use the personal **a** when necessary.

—¿Qué miras? ¿A quién miras? (un periódico / los chicos)
—Miro un periódico. Miro a los chicos.

1. ¿Qué buscan ellos? ¿A quién buscan? (Pablo / entradas)
2. ¿Qué esperas? ¿A quién esperas? (el autobús / mis primos)
3. ¿Qué quiere ver usted? ¿A quién quiere ver? (señor Ortega / una película)
4. ¿Qué escuchas? ¿A quién escuchas? (mis amigos / música)
5. ¿Qué miran ustedes? ¿A quién miran? (el periódico / Pablo)

6 Conversación • Al teléfono

Work with a partner. Over the telephone, you decide to go to the movies. Discuss what movie you are going to see, what kind of movie it is, where it's shown, and at what time you are going. Report your decision to the class.

7 Actividad • ¡A escribir!

Write a dialog based on your telephone conversation with your friend.

8 Pronunciación, lectura, dictado

1. Listen carefully and repeat what you hear.
2. The sound of the Spanish consonant **g** before **a, o, u**. Listen, then read aloud.

    regular   gusto   lugar   gordo   Miguel   Guillermo   ganas   alguno

3. Copy the following sentences to prepare yourself to write them from dictation.

    No tengo ganas de jugar golf hoy.
    Me gusta mucho ir al cine con mi amigo Gustavo.
    ¡Magnífico! El domingo salgo con Gregorio.
    ¡Qué guapo y delgado es Guillermo Rodríguez!

¿LO SABES?

Let's review some important points you have learned in this unit.

SECTION A

When you receive an invitation, how do you accept or decline the invitation?
First, accept two of the following, and then turn two down, explaining why.

1. Voy al parque. ¿Vienes?
2. ¿Quieres salir el sábado?
3. Hay una fiesta el viernes, ¿vas?
4. Vamos al cine. ¿Quieres ir?

How would you ask friends to go to a concert with you, to go out to eat, to go to a dance, or to take a walk?
Each invitation is turned down. How do you express your regrets?

Can you talk about who goes out with whom, and how often?
Form as many phrases as you can with the elements below, using the verb **salir.**

mi prima	bastante	tus	primos
los chicos	a veces	mis	chicos
tu hermana	mucho	sus	padres
yo / tú	todo el tiempo	nuestros	amigos

When a new friend asks you about going out, what do you say?
Answer the following.

1. ¿Sales mucho?
2. ¿Qué días sales?
3. ¿Cuántas veces por semana sales?
4. ¿Con quién sales?

SECTION B

You want to know what your friends are going to do for the weekend.
Write down five questions you might ask them.

Are you able to suggest seeing different kinds of movies?
Replace the words in italics with five alternatives.

—¿Y si vemos *una cómica?*

SECTION C

How would you interrupt politely or excuse an action you wish to take?
Choose the expression that best applies to the following situations.

Mira   Oye   Permiso, por favor   Perdón

1. The bus is crowded and you want to get off.
2. Ask a friend where to get off.
3. You need to interrupt a conversation.
4. You're passing by the movie house with a friend.
   The movie that you want to see is announced.

Do you know how to ask for information?
Using **saber** and **conocer,** write down five questions to find out the date, time, and place of a party, and how to get there.

VOCABULARIO

SECTION A

el **baile** *dance*
bastante *a lot*
el **café** *coffeeshop*
el **cine** *movies, movie theater*
el **concierto** *concert*
¿cuántas veces? *how many times?*
dar una vuelta *to go for a walk*
decir *to say*
la **discoteca** *disco*
entrevistar *to interview*
esta noche *tonight*
esta tarde *this afternoon*
el **examen** *exam*
la **fiesta** *party*
el **fin de semana** *weekend*
el **helado** *ice cream*
la **juventud** *youth*
lo que *what, that*
lo siento *I'm sorry*
el **parque** *park*
pasear *to go for a walk*
la **piscina** *pool*
poder (ue) *to be able, can*
por semana *per week*
¡qué lástima! *what a shame!*
salir *to go out*
sencillamente *simply*
tener ganas de *to feel like*
tener que *to have to*
todo, -a *all*
todo el tiempo *all the time*

tomar *to have (eat or drink)*
la **vez (pl. veces)** *time*
dos veces *twice*
una vez *once*
volver (ue) *to return*

SECTION B

el **amor** *love*
la **aventura** *adventure*
¡basta de . . . ! *enough . . . !*
las **bodas de plata** *silver wedding anniversary*
la **ciencia-ficción** *science fiction*
la **clase** *kind*
cómico, -a *comic, comical*
el **crimen** *crime*
dar una película *to show a movie*
detenido, -a *suspended*
el **dibujo animado** *animated cartoon*
la **historia** *story*
el **lío** *complication*
loco, -a *crazy*
mejor *better, best*
mejor . . . *it would be better to . . .*
la **película** *film, movie*
la **película de terror** *horror movie*
la **película musical** *musical*
la **película del oeste** *Western*

la **película policial** *detective movie*
pensar (ie) *to think, plan*
la **plata** *silver*
el **programa** *program*
el **ruido** *noise*
si *if*
¿si vamos . . . ? *what if we go . . . ?*
el **sueño** *the dream*
uno, -a (de) *one*
voy a *I am going to (to indicate intention)*

SECTION C

bajar *to get off*
conocer *to know, meet, be acquainted with*
¡cuánta gente! *what a lot of people!*
la **entrada** *admission ticket*
la **fila** *line*
la **gente** *people*
más tarde *later*
el **minuto** *minute*
la **parada** *stop*
permiso *excuse me*
próximo, -a *next*
saber *to know (a fact)*
saber (+ inf) *to know how (+ inf)*
el **teatro** *theater*
la **ventanilla** *ticket window*

ESTUDIO DE PALABRAS

1. Review the vocabulary list above and find all the places where people go when they go out to enjoy themselves. Make a list of the places.

2. List all the words and phrases you can use to describe the different types of movies you can see.

VAMOS A LEER

Antes de leer

You're all set to go to the movies and want to know at what time the show starts. Before looking at the ads in today's newspaper, you should be aware that in Spain and South America the 24-hour clock is used to express time. The 24-hour system goes from 0:01 (for 12:01 A.M.) to 24:00 (for midnight). So, to find out any time in the afternoon, add 12 hours to your P.M. time or subtract 12 hours from theirs.

¿Qué dan hoy?

Read the movie ads and decide what film you would like to see.

---

aclamada *acclaimed*   **amada** *loved*   **púrpura** *purple*   **estreno** *premiere*   **ha empezado** *has begun*   **invasores** *invaders*
vuelve *returns*

Guía de espectáculos°

Cervantes. Tejas 2
Teléfono: 37-2390
Estreno nacional
Rambito y Rambón, su primera misión
Divertida comedia.
A las 16:40, 19:50 y 23.

Ateneo. Cerros 23
Teléfono 31-1045
Para chicos y grandes°.
El cuento° del Mago° de Oz
A las 13:25, 16:10, 18:50.
Las aventuras de Mónica y sus amigos
A las 14:45 y 17:30.

Capitol 2. Lavalle 315
Tel. 22-4372. Un filme para toda la familia.
Ralph Macchio
Pat Morita
El Karate Kid II
A las 13:10, 15:35 y 17:50. Sábado 20:20.

Atlas Santa Cruz.
Santa Cruz 201.
Tel. 332-1836.
Miss Mary
Con Julie Christie,
Nacha Guevara. Un filme de María L. Bemberg. A las 13:50, 15:25, 17:50 y 20:15.

Paramount.
Corrientes 98
El color púrpura
Basada° en la historia de Alice Walker.
Ganadora° del premio Pulitzer. Noticiero°, a las 18:50 y 22 horas.

Coliseum. Tetuán 114.
Tel 91-3442. Película de emocionantes aventuras.
Indiana Jones y el templo de la perdición°
Lunes a viernes 13:30, 17:55, 20:15, 22:40.
Sábado y domingo 17:30, 20:00, 22:45.

Lavalle. Princesa 7
Teléfono: 84-8888
Admiradora secreta
A las 17:55, 20:10 y 22:23.
Sábados función a la 1:20.

Filmoteca 1. Corrientes 654 Tel. 44-6676. Un filme de Alan Parker.
Pink Floyd (*The Wall*)
Una mezcla° fascinante de música, rock futurista, juegos de luces°, sonidos° y dibujos. La película musical más sensacional de la historia del cine. A las 15, 17, 19:21, 23 Viernes y sábados 1:20.

Broadway. Narváez 478 Teléfono 99-1660.
Locademia de policía
Una vez más las extravagantes aventuras de los policías de esta singular academia.

Actividad • Charla

Work with a partner. You're reading the newspaper together and considering the ads above. Decide on a movie you both want to see. Explain why you want to see it. Make plans regarding the day and time you wish to go.

---

espectáculos *shows* **grandes** *adults* **cuento** *story* **mago** *wizard* **basada** *based* **ganadora** *winner*
noticiero *newsreel* **perdición** *doom* **mezcla** *mixture* **luces** *lights* **sonidos** *sounds*

El regalo 📼

Daniel y Adriana están muy preocupados. La policía los busca°. ¿Quién va a creer que ellos son inocentes y que los verdaderos° criminales son el piloto y la aeromoza?

ADRIANA   No debemos salir. Tenemos que esperar.
  DANIEL   Pero tenemos que ir a la escuela. No podemos faltar° a clase.
ADRIANA   Y vamos directamente° a casa después del colegio.

En la clase de matemáticas dos amigos le preguntan a Daniel:

  AMIGO   Oye, ¿quieres ir con nosotros al cine esta noche? En uno de los cines del centro dan una película nueva. Es de aventuras.
  DANIEL   Lo siento. No puedo. Quiero, pero no puedo.
  AMIGO   ¿Y mañana? ¿O el sábado?
  DANIEL   No sé, estoy castigado°. Tal vez° dentro de dos o tres semanas.
  AMIGO   ¡Tanto tiempo! ¡Es como estar en la cárcel°! Tus padres son muy estrictos, ¿no?

Una amiga le habla a Adriana de sus planes para el fin de semana. Va a ir a una discoteca con unos amigos y después a una fiesta que va a estar estupenda.

---

los busca *is looking for them*   **verdaderos** *true*   **faltar** *miss*   **directamente** *directly*   **castigado** *punished*
tal vez *perhaps*   **cárcel** *jail*

AMIGA	¿Pasamos por tu casa a las nueve?
ADRIANA	No, este fin de semana, mejor estudio.
AMIGA	¿En serio?° Estás muy cambiada°, Adriana.

Más tarde llega otra amiga.

| AMIGA | ¿Sabes? El viernes vamos a escuchar al grupo español. Uno de los músicos te quiere conocer. Se llama Esteban Arévalo. ¿Te compro una entrada? |

Adriana no sabe qué hacer. Ella también quiere conocer a Esteban Arévalo . . .
pero . . . no puede aceptar la invitación. Esa noche los chicos están aburridos.

ADRIANA	Yo quiero ir a ese concierto el viernes.
DANIEL	Yo sé por qué. Quieres conocer a "El Gato"°.
ADRIANA	¿Cómo? ¿A quién?
DANIEL	A Esteban Arévalo. Ese chico que tiene un ojo verde y otro azul, como los gatos exóticos.
ADRIANA	¡Estás loco! Es un muchacho muy guapo.
DANIEL	Sí, estoy loco. Es verdad. Los dos estamos locos porque queremos salir y no podemos. Hace ocho días que estamos en esta cárcel.
ADRIANA	Por lo menos° la comida de esta cárcel no es mala. Pero . . .

Los dos se miran°. Piensan en lo mismo°.
Existe una diversión: el televisor. No pueden
resistir la tentación. Allí está en un rincón°,
esperando°.

Actividad • Decisiones

Adriana and Daniel are trying to decide what to do. What do you think is best
and why? You can give them some other choices also.

1. ¿Debemos ir a la escuela?
2. ¿Podemos salir?
3. ¿Miramos televisión?

4. ¿Podemos invitar a nuestros amigos a ver el televisor secreto?
5. —Ustedes pueden . . .

¿en serio? *seriously?*   cambiada *changed*   gato *cat*   por lo menos *at least*   se miran *look at each other*   lo
mismo *the same thing*   rincón *corner*   esperando *waiting*

Bienvenida

Repaso

SHOPS   TIENDAS

RESTAURANTS   RESTAURANTES

BOARDING GATES PUERTAS DE EMBARQUE

La sala de espera

Aeropuerto Kennedy, Nueva York.

Miguel Hernández y su papá esperan a Elena, una prima de Costa Rica. Ella va a pasar un mes del verano con ellos en Nueva York.

MIGUEL   ¿Dónde está la aduana?
          Elena tiene que pasar por
          la aduana, ¿no?
SEÑOR HERNÁNDEZ   Sí, pero mira, allí está . . .

SEÑOR HERNÁNDEZ   ¡Elena! ¡Elena! ¿Cómo estás?
                   ¿Qué tal el vuelo?
                   ¿Conoces a tu primo, Miguel?

ELENA   Mucho gusto, Miguel.
         ¡Pero qué alto y guapo!
         Y, ¿cómo está tía Isabel?

MIGUEL   Muy bien. Está en casa. ¿Tienes
         hambre? El almuerzo va a ser muy
         bueno. ¿Y tu equipaje?

ELENA   Aquí está. Creo que tengo todo: mi
         diccionario—no hablo inglés muy
         bien—y el pasaporte en el bolsillo,
         la cámara. Y tú, Miguel, ¿tienes
         las maletas?

SEÑOR HERNÁNDEZ   Sí, tenemos todo. Vamos al carro.

2   Actividad • No es así

Make these sentences true according to the conversation you have just read.

1. Miguel vive en Puerto Rico.
2. Elena viene en autobús.
3. Elena es la abuela de Miguel.
4. Es otoño.
5. Elena es de España.

6. Elena tiene que pasar por la cafetería.
7. La mamá de Miguel se llama Ana.
8. La tía está en el aeropuerto.
9. Elena habla inglés muy bien.
10. Van a casa en autobús.

Actividad • Charla

Work with a classmate. Imagine that one of your favorite relatives is coming to visit. Describe the relative to your partner. Say how old he or she is, and tell where she or he lives. Then each of you should be prepared to describe the other's relative to the class.

> —Mi prima Dolores tiene diecisiete años. Es alta y pelirroja. Es inteligente, bonita y muy simpática. Vive con su familia en Miami.

4 Actividad • ¡A escribir!

Write down the description of your classmate's relative and then describe your relative also.

5 SITUACIÓN • Dos fiestas

Miguel y Elena, su prima de Costa Rica, conversan.

MIGUEL   Elena, ¿sabes que mañana es la fiesta, no? Viene toda la familia: los abuelos, los tíos de Nueva Jersey, los primos . . . y todos nuestros amigos.

ELENA   ¡Qué divertido! Mira, ya no necesito el diccionario inglés/español. Hablo un poco de inglés y muchos de tus amigos quieren practicar español.

Con los amigos norteamericanos de Miguel.

BILL   Dan una película de ciencia-ficción en el cine Roma. ¿Quieren ir?
BETH   ¡Ay no! ¿Por qué no vamos a la película nueva de Matt Dillon?
ERIC   Yo no puedo ir. El domingo voy con mi primo.
KAREN   ¡Tengo una idea! ¿Por qué no vamos a casa? Tengo unos discos nuevos.
MIGUEL   ¿Qué te parece, Elena?
ELENA   ¡Estupendo!

Los chicos llegan a casa de Karen que le da a Elena una fiesta sorpresa.

KAREN   A la derecha, por favor, vamos a la sala de estar.
ELENA   ¡Oh! Una fiesta . . . y están todos nuestros amigos. ¡Qué sorpresa!
TODOS   ¡Buena suerte, Elena!
ELENA   ¡Qué emoción! Ustedes tienen que venir un día a casa en Costa Rica. *Thank you all* . . . mucho.
BILL   ¿Elena, ahora quieres . . . *uh* . . . *uh* . . . *dance?*
ELENA   ¿Bailar? Sí, con mucho gusto, Bill.

¡Y la fiesta empieza!

6 Preguntas y respuestas

1. ¿Quiénes van a ir a la fiesta?
2. ¿Necesita Elena un diccionario? ¿Por qué?
3. ¿Qué quieren practicar los amigos de Miguel?
4. ¿Qué dan en el cine Roma?
5. ¿Adónde va a ir Eric el domingo? ¿Con quién?
6. ¿Adónde quiere ir Karen? ¿Por qué?
7. ¿Dónde están los amigos?
8. ¿Para quién es la fiesta?
9. ¿Adónde invita Elena a sus amigos?
10. ¿Bill quiere cantar?

7   Actividad • Charla

With a partner, try this quiz. One partner names a popular film, and the other tells in Spanish the film's category. Switch roles. Then try to do the same with **un programa de televisión.** Use these categories:

Película (o programa)

de aventuras   cómica   policial   de dibujos animados   de ciencia-ficción

musical   **de** amor   de terror

8   Actividad • ¡A escribir!

You receive five different invitations. Pick a suitable response from the column on the right and write it out. Use each response just once.

1. Voy a una fiesta en casa de Karen. ¿Quieres venir?
2. ¿Puedes salir esta tarde?
3. ¿Quieres ir a un concierto hoy?
4. ¿Vamos al cine esta noche?
5. Voy a comprar discos. ¿Quieres venir?

a. Sí, hay una película muy buena en el cine Roma.
b. No, no puedo. No tengo dinero.
c. Sí, me gusta mucho bailar. ¿A qué hora es?
d. No puedo. Tengo que estudiar.
e. No, gracias. No me gusta la música.

9   Actividad • Fotos

Back in Costa Rica, Elena shows her family some of the many photos she took on her vacation. What does she say about each one? Match her comments with the appropriate picture.

1. La fiesta es en la sala de estar.
2. Llego con dos maletas, la cámara, el pasaporte y mi diccionario.
3. Una fiesta fantástica en casa de Karen.
4. Miguel es alto y guapo.
5. El aeropuerto Kennedy es muy grande.
6. Están en fila para comprar entradas para un concierto.

San José, 3 de octubre

Querido Miguel:

Tienes que venir a Costa Rica. ¿Por qué no vienes en las vacaciones de diciembre? Todos mis amigos te quieren conocer. Vamos a dar muchas fiestas en casa.

Aquí tienes fotos de casa. En la foto de la familia, mi hermano, Roberto, está al lado de mamá. Los chicos altos son los hijos de mis tíos. Ellos viven en Honduras.

Miguel, ¿sabes que en la clase de inglés soy la mejor?

Recuerdos a mis tíos.

Un abrazo,
Elena

11 Actividad • Para completar

Complete the following sentences according to Elena's letter.

1. Elena escribe a . . .
2. Ella invita a Miguel a . . .
3. Todos los amigos de Elena quieren . . .
4. Van a dar . . .
5. Con la carta van fotos de . . .
6. En la foto Roberto está . . .
7. Los chicos altos viven en . . .
8. En la clase de inglés Elena es . . .

Viñeta cultural 2

Paisajes

The Iberian Peninsula juts out into the Atlantic Ocean, separated from the rest of Europe by **Los Pirineos,** a chain of rugged mountains. Spain, which shares the Peninsula with Portugal, is a country of varied landscapes *(paisajes)*—mountains and plains, rocky coastlines, and sandy beaches. Its people have varying customs and divided loyalties, but the wonder and mystery of this ancient country remain unchanged.

❶ Una región agrícola en las Islas Canarias, España

❷ Galicia, al noroeste de España

❸ Una granja típica en los Pirineos, España

The countryside of Castile, with its many windmills, reminds us of Don Quixote, the famous character of Cervantes' novel. Castile consists of a huge, dry plateau called the **Meseta** that is broken by rolling hills and low mountains.

❶ Andorra, pequeño país en los Pirineos
❷ Provincias Vascongadas, España
❸ Un molino de viento en la tierra de Don Quijote, Castilla, España

When the Spaniards explored the Americas, they brought their language, their heritage, and their architectural skills. As far back as the 1400s, they built many towns, missions, and churches, some of which still stand today in Texas, California, New Mexico, Arizona, and Puerto Rico.

❶ Misión de Carmel en California, construida por los españoles alrededor de 1700

❷ Misión de San Javier del Bac en Tucson, Arizona

❸ El Álamo en San Antonio, Texas, fundado por los españoles alrededor de 1700

❹ El Yunque, Puerto Rico

There were highly advanced Indian cultures in the Americas before Columbus. Between 300 and 1000 A.D., Mexico was an important cultural center where several highly developed Indian civilizations flourished. The remains of the ancient Mayan civilization can still be seen at places on the Yucatan Peninsula, such as the city of Chichén Itzá.

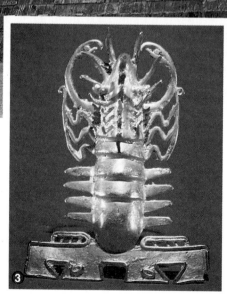

❶ Pirámide maya en Tikal, Guatemala, Centroamérica

❷ Ruinas de Chichén Itzá en Yucatán, México

❸ Pendiente de oro de la época precolombina, Costa Rica

Central America is about 1,100 miles long. At its widest point, it is 300 miles from coast to coast. At its narrowest point, which is only 30 miles wide, lies the Panama Canal. Rugged mountains crisscross all seven countries, and many of them are volcanoes. Most Central Americans earn their living on farms, supplying the world with coffee, bananas, cacao, sugar cane, and tobacco.

❶ Volcán Poás, Costa Rica

❷ Una hacienda ganadera en Costa Rica

❸ El canal de Panamá une el Atlántico con el Pacífico

❹ Una casa de campo en Costa Rica

The South American continent extends almost 5,000 miles from the jungles of Colombia in the north to the icy waters of Antarctica in the south. On this continent, you will find a great variety of landscapes and climates. Along the west coast lies the **Cordillera de los Andes,** which is strewn with volcanoes, torn into separate ranges by violent river torrents, and capped by glaciers. This cordillera is the longest unbroken mountain range in the world.

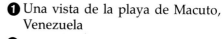

❶ Una vista de la playa de Macuto, Venezuela

❷ La cosecha de café, Colombia

❸ Niños trabajando en una granja de Colombia

❹ La Cordillera de los Andes en Colombia

❺ Valle del Cauca, Colombia

❶ Machu Picchu, la ciudad perdida de los incas en Perú

❷ El río Amazonas de Suramérica

❸ Puente colgante en el Perú

❹ Lago Titicaca, Bolivia

❺ Rebaño de ovejas en una hacienda de Chile

Argentina, Chile, and Uruguay, the countries in the southern tip of South America, are in a temperate zone opposite that of the United States. Therefore, their winter is in June, July, and August. There you can find magnificent beaches, glaciers, mountains, and waterfalls such as Iguazú Falls.

❶ Vista de la Patagonia, Chile

❷ Territorio de la Tierra del Fuego, Argentina

❸ Viña del Mar, Chile

❹ Cataratas de Iguazú, Argentina

TERCERA PARTE

¡Buen provecho!

¡Tacos! ¡Enchiladas! ¡Churros y chocolate! ¡Paella! ¡Arroz con pollo! Sampling the food of other countries is an adventure you can have without leaving home. If you like to cook, read one of the recipes in this unit and prepare a genuine *comida española* for your friends. You can also visit one of the many Spanish or Mexican restaurants in this country. If you are able to visit other Spanish-speaking nations, many more delights await you. All you need is the willingness to try new things and a readiness to understand the customs of those around you.

In this unit you will:

SECTION A	say what foods you like and don't like
SECTION B	select the food you like . . . express your enjoyment of food
SECTION C	say you're hungry or thirsty . . . ask for what you need at the table
TRY YOUR SKILLS	use what you've learned
VAMOS A LEER	read for practice and pleasure

237

Service in the restaurants of Spain and of other Spanish-speaking countries is usually courteous and efficient, but not hurried. You'll be able to enjoy a new and delicious experience if you don't mind waiting.

A1   ¿Qué comemos hoy?

Los señores Álvarez escriben sobre los restaurantes de San Antonio para una guía turística. ¿Qué van a comer hoy? ¿Comida española, tex-mex, del Caribe, pizza o hamburguesas?

CAMARERA	¿Desean ver el menú? El plato del día es pollo con cebolla y salsa de tomate.
SR. ÁLVAREZ	A mí no me gustan las cebollas. ¿Hay sopa?
SRA. ÁLVAREZ	Queremos probar algo típico tex-mex.
CAMARERA	¿Puede ser chile con carne?

CAMARERA	¿Y de postre, señores?
SRA. ÁLVAREZ	Un helado de chocolate, por favor, y café con leche.
SR. ÁLVAREZ	Fruta y té con limón para mí. Estoy a dieta.

CAMARERO	¿A ustedes les gustan las enchiladas? Es una especialidad de la casa.
SRA. ÁLVAREZ	Sí, me gustan mucho. Quiero dos de carne y una de queso.
SR. ÁLVAREZ	Y para beber, agua mineral.

SRA. ÁLVAREZ	¡Qué rápido cenamos aquí!
SR. ÁLVAREZ	Sí, voy a pagar la cuenta.
SRA. ÁLVAREZ	¿Cuánto dejamos de propina?
SR. ÁLVAREZ	¡No sé cuánto . . . ni dónde!

A2 Actividad • No es así

Change the following sentences as necessary to make them true according to A1.

1. Los señores Álvarez escriben un diccionario de la comida del Caribe.
2. En **Sombrero Rosa** el plato del día es pizza con cebolla.
3. Al señor Álvarez le gustan las cebollas.
4. Desean tres enchiladas de queso y té con limón.
5. De postre, la señora come fruta.
6. La señora está a dieta. Desea agua mineral con limón.
7. El señor no tiene la cuenta.
8. Los señores Álvarez dejan la propina en la mesa.

A3 Actividad • Conversación

Pair up with a partner and look over the pictures in A1. Then ask each other these questions.

1. ¿Vas tú a restaurantes a veces? ¿A qué restaurante vas?
2. ¿Tienes un restaurante favorito? ¿Cuál es?
3. De los restaurantes, ¿cuál te gusta más?
4. ¿Qué clase de comida te gusta?
5. ¿Cuál te gusta más: la sopa o el postre?

A4 Actividad • ¡A escribir!

Using the questions and answers to A3 as a guide, prepare a brief composition about the dinner you had at a restaurant.

A5 ¿Sabes que . . . ?

A **café** in Spanish-speaking countries is a place that serves sodas, coffee and tea, and other drinks; sandwiches and other light snacks, fruit, fruit juices, ice cream, and pastries. It usually has some tables and chairs on the sidewalk in front and others inside where there is also a small bar, a television set, a pay telephone, rest rooms, and in some countries, video game machines. In the evening, friends meet in their favorite **café**, play the video games or just chat and have a soda.

Comemos por la mañana, al mediodía, por la tarde y por la noche.
A la hora de la merienda, o entre comidas, lo mejor es un bocadillo y
un vaso de leche o de jugo.

Por la mañana, en el desayuno, nos gusta . . .

tomar café con leche o chocolate, comer pan con mantequilla, jalea o mermelada.

Al mediodía, en el almuerzo, nos gusta . . .

En el almuerzo, a mí me gusta . . .

un bistec o pescado, arroz, verduras y un
postre. Nuestro postre favorito es el flan.
A nosotros nos gusta una comida completa.

comer un bocadillo. Me gustan los bocadillos
de jamón y queso, con lechuga, tomate y
mayonesa. Las papas fritas me encantan.

Por la noche, para la cena, en casa les gusta . . .

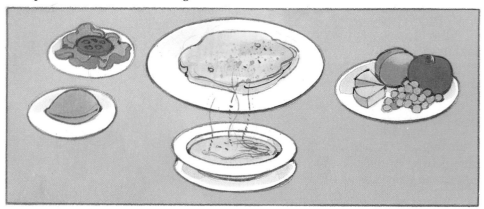

una comida ligera: tomar sopa, comer una tortilla con ensalada, pan, queso y fruta.

A7 Actividad • No es así

Change the following sentences to make them true according to A6.

1. Como papas fritas en el desayuno.
2. Nuestro postre favorito es la sopa.
3. A mí me gusta un bocadillo de arroz en el almuerzo.
4. A la hora de la merienda lo mejor es un bistec.

A8 Actividad • ¡El menú está malo!

The menu printer mixed up the meals, the hours, and the menu items.
Rearrange the three columns
as you think best.

RESTAURANTE ESTRELLA

Desayuno	cinco de la tarde	refrescos bistec postre
Almuerzo	ocho de la noche	chocolate café con leche
Cena	una de la tarde	bocadillo jugo o leche
Merienda	de ocho a nueve de la mañana	sopa ensalada

A9 Actividad • ¿A qué hora comes?

Talk with a classmate about food and meals. Ask each other the following questions:

1. ¿A qué hora tomas el desayuno?
2. ¿Qué toman en tu casa en el desayuno? ¿Leche, jugo, café?
3. ¿Cuál es la hora del almuerzo en la escuela? ¿Y en tu casa?
4. ¿Tomas sopa en el almuerzo o en la cena?
5. ¿Comes ensalada en el almuerzo o en la cena?
6. ¿Cenas en tu casa? ¿Cuándo cenas en un restaurante?
7. ¿Tomas una merienda al volver de la escuela?
8. ¿A qué hora cenan en tu casa?
9. ¿Te gusta cenar tarde o temprano?
10. ¿Comes entre comidas? ¿Qué comes, un bocadillo?

A10 Actividad • ¡A escribir!

Using your answers to A9 as a guide, prepare a brief composition about meals at
home. Start with **"En mi casa, tomamos el desayuno a las . . . "**

ESTRUCTURAS ESENCIALES
The verb gustar

1. In Unit 3, you first used **gustar** to talk about liking something, and you learned to use **me, te,** and **le** to indicate the person who does the liking.

Me gusta comer.	*I like to eat.*
Te gusta el helado.	*You like ice cream.*
Le gusta la sopa.	$\begin{cases} She \\ He \\ You\ (Ud.) \end{cases}$ *likes soup.*

2. Use **nos** or **les** when more than one person likes something.

Nos gusta comer.	*We like to eat.*
Les gusta el helado.	$\begin{cases} They \\ You\ (Uds.) \end{cases}$ *like ice cream.*

3. Only two forms of the verb **gustar** are used. Use **gusta** if what is liked is singular. Use **gustan** if what is liked is plural.

A Luisa le gusta el helado.	*Luisa likes ice cream.*
Me gustan las enchiladas.	*I like enchiladas.*
Nos gustan los restaurantes españoles.	*We like Spanish restaurants.*
Te gustan las frutas.	*You like fruit.*

4. To say that people don't like something, place **no** before **me, te, le, nos, les.**

No me gusta el helado.	*I don't like ice cream.*
No nos gustan las enchiladas.	*We don't like enchiladas.*

5. For clarification or emphasis, you can add **a** + prepositional pronoun.

¿Yo? **A mí** me gusta el helado.
¿Tú? **A ti** no te gusta la cebolla.
A ella le gusta el helado.
A él le gustan las enchiladas.
A Ud. le gusta comer pescado.
A nosotros nos gusta estudiar.
A ellas les gustan los restaurantes mexicanos.
A Uds. les gusta la clase de español.
A Pepe le gusta comer.

Notice that the prepositional pronouns are the same as the subject pronouns, except that **mí** replaces **yo,** and **ti** replaces **tú.**

A 12   Actividad • ¿Qué les gusta? 🔲

Say what the following people like to do. Follow the model.

—Anita (jugar tenis)
—A Anita le gusta jugar tenis.

1. Mi hermano (bailar)
2. Tomás y Dora (las enchiladas)
3. Ellos (ir al cine)
4. Nosotros (la ensalada)
5. Carolina (el postre)
6. Yo (los bocadillos de jamón y queso)

Actividad • Combinación

Make up 10 sentences using items from each column.

—A ellos no les gusta la fruta.

| A mí   A ti
A él   A ella
A usted
A nosotros
A ellos   A ellas
A ustedes
A mis amigos | (no) | les
te
me
le
nos | gusta(n) . . . | el pollo   el café con leche
la cebolla la fruta el queso
el té con limón   la carne
el pan con mantequilla comer
la mayonesa   las papas fritas
el jugo   el arroz
los postres   las verduras
los helados   la ensalada |

A 14 ¡Están seguros! *They're sure!*

Make these sentences more emphatic by using a prepositional pronoun.

—No te gusta bailar.   —A ti no te gusta bailar.

1. Le gusta el jugo.
2. Me gusta comer.
3. Les gusta la ensalada.
4. Te gustan los postres.

5. No nos gusta la cebolla.
6. No les gustan las verduras.
7. No nos gusta dejar propina.
8. Te gustan los helados.

9. Le gusta el pan con mantequilla.
10. Me gustan los postres.
11. No me gusta la cebolla.
12. No les gusta el arroz.

A 15 SE DICE ASÍ
Saying what you like and don't like

	¿Qué te gusta a ti y qué no?	A mí me gustan las enchiladas. A mí no me gusta el mole.
	¿Qué les gusta a ustedes y qué no?	A nosotros nos gustan los postres. A nosotros no nos gusta la fruta.

A 16 Actividad • Charla

Get together with two or three classmates, talk about what foods you like and don't like. The list of foods in the last column of A13 may jog your memory. Report to the class who likes what, and who dislikes what.

—A mí me gusta la cebolla. ¿Y a ustedes?   —Sí, a nosotros nos gusta también.

A 17 Actividad • ¡A escribir!

Write two lists of the foods in A13—those you like and those you don't. Compare your likes and dislikes with those of your friends.

—A mí me gusta(n) . . . y a mis amigos les gusta(n) . . . también.
—A mí me gusta(n) . . . pero a mis amigos no les gusta(n) . . . .

A 18 Actividad • ¿Y en tu casa?

Pair up with a partner and ask each other the following.

¿Qué comen en tu casa?
¿Qué comida(s) le(s) gusta(n) . .

. . . a tu papá?
. . . a tu mamá?
. . . a tus hermanos?
. . . a tus hermanas?
. . . a ti?

sopa hamburguesas verduras pollo
queso helados postre
bocadillos pan con mantequilla
arroz carne

A 19 Actividad • ¡A escribir!

¿Les gusta o no? Write down the conversation you had with your partner. Talk about what you eat at home and your family's likes and dislikes about food.

A 20 ¿Sabes que . . . ?

Dishes like **arroz con pollo,** *chicken with rice,* are served in most Spanish-speaking countries. But many countries have a special dish. In Spain, for example, some people have **chocolate y churros** (doughnut-like pastries with no hole) for breakfast or snacks. **Paella,** associated with the city of Valencia, is another famous Spanish dish: it consists of a large platter of seafood, chicken, and saffron-colored (yellow) rice. **Tacos** (folded and filled corn tortillas) and **enchiladas** (rolled tortillas filled with meat or cheese, fried, and served with a chile sauce) are two of the scores of foods for which Mexico is famous. Sometimes foods are the same, but the names are different—potatoes, for example, are **patatas** in Spain and **papas** in the Americas. The vocabulary of food in Spanish is large. If you'd like to learn even half the words, get ready for a lifetime of good eating!

A 21 Comprensión

Food, meals, and restaurants . . . do they like it or not?

	0	1	2	3	4	5	6	7	8	9	10
Le(s) gusta(n)											
No le(s) gusta(n)	✔										

Actividad • ¡A escoger!

The waiter is talking to you. Choose the appropriate response.

1. ¿Qué desean ustedes?
• No me gusta la cebolla.   • Chile con carne, por favor.
2. Hay enchiladas de queso y de carne.
• Dos de queso.   • No me gustan las verduras.
3. El plato del día es pollo.
• La sopa no me gusta.   • Bueno, y para beber un refresco.
4. ¿Y de postre?
• Pollo con salsa.   • Helado de chocolate.
5. ¿Más café?
• Un poco, por favor.   • Me gusta el café.
6. ¿Algo más?
• No, gracias. La cuenta, por favor.   • La propina.
7. La cuenta, señores.
• No me gusta.   • Gracias.
8. Gracias, buenas noches.
• ¿Tienen chile con carne?   • Buenas noches.

A23 **Actividad • El restaurante**

To create the atmosphere of a restaurant, write out a menu in Spanish, make out a bill, and bring props from home if you can. Work with two of your classmates. Two of you will be the customers at a restaurant. The other one will be the waiter or waitress. Add your own ideas to the following.

The customers:

• Enter the restaurant and ask for a table.
• Ask for the menu.

• Listen to the specials, decide what to have, and order their food.
• Eat. Make comments about the food. Call the waiter or waitress to order dessert. Ask for the bill.
• Look at the bill. Discuss how much tip to leave. Say good night and leave.

The waiter or waitress:

• Seats the customers.
• Brings the menu, and says what the specials of the day are.
• Takes their order. Asks what they want to drink.
• Brings dessert and the bill.

• Thanks the customers, and says good night.

A24 **Actividad • ¡A escribir!**

Write your restaurant scene in dialog form.

Picnics are great fun and are popular in Spanish-speaking countries. La tortilla, Spanish omelette, is a favorite dish since it is good hot or cold.

B1 Un picnic

ELENA ¿Qué haces?
CARLOS Preparo una tortilla para el picnic.
ELENA ¡Estupendo! A todos nos gusta la tortilla. Es muy rica. ¿Te ayudo?
CARLOS ¿Por qué no cortas estas patatas y esas cebollas en trozos pequeños? Después voy a freír todo.
ELENA Bueno, a lo dicho, hecho. ¡Ay!
CARLOS ¿Por qué lloras, Elena?
ELENA ¡Son las cebollas por supuesto! Y ahora, ¿qué?

CARLOS Ahora bato los huevos, añado las patatas y las cebollas y cocino todo en esta misma sartén. Tiene que dorarse de los dos lados. ¡Y aquí está nuestra tortilla!
ELENA ¡Ay, qué hambre tengo!

B2 Actividad • ¿Es cierto o no?

Say whether the following statements are correct or not according to B1.
Correct the statements that aren't true.

1. La tortilla es para un picnic.
2. Carlos va a hacer enchiladas.
3. A Elena no le gusta la tortilla.
4. Elena corta la fruta.

5. Carlos va a freír todo en una sartén.
6. Él bate las patatas y añade los huevos.
7. ¡Aquí está nuestra cocina!
8. Elena no tiene hambre.

Miguel compra las frutas. Va a aquella frutería grande de la esquina.

Alicia hace bocadillos de jamón y queso, de pollo y de atún. ¡Qué sabrosos!

Sofía compra pasteles en una pastelería muy buena.

Manuel trae los refrescos.

¡Buen provecho! 247

Preguntas y respuestas

Answer in complete sentences. Base your answers on B3.

1. ¿Qué compra Miguel? ¿Dónde?
2. ¿Qué más hay allí?
3. ¿Qué prepara Alicia? ¿De qué son?
   ¿Cómo son?
4. ¿Qué compra Sofía? ¿Dónde?

5. ¿Sabes qué lleva ella al picnic?
6. ¿Y Manuel, qué lleva?
7. ¿Dónde tiene él todo?
8. ¿Cómo va a ser el picnic?

B5 ESTRUCTURAS ESENCIALES
The verb hacer, *to do, to make*

hacer *to do, to make*			
Hago	un postre.	**¿Hacemos**	un picnic?
¿Haces	bocadillos?	**¿Hacéis**	la comida?
Hace	un flan.	**Hacen**	la tortilla.

The present-tense forms of **hacer** are all regular except the **yo** form: **hago.**

The verb **hacer** is equivalent to two English verbs: *to do,* and *to make.*

—María, ¿qué **haces**?
—**Hago** la tarea.

—María, what are you doing?
—I'm doing homework.

—Enrique, ¿qué **haces**?
—**Hago** una tortilla de patatas.

—Enrique, what are you making?
—I'm making a potato omelet.

B6 Actividad • ¿Qué hacen?

Everybody has to make something for the picnic. Supply the missing forms of
hacer to complete the conversation.

1. Carlos Y Elena _____ una tortilla.
2. Alicia _____ bocadillos.
3. ¿ _____ ustedes un pollo?

4. No, nosotros _____ una
   ensalada.
5. ¿Qué _____ tú?

6. Yo _____ un flan.
7. Y yo, ¿qué _____ ?
8. Tú puedes _____ una tarta.

B7 Actividad • ¿Quién lo hace?

Using forms of **hacer,** say who makes what for the family picnic.

—¿La ensalada? —Celia y Raúl.
—Ellos hacen la ensalada.

—¿El pollo? —Mamá.
—¿La tortilla? —Carlos y yo.
—¿Los bocadillos? —Tú.

—¿La tarta? —Yo.
—¿El flan? —Alicia y tú.
—¿La ensalada? —Celia y Raúl.

—¿El arroz? —Pedro.
—¿Los pasteles? —Ramón
   y yo.

B8 Actividad • Charla

Plan a picnic with two or three classmates. Discuss a good place, date, and time.
Make up a shopping list and decide who should do what. Then report your plans
to your classmates.

B9 Actividad • ¡A escribir!

Nuestro picnic. Write down the plans that you and your classmates made for a picnic in B8.

B10 ESTRUCTURAS ESENCIALES
Demonstrative adjectives

		Singular		Plural	
this/these	Masculine	**este**	chico	**estos**	chicos
	Feminine	**esta**	chica	**estas**	chicas
that/those	Masculine	**ese**	chico	**esos**	chicos
	Feminine	**esa**	chica	**esas**	chicas
	Masculine	**aquel**	chico	**aquellos**	chicos
	Feminine	**aquella**	chica	**aquellas**	chicas

1. Demonstrative adjectives are usually placed before the noun they modify. Like other adjectives in Spanish, they agree in gender and number with the noun.

2. Demonstrative adjectives point out people and things. The **este** forms correspond to the English *this, these.* The **ese** and **aquel** forms correspond to *that, those.* The difference is that **aquel** suggests greater distance from both speaker and listener than does **ese.**

B11 Actividad • En la frutería

Work with a classmate. One of you is the customer; the other is the clerk at a fruit stand. Tell the clerk you want a kilo of the various fruits you point to. The clerk will show you the fruit to make sure it is what you want. Switch roles.

las uvas   —Un kilo de esas uvas, por favor.
          —¿Estas uvas?

1. las manzanas
2. las fresas
3. los limones
4. los tomates
5. los plátanos
6. los melocotones
7. las cerezas
8. las naranjas

B12 Actividad • En el restaurante

Tell the waiter where you would like to sit. Use an appropriate form of **aquel.**

entrada   —Cerca de aquella entrada, por favor.

1. puerta
2. mesa
3. señoritas
4. señor
5. chicos
6. chicas

Who is preparing a picnic?

	0	1	2	3	4	5	6	7	8	9	10
Sí	✔										
No											

B 14 ¿Sabes que . . . ?

Kilos y litros. The metric system is used in Spanish-speaking countries to measure weight and volume. A 150-pound track star weighs 68 **kilos**—a kilo is 2.2 pounds. Potatoes, meat, and other items are bought by the kilo. Smaller amounts are measured in **gramos;** 1000 grams equal 1 kilo, and 28.3 grams equal 1 ounce.

Milk, water, wine, and other liquids, including gasoline, are all measured in **litros.** A liter is slightly larger than a quart. Cookbook recipes specify small amounts in **cucharadas y cucharaditas,** *tablespoons and teaspoons.*

B 15 SE DICE ASÍ
Selecting what you like

—(Señor, quiero) Este bizcocho, por favor.	
¿Quiere . . . ?	Sí, gracias Sí, y también . . . No, gracias. No, . . . esa No, mejor esos . . .

B 16 Actividad • Charla

Work with a partner. Take turns playing customer and vendor. Pick five of the items listed below. The vendor makes suggestions about what items to buy. The customer selects what he or she wants. Use as many of the expressions in B15 as possible.

—¿Quieres estas manzanas?

—Sí, y también . . .
—No, mejor esas naranjas.

tomates   jugo   manzanas   naranjas   fresas   tarta
postre   pan   jalea   patatas   bizcocho   bocadillo
verduras   refrescos   pasteles   huevos

B 17 Actividad • ¡A escribir!

Write a dialog based on the suggestions from your classmate, and the selections you made in B16.

B 18 Actividad • La frutería

Work with a partner. One of you is the vendor, and the other is the customer. The vendor makes suggestions, using **este, estos, esta, estas.** The customer indicates another choice using **ese, esos, esa,** or **esas.** Then switch roles.

—¿Quiere / plátanos?   —No, quiero / melocotones.
—¿Quiere estos plátanos?   —No, quiero esos melocotones.

1. —¿Lleva / melón?   —No, / sandía, por favor.
2. —¿Le gustan / naranjas?   —No, quiero / plátanos.
3. —¿Compra / piña?   —No, mejor / cerezas.
4. —¿Le gustan / manzanas?   —No, llevo / plátanos.
5. —¿Quiere / uvas?   —No, quiero / melones.
6. —¿Va a llevar / peras?   —No, / melocotones, por favor.
7. —¿Lleva / pastel de fresa?   —No, voy a llevar / bizcocho.
8. —¿Quiere / tarta?   —No, mejor / pasteles.

B 19 Actividad • ¿Quieres frutas?

Now the vendor asks the questions in B18 again, this time using **ese, esos, esa,** and **esas.** The customer answers using **aquel, aquella, aquellos,** and **aquellas.**

—¿Quiere / plátanos?   —No, quiero / melocotones.
—¿Quieres esos plátanos?   —No, quiero aquellos melocotones.

B 20 ¿Sabes que . . . ?

Mexican tortillas are flat corncakes used instead of bread. In Spain, a tortilla is an omelette. Potatoes and onions are thinly sliced and cooked in oil. When tender, the potatoes are drained and added to a bowl of beaten eggs, which are then cooked, completing the tortilla.

B 21 Actividad • ¿Qué compramos?

Work with one or two of your classmates. You are at the store getting food for a picnic. Discuss what to buy. Then report to the class what food you're buying.

—¿Compramos este melón o aquellos
   plátanos?
—Mejor, esas naranjas.
—¿Por qué no llevamos esos pasteles de
   manzana?
—Bueno, compramos los pasteles.

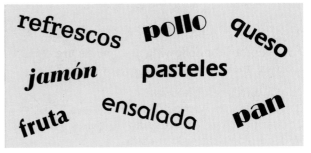

saying you're hungry or thirsty . . . asking for what you need at the table . . . expressing your enjoyment of food.

Once you've shopped for the ingredients and made your picnic food, it's time to have the picnic. Is anybody hungry or thirsty?

C1   Y por fin, ¡el picnic! 📼

MIGUEL   La sal, por favor. ¡Esta tortilla está perfecta! Pero, ¿dónde está Manuel con los refrescos? Tengo mucha sed.

ELENA   ¡Paciencia! Comes por tres, ¿sabes? ¡Ah, aquí viene!

MANUEL   ¡Hola! ¡Cuánto tráfico! ¿Pongo la mesa? ¿Dónde van los refrescos?

ELENA   La mesa ya está.

MIGUEL   Los refrescos, aquí, por favor, a mi lado.

ELENA   No, a tu lado, no. Miguel, ¿por qué no pones los refrescos debajo de ese árbol?

ALICIA   Debes tener hambre, Manuel. ¿Quieres un bocadillo? ¿De queso o de jamón?

MANUEL   De jamón, por favor. . . . ¡Qué rico está! Gracias, Alicia.

CARLOS   Este picnic necesita música. Miguel, ¿por qué no pones este casete? ¿Quieres bailar, Alicia?

ALICIA   ¡Cómo no! Es mi canción favorita.

MIGUEL   Buena idea. Vamos, Elena. Si bailas conmigo, no como más.

ELENA   ¡No hay más remedio! Vamos, Miguel.

C2   Actividad • ¿Es cierto o no? 📼

Say whether the following statements are correct or not according to C1.
Correct the statements that aren't true.

1. ¡La tortilla está horrible!
2. ¿Dónde está Manuel? Tiene los bocadillos.
3. Manuel come un bocadillo de queso.
4. Este picnic necesita música.

5. A Alicia no le gusta la canción.
6. A Miguel no le gusta bailar.
7. Miguel va a bailar con Alicia.

C3 Preguntas y respuestas

Answer the following questions about C1.

1. ¿Le gusta a Miguel la tortilla? ¿Cómo sabes?
2. ¿Por qué espera Miguel a Manuel?
3. ¿Por qué llega tarde Manuel?
4. ¿Dónde ponen la comida? ¿Y los refrescos?

5. ¿Qué come Manuel? ¿Le gusta? ¿Cómo sabes?
6. ¿Qué necesita el picnic?
7. ¿Quiere bailar Alicia? ¿Por qué?
8. ¿Con quién baila Alicia? ¿Y Elena?

C4 SE DICE ASÍ
Talking about whether people are hungry or thirsty

¿Tienes sed, Miguel?	Sí, tengo mucha sed.
Are you thirsty, Miguel?	Yes, I'm very thirsty.
Elena no tiene hambre ahora.	Yo, sí. Tengo mucha hambre.
Elena is not hungry now.	I am. I'm very hungry.

C5 Actividad • Charla

With a classmate, discuss whether you are hungry or thirsty, where you want to go, and what you want to eat.

—¿Tienes hambre, Carmela?

Sí, tengo mucha hambre.

¿Comemos un bocadillo en este café?

No, mejor vamos al café Valencia. Tienen unas tartas deliciosas.

C6 Actividad • ¡A escribir!

Write a dialog of at least four exchanges based on the Charla in C5.

C7 ¿Sabes que . . . ?

Chocolate is an extract from the seeds of the cacao tree. When Columbus discovered the New World in 1492, he also found cacao growing there, but the importance of the plant wasn't immediately recognized.

In 1519, when Hernán Cortés began the Conquest of Mexico, he learned that the Aztec Emperor, Moctezuma, and the nobles of his court were very fond of drinking chocolate. These Spanish explorers brought the drink back to Spain, where it became very popular. It was so highly prized that Spanish officials kept the recipe a secret for a hundred years.

¡Buen provecho!   253

poner *to place, to put*			
¿Pongo	la comida allí?	**¿Ponemos**	los huevos en la sartén?
¿Pones	un casete?	**Ponéis**	todo debajo del árbol.
Pone	música.	**Ponen**	los refrescos en el coche.

The present-tense forms of **poner** are regular except the **yo** form: **pongo.** The expression **poner la mesa** means *to set the table.* However, when you put something on the table, you say: **poner en la mesa.**

C9 Actividad • Combinación

¿Qué ponen en la mesa? Form sentences using an item from each box. Add the appropriate form of **poner** and **en la mesa** to all your sentences.

—Ella pone las manzanas en la mesa.

Tú		**Felipe y yo**
Papá	**Ella**	**Mamá**
Manuel y Elena		**Yo**
Nosotros		**Ustedes**

los bocadillos	**los pasteles**
la fruta	**el agua**
los refrescos	**las manzanas**
la tortilla	**la sal** **el pan**

C10 Actividad • ¿Quién pone la mesa?

Who's setting the table? Complete this conversation using appropriate forms of **poner.**

1. Yo no ____ la mesa. ¿ ____ tú la mesa?
2. No, Julián y Elvira ____ la mesa.
3. ¿Nosotros? ¡No! Nosotros no ____ la mesa. Mejor, ustedes ____ la mesa.
4. ¿Por qué no ____ tú la mesa?

5. ¿Y Daniel? No, él no ____ la mesa. A él no le gusta ____ la mesa.
6. ¿Quién? ¿Yo? ¡Nunca! Yo no voy a ____ la mesa. Los chicos ____ la mesa.

C11 Actividad • ¿Dónde ponemos la comida?

You are organizing a picnic. Help place the food everybody is bringing in the right place. Answer your friends' questions using as many expressions as you can from the list on the right.

¿Dónde pongo . . .

los refrescos	**los bocadillos**
el queso	**el jamón**
la lechuga	**el tomate**
el pan	**la fruta**
las tartas . . . ?	

delante de   arriba de   a la izquierda de
allí
detrás de   debajo de   detrás de   aquí
entre   a la derecha de   al lado de

Para el desayuno pongo:

vaso para el jugo, platillo para el pan y la mantequilla

plato hondo para el cereal, cuchara y servilleta

taza con platillo, y cucharita para el azúcar

Para el almuerzo ponemos:

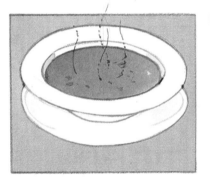

plato hondo para la sopa

platillo para el bocadillo y servilleta

sal, pimienta, mostaza y catsup

Para la comida o para la cena ellos ponen:

platillo para la ensalada, plato llano para la comida

tenedor, cuchillo, dos cucharitas, servilleta

vaso para el agua y platillo para el postre

Actividad • Combinación

Match items in the two boxes.

—Por favor, necesitamos una taza para el té.

Por favor, necesitamos . . .		**para . . .**	
un cuchillo	un plato llano	*la sopa.*	*la leche.*
una cuchara	un vaso	*la tortilla.*	*la carne.*
un tenedor	un platillo	*el cereal.*	*el azúcar.*
una taza	una cucharita	*el postre.*	*la ensalada.*
un plato hondo		*el té.*	

C14 Actividad • ¡A escoger!

Choose the food for which the dish or flatware makes most sense.

1. **Plato hondo** • sopa • ensalada • bocadillo
2. **Vaso** • pollo • jugo • ensalada
3. **Tenedor** • sopa • helado • carne
4. **Cuchillo** • carne • cereal • huevos
5. **Platillo** • jugo • ensalada • agua
6. **Cucharita** • bocadillos • tortilla • postre
7. **Plato llano** • carne • cereal • sopa
8. **Taza** • pollo • tortilla • chocolate

C15 Actividad • ¡Camarero, por favor!

The service at the restaurant is absolutely terrible! All the customers are complaining. Complete the sentences with the names of the missing objects.

—Tengo el jugo, pero no tengo _____ .
—¿Cómo como la sopa? Necesito una _____ .
—Aquí hay dos tenedores, pero no hay _____ para la carne.
—Y mi _____ de leche, ¿dónde está?
—¡Por favor! No puedo comer el pollo con una _____ de sopa.
—¿Cómo pongo el azúcar en el té? No tengo _____ .
—Sí, tengo la leche, pero, ¿dónde está el _____ para el cereal?
—Me gusta la taza, es muy bonita. ¡Qué pena! No tiene _____ .
—¿Con qué corto la carne? ¿Con la _____ ?

C16 Actividad • Charla

Work with a partner. One of you is a customer; the other is a waiter or waitress. Practice making some of your own complaints at the restaurant referred to in C15. Switch roles. Repeat your complaints for your classmates.

C17 Actividad • ¡A escribir!

Lista de quejas. Prepare a list of all the complaints you had in C16.

C18 Actividad • Falta algo

Supply the missing forms of the verb **poner.**

1. Ellos / la mesa.
2. Yo / el tenedor a la izquierda del plato.
3. Carlos quiere / la mesa.
4. Tú / los platos.

5. ¿Dónde / yo el vaso?
6. Ustedes no / las servilletas en la mesa.
7. Tú y yo / los vasos.
8. ¿ / usted la cucharita al lado del cuchillo?

 C19 Comprensión

What do they need?

	0	1	2	3	4	5	6	7	8	9	10
cuchillo	✔										
cuchara											
tenedor											
cucharita											

 C20 SE DICE ASÍ
Expressing your enjoyment of food

> ¡Esta sopa está muy sabrosa!
> ¡Estos bocadillos están muy buenos!
> ¡Estas uvas están muy ricas!
> ¡Este bizcocho está delicioso!
> ¡Estos pasteles están exquisitos!
> ¡Qué buenos están estos bocadillos!

Use adjectives like **sabroso** or **exquisito** to express how much you like particular dishes. Make sure your adjective agrees with the noun it modifies.

 C21 Actividad • Reacciones

You are eating with some Spanish-speaking friends. Compliment the hostess when she asks your opinion about the food.

¿La sopa? (buenísimo)   —Esta sopa está buenísima.

1. ¿La sopa?   (delicioso)
2. ¿El pollo?   (rico)
3. ¿La salsa?   (buenísimo)
4. ¿La carne?   (sabroso)
5. ¿La ensalada? (muy rico)
6. ¿Los helados? (fantástico)
7. ¿La tortilla? (sabroso)
8. ¿El flan?   (delicioso)
9. ¿El postre?   (muy bueno)
10. ¿Los plátanos? (muy rico)

¡Buen provecho! 257

Actividad • ¡Vamos a comer!

Work with a partner. You're going to have a meal together. Decide what meal you're going to have (breakfast, lunch, or dinner), at what time, and where. Make a shopping list for everything you need for your meal. You'll find some suggestions below.

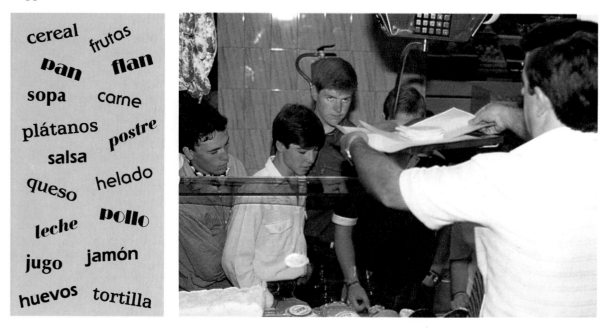

cereal frutas pan flan sopa carne plátanos postre salsa queso helado leche pollo jugo jamón huevos tortilla

C23 Actividad • ¿A cuánto están? *How much are they?*

You and your classmate go shopping together. Prepare a shopping list using some of the items in C22. Talk about what to buy. Follow the model replacing the underlined words with items from your shopping list. Add your own ideas.

—¿A cuánto están <u>estos plátanos</u>?

—¿Llevamos <u>este queso o esa salsa</u>?

—<u>Ese pescado</u> parece muy bueno.

—¡Mira <u>aquellos postres</u>! Parecen <u>deliciosos.</u>

C24 Actividad • La comida

Together with your partner, talk to your classmates about the meal you're planning and the food you bought. Talk about how much you like the different foods. If you don't like one of the foods, say what you think of it.

C25 Actividad • ¡A escribir!

Una comida buenísima. Write down the shopping list you made with your classmate in C22. Then write the conversation you had when you went shopping together. You can substitute items and include comments from the vendor at the food store also.

1 ¿Dónde comemos? 📼

Before going to the movies with a friend, you might want to eat something first.
Where would you like to go?

RICARDO Alicia, la película no empieza hasta las nueve y yo tengo hambre ahora.

ALICIA ¿Quieres ir a la cafetería a ver que tienen hoy?

RICARDO Ya sabes, siempre el mismo menú: bocadillos, hamburguesas, ensaladas.

ALICIA ¿Por qué no vamos mejor a un restaurante?

RICARDO ¡Buena idea! A mí me gusta mucho la comida mexicana, ¿y a ti?

ALICIA A mí también. Conozco un lugar donde hacen unas enchiladas deliciosas, y no está lejos de aquí.

RICARDO ¡Fantástico! Pero no tengo mucho dinero.

ALICIA Yo tengo bastante. Esta vez pago yo, tú pagas otro día.

RICARDO De acuerdo. Vamos entonces.

2 Preguntas y respuestas

Answer the questions according to ¿Dónde comemos?

1. ¿Qué van a hacer Ricardo y Alicia a las nueve?
2. ¿Por qué quiere ir a comer Ricardo?
3. ¿Qué comida tienen en la cafetería?
4. ¿Qué lugar conoce Alicia?
   ¿Qué comida hacen allí?
5. ¿Está el restaurante lejos?
6. ¿Qué problema tiene Ricardo?
7. ¿Quién va a pagar? ¿Por qué?
8. ¿Van a salir los chicos otro día?
   ¿Cómo sabes?

Actividad • ¿Qué vamos a comer hoy?

• Plan a breakfast and a supper, either just for yourself or for you and one friend or more. In Spanish, write out the menu for each meal. You can use some of the dishes from Skills 4 in your plan.
• Now make up a shopping list in Spanish of the things you need for the two meals.
• Tell the class what was on your shopping list and what you planned for each meal.

4 Actividad • ¿Qué pedimos? *What do we order?*

Four of your friends are going to have lunch in a restaurant. Josefina, who likes chicken, wants to try Mexican food. Blanca is dieting. Rafael, a vegetarian, won't eat meat, not even chicken. Manuel is hungry and likes everything. Order a meal for each of them.

pescado *hamburguesas* *jugos* *ensalada* *pollo con cebollas* *bizcocho* *tarta de manzanas* *flan* *helado* *arroz* *bistec* *frijoles* *gaseosas* *enchiladas* *papas fritas* *pasteles* *refrescos* *chile con carne* *fruta* *sopa de verduras*

5 Actividad • Charla

With a classmate, ask and answer these questions.

1. ¿Te gusta comer en restaurantes o te gusta más comer en casa?
2. ¿Tienes un restaurante favorito? ¿Cuál es? ¿Por qué te gusta?
3. ¿Te gusta la comida mexicana?
4. ¿Cuál es tu comida favorita?
5. ¿Qué comes en el desayuno?
6. ¿Y en el almuerzo?

6 Actividad • Una comida revuelta *Scrambled meal*

Change words and expressions in the following dialog so that it makes sense.

CAMARERO   ¡Buenas noches, señores!
CLIENTE 1   Una cocina para tres, por favor.
CAMARERO   ¡Bien, aquí está la cuenta!
CLIENTE 2   ¿Cuál es la cuchara del día?
CAMARERO   Arroz con tenedores.
CLIENTE 1   ¡Ay! No me gusta el arroz. Una sartén con cebolla, por favor.
CAMARERO   ¿Y de beber, señora?
CLIENTE 2   Tengo sed. Tomates, por favor.
CLIENTE 3   No tengo servilleta para cortar la carne. Una servilleta, por favor.
CAMARERO   Bien, vuelvo enseguida.

(El camarero vuelve con la comida y los clientes bailan.)

CAMARERO   ¡De postre tenemos una propina fantástica!
CLIENTE 1   No, gracias, para mí té con verduras.
CLIENTE 2   Para mí, café.
CLIENTE 3   Es todo, ¡la mesa por favor!

7 Actividad • Vamos a comer bien *Let's eat right*

After correcting the dialog in Activity 6, practice with three classmates and then present it to the class.

8 Actividad • Una clase de cocina

The following are the responses given by four students. They were asked to talk briefly about their recipes and skills. One of them attends a cooking class. Can you tell which one?

Me llamo Alicia Martínez. A mí me gustan las sopas. Creo que una buena sopa debe tener de todo. Yo sé hacer una sopa de carne y tomates buenísima. Saber cocinar bien es muy importante.

Soy Ramón Ballesteros. Una persona que no sabe hacer postres, no sabe cocinar. Para hacer mi postre favorito, pongo tres huevos y una taza de azúcar en un plato grande. Añado mostaza y una cebolla cortada.

Mucho gusto, Concepción Vázquez. A mí no me gusta cocinar. Me gusta poner la mesa. La presentación artística de la comida es muy importante. Siempre uso platos y vasos elegantes. Comer con servilletas feas es horrible.

Si a ustedes les gusta mucho comer, cenar tarde no es bueno. A mí me gusta una cena ligera: un trozo grande de carne con cuatro o cinco papas, un plato de arroz . . . postre. Tengo hambre. Me llamo Félix Villa. Gracias.

9 Pronunciación, lectura, dictado

1. Listen carefully and repeat what you hear.

2. The sound of the Spanish consonant **r**. Listen, and then read aloud.

> servilleta tenedor por favor charlar remedio
> propina postre fruta pregunta arriba

> Ricardo, vas a necesitar una sartén más grande para freír esos huevos.
> Vamos a preparar una tortilla para el almuerzo del martes.

3. Copy the following sentences to prepare yourself to write them from dictation.
> Por favor, ¿nos puede comprar tres refrescos de naranja?
> Creo que te va a gustar ese postre de frutas.
> El arroz en este restaurante es muy rico.
> Hace mucho calor para tomar chocolate con churros.

¿LO SABES?

Let's review some important points you have learned in this unit.

When you are in a Spanish restaurant, can you order food at different times of the day?
Order in Spanish something you might want for breakfast, something for lunch, and something for dinner.

Do you know how to talk about the foods you like and dislike?
Using **A mí me gusta(n)** and **A mí no me gusta(n),** mention five types of food you like and five you don't.

Can you say what you would like to have for breakfast, lunch, and dinner and what your friends and family would like (or wouldn't like) to have for each meal if you were in a Spanish country?
First, make a list of the different types of food you have for each meal, then say who likes them and who doesn't.

Can you talk to a friend who is organizing a picnic and find out information about it?
Write down five questions you might ask.

When organizing a picnic, can you say how you're going to contribute?
Make five sentences talking about what you are bringing and the steps that you'll follow to get it.

Can you choose items at the food store, fruit stand, or pastry shop?
Write down five of your selections, using forms of **este** or **ese.**

Are you able to tell the store clerk what you really want?
Answer these suggestions with **no,** and indicate what you want instead.

¿Esas peras?   ¿Esta piña?   ¿Esas uvas?
¿Estos melocotones?   ¿Esta tarta?   ¿Ese bizcocho?

When you are in a Spanish-speaking environment and you want a glass of water and something to eat, what would you say?
Make up four sentences.

Do you know how to ask in Spanish for something you need at the table?
Ask for:

a cup   a knife   a napkin   a glass   a fork
a small plate   a dish   a spoon   a small spoon

Can you complain in Spanish about the food or the service?
Write down five complaints you might have.

Do you know different ways to say how much you like the food?
You are having a meal with a Spanish-speaking family. What would you say about . . .

la sopa   el arroz   el flan   la carne   las verduras   la tarta

VOCABULARIO

SECTION A

a dieta   *on a diet*
el agua (f.)   *water*
el arroz   *rice*
el bistec   *beefsteak*
el bocadillo   *snack; sandwich*
¡Buen provecho!   *Enjoy it!*
el café   *coffee*
la camarera   *waitress*
el camarero   *waiter*
el Caribe   *Caribbean*
la carne   *meat*
la cebolla   *onion*
la cena   *dinner, supper*
cenar   *to have dinner*
la cocina   *cooking, cuisine*
la comida   *food; meal; dinner*
completo, -a   *complete*
¿cuánto?   *how much?*
la cuenta   *bill, check*
el chile con carne   *dish of beans, ground beef, and chilies*
el chocolate   *chocolate*
dejar   *to leave (behind)*
desayuno   *breakfast*
desear   *to like, want*
encantar   *to delight*
la enchilada   *rolled tortilla filled with meat or cheese*
la ensalada   *salad*
la especialidad   *specialty*
el flan   *baked custard*
los frijoles   *beans*
la fruta   *fruit*
la guía   *guidebook*
gustar   *to like*
les gusta(n)   *you (they) like*
nos gusta(n)   *we like*
la hamburguesa   *hamburger*
la jalea   *jelly*
el jamón   *ham*
el jugo   *juice*
la leche   *milk*
la lechuga   *lettuce*
les   *you (pl.), them*
ligero, -a   *light (meal)*
el limón   *lemon*
la mantequilla   *butter*
la mayonesa   *mayonnaise*
el mediodía   *noon*
lo mejor   *the best (thing)*
el menú   *menu*
la merienda   *snack, light meal in the afternoon*
la mermelada   *marmalade*
la mesa   *table*
mí   *me*

el mole   *spicy chocolate sauce*
ni   *neither, nor*
nos   *us*
pagar   *to pay*
el pan   *bread*
las papas fritas   *french fries*
el pescado   *fish*
el peso   *monetary unit of Mexico, Bolivia, Chile*
el plato del día   *specialty of the day*
el pollo   *chicken*
el postre   *dessert*
de postre   *for dessert*
principal   *main*
probar   *to try*
la propina   *tip*
el queso   *cheese*
el restaurante   *restaurant*
rosa   *pink*
la salsa   *sauce*
sobre   *about*
la sopa   *soup*
te   *you*
el té   *tea*
ti   *you*
típico, -a   *typical*
el tomate   *tomato*
la tortilla   *omelette*
turístico, -a   *touristic*
el vaso   *glass*
la verdura   *green vegetable*

SECTION B

a lo dicho, hecho   *no sooner said than done*
añadir   *to add*
aquel, aquella   *that*
aquellos, -as   *those*
el atún   *tuna*
ayudar   *to help*
batir   *to beat*
el bizcocho   *cake*
buenísimo, -a   *very good*
la cereza   *cherry*
cocinar   *to cook*
cortar   *to cut*
delicioso, -a   *delicious*
dorarse   *to brown*
ese, -a   *that*
esos, -as   *those*
este, -a   *this*
estos, -as   *these*
freír   *to fry*
la fresa   *strawberry*
la frutería   *fruit store*

la gaseosa   *soda*
hacer   *to do, make*
el huevo   *egg*
el kilo   *kilogram (2.2 pounds)*
el lado   *side*
llevar   *to take*
llorar   *to cry*
la manzana   *apple*
el melocotón   *peach*
el melón   *melon*
mismo, -a   *same*
la naranja   *orange*
parecer   *to seem*
el pastel   *pie; cake*
la pastelería   *pastry; pastry shop*
la patata   *potato (Spain)*
la pera   *pear*
la piña   *pineapple*
el plátano   *banana; plantain*
preparar   *to prepare*
rico, -a   *tasty, delicious (food)*
sabroso, -a   *tasty, delicious*
la sandía   *watermelon*
la sartén   *frying pan*
la tarta   *tart, pastry*
trae   *brings*
el trozo   *piece*
la uva   *grape*

SECTION C

el árbol   *tree*
el azúcar   *sugar*
la canción   *song*
cómo no   *of course*
conmigo   *with me*
la cuchara   *spoon*
la cucharita   *teaspoon*
el cuchillo   *knife*
debajo (de)   *under*
la mostaza   *mustard*
no hay más remedio   *it can't be helped*
la paciencia   *patience*
la pimienta   *pepper*
el platillo   *saucer, small plate*
el plato   *dish, plate*
el plato hondo   *soup dish*
el plato llano   *dinner dish*
poner   *to put*
poner la mesa   *to set the table*
la sal   *salt*
la servilleta   *napkin*
la taza   *cup*
el tenedor   *fork*
tener (mucha) sed   *to be (very) thirsty*

VAMOS A LEER

Antes de leer

Try to read the recipe without looking at the glossary. Remember, many quick readings will improve your reading skills, vocabulary mastery, and enjoyment more than one painstaking reading during which you look up every word you are not sure of.

Tortilla de patatas a la española *(para 6 personas)*

8 huevos
2 cebollas
1 kg. de patatas

2 tazas de aceite°
(½ litro)
sal

Pelar° las patatas, lavarlas° y cortarlas fino°. Cortar las cebollas en trozos pequeños. Calentar° el aceite y freír las patatas y las cebollas; moverlas° y echarles° un poco de sal. Una vez fritas°, poner en un colador y quitar° el aceite de la sartén. Batir los huevos con un poco de sal, echar las patatas y las cebollas en el mismo plato de los huevos y moverlas con un tenedor. En una sartén grande poner 3 cucharadas de aceite. Calentar el aceite y añadir los huevos con las patatas y cebollas.

Mover la sartén para que no se pegue° la tortilla. Cuando se dore° bien, voltearla° en un plato y cocinar del otro lado. Servir° fría o caliente.

Actividad • No es así

Change the following statements so they agree with the **tortilla** recipe.

1. Poner el agua en la sartén a calentar.
2. Echar un poco de azúcar a las patatas.
3. Echar las patatas y cebollas en la misma taza de los huevos.
4. Batir los huevos con un cuchillo.

5. Añadir la sal al aceite cuando está frío.
6. Cuando la tortilla se dore, voltearla en una cuchara.

Actividad • La tortilla de patatas

Are you a good cook? Do you want to follow the recipe and make your own **tortilla?** Make it and share it with your friends. Good luck!

---

aceite *oil*   **pelar** *to peel*   **lavarlas** *wash (them)*   **cortarlas fino** *cut (them) into thin slices*   **calentar** *to heat*
moverlas *stir (them)*   **echarles** *add to them*   **fritas** *fried*   **quitar** *remove*   **pegue** *stick*   **se dore** *it turns brown*
voltearla *turn it over*   **servir** *serve*

De compras°

Before making the **tortilla,** you have to shop for the ingredients. Check the prices first, so you don't pay more than you should.

SEÑORA	¿A cuánto están las cebollas hoy?
VENDEDOR	A cuarenta pesos la libra, señora.
SEÑORA	¿Cómo? En la Calle Ocho las venden a treinta y cinco la libra.
VENDEDOR	Entonces, señora, ¿por qué no las compra allí?
SEÑORA	Es que allí no tienen más cebollas hoy.
VENDEDOR	Pues, señora, cuando yo no tengo cebollas, también las vendo a treinta y cinco.

Actividad • Charla

With a partner, prepare a scene similar to **De compras.** Change produce, price, and location. Then present it to your class.

El plátano

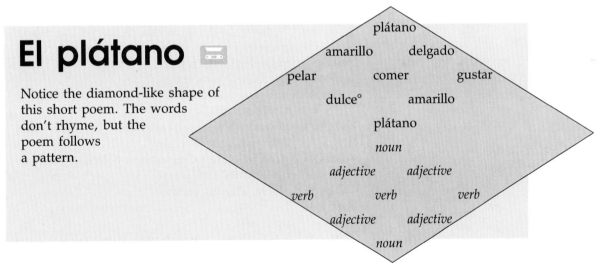

Notice the diamond-like shape of this short poem. The words don't rhyme, but the poem follows a pattern.

Actividad • ¡A escribir!

Write your own diamond-shaped poem in Spanish. Follow the pattern of the words above when preparing your poem.

---

de compras *shopping*   **dulce** *sweet*

¡Buen provecho!   265

El regalo ▭

¡Hay otro botón° en el televisor! ¿Para qué es el nuevo botón? Los chicos no saben.
Daniel juega con el botón, lo aprieta°, y . . . ¡no pasa nada°!

DANIEL   Mira, Adriana, el Canal 17. Hay un programa sobre El Paso,
          un programa de Texas.
ADRIANA   ¡Ah, sí! El Canal 17, ¿no? Pero, Daniel, ¡por favor! Después, tenemos que
          ir a Texas, y, ¿cómo volvemos a casa? No, mejor miramos otro canal.

Pero, ¡ya es tarde! Los chicos llegan a El Paso con el televisor. Esta vez, el televisor
va con ellos. Ahora, ya saben para qué pueden usar el nuevo botón. Por suerte,
con el nuevo botón, no van a tener problemas para volver a México.

En El Paso

DANIEL   Tengo hambre y sed. ¿Dónde podemos comer?
ADRIANA   No sé. Además°, ¿a qué restaurante vamos a ir si no tenemos dinero?

Pasa un joven°. Él escucha la conversación de los dos hermanos. Es muy amable.

JOVEN   ¡Hola chicos! ¿Qué tal? ¿Ustedes buscan un
          lugar para comer? Yo conozco un restaurante
          mexicano muy cerca de aquí.
DANIEL   Muchas gracias. ¿Cómo se llama el restaurante?
ADRIANA   ¿Y dónde está?
JOVEN   Se llama **El refugio.** Está detrás de esa tienda
          grande. Pueden ir por esa calle, a la derecha.
ADRIANA   **¿El refugio?** Gracias.
JOVEN   De nada. Hasta luego.
ADRIANA   ¡Los texanos son tan simpáticos! Y guapos
          también, ¿no?
DANIEL   Sí, no son flacos° ni feos como tú. Pero, mira,
          Adriana, ¿qué hay ahí?
ADRIANA   ¡Una billetera°! Creo que es del chico guapo,
          del texano.
DANIEL   ¿Tiene identificación?
ADRIANA   No, no tiene, pero . . . tiene dinero, y . . .
          ¡mucho!
DANIEL   ¡Qué suerte! Ahora podemos ir a comer. Vamos
          a **El refugio,** ¿no? ¿Qué te parece?
ADRIANA   Por supuesto. No conocemos otro restaurante.
          ¡Vamos!

---

botón *button*   **aprieta** *presses*   **no pasa nada** *nothing happens*   **además** *besides*   **pasa un joven** *a young man passes by*
flacos *skinny*   **billetera** *wallet*

En El refugio

En el restaurante, Daniel y Adriana esperan la comida. Unos mariachis° llegan a
El refugio. Van a tocar música y a cantar. Los músicos miran a los dos hermanos,
y empiezan a cantar:

> No pueden volver a casa,
> tienen que esperar.
> No pueden volver a casa,
> deben cruzar el mar°.
>
> Cerca de la Puerta del Sol°,
> para ustedes hay una flor°.
> Allí van, van muy rápido,
> con su televisor.

DANIEL Adriana, esa canción° es para nosotros.
Debemos ir a Madrid inmediatamente.
¡Vamos rápido!

ADRIANA Un momento, Daniel. Ahí viene el
camarero con la comida. ¿Por qué
no comemos primero? Yo tengo hambre.

DANIEL Tú también escuchaste° la canción.
Es un mensaje° para nosotros. Con el
Canal 17, estamos en Madrid en un
minuto.

ADRIANA Pero, ¿qué vamos a hacer en Madrid?
¿Vamos a buscar una flor en la
Puerta del Sol? ¡Es imposible, Daniel!

Actividad • ¿Quiénes hablan?

Which of the characters from **El regalo** might say or think each of the following?
Why? Justify your choices in Spanish.

1. Yo no quiero mirar el Canal 17.
2. ¿Dónde hay un restaurante? Tengo hambre.
3. Yo también tengo hambre, pero no tenemos dinero.
4. Estos chicos buscan un restaurante.
5. Se llama **El refugio.** Pueden llegar por esa calle.
6. ¡Qué joven tan guapo!
7. ¡Qué suerte! ¡Vamos a comer!
8. Mejor, esperamos. Ahí viene el camarero.
9. Tú escuchaste la canción. Tiene un mensaje para nosotros.
10. ¿Una flor en la Puerta del Sol? ¡Imposible!

---

mariachis *Mexican band*   **cruzar el mar** *to cross the sea*   **Puerta del Sol** *famous plaza in Madrid*   **flor** *flower*
canción *song*   **escuchaste** *you heard*   **mensaje** *message*

UNIDAD **10**

Un viaje estupendo

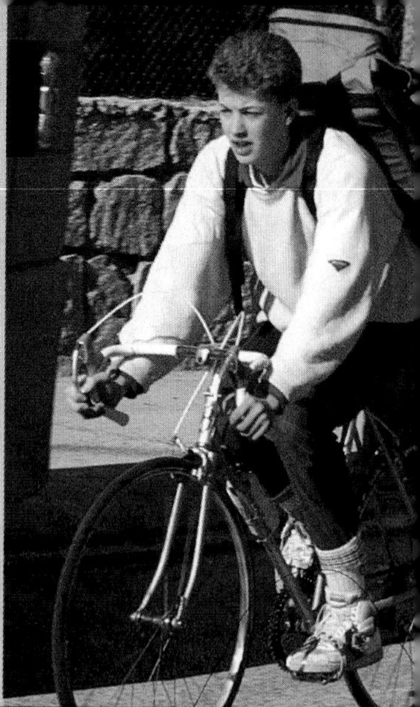

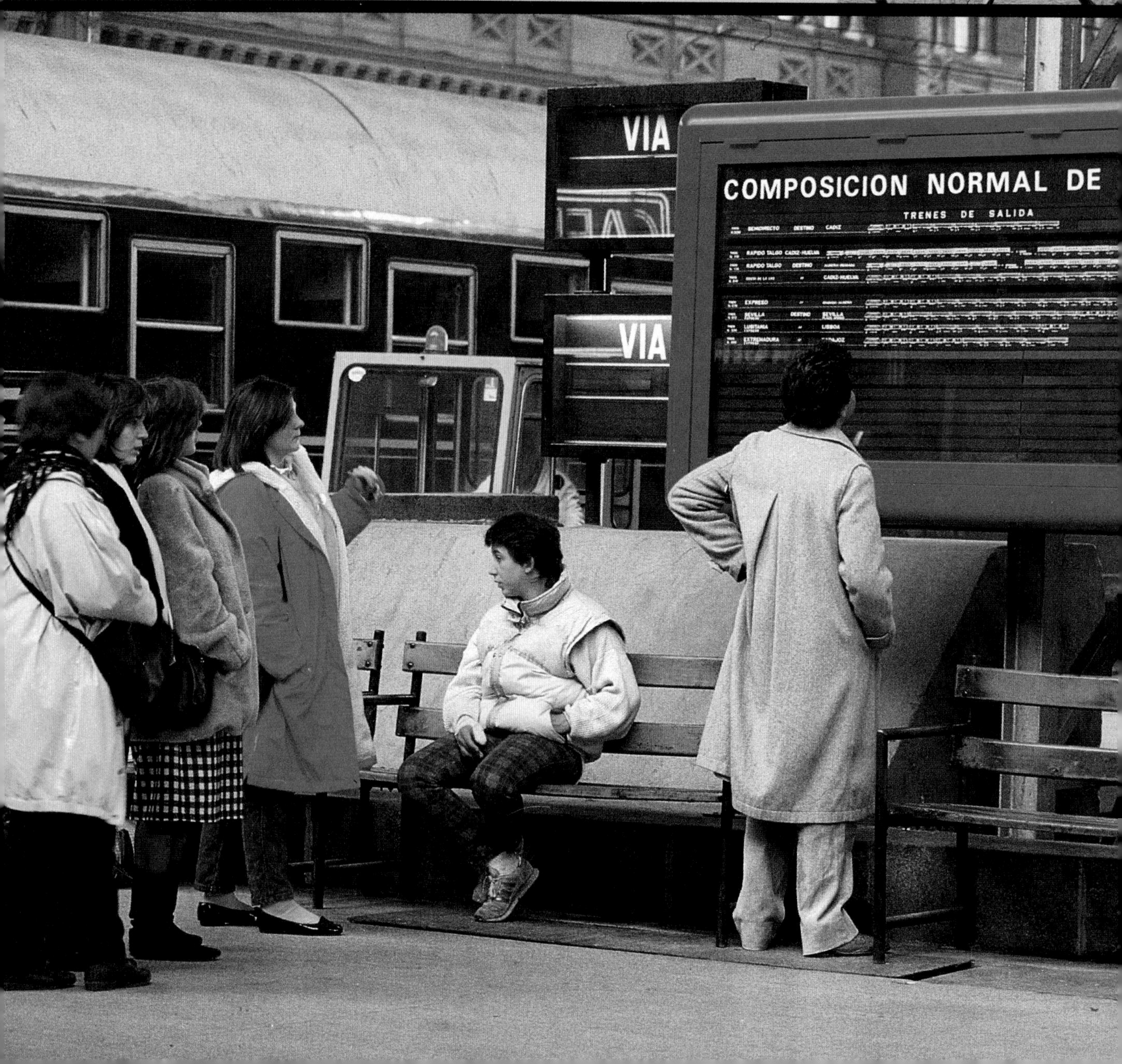
VIA
COMPOSICION NORMAL DE
TRENES DE SALIDA
VIA

Isn't it time you started thinking about taking a trip yourself? For example, you might consider applying as an exchange student to Mexico, Spain, or some other Spanish-speaking countries. Ask your teacher what exchange programs may be open to you— if not for this year, then for the future. You might also consider traveling on your own, either with a group of friends or with your family. Making plans for a big trip is part of the excitement.

In this unit you will:

SECTION A	talk about what you did yesterday, the day before, and last summer
SECTION B	ask for information about something that happened in the past
SECTION C	ask whether or not someone did something
TRY YOUR SKILLS	use what you've learned
VAMOS A LEER	read for practice and pleasure

Traveling to a foreign city, seeing the landmarks—that's something to look forward to. When Madrid is the city you plan to visit, you're in for a special treat. Madrid is one of the great capital cities of the world, with fabulous avenues, palaces, parks, museums, stores, and a wonderful, fun loving population of over 3 million people. You'll have a great deal to tell your friends when you return!

A1 El diario de Pilar 📼

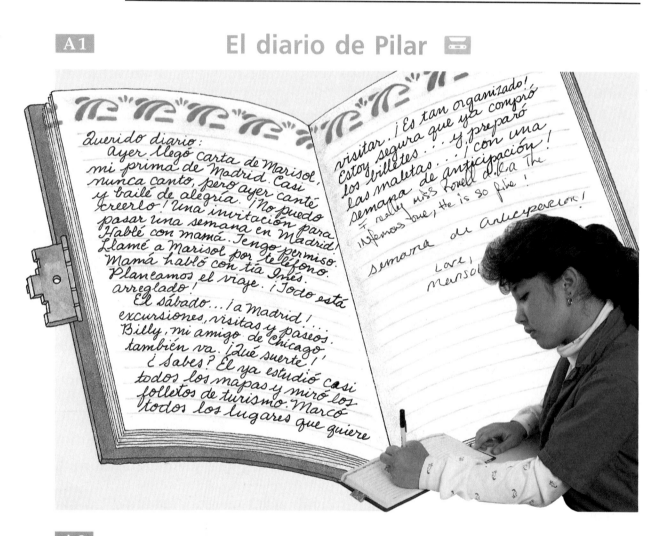

Querido diario:
    Ayer llegó carta de Marisol,
mi prima de Madrid. Casi
nunca canto, pero ayer canté
y bailé de alegría. ¡No puedo
creerlo! Una invitación para
pasar una semana en Madrid!
Hablé con mamá. Tengo permiso.
Llamé a Marisol por teléfono.
Mamá habló con tía Inés.
Planeamos el viaje. ¡Todo está
arreglado!
    El sábado... ¡a Madrid!
excursiones, visitas y paseos.
Billy, mi amigo de Chicago,
también va. ¡Qué suerte!
¿Sabes? Él ya estudió casi
todos los mapas y miró los
folletos de turismo. Marcó
todos los lugares que quiere

visitar. ¡Es tan organizado!
Estoy segura que ya compró
los billetes... y preparó
las maletas... ¡con una
semana de anticipación!
I really miss Lowell d. L. a The
I always love, He is so fine !

semana de Anticipacion!
Love,
Marisol

A2 Actividad • Para completar

Complete these sentences to make them agree with **El diario de Pilar.**

1. Ayer _____ carta de Marisol, mi prima de _____ .
2. Canté y _____ de alegría.
3. _____ con mamá. Tengo _____ .
4. Llamé a _____ por _____ .
5. Y _____ . . . ¡a Madrid!
6. Billy, mi _____ de Chicago, también _____ .
7. ¿Sabes? Él ya _____ casi todos los mapas.
8. Estoy segura que ya _____ los billetes.

Actividad • Combinación

See how many logical sentences you can form by choosing items from both columns.

Ayer llegó	los lugares que quiere visitar.
Canté y bailé	todos los mapas.
Llamé a Marisol	los folletos de turismo.
Billy ya estudió	de alegría.
Él miró	por teléfono.
Mareó todos	las maletas.
Estoy segura que ya	carta de Marisol.
También preparó	compró los billetes.

A4 Preguntas y respuestas

Answer the following questions according to **El diario de Pilar.**

1. ¿Dónde escribe Pilar?
2. ¿Quién es Marisol?
3. ¿Dónde está Marisol?
4. ¿Para qué es la invitación?
5. ¿Puede ir Pilar a Madrid? ¿Por qué?
6. ¿Cuándo va a ir Pilar a Madrid?
7. ¿Con quién va a ir?
8. ¿Qué va a hacer Pilar en Madrid?
9. ¿Cómo se llama el amigo de Pilar?
10. ¿Es él de Madrid?

A5 ¿Sabes que . . . ?

Madrid, the capital of Spain, is a center of industry and communications, much like Chicago and New York. Primarily, however, it is Spain's administrative and governmental center, parallel to Washington, D.C. The Royal Palace, courts, ministries, and other governmental buildings are in Madrid. Spain's formal chief of state is the king: **el Rey** Juan Carlos. Spain's parliament, called **las Cortes,** elects a president of the government, whose responsibilities resemble those of the British prime minister.

ESTRUCTURAS ESENCIALES
The preterit (past tense) of regular -ar verbs

In order to express past actions you need to use a verb in the past tense: *I went to the movies yesterday.* In Spanish one such past tense is the preterit tense. It corresponds to the English simple past tense.

hablar *to talk*		
Yo	**hablé**	con Marisol.
¿Tú	**hablaste**	con tía Inés?
Usted, él, ella	**habló**	por teléfono.
Nosotros(as)	**hablamos**	ayer.
¿Vosotros(as)	**hablasteis**	con el aduanero?
Ustedes, ellos(as)	**hablaron**	anoche.

1. The verb forms in the chart are the preterit tense forms of the regular verb **hablar.** They express actions that took place and were completed in the past: **Hablé** con Marisol. *I talked with Marisol.*

2. You can produce the preterit forms of most other regular **-ar** verbs by adding the following endings to the stem:

> **-é, -aste, -ó, -amos, -asteis, -aron**

When you add **-é** to the stem **habl-,** you get **hablé,** *I talked, I spoke.* The regular verb **planear** is conjugated like **hablar.** For example, when you add **-aste** to the stem **plane-,** you get **planeaste,** *you* (**tú**) *planned,* and so on.

3. Notice that the **yo** and the **usted, él, ella** forms have written accents.

> **Yo hablé.**
> **Ella habló.**

4. The **nosotros(as)** forms of **-ar** verbs are the same in the preterit and the present. Other words in the sentence usually make clear whether you are talking in the present or the past.

> **Hablamos** con Billy ahora.   *We are talking to Billy now.*
> **Hablamos** con Billy ayer.   *We talked to Billy yesterday.*

Actividad • ¿Qué planearon?

Using the preterit of **planear,** say who planned what.

> ¿El viaje? Nosotros.
> —Nosotros planeamos el viaje.

1. ¿El paseo? Yo.
2. ¿La comida? Mamá.
3. ¿La excursión? Nosotros.
4. ¿La visita? Los chicos.
5. ¿El menú? Teresita.

6. ¿El viaje? Tú.
7. ¿El baile? Ustedes.
8. ¿El concierto? La profesora.
9. ¿La fiesta? Mis primos.
10. ¿El horario? El señor Valdez.

A8 Actividad • ¿Con quién hablaste?

Complete the following, using the preterit tense of **hablar.**

—¿ ____ (tú) con Marisol?
—No, yo no ____ con ella.
—¿ ____ mamá con ella?
—Sí, creo que mamá ____ con ella.
—¿Con quién ____ ustedes?

—(Nosotros) ____ con la tía Inés.
—Pero, ¿ ____ ustedes con Marisol también?
—Sí, (nosotros) ____ con Marisol, y
  Marisol ____ con Pilar.

A9 SE DICE ASÍ
*Saying what you usually do and then saying what
you did at specified times in the past*

Canto **a menudo** y **ayer también** canté.	*I often sing, and I also sang yesterday.*
Casi siempre canto, **pero ayer** no canté.	*I almost always sing, but I didn't sing yesterday.*
Casi nunca canto, **pero ayer** canté.	*I rarely sing, but I sang yesterday.*
Estudiamos **todos los días.**	*We study every day.*

A10 Actividad • Ayer también

Complete the following sentences using the preterit of the underlined verbs.

<u>Hablo</u> a menudo en español y ayer también . . .
Hablo a menudo en español y ayer también hablé.

1. Nosotros <u>estudiamos</u> a menudo. Ayer también . . .
2. Marisol casi siempre <u>llama</u>, pero ayer no . . .
3. Tú a menudo <u>compras</u> discos. Ayer también . . .
4. Casi siempre <u>miro</u> televisión, pero ayer no . . .
5. <u>Cantan</u> casi siempre en español, pero ayer no . . .
6. Ella a menudo <u>espera</u> en la cafetería. Ayer también . . .

A11 Actividad • Todos los días y ayer

Team up with a partner. Using **siempre** or **todos los días,** ask whether the people usually do what is mentioned. Your partner will answer negatively following the model.

Los chicos bailan.

—¿Bailan los chicos siempre?
—No, no bailan siempre,
  pero ayer bailaron.

1. Pilar canta y baila.
2. Ella habla con su tía.
3. Pilar llama a su prima.
4. Ellos escuchan música.

5. Billy estudia con sus amigos.
6. Ellas miran televisión.
7. Marisol toma fotografías.
8. Los chicos montan en bicicleta.

Un viaje estupendo   273

Actividad • ¡A escribir!

La rutina. Write down what you usually do every day and what you did or didn't
do yesterday. Use the expressions you learned in A9.

—Todos los días preparo las tareas, y ayer también preparé las tareas.
（pero ayer no preparé las tareas.）

A 13 **Conversación • Ayer y hoy**

Pair up with a classmate, talk about what you do every day
and what you did yesterday.

—¿Escuchas música
todos los días?

—¿Y ayer escuchaste
música?

• Sí, escucho música siempre.
• No, no escucho música
todos los días.

• Sí, ayer también escuché
música.
• Ayer no escuché música.
• No, ayer no escuché música.

llamar por teléfono

pasear **preparar las tareas**

tomar el autobús

estudiar español

hablar con tus amigos

trabajar con la computadora

mirar televisión

montar en bicicleta

A 14 **SITUACIÓN • Conversación de dos minutos**

Carlos llama por teléfono a Isabel en un mal momento. Isabel está a punto de
salir para el aeropuerto.

CARLOS ¡Hola, Isabel! ¿Cómo estás?
ISABEL ¡Apuradísima! No puedo hablar
ahora. Salimos para el aeropuerto
dentro de dos minutos. Vamos a
Barcelona.
CARLOS ¿A Barcelona?

ISABEL Sí. Vamos a visitar a la abuela.
Mamá reservó los billetes de avión
la semana pasada. Papá y mamá
llamaron a la abuela anoche. Papá
regresó de la oficina hace una hora.
El taxi ya llegó . . . y yo todavía
tengo que hacer mi maleta. ¡Adiós!

A15 Preguntas y respuestas

Answer the following questions according to A14.

1. ¿Cómo está Isabel? ¿Por qué?
2. ¿Puede ella hablar mucho? ¿Por qué?
3. ¿Adónde va ella?
4. ¿Qué va a hacer allí?
5. ¿Qué reservó la mamá de Isabel? ¿Cuándo?

6. ¿A quién llamaron? ¿Cuándo?
7. ¿Está el papá en la oficina todavía?
8. ¿Dónde está el papá?
9. ¿Cuándo regresó?
10. ¿Cómo van al aeropuerto?

A16 Actividad • ¡A escoger!

Choose the option that best completes each statement according to A14.

1. Isabel dice que está
   • muy bien.   • apuradísima.   • con su mamá.
2. Isabel y sus papás salen para
   • la oficina.   • la casa de Carlos.   • el aeropuerto.
3. Ellos salen para Barcelona
   • dentro de dos minutos.   • mañana.   • el sábado.
4. Van a Barcelona para
   • trabajar.   • visitar a la abuela.   • visitar a Carlos.
5. Mamá reservó los billetes
   • hace una hora.   • la semana pasada.   • hace dos minutos.
6. Llamaron a la abuela
   • la semana pasada.   • hace una hora.   • anoche.
7. Papá regresó de la oficina
   • anoche.   • hace cinco minutos.   • hace una hora.
8. Yo no terminé
   • de hacer mi maleta.   • de hablar por teléfono.   • de hablar con Carlos.

A17 ¿Sabes que . . . ?

Barcelona, Spain's second-largest city, is a center of industry and a beautiful port on the Mediterranean Sea. Famous especially for its painters, architects, and sculptors, Barcelona is the capital of Cataluña, one of the 17 regions into which Spain is divided. The Catalan language is spoken along with Spanish throughout the region.

ESTRUCTURAS ESENCIALES
Expressing how long ago something happened

Isabel llegó **hace** { mucho tiempo. / quince días. / una hora. }   **Hace** { un mes / una semana / poco tiempo } **que** Isabel llegó.

subject + verb in the preterit + **hace** + expression of time	**Hace** + expression of time + **que** + subject + verb in the preterit

Use **hace** + time expression or **hace** + time expression + **que** to indicate how long ago an action took place. Notice that in both cases the verb of the sentence is in the preterit.

A 19 Actividad • ¡Cómo pasa el tiempo!

Form sentences with **hace** and **que** to indicate how long ago the events happened.

> Hoy es lunes 16. José llegó el lunes 2.
> **Hace** dos semanas **que** llegó.

1. Son las doce. El autobús llegó a las once.
2. Hoy es miércoles. Isabel compró los billetes el miércoles pasado.
3. Hoy es el 5 de marzo. Marisol visitó a sus primos el 2 de marzo.
4. Hoy es el 4 de abril. Daniel llamó a su tía el 20 de marzo.
5. Es la una. Paco preparó las maletas a las doce.
6. Hoy es sábado. Mis padres hablaron con los chicos el sábado pasado.
7. Son las cuatro. La excursión terminó a las tres.
8. Hoy es el 8 de mayo. Los chicos estudiaron los mapas el 8 de abril.

A 20 Comprensión

Are they talking in the present or the preterit?

	0	1	2	3	4	5	6	7	8	9	10
Present	✔										
Preterit											

A 21 Conversación • El viaje

Work with a partner. Imagine that you are coming back from a trip to one of the places in the pictures on the next page—or to another place you have visited. In at least 10 sentences, tell your partner what you did there. Ask your classmate about his or her trip, using each of the verbs below.

¿Paseaste . . . ? ¿Tomaste . . . ? ¿Entraste . . . ?
¿Visitaste . . . ? ¿Miraste . . . ? ¿Compraste . . . ? ¿Hablaste . . . ?
¿Cambiaste . . . ?

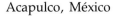

Acapulco, México

Ask your partner:

¿Cuándo visitaste . . . ?
¿Cuánto tiempo pasaste allí?
¿Qué lugares visitaste?
¿Compraste algo?
¿Qué compraste?
¿Cuándo regresaste?

Barcelona, España

Madrid,
España

San Juan, Puerto Rico

San Francisco,
California

A 22 Actividad • ¡A escribir!

Prepare a written report about an imaginary trip to Mexico, Spain, or Puerto Rico.
Present your report orally in class.

A 23 Actividad • Una confusión

Make sense out of the following phone conversation, putting the lines in their correct order.

—Muy bien, ¿y tú?
—¿Te gustó?
—Diez días. Visitamos a la abuela, y a mis tíos también.
—Sí, ¿hablamos mañana? Tengo que salir ahora.
—¡Hola Carlota! ¿Cómo estás?
—Muy bien también. Regresamos ayer de Barcelona.
—Me gustó mucho. Visitamos la ciudad.
—¿Compraste muchas cosas?
—Bueno, hasta mañana.
—¿Cuánto tiempo pasaron en Barcelona?

It's always exciting to receive long-distance calls from close friends or favorite relatives. If they're on a trip, we want to find out what places they've seen, where they went, and how everything is.

B1 Pilar llama desde Madrid 📼

Pilar llama a su casa. Su hermana Socorro contesta el teléfono. Socorro quiere saber todo lo que pasa. Pregunta sin parar.

Socorro	Sí, ya viene, pero, antes, ¿qué tal el viaje? ¿Adónde fueron hoy? ¿Qué hicieron?
Pilar	Fuimos primero a casa de los tíos. Dejamos nuestras cosas allí. Hablamos mucho. Hicimos planes también.
Socorro	Ya sé, ya sé . . . , pero, ¿qué más hicieron?
Pilar	Hicimos muchas cosas.
Socorro	¿Fueron a la Gran Vía?
Pilar	No, fuimos en moto hasta la Puerta de Alcalá. Caminamos mucho. Después fuimos al Parque del Retiro. Remamos en el estanque. ¡Pasamos un día fantástico!
Socorro	¡Qué envidia! Aquí viene mamá. ¡Hasta mañana!
Pilar	¡Adiós, Socorro!

Socorro ¡Hola, Pilar! ¿Cómo estás? ¿Y Billy? ¿Cómo llegaron? ¿Les gusta Madrid?

Pilar Estamos muy bien, Socorro. ¿Está mamá?

Actividad • ¡A escoger!

Choose the most appropriate option to complete each statement according to B1.

1. Pilar llama
   • a casa de sus tíos.   • a su casa.   • al Parque del Retiro.
2. Socorro es
   • la hermana de Pilar.   • su mamá.   • su tía de Madrid.
3. Socorro quiere
   • saber dónde está Pilar.   • hablar con su mamá.   • saber todo lo que pasa.
4. Pilar y Billy fueron a la Puerta de Alcalá
   • en autobús.   • en bicicleta.   • en moto.
5. Pilar y Billy remaron
   • en la Gran Vía.   • en el estanque del parque.   • en casa de los tíos.
6. Pilar está
   • en Madrid.   • en casa de Billy.   • en el estanque.
7. Pilar y Socorro van a hablar
   • mañana.   • después.   • dentro de cinco minutos.
8. Aquí viene
   • Socorro.   • Billy.   • mamá.

B3 Actividad • ¿Es cierto o no?

Change the following sentences to make them true according to B1.

1. Pilar llama desde Sevilla.
2. Su mamá contesta el teléfono.
3. Pilar y Billy están en Madrid.
4. Pilar quiere hablar con su ~~papá.~~ *mamá*
5. Pilar y Billy dejaron sus cosas en la Gran Vía.

casa de los tíos

6. Hoy fueron en moto hasta la Puerta de Alcalá.
7. Después fueron a la Gran Vía.
8. Más tarde remaron en el estanque.

B4 ¿Sabes que . . . ?

European cities in the Middle Ages were surrounded by walls with large entrance gates, or **puertas.** As the cities' boundaries grew outward, the old walls eventually disappeared, but many of the old **puertas** remained. Madrid's oldest gate, **la Puerta del Sol,** is actually in the center of the city, where all subway lines and many bus routes originate. **La Puerta de Alcalá,** an 18th-century triumphal arch now surrounded by flowers, is another reference point. **La Gran Vía** is the central avenue in the heart of Madrid, lined with elegant shops, theaters, and cafés. Madrid also has many lovely parks: the biggest is **el Parque del Retiro,** with over 200 acres of lofty trees, flowers, secluded walks and gardens. It has a small lake where visitors may rent rowboats, and two buildings where art shows are held.

ESTRUCTURAS ESENCIALES
The preterit of hacer

hacer *to do, to make*			
Hice ᵞᵒ	la comida.	**Hicimos** ⁿ	unos bocadillos.
¿Hiciste	el viaje?	**¿Hicisteis**	muchas cosas?
Hizo	planes.	**Hicieron**	una excursión.

1. The preterit forms of **hacer** are irregular.

Hizo muchas cosas ayer.   *He (She) did many things yesterday.*
Hicimos unos bocadillos anoche.   *We made some sandwiches last night.*

2. The **usted, él, ella** form is **hizo.**

3. Notice that **hice** and **hizo** are stressed on the stem. Neither has a written accent.

B6 Actividad • Una excursión

A group of friends and relatives are going on an excursion. Using the preterit of **hacer,** say who went on the excursion.

Ustedes—Ustedes hicieron la excursión.

1. Mamá   **4.** Los chicos   **7.** Yo
2. Usted   **5.** Tú   **8.** Mi hermano Javier
3. Pepe y yo   **6.** Ustedes   **9.** Mis tíos

B7 Actividad • ¿Qué hicieron?

Complete the following using the preterit of **hacer.**

—¿Qué ____ ustedes el domingo?
—Nosotros ____ una excursión estupenda. Mi hermana ____ todos los planes.
Rosario ____ la comida. Catalina y Julián ____ unos bocadillos.
—¿Qué tiempo ____ ?
—____ muy buen tiempo. Todos nosotros ____ algo.
—Y tú, ¿qué ____ ? ¿ ____ tú la comida?
—No, yo ____ todos los planes para la excursión.

B8 Actividad • Charla

¿Qué hiciste el fin de semana? Work with a partner. Talk about what
you did last weekend.

—¿Qué hiciste?   —¿Una excursión?   —¿Adónde?
—¿Con quién?   —¿Visitaste a tus amigos?   —¿Estudiaste?

B9 Actividad • ¡A escribir!

Prepare a written report of the conversation you had with your partner in B8.

ESTRUCTURAS ESENCIALES
The preterit of ir

ir *to go*			
Fui	a su casa.	**Fuimos**	en autobús.
Fuiste	en bicicleta.	**¿Fuisteis**	a pie?
Fue	al cine.	**Fueron**	a la Gran Vía.

The preterit forms of **ir** are irregular.

B 11 Actividad • Combinación

Let's see how many sentences you can prepare by matching the persons on the left with the activities on the right.

Marisol y yo	
Pilar	fue a la Gran Vía.
Los chicos	fuimos a casa de Javier.
Tú	fuiste al cine.
Yo	fui al Parque del Retiro.
Javier y tú	fueron a dar una vuelta.

B 12 Actividad • ¿Adónde fueron?

It seems that everybody went somewhere last Sunday. With a partner, read the dialog, supplying the missing preterit forms of **ir**.

—¿Adónde ____ (tú) el domingo pasado?
—(Yo) ____ a casa de los tíos.
—¿Y Billy, adónde ____ ?
—Billy ____ a un concierto.
—¿ ____ ustedes al cine después?
—No, Billy ____ a la Gran Vía.

—Tía Inés y yo ____ a dar una vuelta.
—¿Y tú, adónde ____ ?
—Yo ____ al parque.
—¿Con quién ____ ?
—(Yo) ____ con mi amiga Carmen.

B 13 Actividad • Fuimos anoche

Work with a partner. Ask each other these questions. Answer using **No**, the preterit of **ir**, and **anoche.**

—¿Vas al cine?   —No, fui anoche.

1. ¿Van los chicos a casa de los tíos?
2. ¿Va Pilar al cine?
3. ¿Vas tú al concierto?
4. ¿Van ustedes a la Gran Vía?

5. ¿Vamos al cine?
6. ¿Vas tú a la Puerta de Alcalá?
7. ¿Van Isabel y Julio?
8. ¿Va tu hermana?

Actividad • ¿Cómo fueron?

Using items from both columns and the preterit of **ir,** say how everybody got to
the party last night in honor of tía Inés.

Rosario—en metro   —Rosario fue en metro.

Rosario *Los chicos* *Alberto y Julián* *Nosotros* *Yo* *Los abuelos* *Usted* *La señora Pérez* *Tú*	**a pie** **en coche** **en autobús** **en metro** **en bicicleta** **en moto**

B15   Actividad • ¡A escribir!

Think of a party you went to recently. Write a list saying how everybody that you
remember got to the party.

B16   Conversación • Ayer, anoche y la semana pasada

Find out from five friends what each one did yesterday, last night, and last week.
Report your findings to the class.

— ¿Qué hiciste?
— ¿Adónde fuiste?
— ¿Cómo fuiste?
— ¿Con quién fuiste?

Ayer El domingo
El fin de semana pasado   Anoche
El sábado

B17   Actividad • ¡A escribir!

Prepare a written report of your findings in B16.

Which segments of the conversation are in the present or the preterit?

	0	1	2	3	4	5	6	7	8	9	10
Present											
Preterit	✔										

B 19 Actividad • ¿Adónde fueron?

Say who went where using elements from the two boxes below. You can
also add how and when they went. Form as many sentences as you can.

¿Quién?   ¿Adónde?

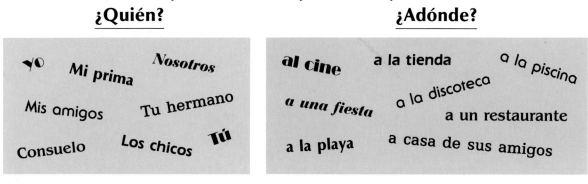

B 20 Actividad • La ruta

Describe to a partner or the entire class how you got to a place and what you did
there. Use the map and the description as a model. Some possibilities: when you
went to a store, to a party, to the house of a friend or relative. . . .

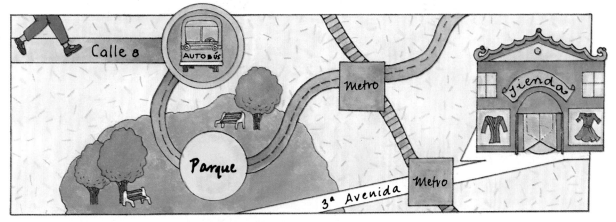

Fui a pie hasta la calle 8. Allí tomé el autobús y fui al parque. Después fui en
metro hasta la Tercera Avenida. Caminé por la Tercera Avenida hasta la tienda.
Compré muchas cosas.

B 21 Actividad • ¡A escribir!

Draw a map of the route in B20 and write a description of the trip, using at least
eight sentences.

Getting ready for a weekend excursion sometimes seems to take as much energy and time as preparing for a much longer trip. It may be better to remain calm and do less planning—if we forget to pack something, we can live without it for two days.

C1 Un viaje corto

La mamá de Socorro quiere saber si está todo listo para el viaje a Granada.

MAMÁ Socorro, ¿tienes los billetes?
SOCORRO Sí, mamá, los tengo aquí.
MAMÁ ¿Hiciste las maletas?
SOCORRO Sí, mamá, las preparé.
MAMÁ ¿Y los regalos?
SOCORRO Están todos.
MAMÁ ¿Te llamó tu hermano?
SOCORRO Sí, me llamó esta mañana.
MAMÁ ¿Llamaste al taxi?
SOCORRO Sí, ya lo llamé.
MAMÁ Bueno, ¿qué más? . . . ¿Tiene tu papá nuestro número de teléfono?
SOCORRO Sí, lo tiene. Mamá, ¡por favor!, ¡sólo vamos a Granada por dos días!

Señor Jiménez
Granada
958 432-31-71

C2 ¿Es cierto o no?

Change the following statements to make them true according to the dialog in C1.

1. Socorro no tiene los regalos.
2. Ella hizo las maletas.
3. Socorro llamó a su hermano.
4. El hermano de Socorro llamó por teléfono.
5. Van a ir al aeropuerto en metro.
6. El papá de Socorro no va con ellas.
7. Socorro y su mamá van a Córdoba.
8. Socorro y su mamá van por una semana.

C3 Actividad • ¡A escoger!

Choose the most appropriate option to complete each statement according to C1.

1. Socorro tiene
 • los billetes. • los números. • los teléfonos.
2. Ella preparó
 • la comida. • las maletas. • las tareas.
3. El hermano de Socorro
 • llamó al taxi. • llamó por teléfono. • llamó ayer.
4. La mamá de Socorro _____ saber si no falta nada.
 • va a • puede • quiere
5. ¿Está todo listo para
 • el taxi? • el viaje? • tu hermano?
6. Socorro llamó
 • al taxi. • al papá. • al hermano.
7. ¿Tiene papá nuestro
 • billete? • asiento? • número?
8. Socorro y su mamá van de viaje
 • por dos semanas. • por dos días. • por tres días.

C4 ¿Sabes que . . . ?

In the eighth century, Moorish warriors from North Africa invaded Spain and eventually conquered nearly all of it. Spain's Moorish kingdoms became the richest states in Europe and centers of world learning. Granada, capital of the last Moorish state in Spain, was reconquered by the Christians in 1492, the year Colón discovered America. Every year tourists by the millions visit its surviving palaces and gardens, specifically the **Alhambra** and **Generalife,** situated in the foothills of the spectacular snowcapped Sierra Nevada mountains.

ESTRUCTURAS ESENCIALES
Direct-object pronouns

In Unit 7, you began to use sentences that include direct objects. The verb in such sentences expresses an action, and the direct object indicates who or what gets acted upon.

Billy compra **el billete.**   *Billy buys the ticket.*
Pilar llamó **a su hermana.**   *Pilar called her sister.*

The *ticket* gets bought. The *sister* gets called. They are the direct objects. When the direct object refers to a person, you need to use the personal **a** before it.

You can also replace the direct object with a direct-object pronoun.

	Singular		*Plural*
me	me	**nos**	us
te	you (*fam.*)		
lo	him, you (*m.*), it (*m.*)	**los**	them, you (*m.*)
la	her, you (*f.*), it (*f.*)	**las**	them, you (*f.*)

1. The direct-object pronouns **me, te,** and **nos** are the same for both masculine or feminine nouns.

Sí, yo vengo.   Marisol **me** llamó.   *Marisol called me.*
Sí, tú vienes.   Marisol **te** llamó.   *Marisol called you.*
Sí, nosotros venimos. ⎫
Sí, nosotras venimos. ⎬   Marisol **nos** llamó. *Marisol called us.*

2. The pronouns **lo, la, los,** and **las** correspond to English *him, her, it, them,* and *you* (**usted, ustedes**). They reflect the gender and number of the direct-object persons or things.

Billy compra **el billete.** Billy **lo** compra.   *Billy buys it.*
Pilar llamó **a su hermana.** Pilar **la** llamó.   *Pilar called her.*
¿Conoces **a mis primos?** Sí **los** conozco.   *Yes, I know them.*
Marisol espera **a sus amigas.** Marisol **las** espera.   *Marisol is waiting for them.*

3. Place the direct-object pronoun right before the conjugated verb.

Yo llamé **a Carmen.**   *I called Carmen.*
Yo   **la**   llamé. *I called her.*

4. In negative sentences **no** must precede the direct-object pronoun.

Yo **no** llamé **a Carmen.**   *I did not call Carmen.*
Yo **no**   **la**   llamé. *I did not call her.*

Actividad · ¿Me escuchaste? 🎞️

While you were away on a trip, your family sent you a cassette recording. Everybody wants to know whether you heard what they had to say.

—¿A tía Inés?   —¿Escuchaste **a tía Inés?**   —Sí, **la** escuché.

1. ¿Al tío?   3. ¿A tus primos?   5. ¿A mí?   7. ¿A tu papá?
2. ¿A la abuela?   4. ¿A Susana?   6. ¿A nosotros? 8. ¿A tu hermano?

Answer the following questions using the direct object pronouns, **lo**, **la**, **los**, or **las**.

> —¿Dejaste **las maletas?**
> —Sí, **las** dejé.

1. ¿Planeaste el viaje?
2. ¿Estudiaste los mapas?
3. ¿Miraste los folletos?
4. ¿Reservaste los billetes?
5. ¿Llamaste a tus amigos?
6. ¿Llamaste a tía Inés?
7. ¿Compraste los billetes?
8. ¿Hiciste las maletas?

C8 Actividad • ¿Cuándo lo hiciste?

Imagine you're going on a trip. On your way to the airport, you meet a friend who is also going there. Ask each other the following questions. Include in your answer the direct-object pronouns **lo**, **la**, **los**, or **las**.

> —¿Cuándo planeaste **el viaje?**

> —**Lo** planeé el mes pasado.

1. ¿Cuándo preparaste este viaje?
2. ¿Cuándo estudiaste los mapas?
3. ¿Cuándo miraste los folletos?
4. ¿Cuándo cambiaste el dinero?
5. ¿Cuándo reservaste los billetes?
6. ¿Cuándo compraste el diccionario?
7. ¿Cuándo hiciste las maletas?
8. ¿Cuándo llamaste al taxi?

> *hace un mes*   hace quince días
> *el mes pasado*   **ayer**   anoche
> hace un año   la semana pasada
> hace una semana

C9 Actividad • ¡A escribir!

Using your answers to the questions in C8 as a base, prepare a brief paragraph about the trip.

C10 Actividad • ¿Dónde lo compraste?

You bought a lot of things during your trip. Say where you bought them.

> revistas / Madrid   —¿Las revistas?, **las** compré en Madrid.

1. libros / Gran Vía
2. diccionario / una librería
3. casetes / la calle
4. billetes / el teatro
5. mapa / Casa Suárez
6. cartera / una tienda
7. postales / el Prado
8. discos / el Rastro

¿Sabes que . . . ?

Madrid's **Museo del Prado** is one of the world's leading art museums. Great paintings by Diego Velázquez, El Greco, Francisco Goya, and other Spanish masters are displayed, along with major works of the Flemish and Italian schools.

Another famous attraction in Madrid is **El Rastro,** a flea market where each Sunday determined shoppers sift through an endless jumble of odds and ends. With luck, spending very little money, you may walk away with a rusty but working bicycle, a lovely antique brooch, or a fine group portrait of forgotten statesmen by an anonymous painter.

 Comprensión

Appropriate or inappropriate?

	0	1	2	3	4	5	6	7	8	9	10
Sí	✔										
No											

 SE DICE ASÍ
Discussing whether or not something has already been done

¿Ya contestaste la carta?	Sí, ya la contesté.
	No, no la contesté.

Use **ya** (*already*) in your questions and affirmative answers.

C14 Actividad • Sí, ya lo hice

You and your friends are getting ready for a bicycle trip. Answer the following questions about the trip saying yes, you've already done it, and your friends have too. Use **lo, la, los,** or **las** in your answers.

—¿Ya planeaste **el viaje?** ¿Y tus amigos?
—Sí, ya **lo** planeé. Y ellos **lo** planearon también.

1. ¿Ya estudiaste la ruta?
2. ¿Ya miraste los mapas?
3. ¿Ya llevaste el dinero?
4. ¿Ya llamaste a tus primos?
5. ¿Ya compraste la comida?
6. ¿Ya hiciste los bocadillos?

C15 Actividad • No, no lo hice

Now, answer the questions in C14, saying that you haven't done it.

—¿Ya planeaste **el viaje?**   —No, no **lo** planeé.

C16 Actividad • ¿Ya lo hiciste o no lo hiciste?

You and a classmate are getting ready for a trip. Ask each other:

1. ¿Preparaste las cosas?
2. ¿Compraste los billetes?
3. ¿Hiciste la maleta?
4. ¿Miraste los folletos?
5. ¿Estudiaste el mapa?
6. ¿Llamaste a tus amigos?
7. ¿Llamaste a tu papá?
8. ¿Escribiste los números de teléfono?

C17 Actividad • ¡Ya lo hice todo!

Before leaving, go over your checklist and say you already did each thing.

llamar / papá   —Ya lo llamé.

1. contestar / carta
2. comprar / billetes
3. cambiar / cheque
4. llamar / abuela
5. comprar / regalos
6. estudiar / mapa
7. hacer / maletas
8. llamar / taxi

C18 Actividad • ¡A escribir!

Write a list of all the things you did in preparation for a trip. Use your answers to C17 as a guideline.

C19 Actividad • Una conversación telefónica

Work with a partner. You are away on a trip and you call home. Your partner answers the phone and asks you about your trip. Switch roles.

¿Con quién fuiste?   ¿A una tienda?   ¿Cómo fuiste?   ¿Cómo estás?
¿Qué compraste?   ¿Qué me compraste?
¿A un concierto?   ¿Fuiste a un parque?   ¿Al teatro?   ¿Qué hiciste?   ¿Al cine?
¿Me compraste algo?   ¿Adónde fuiste?

TRY YOUR SKILLS

using what you've learned

1 Recuerdos de Madrid

Desde Madrid, Pilar y Billy escriben postales.

Parque del Retiro, Madrid

Querida Isabel,
¿Cómo estás? Te escribo desde Madrid. Me invitó mi prima Marisol. ¡Es una chica estupenda! Mi amigo Billy también está aquí. Llegamos ayer, y vamos a estar una semana en Madrid.
Hasta la próxima,
Pilar

Isabel Zaldivar
Calle Mirand
San Jua

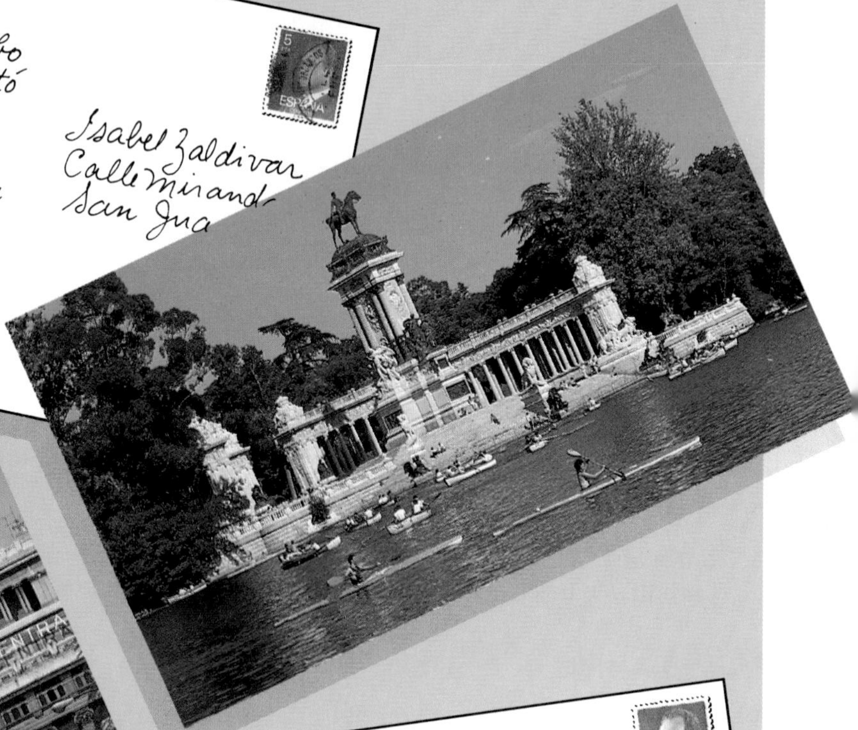

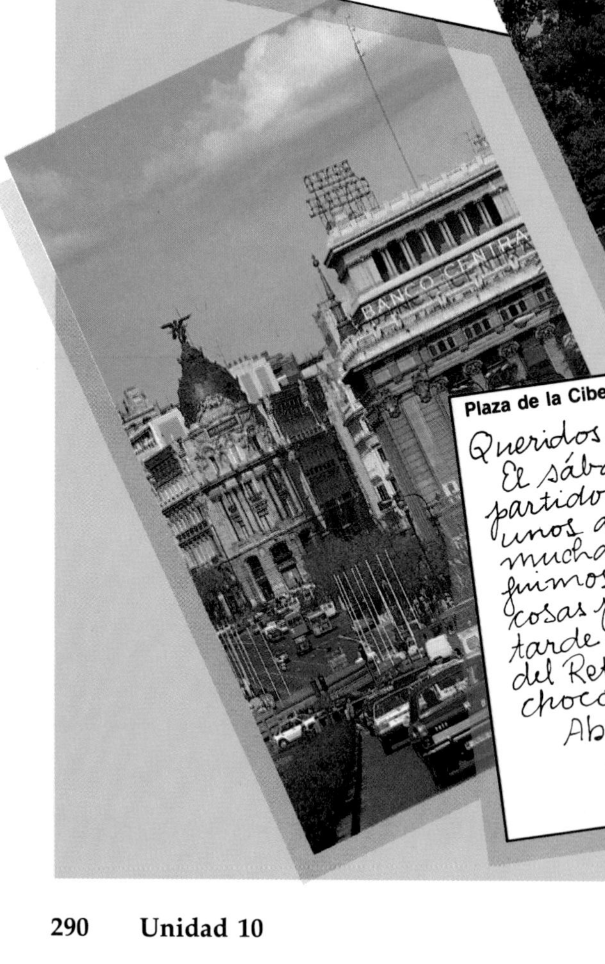

Plaza de la Cibeles, Madrid

Queridos papá y mamá,
El sábado fui a un partido de fútbol con unos amigos de aquí. Tomé muchas fotos. El domingo fuimos al Rastro. Compré cosas para todos. Por la tarde fuimos al parque del Retiro y tomamos chocolate con churros.
Abrazos para toda la familia, Billy

Familia Jones
88 Milan Circle
Chicago, Illinois
60665

U. S. A.

2 Actividad • ¿Es cierto o no?

Change the following sentences to make them true according to Pilar's and Billy's postcards.

1. Pilar escribe desde Sevilla.
2. Marisol es una chica estupenda.
3. Pilar y Billy llegaron la semana pasada.
4. Pilar escribe a una amiga.
5. El sábado Billy fue a un partido de fútbol.
6. Por la noche él fue al Rastro.
7. En el parque los chicos tomaron sopa.
8. Billy tomó muchas fotos.

3 Preguntas y respuestas.

Pair up with a partner. Ask each other the following questions.

1. ¿Desde dónde escribe Pilar?
2. ¿A quién escribe?
3. ¿Conoce Isabel a Pilar?
4. ¿Adónde fue Billy el sábado? ¿Con quién fue?
5. ¿Adónde fue él el domingo?
6. ¿Qué compró él allí?
7. ¿Adónde fueron el domingo por la tarde?
8. ¿Qué tomaron después?

4 Actividad • Charla

With a partner, talk about what you did last weekend, last week, and last summer.

—¿Adónde fuiste?
—¿Con quién?
—¿Qué hiciste allí?
—¿Compraste algo? ¿Qué?

el verano pasado
el fin de semana pasado
la semana pasada

5 Actividad • Postales

You're away on a trip. Write two postcards to different friends or to members of your family. Tell your friends what you did, what you saw, where you went and with whom, and what you bought during your trip.

6 Pronunciación, lectura, dictado

1. Listen carefully and repeat what you hear.

2. The Spanish consonants **z** and **s** have the same sound. Listen, then read aloud.

cerámica   cine   gracias   cereza
enseguida   reservar   pesetas   clase
bolsillo   sol   Susana   sandía
azul   zanahoria   empezar   almorzar

3. Copy the following sentences to prepare yourself to write them from dictation.

El señor González regresó de la oficina muy cansado.
La clase de educación física no es difícil.
La señorita de los zapatos azules es muy simpática.
La excursión sale el siete de marzo.

¿LO SABES?

Let's review some important points you have learned in this unit.

SECTION A

Can you talk about what you did early this morning, yesterday, or last week?
Mention five things you did yesterday, using:

hablar   llamar   mirar   estudiar
comprar   preparar   planear   tomar

Are you able to find out if somebody did the same things you did yesterday?
Write down five questions you might ask.

Using *también* and *pero*, can you talk about what you do every day and say whether you did or didn't do the same thing yesterday?
Form five sentences.

SECTION B

What do you ask somebody who is just back from a trip?
Ask five questions.

Do you know how to talk about a trip you've just taken?
Briefly describe to a friend what you did on your trip.

Are you able to talk about the route you took this morning going to school or this afternoon coming back home?
Did you walk? Did you take a train or a bus? What streets did you take? Did you go past any important landmarks?

SECTION C

Do you know how to refer to people and things, using *lo, la, los,* and *las*?
Answer the following. Use **lo, la, los,** and **las.**

1. ¿Reservaste el billete?
2. ¿Tienes el pasaporte?
3. ¿Compraste los regalos?
4. ¿Estudiaste el mapa?
5. ¿Hiciste las maletas?
6. ¿Llamaste al taxi?

Can you talk about what you've already done today?
Using **ya,** make up five sentences.

VOCABULARIO

SECTION A

la **alegría** *happiness*
anoche *last night*
apuradísimo, -a *in a big hurry*
arreglado, -a *arranged*
ayer *yesterday*
el **billete** *ticket*
con una semana de anticipación *a week ahead of time*
creer *to believe*
creerlo *to believe it*
el **diario** *diary*
estar a punto de *to be about to*
la **excursión** *excursion, pleasure trip*
el **folleto** *brochure*
hace una hora *an hour ago*
hacer la maleta *to pack a suitcase*
la **invitación** *invitation*
lo *it*

marcar *to mark*
la **oficina** *office*
organizado, -a *organized*
pasado, -a *last, past*
la semana pasada *last week*
el **paseo** *sightseeing trip*
el **permiso** *permission*
planear *to plan*
querido, -a *dear*
regresar *to return*
reservar *to reserve*
seguro, -a *sure*
terminar *to finish*
todavía *still*
el **turismo** *tourism*
el **viaje** *trip*
ya *already*

SECTION B

antes *before*
caminar *to walk*
desde *from*
la **envidia** *envy*

¡qué envidia! *what envy (I feel)! what luck!*
el **estanque** *pond*
hasta *as far as*
la **moto** *motorcycle*
parar *to stop*
el **plan** *plan*
preguntar *to ask*
remar *to row*
sin *without*
sin parar *without stopping*
ya viene *he(she) is coming*

SECTION C

corto, -a *short*
la *you (pol. sing.), her, it*
las *you (pl.), them*
listo, -a *ready*
lo *you (pol. sing.), him, it*
los *you (pl.), them*
¿Qué más? *What else?*
el **regalo** *present*
la **ruta** *route*

ESTUDIO DE PALABRAS

1. Make a list of all the travel words in the unit vocabulary. Arrange them in meaningful groups to help you remember them—all the words about planning in one group, all the words about packing in another.

2. Then go through the unit list and collect all the new verbs. Verbs are the heart of your sentences—learn them well.

VAMOS A LEER

Antes de leer

As you read, do you say the words to yourself or move your lips? Put your finger on your lips while reading this travel brochure. If you're moving your lips, you are reading at a slower pace than you should.

¡A España!

ESPAÑA TE ESPERA SIEMPRE . . .

¡¡Viva° España!!
Valencia te brinda°
su imaginación
con arte en una
explosión de luz,°
flores y color.
Participa de° esta
imagen fascinante
y no olvides°
comer una
suculenta
PAELLA.

Las Fallas° de Valencia empiezan una semana antes de la fiesta de San José, el 19 de marzo. La primavera va a empezar y los valencianos° la saludan° con hogueras°. En cada esquina de la ciudad hay una falla y a la medianoche° del día 19, se queman° todas las fallas al mismo tiempo. Entonces la ciudad parece arder° por todas partes.

La paella, un delicioso plato original de Valencia, tiene hoy en día fama internacional. Los ingredientes básicos son arroz amarillo, pollo, mariscos° y legumbres°.

Preguntas y respuestas

Answer the questions about what you have read.

1. ¿Cuándo empiezan las Fallas?
2. ¿Qué estación del año va a empezar?
3. ¿Cómo la saludan los valencianos?
4. ¿Qué hay en cada esquina de la ciudad?
5. ¿Cuándo se queman las fallas?
6. ¿Qué plato valenciano tiene fama internacional?
7. ¿Cuáles son sus ingredientes básicos?

Actividad • Un anuncio *An ad*

Write a short ad about your city or town for a tourist brochure. Mention an important date or celebration in your town and say how it's celebrated. Talk about tourist attractions and places of interest in or near your town.

¡viva! *long live!* **brinda** *offers* **luz** *light* **participa de** *share in* **no olvides** *don't forget* **fallas** *giant figures* **valencianos** *natives of Valencia* **la saludan** *greet it* **hogueras** *bonfires* **medianoche** *midnight* **se queman** *are burned* **arder** *to burn* **mariscos** *seafood* **legumbres** *vegetables*

Guía turística de nuestra galaxia 📼

Folleto° imaginario para viajes del futuro.

1. Estación interplanetaria
×32—Amplio estacionamiento°
para su nave°—cómodos
restaurantes con la más amplia
variedad° de píldoras°
alimenticias°.

2. Centro comercial galáctico.
El último grito° de la moda
en trajes espaciales.

3. Museo interplanetario
—Reproducción de la primera
estación lunar—Amplio archivo°
fotográfico— Una experiencia
fascinante para toda la familia.

**4. Transbordador de la
amistad°**—Un robot
guía lo acompañará°
en una visita
inolvidable° a la
Casa-Museo "E.T."

**5. Zoológico de la Vía
Láctea°**—Una fascinante
colección de especies
animales, desde° un
monstruo de Hollywood
hasta° un elefante violeta
de Júpiter.

Actividad • Información, por favor

You are in charge of information at the intergalactic tourist center. Answer these
tourists' questions, giving all the information you can, according to **Guía turística.**

1. ¿Dónde puedo estacionar mi nave?
2. ¿El restaurante, por favor?
3. Necesito un traje espacial.
4. Queremos mirar fotografías.

5. ¿Dónde puedo ir con mis hijos?
6. ¿Podemos visitar la Casa-Museo "E.T."?
7. ¿La colección de animales?
8. ¡Píldoras alimenticias, por favor!

Actividad • Charla

You and your partner have just come back from a galactic trip. Talk to your
partner about the places you visited and what you saw there, and ask him or her
about the places he or she visited.

---

folleto *brochure* **amplio estacionamiento** *ample parking* **nave** *(space)ship* **variedad** *variety* **píldoras**
alimenticias *food capsules* **el último grito** *the last word* **archivo** *file* **transbordador de la amistad** *friendship carrier*
lo acompañará *will accompany you* **inolvidable** *unforgettable* **Vía Láctea** *Milky Way* **desde . . . hasta** *from . . . to*

Un viaje estupendo **295**

El regalo

En El Paso, Daniel y su hermana deciden ir a Madrid. Deben buscar la flor° de la canción° de los mariachis°. Los chicos prenden° el televisor.

DANIEL   Hoy no hay ningún° programa de España en el Canal 17. No podemos ir.

ADRIANA   Pero, este programa es de México, Daniel. ¿Por qué no vamos a casa?

DANIEL   ¿Crees que es una buena idea? . . . Bueno, está bien. Regresamos a México.

Al día siguiente, en México, los chicos encuentran° un programa sobre Segovia. Allí van los dos hermanos. Dan una vuelta por la ciudad, y llegan a la parte antigua°.

DANIEL   ¡Qué ciudad tan bonita! ¿A ti te gusta, Adriana?

ADRIANA   Me gusta mucho. Aquí, en la parte antigua, me parece estar en el pasado . . . ¡Oh, Daniel! Ahí hay un autobús para Madrid. Sale pronto°, ¿lo tomamos?

Los chicos llegan a Madrid y toman un taxi.

DANIEL   A la Puerta del Sol, por favor.

TAXISTA   Bien, llegamos pronto°. Ahora estamos en el centro de Madrid. Es como una rueda°, los números de las calles empiezan aquí.

Los chicos bajan° del taxi. Hay mucho tráfico y mucha gente en las calles. Pero, ¿cuál es la flor que deben encontrar, la flor de la canción de El Paso?

ADRIANA   Ahora, ¿qué? ¿Por qué hicimos este viaje tan loco?

DANIEL   Porque es nuestro destino y yo soy un genio.

ADRIANA   Sí, sí, ya me convenciste°. ¡Daniel! ¡Mira a esa mujer!° La que está enfrente del° banco. Creo que la conozco, es . . .

DANIEL   ¡Tienes razón! Es la aeromoza°, la mujer del secuestro° del vuelo 28. Debe estar en Madrid porque ese vuelo es de México a Madrid.

ADRIANA   ¡Cuidado!° Si ella nos ve y nos reconoce°, puede hacer cualquier° cosa . . .

DANIEL   Mira, ella va a cruzar° la calle. ¿La seguimos?°

---

flor *flower*   **canción** *song*   **mariachis** *Mexican band*   **prenden** *they turn on*   **no hay ningún** *there isn't any* **encuentran** *they find*   **antigua** *old*   **pronto** *soon*   **rueda** *wheel*   **bajan** *get out*   **me convenciste** *convinced me* **mujer** *woman*   **enfrente del** *in front of*   **aeromoza** *flight attendant*   **secuestro** *hijacking*   **¡cuidado!** *be careful!*   **nos reconoce** *recognizes us*   **cualquier** *any*   **cruzar** *to cross*   **¿la seguimos?** *do we follow her?*

La aeromoza camina hasta la esquina y sube a° un coche. El chófer es un hombre°
rubio—el mismo del aeropuerto de México. ¡Es Héctor Ríos!, el cómplice° de la aeromoza.

De repente°, la aeromoza mira hacia° donde están Daniel y Adriana y grita° algo.
El coche va hacia los dos muchachos como una bala°. Un segundo° coche viene
por la derecha. Los dos vehículos chocan°.

Todo pasa tan rápido que Daniel y Adriana están paralizados. La gente se acerca°;
en pocos minutos llega la policía. El conductor del segundo coche habla con la
policía. Camina hacia Daniel y Adriana y los saluda con gran emoción. Adriana lo
reconoce inmediatamente: es el joven° guapo de El Paso.

ADRIANA	Daniel, ¡el joven de El Paso!
DANIEL	¿Qué hace él aquí?
JOVEN	¡Bienvenidos a Madrid!
DANIEL	Gracias . . . , pero, ¿quién eres tú?
JOVEN	Me llamo Omar Ramos.
ADRIANA	¿Ramos? ¿Como el piloto del vuelo 28?
JOVEN	Sí. El piloto Héctor Ramos Velázquez es mi padre. Ustedes lo ayudaron muchísimo.
DANIEL	¿Lo ayudamos? ¿Cómo?
JOVEN	Ustedes le salvaron la vida°. Salvaron la vida de mi padre.

Actividad • No es así

Correct the following statements, according to **El regalo.**

1. Daniel y Adriana deciden ir a Madrid para ver un programa sobre España.
2. Los hermanos toman un avión en El Paso para ir a Madrid.
3. Ellos encuentran un programa de España en El Paso.
4. En Segovia pueden ver un programa sobre México.
5. En la parte antigua de México, Adriana cree estar en el futuro.
6. Ellos no toman el tren para Madrid porque sale tarde.
7. La mujer que está enfrente del banco es la madre del piloto del vuelo 28.
8. La aeromoza camina hasta el banco y sube a un autobús.
9. El joven de El Paso es primo del piloto.
10. Daniel y Adriana salvaron la vida del tío de la aeromoza.

---

sube a *gets into*	**hombre** *man*	**cómplice** *accomplice*	**de repente** *suddenly*	**hacia** *towards*	**grita** *yells*	**bala** *bullet*
segundo *second*	**chocan** *collide*	**se acerca** *come near*	**joven** *young man*	**le salvaron la vida** *saved his life*		

UNIDAD 11

¡Vamos de compras!

Do you like to shop? In Spanish-speaking countries, shopping can be a wonderful adventure. For very little money, you can often find beautiful clothing, handicrafts, and gifts. In the larger stores, the merchandise usually has price tags and the prices are fixed, but that's not the case in the public markets or in small shops. There you can watch lively scenes of *regateo* (bargaining), and try bargaining yourself.

In this unit you will:

SECTION A	make comparisons . . . talk about differences in quality and price
SECTION B	discuss prices . . . bargain
SECTION C	say what you did . . . talk about future plans
TRY YOUR SKILLS	use what you've learned
VAMOS A LEER	read for practice and pleasure

making comparisons . . . talking about differences in quality and price

The **Palacio de Hierro** *is one of the great old department stores in Mexico City. As the city grew, the store opened branches in shopping centers on the outskirts. Let's visit the super-modern* **Palacio de Hierro** *in* **Perisur,** *a shopping center on the* **Periférico,** *the freeway that encircles the ever-growing metropolis.*

A1   ¿Lo compramos? 📼

SEÑORA	Señorita, por favor.
VENDEDORA	¿Qué desea, señora?
SEÑORA	Ese plato de cerámica, por favor.
VENDEDORA	¿Cuál, el pequeño o el grande?
SEÑORA	Los dos . . . Este plato es más grande que ése, pero cuesta menos, ¿por qué?
VENDEDORA	El más pequeño está hecho a mano. El grande es una imitación. No es de cerámica, es de plástico.
SEÑORA	¡Oh, no! Yo quiero uno de cerámica, pero más barato que éste. ¿Y ése de allá?
VENDEDORA	Cuesta igual que el de cerámica.
SEÑORA	¡Oh! ¿Valen lo mismo? Muchas gracias.

EMILIO	¿Qué te parece, Diego? ¿Qué cinturón llevamos?
DIEGO	No sé, pero a mí me gusta más el oscuro. Es más largo y más bonito que el claro.
EMILIO	El claro no me gusta nada. El oscuro está bien, ¿no?
DIEGO	No está mal, pero es más caro que el otro.
EMILIO	¡No importa! Es bien lindo y es de cuero.

CLARA	¡Mira esta blusa! Es una preciosura. Es de algodón. Está bordada a mano. ¿La compro?
MARIANA	¡Buena idea! Voy a preguntar el precio. Por favor, señorita, ¿cuánto vale esta blusa en dólares?
VENDEDORA	Veinte dólares, señorita.
CLARA	Bueno, está bien. ¿Puedo pagar con tarjeta de crédito?
VENDEDORA	Sí, cómo no. En la caja, por favor.

A2 Actividad • ¿Es cierto o no?

Correct the following sentences to make them agree with the dialog in A1. Some of them are correct already.

1. La señora quiere ver unos platos de plástico.
2. Ella quiere ver el plato pequeño.
3. El plato pequeño es más barato.
4. El plato grande está hecho a mano.
5. El plato grande es de cerámica.
6. A Diego le gusta el cinturón más claro.
7. El cinturón claro es más pequeño que el oscuro.
8. Mariana sabe el precio de la blusa.
9. La blusa vale cincuenta dólares.
10. Clara no puede usar su tarjeta de crédito.

A3 Actividad • ¡A escoger!

Choose the best option to complete the following sentences according to ¿**Lo compramos?**

1. La señora quiere comprar
   • un plato de cerámica.   • un cinturón.   • una blusa.
2. El plato pequeño cuesta más que
   • el grande.   • el de cerámica.   • el cinturón.
3. El cinturón oscuro es
   • más barato.   • más caro.   • una imitación.
4. Ellos van a llevar
   • unos platos.   • una blusa.   • un cinturón.
5. El cinturón es de
   • plástico.   • cuero.   • algodón.
6. A Clara le gusta
   • una blusa bordada.   • un cinturón.   • un plato de cerámica.
7. La blusa es de
   • plástico.   • algodón.   • cuero.
8. Clara dice que va a pagar
   • con un cheque.   • con dinero.   • con tarjeta de crédito.

A4 SE DICE ASÍ
Asking and expressing opinions

—Y a ti, ¿qué te parece? (¿qué crees?) (¿qué piensas?)	¡Buena idea! ¡Está(n) bien! No está(n) mal . . .	(It's a) good idea! It's (They're) all right! It's not (They're not) bad . . .
—Y a usted, ¿qué le parece? (¿qué cree?) (¿qué piensa?)	Me gusta(n) más . . . No me gusta nada. No sé. No sé, pero . . .	I like it (them) more . . . I don't like it at all. I don't know. I don't know, but . . .

¡Vamos de compras!   301

A5 Actividad • ¿Qué te parece?

You go shopping with a friend. Ask each other's opinion about what you're buying. Then write down your conversation.

—¿Qué te parece esta raqueta?

—¿Qué crees?

—¿Qué piensas?

• Está bien.

• No está mal.

• No sé, pero . . .

• Me gusta más . . .

A6 ESTRUCTURAS ESENCIALES
Comparisons with **más** *and* **menos**

1. In Spanish, to make comparisons with adjectives, use the following formula:

más **menos** + adjective + **que**	*more* *less* + adjective + than

El cinturón oscuro es **más** bonito **que** el claro.
The dark belt is more attractive than the light one.

El plato de plástico es **menos** caro **que** el de cerámica.
The plastic plate is less expensive than the ceramic one.

2. Que is the equivalent of *than* in English. It can be followed by a noun or a subject pronoun.
Compro menos ropa **que tú.** *I buy less clothing than you.*
Tú eres más alto **que yo.** *You are taller than I.*

3. Before a number or an expression of quantity, use **de** instead of **que.**
Cuesta **más de** ochenta pesos. *It costs more than eighty pesos.*
Cuesta **menos de** diez dólares. *It costs less than ten dollars.*

A7 Actividad • ¿Qué es más caro?

You are at the store. Compare prices. (Use your own judgment in determining whether the first item is more or less expensive than the second item.)

cinturón / cartera   —El cinturón es más barato que la cartera.
　　　　　　　　　　　—La cartera es más cara que el cinturón.

1. zapatos / botas
2. taza / plato
3. guantes / pañuelos
4. discos / casetes

5. revistas / libros
6. cinturón / blusa
7. raqueta / bate

8. estéreo / televisión
9. tartas / pan
10. fresas / uvas

abrigo   chaqueta de lana   suéter   calcetines

pantalones

saco

jeans   corbata   camisa   traje

sombrero   zapatos   vestido
de algodón   falda

pañuelo de seda   blusa   traje de baño

A 9   Práctica • ¡A escoger!

Choose the best option to complete these sentences according to the window display in A8.

1. La chaqueta es de
   • lana.   • algodón.   • seda.
2. La falda está
   • al lado de los zapatos.   • a la derecha del vestido.   • entre los pañuelos y las blusas.
3. Los jeans están
   • debajo del sombrero.   • a la izquierda de la corbata.   • detrás del traje de baño.
4. Hay pañuelos de seda de color
   • verde claro.   • amarillo oscuro.   • azul y blanco.
5. Las camisas son
   • blancas.   • azules.   • verde claro.
6. Venden vestidos de
   • seda.   • lana.   • algodón.
7. Los calcetines están
   • cerca de la corbata.   • detrás del sombrero.   • al lado del suéter.
8. Venden zapatos de color
   • verde oscuro.   • marrón.   • verde claro.

A 10   Actividad • Voy a comprar . . .

You have some money to spend on clothes. Decide what you want to buy for yourself in the store, based on what you see in A8. After making your choices, discuss them with a classmate.

A 11 Actividad • ¡A escribir!

Write the conversation you had with your classmate in A10. Mention what you are going to buy and write about what your friend is going to buy also.

A 12 ¿Sabes que . . . ?

You want to try on one of those sweaters? **¿Qué talla necesitas?** *What size do you need?* In Spanish-speaking countries, clothing sizes are marked in the metric system. Find your sizes in the following tables and write them down where you can use them when you travel.

Tallas para señoras						
Vestidos, Trajes y Abrigos						
Métrico:	36	38	40	42	44	46
EE.UU.:	8	10	12	14	16	18
Blusas y Suéteres						
Métrico:	40	42	44	46	48	50	52
EE.UU.:	32	34	36	38	40	42	44
Zapatos						
Métrico:	35 35 36 37 38 38 38¹/₂ 39 40						
EE.UU.:	5 5¹/₂ 6 6¹/₂ 7 7¹/₂ 8 8¹/₂ 9						

Tallas para señores						
Trajes, Suéteres y Abrigos						
Métrico:	44	46	48	50	52	54	56
EE.UU.:	34	36	38	40	42	44	46
Camisas						
Métrico:	36	37	38	39	40	41	42
EE.UU.:	14 14¹/₂ 15 15¹/₂ 16 16¹/₂ 17						
Zapatos						
Métrico:	39 40 41 42 43 43 44 44 45						
EE.UU.:	7 7¹/₂ 8 8¹/₂ 9 9¹/₂ 10 10¹/₂ 11						

A 13 Comprensión

Listen to the conversation, then check **Sí** or **No**.

	0	1	2	3	4	5	6	7	8	9	10
Sí	✔										
No											

A 14 Actividad • Charla

A new student enrolled in your class today. He or she doesn't know your home, family, friends, or hobbies. Using **más que** and **menos que,** talk about brothers, sisters, friends, sports figures, movies, records, songs. . . .

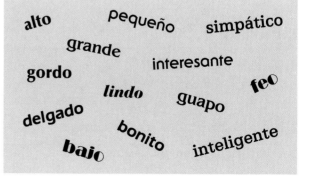

A 15 SE DICE ASÍ
Asking and saying what something is made of

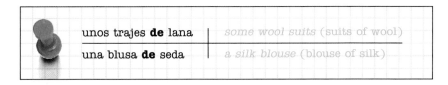

| | unos trajes **de** lana | some wool suits (suits of wool) |
| | una blusa **de** seda | a silk blouse (blouse of silk) |

To say what something is made of, use **de** + the noun naming the material.
To find out what something is made of, ask: **¿De** qué es (son)?

A 16 Actividad • ¿Qué compraste?

Yesterday you went shopping. Say you bought the items listed, adding a phrase
to show what material each is made of.

un abrigo   —Ayer compré un abrigo de lana.

1. una blusa   **3.** una camisa   **5.** unos zapatos
2. unos calcetines   **4.** una cartera   **6.** una chaqueta

A 17 ESTRUCTURAS ESENCIALES
Demonstrative pronouns

¿Un traje?		**éste / ése / aquél.**		*this / that* (one).
¿Una falda?	Llevo	**ésta / ésa / aquélla.**	*I'll take*	
¿Unos zapatos?		**éstos / ésos / aquéllos.**		
¿Unas camisas?		**éstas / ésas / aquéllas.**		*these / those.*

In Unit 9 you began to use demonstrative adjectives. Demonstrative pronouns are the same
words, with the nouns deleted. But when you write them as pronouns, add written accents.

	adjective	*noun*		*pronoun*
	este	traje	⟶	**éste.**
Llevo	esa	camisa	⟶	**ésa.**
	aquel	pañuelo	⟶	**aquél.**

A 18 Actividad • No, quiero ésa

The customer never wants what the clerk suggests. Play the role of the customer.
Work with a partner. Switch roles.

—¿Quiere **esta** blusa?

—No, quiero **ésa.**

| traje | pantalones | camisas | platos | cinturón | zapatos |
| cartera | suéter | maleta | libro | revistas | calcetines |

Actividad • No, aquélla 🔲

Go over the items in A18, following the model given below.

—¿Lleva **esos** pañuelos?

—No, llevo **aquéllos.**

A 20 Actividad • Conversación

Work with a partner. Be a difficult customer. When the clerk shows you something, ask about several other items—the more the better. Switch roles.

—Estos zapatos cuestan 30 dólares.
—¿Y ésos? ¿Y aquéllos de cuero? ¿Y ésos de tenis? ¿Y éstos blancos?

1. Esa blusa cuesta lo mismo.
2. Este plato de cerámica cuesta menos.
3. Aquel traje está hecho a mano.
4. Estos cinturones son de cuero.

5. Estas faldas son de algodón.
6. Aquellos jeans son muy baratos.
7. Estas tazas valen igual.
8. Esos suéteres son de lana.

A 21 Comprensión 🔲

Adjective or pronoun? Decide which of the two.

	0	1	2	3	4	5	6	7	8	9	10
Accent mark											
No accent mark											

If you buy clothes from a neighborhood shop or a vendor on the street, you can save money. Check for quality and fit and don't forget to bargain—the asking price is usually higher than the seller expects to receive.

B1

¡Es una ganga! ▭

Marisa y su mamá están de compras en La Lujosa, una tienda de barrio.

MAMÁ	¿Le compras dos regalos a Linda, un suéter y una cartera?
MARISA	No, mamá. Compro el suéter para mí y le compro la cartera a Linda. Le mando la cartera por correo, ¿no? ¿Qué te parece? Así la recibe pronto.
MAMÁ	¡Buena idea! Ese suéter te queda muy bien. La cartera es de muy buena calidad. ¿Sabes cuánto cuesta?

MARISA	No. ¿Le preguntamos a la vendedora?
VENDEDORA	¿En qué puedo servirle, señorita?
MAMÁ	¿Cuánto cuesta esta cartera?
VENDEDORA	325 pesos, señora, pero está rebajada a 280 por esta semana. Es una oferta especial. No va a encontrar otra más barata.
MAMÁ	¡280 pesos! Es demasiado cara. Esa cartera no vale tanto. Vamos a otra tienda, Marisa.
MARISA	Por favor, mamá, ¡es una ganga! A Linda le va a encantar.
MAMÁ	No pago más de 200 pesos. (En voz baja.) Pero hijita, tú no sabes regatear. Vas a ver.
VENDEDORA	Perdón, señora. Como a su hija le gusta tanto, le dejo la cartera en 200 pesos. Más barata no puedo.
MAMÁ	Entonces, la llevamos. ¿Le puedo pagar con un cheque?

B2   Preguntas y respuestas ▭

Answer the following questions about B1.

1. ¿Qué compra Marisa?
2. ¿Para quién es el regalo?
3. ¿Cómo le queda el suéter a Marisa?
4. ¿Cuánto cuesta la cartera?
5. ¿A cuánto está rebajada? ¿Por cuánto tiempo?
6. ¿Van ellas a otra tienda? ¿Por qué?
7. ¿Qué piensa Marisa de la cartera?
8. ¿Sabe Marisa regatear?
9. ¿Cuánto pagan por la cartera?
10. ¿Cómo paga la señora?

Pair up with a classmate. Ask each other the following questions.

1. ¿Compras regalos? ¿Te gusta comprar regalos? ¿Por qué?
2. ¿Cuándo y para quién compras regalos?
3. ¿Compras siempre los mismos regalos? ¿Por qué?
4. ¿Qué regalos compras generalmente? ¿Por qué?
5. ¿Te gusta recibir regalos? ¿Cuáles?
6. ¿Regateas generalmente? ¿Te gusta regatear? ¿Puedes regatear? ¿Dónde?

B4 ¿Sabes que . . . ?

In Mexico City, Lima, Bogotá, and other great cities in the New World, the downtown streets and even major avenues in residential sections are crowded with street vendors selling belts and bags, sweaters, blankets, and souvenirs. Theirs are usually the lowest prices in town.

B5 ESTRUCTURAS ESENCIALES
Indirect objects

Le escribo una carta.	*I write her a letter.*
Le escribo una carta **a mi hermana.**	*I write a letter to my sister.*

1. In Units 9 and 10, you learned that the *direct* object indicates who or what gets acted upon by the verb. In the example sentences, **una carta** is what gets written, so it is the direct object.

2. An *indirect* object is the word used to indicate who or what *benefits* from the action of the verb. In the example sentence, the letter is written for the benefit of **mi hermana**—it is written *to* or *for* her. **Hermana,** or the pronoun standing for her, is therefore the indirect object.

3. Indirect-object and direct-object pronouns are the same, except in the third person.

Indirect-Object Pronouns			
Singular		*Plural*	
me	(to) me	**nos**	(to) us
te	(to) you (*informal*)		
	(to) you (*formal*)		(to) you
le	(to) him	**les**	
	(to) her		(to) them (*m. + f.*)

4. Indirect-object pronouns are placed in front of the conjugated verb, even in negative sentences.

Mi hermano no me escribe cartas.

5. The indirect-object pronouns **le** and **les** require clarification when the context does not specify the person to which they refer. Spanish provides clarification by adding **a** + *personal pronoun* or

a + *name of the person.* **Le** escribo una carta. (*to whom? to him? to her?*): **Le** escribo una carta **a mi hermana.** (*to my sister*)

$$
\text{Le escribo}
\begin{cases}
\text{a mi hermano.} \\
\text{a él.} \\
\text{a usted.}
\end{cases}
\qquad
\text{Les escribo}
\begin{cases}
\text{a Marisa y a Linda.} \\
\text{a ellas.} \\
\text{a ustedes.}
\end{cases}
$$

B6 Actividad • ¿Qué les compras?

You've got to buy a lot of gifts. Say that you're going to buy the indicated items. Use a pronoun to mention whom the gift is for.

a mi hermano, un suéter   —Le compro un suéter.

1. a la abuela, un pañuelo de seda
2. a mi amigo Raúl, discos
3. para ti, una chaqueta
4. a mis primos, corbatas
5. a mis padres, una cartera
6. para mí, un casete

B7 Actividad • ¿Lo compraste?

Work with a classmate. You went shopping for everybody. Now that you're back, your classmate checks to see if you remembered everything. Answer each question **Sí** or **No.** Then write down your answers.

Mamá / la revista   —¿**Le** compraste la revista?
                              —Sí, (No, no) **le** compré la revista.

1. Papá / el libro
2. tus hermanos / los casetes
3. tu hermana / un regalo
4. tu prima / el disco
5. tus amigos / los casetes
6. para ti / el suéter
7. tus hermanos y tu hermana / los pañuelos
8. nosotros / los guantes

B8 Comprensión

Are the replies appropriate or inappropriate?

	0	1	2	3	4	5	6	7	8	9	10
Sí											
No	✔										

B9 SITUACIÓN • El estéreo nuevo

Raúl quiere un estéreo nuevo . . . pero, ¿cuándo lo va a poder comprar? ¡El estéreo cuesta más de mil pesos! Raúl hace cuentas.

—Si ahorro veinticinco pesos por semana . . . son cien por mes . . . en un año puedo tener el estéreo . . . ¡No, un año es mucho tiempo! Vamos a ver . . . ahorro el doble: doscientos pesos por mes . . . en dos meses son cuatrocientos . . . sí, en cinco meses, ¡me compro el estéreo!, pero, ¿voy a poder ahorrar?

Actividad · ¡A escoger!

Choose the option that best completes each sentence according to B9.

1. Raúl quiere
   • una bicicleta.   • una cámara.   • un estéreo.
2. El estéreo cuesta
   • más de cien pesos.   • más de diez pesos.   • más de mil pesos.
3. Raúl hace
   • compras.   • cuentas.   • un viaje.
4. Para comprarlo, Raúl
   • tiene que estudiar.   • debe ahorrar.   • va a trabajar.
5. Veinticinco pesos por semana
   • son cien por mes.   • son diez por mes.   • son mil por mes.
6. Doscientos pesos por mes
   • son cien en dos meses.   • son cuatrocientos en dos meses.   • son mil en un mes.

B11 ESTRUCTURAS ESENCIALES
Using the numbers 100 to 1,000

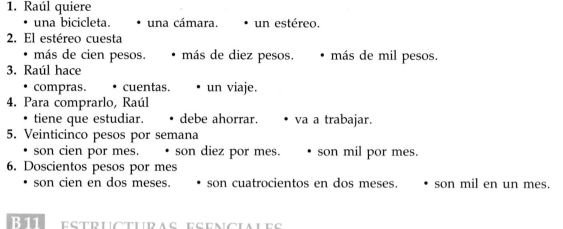

| **100** | **101** | **134** | **200** |
| cien | ciento uno, -a | ciento treinta y cuatro | doscientos, -as |

| **223** | **300** | **400** | **500** |
| doscientos, -as veintitrés | trescientos, -as | cuatrocientos, -as | quinientos, -as |

| **600** | **700** | **800** | **900** | **1,000** |
| seiscientos, -as | setecientos, -as | ochocientos, -as | novecientos, -as | mil |

1. In Unit 2 you saw that **uno** changes its ending to agree with the gender of the noun it modifies.

   un chico, **una** chica, veinti**ún** chicos, veinti**una** chicas
   doscientos treinta y **un** chicos, seiscientas cuarenta y **una** chicas

2. Use **cien** before a noun. It becomes **ciento** when followed by a smaller number.

   cien chicos y **cien** chicas; **ciento un** chicos y **ciento una** chicas

3. Numbers from 200 through 999 have a masculine and a feminine form. The **-os** ending of the hundreds changes to **-as** to agree with a feminine noun.

   quinient**os** chicos, quinient**as** chicas
   cuatrocient**os** tres chicos, cuatrocient**as** tres chicas

4. The word **y** is used only between the tens and the units in numbers above thirty.

   ciento treinta **y** uno   ochocientos cuarenta **y** dos   (BUT: doscientos uno)

5. Periods are often used in Spanish instead of commas to mark off thousands: 2.000 **dos mil.**

Actividad • Precios

You are a clerk in a Latin American store. The customers ask for prices. Answer their questions, reading the price tags.

$ 180   —Ciento ochenta pesos

B 13 Actividad • ¡A escribir!

Write down your answers for B13, writing the quantity in Spanish. Use words, not numbers.

B 14 Actividad • No es así

It's inventory time at the store. You're working with a partner. Correct what he or she says, following the clues.

Cuatrocientos platos (tazas)   —No, son cuatrocientas tazas.

1. Cien libros (revistas)
2. Ciento un discos (cámaras)
3. Seiscientas treinta y tres chaquetas (abrigos)
4. Mil corbatas (pañuelos)
5. Ochocientos veintiocho abrigos (faldas)
6. Doscientos pañuelos (corbatas)

Major cities in the Spanish-speaking world have countless small shops, large department stores and shopping centers, and numerous street vendors. But when you ask people where they get their best bargains, chances are they'll mention some special place you've never heard of before. In Mexico City, bargain hunters flock to **El Monte de Piedad,** a vast pawnshop in the very center of the capital. **El Monte de Piedad** is a good place to start your search for almost anything; if you don't find what you want there, you can try the neighborhood **mercados,** government-sponsored markets.

B16 SE DICE ASÍ
Discussing prices, making a bargain

Cliente	Vendedor
¿Cuánto cuesta / vale? How much does it cost?	Es un regalo. It's practically a giveaway.
Es muy / demasiado caro. It's very / too expensive.	Es muy barato. It's very cheap.
No vale tanto. It's not worth that much.	Es una ganga. Es de muy buena calidad. It's a bargain. It's of very good quality.
No pago más de . . . I'm not paying more than . . .	No va a encontrar uno(a) / otro(a) más barato(a). You're not going to find a cheaper one.

B17 Actividad • ¿Lo compro o no?

Work with two or three classmates. One of you is the salesclerk; the others are customers. Ask what you want. Discuss prices. The clerk helps the customers make decisions.

No pago más de 100 pesos

¡Es una ganga!

Es de muy buena calidad

Es muy caro

No va a encontrar otro más barato

Es un regalo

¿Cuánto cuesta?

No vale tanto

B18 Actividad • ¡A escribir!

Write a conversation between a salesclerk and customers, using your exchanges in B17 as a basis.

B 19   Comprensión

Striking a bargain.

	0	1	2	3	4	5	6	7	8	9	10
Sí	✔										
No											

B 20   Actividad • ¿Qué precio tiene?

Set up an imaginary flea market in class. Bring pictures of items for sale. Establish a fixed maximum price for any item beforehand.

B 21   Actividad • En venta

Make a sign with the pictures of the items you have for sale. Write in Spanish a short paragraph describing each item. Leave prices out of your sign.

B 22   Actividad • ¿Lo llevo o no?

When you find something that you like at the flea market, ask the vendor about price and quality. Compare items, and try your hand at bargaining.

B 23   Actividad • Compras y ventas

• If you sell something, write out a receipt describing the item and showing the price.

• Make a chart for yourself like the one shown below. Compare charts with your classmates. Report to the class everything you bought and sold at the flea market.

	¿Qué?	¿A quién?	¿Cuánto?
Compras			
Ventas			

When you buy something and it doesn't arrive on time, you have to complain to the store and get some action. You need to discuss what you ordered, what you said, and what you wanted.

C1   Sección de quejas y reclamos 📼

El Sr. Gómez no recibió el estéreo que compró. Ahora está en la Sección de quejas y reclamos.

EMPLEADA   ¿Señor?

SR. GÓMEZ   Sí, señorita. Aquí tengo el recibo. Ustedes me prometieron el estéreo para el día 15. Hoy es 25, . . . y no lo recibí.

EMPLEADA   El recibo, por favor. Ah, señor, ¿escribió usted una carta de reclamación?

SR. GÓMEZ   ¡Señorita, por favor! Llamé por teléfono veinte veces, escribí dos cartas la semana pasada . . . , finalmente, decidí venir en persona.

EMPLEADA   ¿Subió usted a la oficina del piso cinco?

SR. GÓMEZ   Sí, ya fui, me mandaron aquí.

EMPLEADA   A ver . . . un momento . . . ¿y quién le vendió el estéreo? Este pedido ya salió . . . usted va a recibir el estéreo mañana, a primera hora . . .

SR. GÓMEZ   Pero, señorita . . . Mi hijo no cumple años mañana . . . ¡su cumpleaños es hoy! ¡Y yo le prometí el estéreo!

C2   Actividad • ¡A escoger! 📼

Choose the best option to complete the following sentences according to **Sección de quejas y reclamos** in C1.

1. El cliente está en la sección de
   • estéreos.   • recibos.   • quejas y reclamos.
2. Le prometieron el estéreo
   • para el día 25.   • para el día 15.   • para hoy.

3. El cliente
   • recibió el estéreo.   • no recibió la carta.   • no recibió su pedido.
4. El señor llamó por teléfono
   • dos veces.   • veinte veces.   • veinticinco veces.
5. Él escribió
   • dos recibos.   • veinte veces.   • dos cartas.
6. El cliente va a recibir el estéreo
   • hoy por la tarde.   • esta noche.   • mañana.
7. El cumpleaños de su hijo es
   • mañana a primera hora.   • hoy.   • esta mañana.

C3   Actividad • Para completar

Complete these sentences to make them agree with C1.

1. Señorita, aquí tengo ____ ____ .
2. Ustedes me prometieron ____ ____ para ____ ____ ____ .
3. Hoy es 25 . . . y no lo ____ .
4. Llamé por teléfono ____ ____ , escribí ____ ____ , ____ decidí venir en persona.
5. ¿Subió usted a la ____ del piso ____ ?
6. Sí, ya fui, me ____ aquí.
7. A ver . . . un ____ , este ____ ya salió.
8. Pero, señorita . . . ¡____ ____ ____ cumple años ____ , su cumpleaños es ____ !

C4   ESTRUCTURAS ESENCIALES
   The preterit of -er *and* -ir *verbs*

	vender *to sell*		**decidir** *to decide*	
yo	**Vendí**	mi bicicleta.	**Decidí**	escribir.
tú	**¿Vendiste**	tus periódicos?	**¿Decidiste**	subir?
usted, él, ella	**Vendió**	su coche.	**¿Decidió**	venir?
nosotros(as)	**Vendimos**	nuestros libros.	**Decidimos**	vender la casa.
vosotros(as)	**¿Vendisteis**	todo?	**¿Decidisteis**	ir?
ustedes, ellos(as)	**Vendieron**	mucho.	**Decidieron**	salir.

1. In Unit 10 you studied the preterit of regular **-ar** verbs. The preterit tense expresses completed past actions. The chart shows the preterit of **vender,** a regular **-er** verb, and **decidir,** a regular **-ir** verb.

2. You can produce the preterit forms of regular **-er** and **-ir** verbs by adding the following endings to the stem:

í, -iste, -ió, -imos,   -isteis,   -ieron

3. Every regular preterit form is stressed on the ending. Notice that the **yo** and **usted/él/ella** forms have written accents.

Yo **vendí** todas las corbatas.   Ella **decidió** comprar el estéreo.

C5 Actividad • En la feria de la clase

The class flea market was a big success. Everybody sold something. Complete the conversation, using the preterit of **vender.**

Raúl / libros y revistas.   —Raúl vendió libros y revistas.

1. ¿Qué / tú?
2. Yo / bocadillos.
3. Nosotros / mucho.
4. ¿Y ustedes, qué / ?
5. Susana y yo / tartas y bizcochos.

6. ¿Quién / discos?
7. Pablo / discos y casetes.
8. Y Mariana, ¿qué / ?
9. Ella / calcetines.
10. Alberto y Graciela / ropa también.

C6 Actividad • Quejas

Everybody is complaining. The things people bought haven't arrived.
Complete using the preterit of **recibir.** Add **no** to all your sentences.

El señor López, los libros
El señor López no recibió los libros.

1. Yo, la cámara
2. Tú, la guitarra
3. Nosotros, el estéreo

4. Mis amigos, la bicicleta
5. Ustedes, la computadora
6. Usted, los discos

7. Angel, la raqueta
8. Marisa y yo, las revistas
9. Tú, el diccionario

C7 Comprensión

Present or preterit?

	0	1	2	3	4	5	6	7	8	9
Present										
Preterit										

C8 Actividad • ¿Qué pasó?

Mr. Gómez is making a complaint at the store. Write out what he says. Use the appropriate forms of these verbs in the preterit. Repetitions are allowed.

> comprar   escribir   ir   mandar   subir
> salir   llamar   prometer   recibir

—Señorita, yo _____ un estéreo el día 15. Hoy es el 25, y yo no _____ el estéreo. El vendedor me _____ el estéreo para el día 19.
—Sí, ¿_____ usted por teléfono?
—Sí, yo _____ la semana pasada, _____ una carta, pero no _____ el estéreo.
—¿_____ usted a la oficina del piso cinco?
—Sí, señorita. _____ y me _____ aquí.
—Bien, señor. Su pedido ya _____ . Lo va a tener mañana a primera hora.
—Pero, ¡yo lo quiero hoy!

Actividad • ¡A escribir!

Use the preterit to tell what happened to Mr. Gómez according to C1. Start with:
El señor Gómez compró un estéreo el día . . .

 Actividad • Charla

Work with a partner. You are the customer and your partner is a clerk in the customer service department of a store. You bought something a month ago, but the store hasn't delivered your order yet. Complain. Switch roles.

 SE DICE ASÍ
Saying what you did and what you are going to do

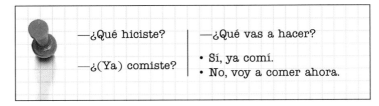

—¿Qué hiciste?	—¿Qué vas a hacer?
—¿(Ya) comiste?	• Sí, ya comí.
	• No, voy a comer ahora.

Use the preterit to say what people did. Use the **ir a** + infinitive construction to say what people are going to do. You can also use the present tense to say what people are doing in the near future: **¿Adónde vas el sábado?**

 Actividad • Charla

Work with a partner. Talk about what you've already done today and what you're planning to do after school or tomorrow.

—¿Le hablaste a ella?

• Sí, ya le hablé.
• No, le voy a hablar después.

¿Caminaste?
¿Fuiste al parque?
¿Comiste?
¿Estudiaste?
¿Hablaste con tus amigos?
¿Corriste?
¿Fuiste a la tienda?
¿Bailaste?
¿Compraste algo?
¿Escribiste?

 Actividad • La fiesta

Your friend is planning a birthday party. Check to see if everything is taken care of. Work with a partner. Ask each other.

1. ¿Ya decidiste a quién invitar?
2. ¿Ya decidiste el día de la fiesta?
3. ¿Ya hiciste la lista de invitados?
4. ¿Ya escribiste las invitaciones?
5. ¿Ya llamaste a todos?
6. ¿Ya compraste la comida?
7. ¿Ya mandaste las invitaciones?
8. ¿Ya recibiste regalos?

C14 Actividad • ¡A escribir!

Write down what you've already done today and what you're planning to do later.

Ya comí.   Voy a mirar televisión.
Ya estudié.   Voy a salir.

C15 Actividad • Charla

El fin de semana pasado y el próximo Work with two or three classmates. Talk about what you did last weekend and what your plans for next weekend are.

—¿Adónde fueron?   —¿Adónde van a ir?
—¿Qué hicieron?   —¿Qué van a hacer?

¿Pasearon?   ¿Van a ir al cine?

¿A quién visitaron?   ¿A qué hora regresaron?

¿Van a salir?

¿Salieron?   ¿Adónde van a comer?   ¿Compraron algo?

¿Van a bailar?

¿Van a estudiar?   ¿Con quién fueron?

¿Cantaron?   ¿Escucharon música?   ¿Van a pasear?

C16 Comprensión

Preterit or future?

	0	1	2	3	4	5	6	7	8	9	10
Preterit											
Future	✔										

C17 Actividad • ¡A escribir!

Write down what you did last weekend and what your plans for next weekend are. You can also talk about what your friends did, and about what their plans are. Follow the chart below as a model.

	El fin de semana pasado	El próximo
Yo		
José		
Carmen		
Luisa		
Felipe		

1   El cliente y el empleado

Pair off with a classmate. One of you will play the part of the client, and the other will be the salesperson. Carry out the following dialog in Spanish. Present your dialog to the class.

Client asks:

- price of item(s) he/she wants.
- what material it is made of.
- what is the lowest price to be paid.
- how good is the quality of item(s).

Salesperson says:

- price of items.
- material and quality.
- lowest possible price.
- client must buy, it's a bargain!

¡Es muy caro!

Es un regalo

¿Cuánto cuesta?

Es de seda

¿Tiene uno más barato?

¿De qué es?

No va a encontrar otro más barato

Es una ganga

¿Es de algodón?

¿Es de buena calidad?

No cuesta mucho

Es de muy buena calidad

2   Actividad • ¡A escribir!

Prepare a written report based on the dialog you had with your partner.

3   Actividad • Conversación

You're coming back from a shopping trip. Work with a partner. Ask each other:

1. ¿A qué tienda fuiste?
2. ¿Es ésa tu tienda favorita? ¿Por qué?
3. ¿Compraste algo? ¿Qué?
4. ¿Cuánto pagaste?
5. ¿Piensas que pagaste mucho? ¿Por qué?
6. ¿Regateaste?
7. ¿Tú te compraste algo? ¿Qué?
8. ¿Compraste algo para tu familia? ¿Qué? ¿Para quién?
9. ¿Compraste algo para tus amigos? ¿Qué les compraste? ¿Por qué?
10. ¿Me compraste algo? ¿Qué? ¿De qué es?

4   Actividad • Talleres gráficos   *Printing shop*

The words for today's comic strip have to be inserted into the bubbles. Tell the artist which speech goes where.

1. Ayer corrí mucho. Estoy cansada.
2. Te compré un regalo.
3. ¡Cincuenta pesos! Es muy caro. Le pago treinta.
4. Cuesta mucho pero es de seda.
5. Muchas gracias. ¿Es una bicicleta?
6. ¡Felipe!, ¿y eso?
7. Fui a patinar el domingo y . . .
8. Tienes doce años y eres más alto que yo.
9. ¡Este disco es fantástico!

5 Actividad • Quejas

While you were away traveling, you bought gifts for the whole family. Six months have passed and the presents have not arrived. Call up the company to complain. Be sure to have the list of items you bought handy. The company representative is going to ask you about your order in detail. Work with a partner. Switch roles.

6 Actividad • ¡A escribir!

The representative told you on the phone to write a letter to the company stating what you bought and when. Do it now, so you can receive your order. Start your letter with: **Señores.**

7 Actividad • Charla

Talk to a partner about what you did last summer and what your plans for your next summer vacation are.

—¿Adónde fuiste en el verano?

—A San Francisco, ¿y tú?

¿Vas a trabajar?
¿Vas a estudiar?
¿Adónde fuiste?
¿Qué hiciste?
¿Adónde vas a ir?
¿Trabajaste?
¿Fuiste a la playa?
¿Vas a ir a nadar?
¿Nadaste?
¿Qué vas a hacer?
¿Estudiaste?

8 Pronunciación, lectura, dictado

1. The Spanish consonants **g** and **j** have the same sound. Listen, then read aloud.

geografía   jardín   gente   naranja   gimnasia   abajo   Argentina

2. The Spanish consonants **b** and **v** have the same sound. Listen, then read aloud.

vaso   bizcocho   invitación   venir   barato   favorito   llevar

Ellos vivieron en Venezuela por veintinueve años.
Le escribimos muchas veces pero nunca recibimos respuesta.

3. Copy the following sentences to prepare yourself to write them from dictation.

Necesito un traje de baño para el verano.
Jorge es un genio en biología.
Julio dejó su tarjeta de crédito en la caja.

¿LO SABES?

Let's review some important points you have learned in this unit.

SECTION A

Do you know how to find out what other people think about something that you're going to buy or do?
Ask five questions to find out somebody else's opinion.
Can you answer those questions yourself when asked to express your opinion?

Are you able to ask the price of different items, when you are at the store?
Ask the price of five different items, then answer those questions as if you were the salesperson.

Do you know how to compare the size and color of different clothing items?
Talk about a shirt, shoes, a dress, a coat, a skirt, socks, or any other clothing item you're interested in buying.
Compare those items and discuss their prices. Say what they're made of.

SECTION B

Do you know how to drive a bargain in Spanish?
Write down five phrases you might use.
Then react to your phrases as if you were the salesperson.

Can you mention some presents you've bought and say whom you gave them to, and name presents that you've received and say who gave them to you?
Make up five sentences. You might want to list the items first.

Can you discuss prices of over a hundred dollars?
Read these numbers aloud in Spanish as if they were **pesos.**

301　　525　　100　　436　　980　　762　　393　　219

SECTION C

Do you know how to make a complaint at the store or over the phone?
You haven't received what you've ordered.
Write down five phrases you might use to complain.

Can you talk about what you did last summer and say what you are planning to do next summer?
Make up five sentences.
Think of five questions you might ask a friend about what he or she did last summer or last weekend and what his or her plans for next summer or next weekend are.

VOCABULARIO

(see p. 310)

SECTION A

el **abrigo** *coat*
el **algodón** *cotton*
allá *(over) there*
aquél, aquélla *that one*
aquéllos, -as *those*
barato, -a *cheap*
la **blusa** *blouse*
bordado, -a *embroidered*
la **caja** *cashier's desk*
el **calcetín** **(pl. calcetines)** *sock*
la **camisa** *shirt*
caro, -a *expensive*
la **cerámica** *ceramics (material)*
claro, -a *light (in color)*
la **corbata** *tie*
¿cuánto vale? *how much does it cost?*
el **cuero** *leather*
la **chaqueta** *jacket*
de *made of*
de plástico *(made of) plastic*
¿de qué es? *what's it made of?*
el (de) *the one (made of)*
ése, -a *that one*
ésos, -as *those*
éste, -a *this one*
éstos, -as *these*
la **falda** *skirt*
hecho, -a a mano *handmade*
igual (que) *the same (as)*
los **jeans** *jeans*
los **jóvenes** *young people*
la **lana** *wool*
largo, -a *long*
lo mismo (que) *the same (as)*
llevar *to take*
la **mano** *hand*
más de . . . *more than . . .*

más . . . que *more . . . than*
más grande que *bigger than*
menos *less*
menos de . . . *less than . . .*
¡no importa! *it doesn't matter!*
no me gusta nada *I don't like it at all*
oscuro, -a *dark*
el **pañuelo** *handkerchief*
los **pantalones** *pants*
la **preciosura** *thing of beauty*
la **ropa** *clothes*
el **saco** *jacket*
la **seda** *silk*
segundo, -a *second*
el **sombrero** *hat*
el **suéter** *sweater*
la **talla** *size*
la **tarjeta de crédito** *credit card*
el **traje** *suit*
el **traje de baño** *bathing suit*
valen *they cost*
el **vestido** *dress*

SECTION B

ahorrar *to save*
así *that way, then*
el **barrio** *neighborhood*
la **calidad** *quality*
dejar *to allow, let*
le dejo la cartera en . . . *I'll let the purse go for . . .*
demasiado *too (much)*
doble *double*
¿en qué puedo servirle? *how may I help you?*
en voz baja *in a low voice*
encantar *to delight*
encontrar (ue) *to find*
especial *special*

estar de compras *to be shopping*
la **ganga** *bargain*
generalmente *generally*
hacer cuentas *to do calculations*
mandar *to send*
los **números del 100 al 1000** *numbers from 100 to 1000* (see p. 310)
la **oferta** *offer*
por correo *by mail*
pronto *soon*
rebajado, -a *reduced (in price)*
recibir *to receive*
regatear *to bargain*
servir *to serve*
te queda muy bien *it looks very nice on you*

SECTION C

a primera hora *as early as possible*
a ver *let's see*
el, la **cliente** *customer*
el **cumpleaños** *birthday*
cumplir años *to have a birthday*
en persona *in person*
elegante *elegant*
la **feria** *fair*
finalmente *finally*
el **pedido** *order*
el **piso** *floor*
prometer *to promise*
la **queja** *complaint*
quinto, -a *fifth*
el **recibo** *receipt*
la **reclamación** *claim*
el **reclamo** *claim*
la **sección de quejas y reclamos** *customer service department*

ESTUDIO DE PALABRAS

Make separate lists of all the items of clothing in the unit list. Add any other clothing words you know and want to remember.

VAMOS A LEER

Antes de leer

To practice reading for information, look at **Festival de super gangas.** In Spanish, write the important facts in the forms of notes. Try to find the Spanish equivalent for the following expressions in the ad without looking at the glosses.

1. long and short sleeves
2. assorted colors
3. beach towels
4. warm-up suits
5. dress shirts
6. giant size

Ropa para toda la familia

FESTIVAL DE SUPER GANGAS

VESTIDOS
MARCAS° FAMOSAS
Algodón, seda
desde
$29.99

GRAN° SELECCIÓN DE CAMISETAS°
Manga° Larga
Todos los tamaños°
$3.33

MEDIAS° PARA HOMBRES
Primera Calidad
Paquete° de 6
$4.99

PIJAMAS
De primera calidad
PARA HOMBRES
Estampados° surtidos
Mangas cortas y largas
$5.99

CAMISAS DE VESTIR° PARA HOMBRES
Mangas cortas
Colores surtidos°
$4.99

PANTALONES DE VESTIR PARA HOMBRES
$9.99
Primera calidad

TOALLAS DE PLAYA°
Tamaño gigante°
colores surtidos
$2.99

TRAJES DE EJERCICIO°
Hombres, Mujeres y Niños
Estilos surtidos
Colores azul, negro y blanco
$7.99

¡A escribir!

Write a short ad for a clothing item. Mention color, size, and price. Make it sound as attractive as you can.

---

gran *great* **camisetas** *T-shirts* **manga** *sleeve* **tamaños** *sizes* **camisas de vestir** *dress shirts* **surtidos** *assorted*
medias *socks* **paquete** *package* **toallas de playa** *beach towels* **gigante** *giant* **marcas** *brands* **estampados** *prints*
trajes de ejercicio *warm-up suits*

De compras en México

La Ciudad de México es moderna y tradicional. Ejemplos de esta combinación son los centros comerciales de la ciudad.

En el centro°, en el Mercado de San Juan, el ambiente° es muy animado°. Desde sus puestos°, los vendedores ofrecen una gran° variedad de productos. Y como allí muchos precios no son fijos°, los mexicanos están acostumbrados a° regatear. ¡Ah . . . qué placer° cuando el vendedor rebaja° los precios!

Al oeste°, en la Zona Rosa, el ambiente es más moderado° y más quieto°. Sus tiendas elegantes ofrecen: carteras, zapatos, ropa, joyas y objetos de alfarería°. Pero la costumbre° de regatear persiste° en esta zona. Y muy a menudo, en una de estas tiendas tan modernas se oye° el intercambio° familiar de: —¿Cuánto cuesta? —¡No, es muy caro! —¡Entonces se lo dejo en . . . !

Actividad • Para completar

Complete the following sentences according to the reading

1. La Ciudad de México es _____ .
2. El ambiente es muy animado en _____ .
3. Desde sus puestos los vendedores ofrecen _____ .
4. Los mexicanos están acostumbrados a _____ .
5. Es un placer cuando el vendedor _____ .
6. En la Zona Rosa el ambiente es _____ .
7. Sus tiendas elegantes ofrecen _____ .
8. La costumbre de regatear _____ .

---

centro *downtown* **ambiente** *atmosphere* **animado** *lively* **puestos** *market booths* **gran** *great* **fijos** *fixed* **estar acostumbrado (-a) a** *to be used to* **placer** *pleasure* **rebaja** *he lowers* **oeste** *west* **moderado, -a** *moderate* **quieto, -a** *quiet* **alfarería** *pottery* **costumbre** *custom* **persiste** *continues* **se oye** *one hears* **intercambio** *interchange*

El regalo 📼

Unos minutos después, Daniel y Adriana ya más calmados°, pueden comprender°
lo que acaba de ocurrir°. La policía arresta a la señorita Flor Gavilán—la aeromoza—
y a su cómplice°, Héctor Ríos. Omar Ramos—el joven° de El Paso—está muy complacido°.

DANIEL   ¡Llegaste en el momento preciso! ¡Nos salvaste la vida°!
ADRIANA   ¿Tú planeaste todo esto?
OMAR   No les puedo explicar° nada ahora. El héroe no soy yo. Ustedes
actuaron estupendamente°.
DANIEL   ¿Qué hacemos ahora?
OMAR   Eso depende de ustedes. Ahora, tengo que irme° . . .
ADRIANA   ¡De nuevo!
OMAR   . . . pero primero, necesito un favor.
ADRIANA   ¡Cómo no!
OMAR   ¿Me pueden devolver° la billetera°? Ustedes saben . . . cuesta mucho
reparar° un coche.

Daniel y Adriana deciden regresar a México con el canal 17. Los dos chicos están
cansados° y Adriana está muy triste°.

DANIEL   ¿Por qué estás triste? Mira, ya estamos en casa. Ahí está El Ángel,
estamos en el mismo centro de México.
ADRIANA   Sí, pero ¿qué pasa ahora? ¿Aquí termina nuestra aventura?
DANIEL   Si quieres, pongo el televisor.
ADRIANA   Ya no me interesa° el televisor. Daniel, ¡cuidado!°

En ese mismo momento unos chicos tratan de apoderarse° del televisor. El
televisor se cae y se hace trizas°.

ADRIANA   ¿Cómo? ¡El televisor no tiene nada adentro°!
DANIEL   Pero, ¿cómo funcionaba°?
ADRIANA   Yo no sé. Ya no tenemos nada. ¿Y la flor° de la canción° en la Puerta
del Sol?, ¿dónde está?
DANIEL   La flor de la canción no es una flor, Adriana. ¿No comprendes? La flor
es una mujer°, la aeromoza, Flor Gavilán. Ella es la "flor" de la Puerta del Sol.
ADRIANA   Y nosotros fuimos a Madrid con el televisor, ¡y la encontramos°!
¡Nosotros encontramos la flor, Daniel! Pero, no tenemos flores, no
tenemos nada. ¿Quién nos va a creer?
DANIEL   Vamos, yo te compro una flor.

Pero, ¿qué pasa? No pueden encontrar flores en ninguna parte°. No hay más
flores en la ciudad.

---

calmados *calmed down*   **comprender** *to understand*   **lo que acaba de ocurrir** *what just happened*   **cómplice** *accomplice*
joven *young man*   **complacido** *pleased*   **nos salvaste la vida** *you saved our lives*   **explicar** *to explain*   **actuaron**
estupendamente *you were fantastic*   **tengo que irme** *I must go*   **devolver** *to return*   **billetera** *wallet*   **reparar** *to repair*
cansados *tired*   **triste** *sad*   **no me interesa** *I don't care*   **cuidado** *be careful*   **tratan de apoderarse** *try to seize*   **se**
cae y se hace trizas *it falls and smashes into pieces*   **adentro** *inside*   **funcionaba** *worked*   **flor** *flower*   **canción** *song*
mujer *woman*   **la encontramos** *we found her*   **ninguna parte** *nowhere*

Adriana y Daniel llegan a su casa. Casi no la reconocen°. Hay flores por todas partes°, miles de flores adentro y afuera°, en las ventanas, en el patio, en la puerta. Y siguen llegando° coches, camiones°, gente en bicicleta, con todas las flores de México para ellos. ¡Adriana y Daniel son los héroes del momento! Pero, no tienen televisor. ¿Qué van a hacer ahora? Sin televisor, sus aventuras terminan . . . ¿o no?

Preguntas y respuestas

Answer the questions according to the reading.

1. ¿A quién arresta la policía?
2. ¿Es el héroe Omar Ramos? ¿Por qué?
3. ¿Por qué necesita Omar la billetera?
4. ¿Cómo está Adriana? ¿Por qué?
5. ¿Dónde están todas las flores?
6. ¿Te gusta el final de la historia? ¿Por qué?

Actividad • Charla

Work with a partner. You should be very well acquainted with **El regalo.** Ask each other questions so that your answers retell the whole story.

—¿Quiénes son Daniel y Adriana?
—¿De dónde son ellos?
—¿Qué reciben los hermanos?

Actividad • ¿Quieres cambiar la historia de Daniel y Adriana?

Imagine a different ending for **El regalo.** Write down your ending. Share it with your class.

---

la reconocen *recognize it*   **por todas partes** *everywhere*   **afuera** *outside*   **siguen llegando** *keep coming*   **camiones** *trucks*

UNIDAD 12

Cartas de México

Repaso

Vista de la Ciudad de México

Ciudad de México
15 de julio

Querida Liliana:
Ayer fuimos en autobús
hasta el Parque de
Chapultepec. De allí
caminamos por el Paseo
de la Reforma hasta la
Zona Rosa. Pasamos un
día fantástico. Te mando
postales, un mapa y
fotos. Regreso la semana
próxima. ¡Qué pena!
Hasta pronto, Gabriela

La Zona Rosa, Ciudad de México

Ciudad de México
20 de agosto

Querido Joaquín:
Ayer pensé mucho en
ti. Fui a un restaurante
mexicano cerca de la
Zona Rosa. Comimos
tacos, pollo y enchiladas.
Todo delicioso y muy
barato. Unos amigos
tocaron la guitarra
y todos cantamos.
Te veo la semana
próxima.
Ignacio

2 Actividad • ¿Es cierto o no? 📼

Change the following sentences to make them true according to Gabriela's and Ignacio's letters.

1. Fuimos en autobús hasta la Zona Rosa.
2. Luego fuimos por el Paseo de la Reforma hasta el parque.
3. Pasamos un día muy aburrido.
4. Te mando postales, unos sellos y tres mapas.
5. Regreso el mes próximo. ¡Qué suerte!
6. Ayer pensé un poco en ti.
7. Fui a un restaurante en el parque.
8. Comimos tacos y chile.
9. Costó muy caro. Unos amigos tocaron el piano.
10. Te veo el año próximo.

3 Actividad • Charla

Work with a partner. Ask each other questions about what Gabriela and Ignacio did in Mexico City.

—¿Adónde fue Gabriela en autobús?
—Fue hasta el Parque de Chapultepec.

—¿Dónde comió Ignacio?
—En un restaurante cerca de la Zona Rosa.

4 Actividad • ¡A escribir!

Think of something special that you did last week, or make up an interesting trip or excursion. Then write to a friend in Spanish telling him or her what you did. You can take into account the following:

• Where did you go? With whom?
• How? By bus, by car, on foot?
• Where did you eat? What?
• How much did it cost?
• Was there any kind of entertainment? What?
• Did you do any shopping? What did you buy?
• Did you have fun? Are you sending something with your letter? What?

5 SITUACIÓN • El diario de Gabriela 📼

Martes por la noche

Queridísimo diario: Hoy por la tarde fuimos en taxi al Museo de Antropología.

MUSEO NACIONAL DE ANTROPOLOGÍA

Caminamos por todas las salas.
Hay veintiséis. Después, en
la tienda compramos libros
y postales. Después del Museo
fuimos al Parque de Chapultepec.
Alquilamos un bote y paseamos.
¡Qué divertido! Comimos unos
tacos y tomamos refrescos.

6 Actividad • Para completar

Complete these sentences according to Gabriela's diary.

1. Gabriela escribe en su diario el _____ .
2. Hoy fueron en _____ al _____ .
3. Caminaron por _____ .
4. Compraron _____ y _____ .
5. Después del Museo fueron al _____ .
6. Los chicos alquilaron _____ y _____ .
7. ¡Qué _____ !
8. Comieron _____ .

7 Actividad • ¡A escoger!

Choose the best option to complete the following sentences according to Gabriela's diary.

1. Fuimos al Museo de Antropología
   • en autobús.   • en taxi.   • a pie.
2. Allí caminamos por
   • el parque.   • todas las salas.   • toda la tienda.
3. También fuimos
   • a la cafetería.   • a la ciudad.   • a la tienda.
4. Después del Museo fuimos
   • a un restaurante.   • a la Zona Rosa.   • al Parque de Chapultepec.
5. Alquilamos un
   • coche.   • bote.   • autobús.
6. Comimos
   • una enchilada.   • frutas.   • unos tacos.

8 · Actividad · Charla

Pair off with a classmate. Take turns asking and answering these questions about Gabriela's diary.

1. ¿Adónde fue Gabriela el martes?
2. ¿Cuándo y cómo fue allí?
3. ¿Cuántas salas hay?
4. ¿Qué compraron en la tienda?
5. ¿Adónde fue ella después del Museo?
6. ¿Qué alquilaron allí Gabriela y sus amigos?
7. ¿Nadaron en el parque?
8. ¿Qué hicieron después?
9. ¿Qué comieron? ¿Pollo?
10. ¿Tomaron leche?

9 · Actividad · Y tú, ¿adónde fuiste?

Now think of a trip you have taken or imagined, and work with your partner on the following questions.

1. ¿A qué ciudad fuiste? ¿Cuándo?
2. ¿Con quién fuiste?
3. ¿Cómo fuiste a la ciudad?
4. ¿Visitaste un museo o viste una exhibición? ¿Cuál?
5. ¿Te gustó? ¿Por qué?
6. ¿Comiste algo? ¿Dónde y qué?
7. ¿Paseaste? ¿Caminaste?
8. ¿Compraste muchas cosas? ¿Qué?

10 · Conversación · El turista y el guía

Team up with a classmate. One of you will play the part of a tourist; the other will be a guide. Pick a place to visit and act out one of the following dialogs in Spanish.

Dialog 1

Visitor asks:
- what sights to see
- how to get around to the different places
- where to go for lunch

Guide suggests:
- four or five different places
- two or three means of transportation
- a soda at one of the plazas and lunch at a restaurant later

Dialog 2

Visitor asks:
- where to go after lunch
- what museum has an interesting exhibit
- what to do after the museum

Guide suggests:
- a stroll in the park or on one of the main boulevards, or a visit to a museum
- a museum and its location
- going to a park and having a soda and something to eat

11 · Proyecto · Una carta

Write a letter about your trip or excursion. Imagine you are sending it to a friend.
Say that you are enclosing postcards, maps, and pictures. Describe them in Spanish.
Make a complete folder to send your friend. Report what you're sending to the class.

Viñeta cultural 3

Festivales

Festivales . . . the word itself brings forth images of color, music, and dance. Spain seems to have festivals for every season and every reason. Many of the festivals celebrate religious holidays; others mark the end of winter and the beginning of spring. In Spain, and throughout the Spanish-speaking world, festivals are occasions when young and old alike rejoice in their heritage.

❶ Festival de los Mariscos en Galicia, España

❷ Festival de Santiago en Galicia, España

❸ La Muñeira, un baile popular de Galicia, España

❹ Festival de San Fermín en Pamplona, España

1. La Jota, un baile folklórico en Aragón, España
2. Festival del Pilar en Aragón, España
3. Celebración del Corpus Cristi en Toledo, España
4. Un desfile de los gigantes en Toledo, España

Brilliant decorations, lively music, costumes, and fireworks are part of almost every festival in Spain. In Valencia, the end of winter is celebrated with a great festival called **Las Fallas.** Enormous wooden and papier-mâché structures, some as tall as three-story buildings, are constructed in the public square.

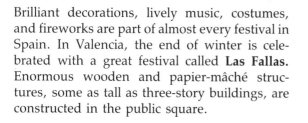

They are decorated with colorful explosives, while chains of smaller firecrackers hang from them in all directions. When the structures are set on fire, the explosives ignite and the firecrackers explode—a spectacular sight to see against a night sky.

1. Fallas de Valencia, España; niñas ofrecen flores a la virgen

2. Presentación de moros y cristianos en Alicante, España

3. Festival de San Juan en Alicante, España

4. Un baile folklórico en las Islas Baleares, España

5. Fiesta de San Miguel en las Islas Baleares, España

Festivales   335

No festival in Spain is complete without flamenco dancing. This unique art form combines guitar playing, singing, chanting, dancing, and staccato hand clapping in a whirlwind of clicking castanets and colorful costumes. It is thought that this dance originated around 1500.

❶ Alegre festival en Castilla, España

❷ Bailando la Jota en Castilla, España

❸ Feria de Andalucía en Málaga, España

❹ Feria de abril en Sevilla, España

❺ El baile flamenco en Sevilla, España

In the United States, Spanish-speaking people celebrate holidays that are traditionally American, such as Thanksgiving and the Fourth of July. They also celebrate festivals that are traditionally Hispanic. On September 15, Mexican Americans celebrate **El Grito,** Mexican Independence Day. And in New York, everyone enjoys the colorful parades during **La semana de la hispanidad** (*Hispanic Week*).

1. Domingo de Ramos en St. Augustine, Florida
2. Festival hispánico en San Antonio, Texas
3. Una obra de teatro en español en Santa Fe, Nuevo México
4. Festival de Lelo Lai en San Juan, Puerto Rico
5. Fiesta mexicana en San Francisco, California

❶ Danza del Quetzal en Puebla, México

❷ Altar en el Día de los Muertos en México

❸ Celebración de los Tres Reyes Magos en México

❹ Día de fiesta en Oaxaca, México

❺ Niños con una piñata en México

Festivals are also important in the culture of Mexico and Central America. In November, Mexicans celebrate **El Día de los Muertos,** a feast day in honor of the dead on which special foods and candies are prepared in the shape of skulls and skeletons. Mexicans also celebrate holidays with fireworks, candy-filled piñatas, and singing mariachis. Piñatas, which most people associate with Mexico, actually originated in Italy in the 1500s. The game today is played much as it was long ago. Everyone is blindfolded and given a stick with which to break the piñata. Once it is broken, a shower of toys, sweets, or other surprises comes tumbling down.

❶ Festival de Quelaquetza en Oaxaca, México

❷ Desfile de muchachas en trajes típicos en Oaxaca, México

❸ Baile de los Conquistadores en Guatemala

❹ Celebración del Día de la Raza en Costa Rica

South America also has its share of festivals, many dating back to pre-Colombian times. In Bolivia, **La fiesta de la cruz** (*Feast of the Cross*) is celebrated on the first weekend in May. Hundreds of people dance in the streets wearing elaborate costumes and masks. In June, on the day of San Juan, most cities in Peru are ablaze with torches and bonfires symbolizing the hope that fires will fend off the cold air of winter.

❶ Festival del Sol en Perú

❷ Celebración religiosa en Lima, Perú

❸ Carnaval de origen pre-colombino en Oruro, Bolivia

❹ Flautista del carnaval en Oruro, Bolivia

❺ Un carnaval festivo en Corrientes, Argentina

FOR REFERENCE

SUMMARY OF FUNCTIONS

The term *functions* can be defined as what you do with language—what your purpose is in speaking. Here is a list of all the functions with the expressions you have learned related to these functions. The number indicates the unit in which the expression is introduced, followed by the section letter and number in parentheses.

EXCHANGING INFORMATION

Asking and giving names
1 (B4) ¿Cómo te llamas tú?
Yo me llamo . . .

Asking and giving someone else's name
1 (B8) ¿Cómo se llama él?
Él se llama . . .
¿Cómo se llama ella?
Ella se llama . . .

Asking someone's age, telling yours
6 (B5) ¿Cuántos años tienes?
Tengo (catorce) años

Asking and saying where people are from
1 (C6) ¿De dónde eres tú?
Soy de . . .
¿De dónde son ellos?
Son de . . .
¿Tú eres de . . . ?
Sí, soy de . . .

Asking for directions
5 (A17) ¿Dónde está(n) . . . ?
¿Está(n) cerca de aquí?
¿Está(n) lejos?

Giving directions
5 (A17) Está abajo.
. . . lejos
5 (A15) . . . allí arriba
. . . detrás de
. . . a la izquierda
. . . al lado de
. . . a la derecha

Asking for information
2 (A10) ¿Cuándo?
¿Cómo?
¿Quién?
¿Qué?
¿Por qué?

¿De dónde?
7 (C8) ¿Sabes si . . . ?
¿Sabes dónde . . . ?
¿Sabes cuándo . . . ?

Telling time
2 (B19) ¿Qué hora es?
¿A qué hora es . . . ?
Es la una.
Son las . . .
A la una.
A las . . .

Discussing prices
2 (C8) ¿Cuánto cuesta(n)?
Cuesta(n) . . .
11 (B16) ¿Cuánto vale?
Es muy caro.
Es demasiado caro.
No vale tanto.
No pago más de . . .
Es un regalo.
Es muy barato.
Es una ganga.

Saying what you usually do
10 (A9) Canto a menudo.
Casi siempre canto.

Expressing how long ago something happened
10 (A18) Isabel llegó hace
. . . mucho tiempo.
. . . quince días.
. . . una hora.
Hace un mes que Isabel llegó.

Discussing whether or not something has already been done
10 (C13) ¿Ya contestaste la carta?
Sí, ya la contesté.
No, no la contesté.

Saying that you know something
7 (C6) Yo sé . . .

EXPRESSING ATTITUDES AND OPINIONS

Asking for and giving an opinion
    7 (B21) ¿Qué piensas?
              Pienso que (no) . . .
              ¿Qué crees?
              Creo que (no) . . .
              ¿Qué te parece?
              Me parece que . . .
   11 (A4) ¡Buena idea!
              ¡Está bien!
              No está mal.
              Me gusta más . . .
              No me gusta nada.
              No sé, pero . . .

Asking what someone or something is like
    6 (B17) ¿Cómo es . . . ?
              ¿Cómo son . . . ?

Telling how something tastes
    9 (C20) ¡Qué sabrosos!
              Son deliciosos.
              ¡Qué rico está!

Asking and saying whether people are hungry or thirsty
    9 (C4) ¿Tienes sed?
              Sí, tengo mucha sed.
              Elena no tiene hambre ahora.
              Yo sí. Tengo mucha hambre.

Asking for advice
    7 (B21) ¿Qué piensas?
              Pienso que (no) . . .
              ¿Qué crees?
              Creo que (no) . . .
              ¿Qué te parece?
              Me parece que . . .

EXPRESSING FEELINGS AND EMOTIONS

Expressing surprise
    2 (B25) ¿Verdad?

Expressing agreement
    3 (C1) De acuerdo.
    6 (C1) Por supuesto.

Expressing disagreement
    2 (B25) Al contrario.

Expressing liking
    3 (A4) Me gusta . . .
    9 (A15) Nos gustan . . .

Expressing dislikes
    3 (A4) No me gusta . . .
    9 (A15) No nos gustan . . .
   11 (A4) No me gusta nada . . .

Expressing strong dislike
    3 (A12) Odio . . .

Expressing preference
    2 (B25) Tu materia favorita
              Es mi . . . preferido(a).
    3 (A12) Me gusta mucho.

Complimenting people
    2 (B25) Eres un genio.
    6 (B1) Es muy inteligente.
              Son bien simpáticos.
              Son cariñosos.
    6 (B21) ¿Tu hermana? ¡Qué linda!
              ¿Tu hermano? ¡Qué guapo!
              ¡Qué chica tan linda!
              ¡Qué chico tan guapo!

Responding to good news
    5 (A1) ¡Qué suerte!

Expressing enthusiasm
    2 (B25) Es muy interesante
    3 (A9) Es divertido.
    3 (A12) Es estupendo.

Expressing lack of enthusiasm
    3 (A9) Es horrible.
    3 (A12) Es aburrido.

Expressing regret
    7 (A14) ¡Qué lástima!
              ¡Qué pena!

PERSUADING

Making suggestions
    5 (C15) ¿Por qué no comemos?
    7 (B15) ¿Tienes ganas de ir al cine?
              ¿Vamos a ver . . . ?
              ¿Quieres ver . . . ?

Suggesting something else
    7 (B8) Vamos a ver (una cómica).
    7 (B15) No, mejor (vamos al parque).
              ¿Por qué no vemos . . . ?
              ¿Y si vemos . . . ?

SOCIALIZING

Saying hello
>1 (A12) ¡Hola!
>>Buenos días.
>>Buenas tardes.
>>Buenas noches.

Saying goodbye
>1 (A1) ¡Hasta luego!
>1 (A10) ¡Hasta mañana!
>1 (A12) ¡Adiós!
>>¡Chao!

Addressing people
>1 (A10) señor + last name
>>señora + last name
>>señorita + last name
>>first name
>11 (A1) Señorita, por favor.
>>¿Qué desea, señora?

Saying please, thank you, and you're welcome
>1 (B6) Por favor
>>Gracias
>>De nada
>3 (B1) Muchas gracias

Getting someone's attention:
getting a friend's attention
>7 (C3) ¡Mira!
>>¡Oye!

getting a stranger's attention
>1 (B8) Por favor, señor (señora, señorita)

Excusing an interruption
>7 (C3) ¡Perdón!
>>¡Permiso, por favor!

Speaking on the phone:
answering the phone
>5 (B19) ¡Diga!
>>¡Hola!
>>¡Aló!
>>Buenas tardes, familia + last name.

asking for someone
>5 (B11) Buenas tardes, ¿el señor + last name?,
>>por favor.

ending a phone conversation
>5 (B11) Adiós.
>>Hasta luego.

Introducing yourself
>1 (B1) Yo me llamo . . .

Responding to an introduction
>1 (B1) Yo me llamo . . . ¡Mucho gusto!
>>Mucho gusto.

Accepting something to eat
>9 (C1) Sí, por favor.
>9 (C4) Yo, sí. Tengo mucha hambre.

Declining something to eat
>9 (B15) No, gracias.

Accepting an invitation
>7 (A9) Sí, fantástico. ¡Vamos!

Declining an invitation
>7 (A9) Lo siento, no puedo.
>7 (A14) No puedo, tengo que estudiar.

Asking "How are you?":
informal
>1 (A4) ¿Qué tal?
>>¿Cómo estás tú?

formal
>1 (A16) ¿Cómo está usted?

Responding to "How are you?"
>1 (A1) Regular.
>>¡Muy mal!
>1 (A4) Bien, gracias.
>5 (A10) Estoy bien, gracias.

Making somebody feel at home
>6 (A10) ¡Bienvenido(a)!
>>¡Pasa!
>>¡Mucho gusto!
>>¡Estás en tu casa!

Accepting hospitality
>6 (A10) ¡Gracias! ¡Es un placer estar aquí!
>>¡Igualmente, señor(a)!
>>¡Usted es muy amable!

Complimenting someone on food
>9 (C1) . . . está perfecto(a).
>>. . . son deliciosos.
>>¡Qué rico(a) está!

GRAMMAR SUMMARY

ARTICLES

DEFINITE ARTICLES

	MASCULINE	FEMININE
SINGULAR	el chico	la chica
PLURAL	los chicos	las chicas

INDEFINITE ARTICLES

	MASCULINE	FEMININE
SINGULAR	un chico	una chica
PLURAL	unos chicos	unas chicas

CONTRACTIONS OF THE DEFINITE ARTICLE

a + el → al
de + el → del

ADJECTIVES

		MASCULINE	FEMININE
Adjectives that end in -o	SING PL	chico alto chicos altos	chica alta chicas altas
Adjectives that end in -e	SING PL	chico inteligente chicos inteligentes	chica inteligente chicas inteligentes
Adjectives that end in a consonant	SING PL	examen difícil exámenes difíciles	clase difícil clases difíciles

DEMONSTRATIVE ADJECTIVES

este			ese		
	MASCULINE	FEMININE		MASCULINE	FEMININE
SINGULAR PLURAL	este chico estos chicos	esta chica estas chicas	SINGULAR PLURAL	ese chico esos chicos	esa chica esas chicas

POSSESSIVE ADJECTIVES

SINGULAR		PLURAL	
MASCULINE	FEMININE	MASCULINE	FEMININE
mi hijo tu hijo su hijo nuestro hijo	mi hija tu hija su hija nuestra hija	mis hijos tus hijos sus hijos nuestros hijos	mis hijas tus hijas sus hijas nuestras hijas

PRONOUNS

SUBJECT PRONOUNS	DIRECT OBJECT PRONOUNS	INDIRECT OBJECT PRONOUNS	OBJECTS OF PREPOSITIONS
yo tú él, ella, Ud. nosotros, -as ellos, ellas, Uds.	me te lo, la nos los, las	me te le nos les	mí ti él, ella, Ud. nosotros, -as ellos, ellas, Uds.

NEGATION:
NEGATIVE WORDS

no nada nunca ni . . . ni

INTERROGATIVES:
INTERROGATIVE WORDS

¿Cómo?	¿De dónde?
¿Cuándo?	¿Por qué?
¿Cuánto?	¿Qué?
¿Cuál?	¿Quién?

COMPARATIVES
COMPARISONS OF UNEQUAL QUANTITIES

más / menos	+	adjective	+	que	más / menos	+	de	+	number (expression of quantity)

REGULAR VERBS

INFINITIVE	PRESENT		PRETERIT	
hablar	hablo hablas habla	hablamos habláis hablan	hablé hablaste habló	hablamos hablasteis hablaron
comer	como comes come	comemos coméis comen	comí comiste comió	comimos comisteis comieron
escribir	escribo escribes escribe	escribimos escribís escriben	escribí escribiste escribió	escribimos escribisteis escribieron

VERB INDEX

The alphabetical list below includes verbs with stem changes, spelling changes, or irregular forms. The page number will guide you to the verb itself or to a verb whose pattern it follows.

Verbs with Irregular Forms

Verbs listed in this section are those that do not follow the usual pattern of **-ar, -er,** and **-ir** verbs. The forms in which the changes occur are printed in **boldface** type.

CONOCER
present   **conozco,** conoces, conoce, conocemos, conocéis, conocen

DECIR
present   **digo, dices, dice,** decimos, decís, **dicen**

ESTAR
present   **estoy,** estás, está, estamos, estáis, están

HACER
present   **hago,** haces, hace, hacemos, hacéis, hacen
preterit   **hice, hiciste, hizo, hicimos, hicisteis, hicieron**

IR
present   **voy, vas, va, vamos, vais, van**
preterit   **fui, fuiste, fue, fuimos, fuisteis, fueron**

PONER
present   **pongo,** pones, pone, ponemos, ponéis, ponen

SABER
present   **sé,** sabes, sabe, sabemos, sabéis, saben

SALIR
present   **salgo,** sales, sale, salimos, salís, salen

SER
present   **soy, eres, es, somos, sois, son**

TENER

present **tengo, tienes, tiene,** tenemos, tenéis, **tienen**

VENIR

present **vengo, vienes, viene,** venimos, venís, **vienen**

Verbs with Stem Changes

The verbs listed in this section are stem changing. Stem changing verbs are those that have a spelling change in the root of the verb. The stem change affects the **yo, tú, él** and **ellos** forms of the present.

Present tense of stem changing verbs

	-ar verbs			-er verbs		-ir verbs
e → ie **pensar**[1]	o → ue **encontrar**[2]	u → ue **jugar**	e → ie **querer**	o → ue **poder**[3]		e → i **servir**
pienso	encuentro	juego	quiero	puedo		sirvo
piensas	encuentras	juegas	quieres	puedes		sirves
piensa	encuentra	juega	quiere	puede		sirve
pensamos	encontramos	jugamos	queremos	podemos		servimos
pensáis	encontráis	jugáis	queréis	podéis		servís
piensan	encuentran	juegan	quieren	pueden		sirven

[1] **empezar (ie)** is conjugated like **pensar**
[2] **probar (ue)** and **costar (ue)** are conjugated like **encontrar**
[3] **volver (ue)** is conjugated like **poder**

NUMBERS

0	cero	18	dieciocho	60	sesenta
1	uno (un, una)	19	diecinueve	70	setenta
2	dos	20	veinte	80	ochenta
3	tres	21	veintiuno(a)	90	noventa
4	cuatro	22	veintidós	100	cien
5	cinco	23	veintitrés	101	ciento uno(a)
6	seis	24	veinticuatro	102	ciento dos
7	siete	25	veinticinco	103	ciento tres
8	ocho	26	veintiséis	200	doscientos, -as
9	nueve	27	veintisiete	201	doscientos uno(a)
10	diez	28	veintiocho	300	trescientos, -as
11	once	29	veintinueve	400	cuatrocientos, -as
12	doce	30	treinta	500	quinientos, -as
13	trece	31	treinta y uno(a)	600	seiscientos, -as
14	catorce	32	treinta y dos	700	setecientos, -as
15	quince	33	treinta y tres	800	ochocientos, -as
16	dieciséis	40	cuarenta	900	novecientos, -as
17	diecisiete	50	cincuenta	1,000	mil

ENGLISH EQUIVALENTS

The following are the English equivalents of the basic material in each section of every unit, with the exception of review units. They are not literal translations but represent what a speaker of English would say in the same situation.

1 ¡HOLA, AMIGOS!

A1 En el colegio

RAMÓN ¡Hola, Anita! ¿Cómo estás?
ANITA Muy bien, Ramón. Gracias, ¿y tú?
RAMÓN ¿Yo? Regular. ¡Hasta luego!
ANITA ¡Chao!
RAMÓN ¡Adiós!

—¿Qué tal?
—¿Yo? ¡Muy mal!
—¡Qué pena!

A10 Saludos

Carmen y el señor Colón
—Buenos días, señor.
—Buenos días, Carmen.
Jorge y la señorita López
—Buenas tardes, señorita.
—¡Adiós! Hasta mañana, Jorge.
Alicia y la señora Valdés
—Buenas noches, señora.
—Buenas noches, Alicia.
—¿Cómo estás tú?

A16 María Luisa y la profesora

SRA. VALDÉS Buenos días, María Luisa. ¿Cómo estás?
MARÍA LUISA Muy bien, señora, gracias. ¿Y cómo está usted?
SRA. VALDÉS Bien, gracias.

B1 En la escuela. En la clase.

RICARDO ¡Hola! Yo me llamo Ricardo. ¿Cómo te llamas tú?
LUPE Me llamo Lupe. ¡Mucho gusto!
RICARDO ¡Mucho gusto! Bueno . . . hasta luego, Lupe.
LUPE Hasta luego, Ricardo.

Él se llama Ricardo.
Ella se llama Lupe.

B6 Después de la clase

En el patio de la escuela.

HI, FRIENDS!

In school

Hi, Anita! How are you?
Very well, Ramón. Thank you. And you?
Me? So-so. See you later!
So long!
Goodbye!

How are things?
(with) Me? Awful!
What a pity!

Greetings

Carmen and Mr. Colón
Good morning, sir.
Good morning, Carmen.
Jorge and Miss López
Good afternoon, miss.
Goodbye! See you tomorrow, Jorge.
Alicia and Mrs. Valdés
Good night, ma'am.
Good night, Alicia.
How are you?

María Luisa and the teacher

Good morning, María Luisa.
How are you?
Very well, ma'am, thank you.
And how are you?
Fine, thank you.

In school. In class.

Hello! My name is Ricardo.
What's your name?
My name is Lupe. Nice to meet you.
Nice to meet you! Well . . . see you later, Lupe.
See you later, Ricardo.

His name is Ricardo.
Her name is Lupe.

After class

In the school courtyard.

ANTONIO	¡Ricardo!, ¡Ricardo!	*Ricardo!, Ricardo!*
RICARDO	¿Sí?	*Yes?*
ANTONIO	¡Oye! Por favor, ¿cómo se llama la chica nueva?	*Hey! Please, what's the new girl's name?*
RICARDO	¿Quién, la chica de Arizona?	*Who, the girl from Arizona?*
ANTONIO	No, la chica de México.	*No, the girl from Mexico.*
RICARDO	Ella se llama Lupe.	*Her name is Lupe.*
ANTONIO	¿Lupe? Gracias, Ricardo.	*Lupe? Thanks, Ricardo.*
RICARDO	De nada, Antonio.	*You're welcome, Antonio.*

C1 ¿De dónde son?

Él se llama Pedro Gómez.
Pedro es de Texas, Estados Unidos.

María Bernal y Carlos Cajal.
Ellos son de España.

Yo me llamo Pablo Matos. Soy de Puerto Rico.
¿De dónde eres tú?

Nosotras somos de México.
Yo me llamo Elena Llansó.
Ella se llama Rosa. ¿De dónde son ustedes?

Where are they from?
His name is Pedro Gómez.
Pedro is from Texas, U.S.A.

María Bernal and Carlos Cajal.
They are from Spain.

My name is Pablo Matos. I'm from Puerto Rico. Where are you from?

We are from Mexico.
My name is Elena Llansó.
Her name is Rosa. Where are you from?

2 EN LA ESCUELA

IN SCHOOL

A1 ¿Cómo vienes a la escuela?
Los estudiantes de la Escuela Secundaria Benito Juárez vienen de muchas partes de la ciudad. Muchos vienen temprano, pero no todos. Algunos vienen tarde hoy. ¿Por qué? Porque el autobús escolar número ocho tiene un problema. Pero, ¡mira!, ahí viene el autobús.

How do you get to school?
The students at the Benito Juárez Secondary School come from many parts of the city. Many come early, but not all. Some are coming late today. Why? Because school-bus number eight has a problem. But, look! Here comes the bus.

ISABEL	Andrés, ¿vienes tú en autobús con Carlos?	*Andrés, do you come by bus with Carlos?*
ANDRÉS	No, yo no vengo en autobús, vengo en auto.	*No, I don't come by bus, I come by car.*
ISABEL	Y ustedes, ¿cómo vienen?	*And you? How do you come?*
RAÚL Y MARTA	Nosotros venimos en metro.	*We come by subway.*
ISABEL	¿Y José? ¿Cuándo viene? ¿Viene él con Carlos?	*And José? When is he coming? Is he coming with Carlos?*
MARTA	Yo no sé.	*I don't know.*
ANDRÉS	Mira, ahí viene José.	*Look, here comes José.*
ISABEL	¿No viene en bicicleta?	*Isn't he coming on his bike?*
RAÚL	No, hoy viene a pie.	*No, today he is coming on foot.*
ISABEL	¡Ah, por fin viene el autobús! ¡Carlos, mi libro de inglés, por favor!	*Ah, the bus is finally coming! Carlos, my English book, please!*

B1 ¿Qué materias tienes hoy?
En el recreo.

ALBERTO	¡Hola, Enrique! ¿Tienes clase de matemáticas?	
ENRIQUE	No, tengo inglés.	

What subjects do you have today?
At recess.
Hi, Enrique! Do you have math class?

No, I have English.

ALBERTO	¿A qué hora?		At what time?
ENRIQUE	A las diez. ¿Y tú?, ¿qué tienes?		At ten o'clock. And you? What do you have?
ALBERTO	Hoy tengo clase de computadoras.		Today I have computer class.
ENRIQUE	¿Hay muchos estudiantes?		Are there a lot of students?
ALBERTO	Como veinte.		About twenty.
ENRIQUE	Y, el profesor, ¿quién es?		And, the teacher, who is he?
ALBERTO	Tenemos una profesora: la señora Suárez. ¿Cuántas materias tienes tú?		We have a female teacher, Mrs. Suárez. How many subjects do you have? (are you taking?)
ENRIQUE	Diez, once . . . no sé. ¿Qué hora es?		Ten, eleven . . . I don't know. What time is it?
ALBERTO	¡Oh! Son casi las diez. ¡Adiós!		Oh! It's almost ten. Goodbye!
ENRIQUE	¡Chao!		So long!

B4 Los números del 0 al 20

cero	once
uno	doce
dos	trece
tres	catorce
cuatro	quince
cinco	dieciséis
seis	diecisiete
siete	dieciocho
ocho	diecinueve
nueve	veinte
diez	

The numbers from 0 to 20

zero	eleven
one	twelve
two	thirteen
three	fourteen
four	fifteen
five	sixteen
six	seventeen
seven	eighteen
eight	nineteen
nine	twenty
ten	

B8 El horario de Enrique

Enrique es estudiante de la Escuela Secundaria Benito Juárez. Tiene un horario fuerte. Hay diez materias, pero no hay clases el sábado.

—Yo tengo otras materias—álgebra a las 4, biología a las 5, filosofía a las 6, francés a las 7, manualidades a las 8, química a las 9 . . .

Enrique's schedule

Enrique is a student at Benito Juárez Secondary School. He has a very heavy schedule. There are ten subjects, but there are no classes on Saturday.

"I have other subjects—algebra at four o'clock, biology at five, philosophy at six, French at seven, industrial arts at eight, chemistry at nine . . .

B25 Diferencia de opiniones

ANDRÉS	¿Qué clase tienes tú ahora?		What class do you have now?
CLARA	Biología, ¿y tú?		Biology, and you?
ANDRÉS	Historia. Con el Sr. Galván. Es mi materia preferida.		History. With Mr. Galván. It's my favorite subject.
CLARA	¿Tú materia preferida? ¡Es muy aburrida! Es difícil. Hay mucha tarea.		Your favorite subject? It's very boring. It's difficult. There is a lot of homework.
ANDRÉS	¡Al contrario! Es fácil. Es muy interesante. Y tu materia favorita, ¿cuál es?		On the contrary! It's easy. It's very interesting. And which is your favorite subject?
CLARA	Química.		Chemistry.
ANDRÉS	Tienes bastante tarea y no es interesante, ¿verdad?		You have a lot of homework and it's not interesting, right?
CLARA	No, es muy interesante.		No, it's very interesting.
ANDRÉS	¿Cuántas materias tienes?		How many subjects do you have?
CLARA	Tengo diez.		I have ten.
ANDRÉS	¿Diez? ¡Eres un genio!		Ten? You are a genius!

C1 ¿Cuánto cuesta?

En una tienda de San Juan, Puerto Rico.

How much does it cost?

In a store in San Juan, Puerto Rico.

Rosa	Miguel, ¡una regla con calcula–dora!	*Miguel, a ruler with a calculator!*
Miguel	¿Sí? ¿Cuánto cuesta?	*Yes? How much does it cost?*
Rosa	Catorce noventa y nueve.	*Fourteen ninety–nine.*
Miguel	Por favor, señor, ¿cuánto cuestan los bolígrafos? No tienen precio.	*Please, sir, how much are the ballpoint pens? They don't have a price.*
Vendedor	Tres por dos pesos.	*Three for two dollars.*
Miguel	Gracias	*Thank you.*
Rosa	Perdón, ¿tiene usted carteras?	*Excuse me, do you have schoolbags?*
Vendedora	Sí, cuestan quince pesos.	*Yes, they cost fifteen dollars.*
Rosa	¡Uy!, no tengo tanto. Gracias, señora.	
Miguel	¿Qué más necesitas?	*What else do you need?*
Rosa	¡Dinero, por supuesto!	*Money, of course!*

C7 Compras para la escuela
—Por favor, ¿cuánto cuesta . . .
    un cuaderno?   un lápiz?
    una goma?   un marcador?
    un compás?
—¡Hay rebajas! Tenemos . . . unos cuadernos, unas revistas, unas plumas, unos lápices, y unos diccionarios en venta.

Shopping for school supplies
Please, how much is . . .
    a notebook?   a pencil?
    an eraser?   a marker?
    a compass?
There are discounts! We have some . . . notebooks, magazines, pens, pencils, and dictionaries on sale.

3 DEPORTES Y PASATIEMPOS

SPORTS AND PASTIMES

A1 ¿Qué deporte te gusta?
¿Qué deporte te gusta, Miguel?
Me gusta el béisbol.
¡No me gusta la gimnasia!

También me gusta mucho el tenis.
¡Y no me gusta correr!
Pero sí me gusta montar en bicicleta.

¿Qué deporte le gusta a Pedro?
A Pedro le gusta nadar.
Pero no le gusta el fútbol.

¿Qué deporte le gusta a Olga?
A Olga le gusta el vólibol.
Pero no le gusta el básquetbol.

What sport do you like?
What sport do you like, Miguel?
I like baseball.
I don't like gymnastics!

I also like tennis very much.
And I don't like to run!
But I really like to ride my bike.

What sport does Pedro like?
Pedro likes to swim.
But he doesn't like soccer.

What sport does Olga like?
Olga likes volleyball.
But she doesn't like basketball.

A9 Pasatiempos
—¿Qué pasatiempo le gusta a Alberto?
—A Alberto le gusta escuchar discos.
  Dice que es divertido.

—¿A Ofelia le gusta estudiar música y cantar?
—No, no le gusta.
  Dice que es muy aburrido.
  Le gusta patinar.

—Y a Pepe, ¿qué le gusta?
—A Pepe, le gusta tocar la guitarra y bailar.
—¿Por qué?
—Dice que es ¡estupendo!

Pastimes
What's Alberto's favorite pastime?
Alberto likes to listen to records.
He says it's fun.

Does Ofelia like to study music and sing?
No, she doesn't like it.
She says it's very boring.
She likes to skate.

And Pepe, what does he like?
Pepe likes to play the guitar and dance.
Why?
He says it's great!

—¿Y a Tato y a Lola?
—A Tato le gusta tomar fotografías.
Pero a Lola le gusta hablar por teléfono.

And Tato and Lola?
Tato likes to take photographs.
But Lola likes to talk on the phone.

—¿Qué te gusta, Luisa?
—Me gusta trabajar y jugar con la computadora. ¡Es fantástico! Y también me gusta mirar televisión.

What do you like, Luisa?
I like to work and play with the computer. It's fantastic! And I also like to watch television.

—Pedro, ¿te gusta mirar televisión también?
—¡No! Odio mirar televisión.
—¿Por qué?
—¡Es horrible!

Pedro, do you like to watch television too?
No! I hate to watch television.
Why?
It's horrible!

A16 El judo

Me llamo Esteban Rodríguez. Mi pasatiempo favorito es el judo. Me gusta practicar judo. Soy cinturón azul. Después del azul vienen el cinturón marrón y el cinturón negro. En el judo hay un cinturón de color diferente para cada categoría. El blanco es para los principiantes y el negro para los más avanzados. No hay cinturón rojo. Hay siete colores en total:

blanco amarillo anaranjado
verde azul marrón negro

Judo

My name is Esteban Rodríguez. My favorite pastime is judo. I like to practice judo. I'm a blue belt. After the blue belt, there's the brown belt and the black belt. In judo there is a different color belt for each category. White is for beginners and black is for the more advanced. There is no red belt.
There are seven colors in all:

white yellow orange
green blue brown black

B1 ¡Un fanfarrón!

Una entrevista imaginaria
Gracias por todo, amigos. Es un honor ser el atleta del año. Pero sí, ¡es verdad! Practico todos los deportes y juego en todas las estaciones. Como todo campeón, gano muchos premios.

A braggart!
An imaginary interview
Thanks for everything, friends. It's an honor to be the athlete of the year. But yes, it's true! I practice all sports and play in all seasons. Like every champion, I win a lot of prizes.

Me gusta mucho el invierno. ¡Soy estupendo en el hielo! Patino muy bien y . . . ¡esquiar es fantástico!

I like winter very much. I'm great on ice! I skate very well and . . . skiing is fantastic!

¡Ah, la primavera! ¡Soy campeón en la cancha de tenis! Ivan Lendl y yo somos amigos. Pero ahora no hablamos de Ivan.

Ah, spring! I'm a champion on the tennis court! Ivan Lendl and I are friends. But we aren't talking about Ivan now.

¿Preguntas, por favor? ¿Me gusta el fútbol? Sí, pero en el otoño.
¿Con quién practico? Diego Maradona y yo practicamos mucho.

Questions, please? Do I like soccer? Yes, but in the fall.
Who do I practice with? Diego Maradona and I practice a lot.

En el verano, participo en los Juegos Olímpicos. Tengo medalla de oro en natación.

During the summer, I take part in the Olympic Games. I have a gold medal in swimming.

¿Mi deporte favorito? ¡Ganar en todo momento! Y, ¡muchas gracias por el trofeo, amigos!

My favorite sport? Winning every time! And, thank you very much for the trophy, friends!

C1 ¿Juegas siempre?

FELIPE ¿Te gusta jugar tenis, Sara?
SARA Sí, a veces juego. No juego a menudo.
FELIPE Yo juego siempre. Juego todos los días.

Do you always play?
Do you like playing tennis, Sara?
Yes, I play sometimes. I don't play often.
I always play. I play every day.

SARA	Necesito practicar más. ¿Jugamos un partido hoy por la tarde?		*I need to practice more. Shall we play a match today in the afternoon?*
FELIPE	Por la tarde, no. ¿Por la noche?		*Not in the afternoon. At night?*
SARA	No, nunca juego por la noche.		*No, I never play at night.*
FELIPE	¿Y mañana por la mañana?		*And tomorrow morning?*
SARA	Bueno, ¡de acuerdo! ¡Hasta mañana!		*Good, agreed! See you tomorrow!*

C9 ¿Qué tiempo hace?

How's the weather?

ANITA	¡Otro día horrible! Hace mal tiempo. Llueve y hace mucho viento.	*Another horrible day! The weather is bad. It's raining and it's windy.*
CONSUELO	Ideal para mirar televisión y escuchar discos.	*It's ideal for watching television and listening to records.*
LUISA	¡Hace frío!	*It's cold!*
CARMEN	Sí, pero no nieva. ¡Estupendo para patinar en hielo!	*Yes, but it's not snowing. It's great for ice-skating!*
FELIPE	¿Hace fresco?	*Is it cool out?*
JULIÁN	No, hace sol y hace calor. ¡Es un día magnífico!	*No, it's sunny and it's hot. It's a magnificent day!*
FELIPE	Por fin hace buen tiempo para la playa.	*At last, the weather is nice for the beach.*

5 EN EL AEROPUERTO

AT THE AIRPORT

A1 ¿Dónde está?

Where is it?

Un grupo de estudiantes llega a Madrid. Vienen en el vuelo 321 de Boston. Entran por la puerta 9. Están en Barajas, el aeropuerto internacional. Van primero a la sección de equipaje. Necesitan un carro para las maletas. Después, a la aduana. ¡Ya está todo! ¿Y ahora? ¡A cambiar de avión o a buscar un taxi!

A group of students arrives in Madrid. They come on flight 321 from Boston. They enter through gate 9. They are at Barajas, the international airport. First they go to the baggage claim area. They need a cart for the suitcases. Then, to customs. Everything's finished! And now? To change planes or look for a taxi!

BRIAN	¡Oh! Mi maleta no está. ¿Dónde está mi maleta?	*Oh! My suitcase is not here. Where is my suitcase?*
ALICE	¿Tu maleta? Allí está.	*Your suitcase? It's over there.*
BRIAN	¡Qué suerte! ¿Tienes tu cámara?	*What luck! Do you have your camera?*
ALICE	Sí, está en mi cartera. Pero, ¿dónde está mi diccionario de español? ¿Y mi mapa?	*Yes, it's in my schoolbag. But, where is my Spanish dictionary? And my map?*
BRIAN	¿Tu diccionario? No sé. ¿No está aquí?	*Your dictionary? I don't know. Isn't it here?*
ALICE	No. ¡Está con el mapa en el asiento del avión!	*No. It's with the map on the airplane seat!*
ADUANERO	Su pasaporte, por favor.	*Your passport, please.*
ALICE	Está en el bolsillo. Aquí tiene, señor.	*It's in my pocket. Here it is, sir.*
ADUANERO	Muchas gracias.	*Thank you very much.*
ALICE	De nada.	*You're welcome.*

A15 En información

At the information booth

Brian y Alice están en información. Tienen muchas preguntas.

Brian and Alice are at the information booth. They have a lot of questions.

BRIAN	Señorita, por favor, ¿dónde está la cafetería?	*Miss, where is the cafeteria please?*
EMPLEADA	La cafetería está allí arriba. ¿Tienen ustedes pesetas?	*The cafeteria is upstairs. Do you have pesetas?*

ALICE	No, señorita. Tenemos cheques de viajero.	*No, miss. We have traveler's checks.*
EMPLEADA	La casa de cambio está detrás de ustedes, a la izquierda.	*The money exchange office is behind you, to the left.*
BRIAN	¿Y el correo?	*And the post office?*
EMPLEADA	Abajo, al lado de los teléfonos y los baños.	*Downstairs, next to the telephones and the bathrooms.*
ALICE	¿Hay una tienda cerca de aquí?	*Is there a store near here?*
EMPLEADA	Sí, señorita, la tienda del aeropuerto está a la derecha.	*Yes, miss, the airport store is to the right.*
ALICE	Muchas gracias, señorita.	*Thank you very much, miss.*

B1 ¿Adónde van?

El profesor quiere saber adónde van los estudiantes. ¡Es muy difícil! Todos van a lugares diferentes.

—¿Adónde vas, Alicia?
—¡Voy a la casa de cambio!
—¿Adónde vas, Brian?
—Voy a la cafetería.
—Jennifer, ¿cómo se llama ella?
 ¿Adónde va?
—Es Gloria. Va al baño.
—George y Mary, ¿adónde van ustedes?
—Vamos a la tienda a comprar algo.

Where are they going?

The professor wants to know where the students are going. It is very difficult! They all go to different places.

Where are you going, Alicia?
I am going to the money exchange office!
Where are you going, Brian?
I am going to the cafeteria.
Jennifer, what is her name?
Where is she going?
She is Gloria. She is going to the bathroom.
George and Mary, where are you going?
We are going to the store to buy something.

B11 Conversación por teléfono

Brian llama por teléfono al señor González. ¡Hay un problema!

Telephone conversation

Brian calls Mr. González on the phone. There is a problem!

SR. GONZÁLEZ	¡Diga!	*Hello!*
BRIAN	Hola. ¿El señor González, por favor?	*Hello. Mr. González, please?*
SR. GONZÁLEZ	Sí, soy yo. ¿Quién habla?	*Yes, speaking. Who is calling?*
BRIAN	Brian Conally.	*Brian Conally.*
SR. GONZÁLEZ	¡Brian! ¿Dónde estás? Tu vuelo llega a las diez de la noche, ¿verdad?	*Brian! Where are you? Your flight arrives at ten o'clock at night, right?*
BRIAN	Bueno, sí y no. El vuelo llega a las diez, pero de la mañana, no de la noche.	*Well, yes and no. The flight arrives at ten o'clock, but in the morning, not at night.*
SR. GONZÁLEZ	¿Entonces llegas mañana?	*Then you arrive tomorrow?*
BRIAN	No, ya estoy en Madrid.	*No, I am already in Madrid.*
SR. GONZÁLEZ	¡Qué confusión! ¡Y son las once!	*What a mixup! And it's eleven o'clock!*
BRIAN	¿Debo tomar un taxi?	*Should I take a taxi?*
SR. GONZÁLEZ	No, esperas allí. Yo voy en mi coche al aeropuerto. Estoy allí dentro de una hora.	*No, you wait there. I'm going in my car to the airport. I'll be there within an hour.*
BRIAN	Gracias, señor. Hasta luego.	*Thank you, sir. See you later.*
SR. GONZÁLEZ	Adiós, Brian.	*Goodbye, Brian.*

B16 ¡Hay problemas con el teléfono!

—¡La comunicación se cortó!
—¿Sí?—¿Bueno?—¡Diga!—¡Hola!—¡Aló!
—¿5237?

There are problems with the telephone!

We were cut off!
Hello!
5237?

—No, 5337. ¡Número equivocado!
—¡Hola, mamá! ¡Habla Paco!
—¡No contestan!
—¡Está ocupado!
—Buenas tardes, señorita González.

No, 5337. Wrong number!
Hello, mom! This is Paco speaking.
No answer!
It's busy!
Good afternoon, Miss González.

C1 En la sala de espera
Brian está en el aeropuerto de Barajas en
Madrid. Alice y otros estudiantes del grupo
esperan la llegada del vuelo para ir a León.
Deben esperar una hora. ¿Qué deciden hacer?

In the waiting area
Brian is at Barajas Airport in Madrid. Alice and other
students from the group are waiting for the arrival of the
flight to León. They must wait for an hour. What do
they decide to do?

BRIAN	¡Tengo mucha hambre! ¿Por qué no subimos a la cafetería a comer y beber algo?
ALICE	¡Estupendo! Pero primero, creo que debemos ir a la casa de cambio.
BRIAN	¿Para qué?
ALICE	Para cambiar un cheque de viajero. ¿Tú vienes, Jennifer?
JENNIFER	No, yo ya tengo pesetas.
MARK	¿Por qué no escribes a casa? Venden postales en la tienda y sellos en el correo.
JENNIFER	¿Una carta a mi familia? Ahora, no. Yo espero aquí. Tengo el periódico de hoy en español.
MARK	Yo no tengo el periódico. ¡Chao!

I am very hungry! Why don't we go up to the cafeteria
to eat and drink something?

Great! But first, I think we should go to the money ex-
change office.
What for?
To cash a traveler's check.
Are you coming, Jennifer?
No, I have pesetas already.
Why don't you write home? They sell postcards at the
store and stamps in the post office.

A letter to my family? Not now. I'll wait here. I have
today's Spanish newspaper.

I don't have a newspaper. 'Bye!

6 LA FAMILIA

THE FAMILY

A1 La visita de Roberto
Roberto, un estudiante norteamericano de Los
Ángeles, llega a la casa de su amigo Antonio
en la Ciudad de México. Va a pasar un mes
de vacaciones con la familia de Antonio.

Roberto's visit
Roberto, a North American student from Los Angeles,
arrives at the home of his friend Antonio in Mexico
City. He is going to spend a month of vacation with
Antonio's family.

ANTONIO	¡Mamá! ¡Mamá! ¿Dónde estás?
MAMÁ	Aquí estoy, Antonio. En la sala. ¡Bienvenido, Roberto! Pasa, por favor. ¿Cómo estás? Mucho gusto.
ROBERTO	Igualmente, señora.
MAMÁ	Estás en tu casa, Roberto.
ROBERTO	Muchas gracias, señora. Usted es muy amable. ¡Es un placer estar aquí con ustedes!
ANTONIO	Con permiso, mamá. Queremos escuchar música. Vamos a mi cuarto.
MAMÁ	¡Un momento, Antonio! ¿Dónde están las cosas de Roberto? ¿Por qué no van a su cuarto primero? Y tú, Roberto, ¿no tienes hambre? ¿Quieres comer algo? ¿Quieres un refresco?

Mom! Mom! Where are you?
I'm here, Antonio. In the living room. Welcome,
Roberto! Come in, please. How are you? Nice to meet
you.
Likewise, ma'am.
Make yourself at home, Roberto.
Thank you very much, ma'am. You are very kind. It's a
pleasure to be here with you!

Excuse us, mom. We want to listen to music. We are
going to my room.

Just a moment, Antonio! Where are Roberto's things?
Why don't you go to his room first? And you, Roberto,
aren't you hungry? Would you like to eat something?
Would you like a soda?

Roberto	No, señora, muchas gracias.		*No, ma'am, thank you very much.*
Antonio	¿Quieres ver tu cuarto, Roberto?		*Would you like to see your room, Roberto?*

B1 Fotos de la familia

Ana María, la hermana de Antonio, y su amiga Gloria, hablan de las fotos que Ana María tiene en su cuarto. Tiene fotos de todos los miembros de la familia.

Family photos

Ana María, Antonio's sister, and her friend Gloria, talk about the photos that Ana María has in her room. She has photos of all the members of the family.

Gloria	Tienes muchas fotografías. ¿Quién es la chica alta y morena? ¿Tu hermana?	*You have a lot of photographs. Who is the tall, dark-haired girl? Your sister?*
Ana María	No, mi hermana Consuelo es baja y rubia. Ella es Luisa, mi prima.	*No, my sister Consuelo is short and blonde. She is Luisa, my cousin.*
Gloria	¿Cuántos años tiene?	*How old is she?*
Ana María	Quince. ¡Es un genio! Es muy inteligente.	*Fifteen. She is a genius! She is very intelligent.*
Gloria	¡Qué fotografía tan bonita! ¿Quién es? ¿Tu padre?	*What a nice photograph! Who is it? Your father?*
Ana María	Sí, es una foto de mi papá.	*Yes, it's a photo of my dad.*
Gloria	¡Qué guapo!	*How handsome!*
Ana María	Mira, aquí está de nuevo, con mi mamá y toda la familia.	*Look, here he is again, with my mother and all the family.*
Gloria	La señora delgada y rubia, ¿quién es? ¡Qué linda!	*The thin, blond woman, who is she? How pretty!*
Ana María	Es mi tía Dolores, la madre de Luisa. Al lado está el esposo, mi tío José.	*She's my aunt Dolores, Luisa's mother. Her husband is beside her, my uncle José.*
Gloria	Y aquí están tus abuelos, ¿no?	*And here are your grandparents, right?*
Ana María	Sí, los padres de mamá. Los dos son bien simpáticos y cariñosos.	*Yes, my mom's parents. They are both very nice and affectionate.*
Gloria	¿Cuántos hijos tienen? ¿Cinco?	*How many children do they have? Five?*
Ana María	No, una hija, mi mamá, y un hijo, mi tío José. El señor pelirrojo es un amigo de ellos. Los otros cuatro son amigos también.	*No, a daughter, my mother, and a son, my uncle José. The redheaded man is a friend of theirs. The other four are also friends.*

B8 Una foto más

Gloria	¡Qué chico tan guapo! ¿Quién es?	*What a handsome boy! Who is he?*
Ana María	El hijo de una amiga de mi mamá. Se llama Anselmo.	*The son of a friend of my mom. His name is Anselmo.*
Gloria	Es muy rubio. Sus padres, ¿son los dos morenos?	*He is very blond. His parents, are they both dark-haired?*
Ana María	El señor de la foto no es su papá. Es su padrastro. Su papá murió. Ahora la mamá está casada de nuevo.	*The man in the photo is not his dad. He's his stepfather. His father died. Now his mom is married again.*

One more photo

B16 ¿Cómo eres tú?

¿alto o baja?
¿gordo o delgada?
¿feo o guapa?
¿moreno, rubia o pelirroja?

What are you like?

tall or short?
fat or thin?
ugly or handsome?
dark-haired, blonde or redheaded?

	¿Cómo son ustedes?	What are you like?
	¿tontos o inteligentes?	dumb or intelligent?
	¿antipáticas o simpáticas?	not nice or nice?
	¿generosos o egoístas?	generous or selfish?
	¿Y cómo eres tú, Roque?	And what are you like, Roque?
	¿Cómo soy yo?	What am I like?
	. . . guapo, inteligente y . . . ¡modesto!	. . . handsome, intelligent, and . . . modest!

C1 La casa de Antonio

Antonio's house

Antonio y Roberto están en la casa de Antonio.

Antonio and Roberto are at Antonio's house.

ROBERTO	Me gusta mucho tu cuarto, Antonio. Es muy cómodo.	*I like your room very much, Antonio. It's very comfortable.*
ANTONIO	¿Quieres ver toda la casa?	*Would you like to see the whole house?*
ROBERTO	¡Por supuesto!	*Of course!*
ANTONIO	Bueno, ¡vamos! Empezamos por la sala de estar.	*Well, let's go! We begin in the family room.*
ROBERTO	¡Qué linda!	*How pretty!*
ANTONIO	Aquí estamos en el comedor. Y, al lado por esta puerta, la cocina.	*Here we are in the dining room. And, beside it through this door, the kitchen.*
ROBERTO	¿Y el baño?	*And the bathroom?*
ANTONIO	Tenemos tres baños. Uno a la derecha de la entrada, otro en el pasillo, y otro en el cuarto de mis padres.	*We have three bathrooms. One to the right of the entrance, another in the hall, and another in my parents' bedroom.*
ROBERTO	¿Dónde estamos ahora?	*Where are we now?*
ANTONIO	En la sala. No usamos mucho este cuarto. Es para cuando vienen visitas. Pasamos nuestro tiempo libre en la sala de estar. Es el cuarto más importante.	*In the living room. We don't use this room much. It's for when visitors come. We spend our free time in the family room. It's the most important room.*
ROBERTO	¿Entramos aquí?	*Should we go in here?*
ANTONIO	¡No, está prohibido! Es el cuarto de mis hermanas.	*No, it's off limits! It's my sisters' bedroom.*
ROBERTO	¡Ya sé! Yo también tengo hermanas. Y vivimos en un apartamento pequeño. ¿Hay un garaje?	*I know! I have sisters too. And we live in a small apartment. Is there a garage?*
ANTONIO	Sí, en el jardín, detrás de la casa. ¿Qué te parece la casa, Roberto?	*Yes, in the garden, behind the house. What do you think of the house, Roberto?*
ROBERTO	Es grande y muy bonita. ¡Y mi cuarto es estupendo!	*It's big and very pretty. And my room is great!*

7 ¡VAMOS A SALIR!

LET'S GO OUT!

A1 ¡A pasear!

Let's go for a walk!

NICOLÁS	Vamos a dar una vuelta.	*We are going for a walk.*
GRACIELA	Yo quiero tomar un helado. ¿Quieren venir?	*I want to have an ice cream. Do you want to come?*
CORINA	Sí, fantástico. ¡Vamos!	*Yes, fantastic. Let's go!*
IGNACIO	No, yo no puedo ir.	*No, I can't go.*
CORINA	¡Qué pena! ¿Qué tienes que hacer?	*What a pity! What do you have to do?*

| IGNACIO | Tengo un examen mañana. Tengo que estudiar esta tarde y esta noche. | *I have a test tomorrow. I have to study this afternoon and tonight.* |

NICOLÁS	Hola, Diego. ¿Qué tal? ¿Vas a la fiesta del sábado en el club?	*Hi, Diego. How are things? Are you going to the Saturday party at the club?*
DIEGO	Lo siento, no puedo.	*I'm sorry, I can't.*
NICOLÁS	¡Qué lástima! ¿Y tu hermana va?	*What a shame! Is your sister going?*
DIEGO	No, no puede. Ella tiene que trabajar el sábado.	*No, she can't. She has to work Saturday.*

A6 ¿Adónde vamos hoy?

¿a la piscina?
¿a una discoteca?
¿al cine?
¿al parque?
¿a la playa?

Where are we going today?
to the swimming pool?
to a disco?
to the movies?
to the park?
to the beach?

A17 ¿Sales mucho?

La revista *Juventud de hoy* entrevista a cuatro estudiantes. Ellos contestan nuestras preguntas:

¿Sales mucho?
¿Cuántas veces por semana sales?
¿Qué te gusta hacer cuando sales?

Do you go out a lot?
The magazine Today's Youth *interviews four students. They answer our questions:*

Do you go out a lot?
How many times a week do you go out?
What do you like to do when you go out?

CRISTINA
Yo salgo bastante, una o dos veces por semana. Voy al cine, a conciertos de rock, o, sencillamente, a casa de mis amigos.

I go out a lot, one or two times a week. I go to the movies, to rock concerts, or to just visit my friends.

ROBERTO
Lo que más me gusta es bailar. Yo voy a bailes y discotecas todo el tiempo. ¡Bailar es fantástico!

What I like the most is to dance. I go to dances and discos all the time. Dancing is fantastic!

RICARDO
Me gusta mucho salir a pasear con otros chicos. Salimos a menudo. Damos una vuelta, si tenemos ganas, vamos a un café, tomamos algo y hablamos mucho.

I like going out for a walk with other boys and girls. We go out often. We go for a walk, if we feel like it we go to a café, we drink something and we talk a lot.

MARTA
Yo salgo todos los domingos. También los sábados por la noche. Me gusta salir los fines de semana porque puedo volver a casa tarde. A veces voy al cine.

I go out every Sunday. Also on Saturday nights. I like to go out on weekends because I can return home late. Sometimes I go to the movies.

B1 ¿Qué vamos a ver?

Paula y Miguel están en el Café Suárez, en Buenos Aires. Dicen que piensan ir al cine, pero, ¿qué van a ver? Miguel mira el periódico.

What are we going to see?
Paula and Miguel are in the Café Suárez, in Buenos Aires. They are saying that they're thinking of going to the movies, but what are they going to see? Miguel looks at the newspaper.

MIGUEL	¿Qué vamos a hacer? ¿Vamos al cine? ¿Qué clase de película quieres ver?	*What are we going to do? Should we go the movies? What kind of movie do you want to see?*
PAULA	¿Qué dan en el cine Belgrano?	*What are they showing at the Belgrano theater?*
MIGUEL	*Detenidos en el tiempo.* ¡Premio de oro, Mar del Plata! Creo que es una película de ciencia-ficción.	Suspended in Time. *Gold prize, Mar del Plata! I think it is a science fiction movie.*

PAULA	¿Y si vamos al Savoy? ¿Qué te parece? ¿Qué dan ahí?	*What if we go to the Savoy? What do you think? What are they showing there?*
MIGUEL	Mmm . . . Aquí está el programa de mañana. Van a dar *Bodas de plata.* ¿Hoy? . . . Hoy dan *Basta de ruido.*	*Mmm . . . Here is tomorrow's program. They are going to show* Silver Wedding Anniversary. *Today? . . . Today they are showing* No More Noise.
PAULA	*¿Basta de ruido?* Me parece que es una musical. Mejor vamos al Belgrano.	No More Noise? *I think that is a musical. We better go to the Belgrano.*
MIGUEL	Bueno, entonces, vamos a ver *Detenidos en el tiempo.* ¡Vamos! La película va a empezar. Son casi las seis.	*Well, then, let's go see* Suspended in Time. *Let's go! The movie is going to start. It's almost six o'clock.*

B8 Mejor una policial

Better a detective film

TERESA	¿Vamos a ver *Sueño de amor?*	*Should we go to see* Dream of Love?
RAQUEL	No, hoy no tengo ganas de ver una película de amor.	*No, today I don't feel like seeing a love story.*
TERESA	¿Y si vemos *El amigo de Frankenstein?*	*What if we see* Frankenstein's Friend?
RAQUEL	¿Una de terror? ¡No! Mejor vemos *Fantasía.*	*A horror movie? No! We better go see* Fantasia.
TERESA	*Fantasía* es de dibujos animados. En el Rex dan una del oeste. ¿Qué te parece?	Fantasia *is an animated cartoon film. They are showing a western at the Rex. What do you think?*
RAQUEL	Si quieres ver una de aventuras, aquí hay una: *Vuelo fantástico.*	*If you want to see an adventure film, here is one:* Fantastic Flight.
TERESA	*¿Vuelo fantástico?* ¡No! Es de ciencia-ficción. Vamos a ver una cómica: *Líos locos.*	Fantastic Flight? *No! It's a science fiction film. Let's go see a comedy:* Crazy Complications.
RAQUEL	*Crimen en el hielo,* ¡la mejor policial del año!	Crime on Ice, *the best detective film of the year!*
TERESA	¿Una policial? ¡Fantástico! ¡Vamos!	*A detective film? Fantastic! Let's go!*

C1 ¡Tito Ortega canta hoy!

Tito Ortega sings today!

En el autobús.

On the bus.

NICOLÁS	¡Mira, Paula! Ahí está Diego. ¡Hola, Diego! ¿Qué tal? ¿Conoces a Paula?	*Look, Paula! There is Diego. Hi, Diego! How are things? Do you know Paula?*
DIEGO	No. ¡Hola! ¿Cómo estás? ¿Adónde van?	*No. Hi! How are you? Where are you going?*
PAULA	Al teatro, a escuchar a Tito Ortega.	*To the theater, to hear Tito Ortega.*
DIEGO	¿Sí?, yo también.	*Really? Me, too.*
NICOLÁS	¡Fantástico! Oye, Diego, ¿sabes dónde tenemos que bajar?	*Fantastic! Listen, Diego, do you know where we have to get off?*
DIEGO	Sí, en la próxima parada, en la calle Sarmiento.	*Yes, at the next stop, at Sarmiento Street.*

Frente al Luna Park.

In front of Luna Park.

DIEGO	¡Cuánta gente! ¡Permiso, por favor!	*What a lot of people! Excuse me, please!*
NICOLÁS	Perdón, señor. ¿Sabe si hay entradas?	*Excuse me, sir. Do you know if there are any tickets?*
SEÑOR	No, nosotros esperamos el autobús.	*No, we are waiting for the bus.*
PAULA	Por favor, señora, ¿sabe cuál es la fila para comprar entradas?	*Please, ma'am, do you know which is the line to buy tickets?*
SEÑORA	Hay entradas en la ventanilla, a la derecha, señorita.	*Tickets are at the ticket window, to the right, miss.*

Unos minutos más tarde.

A few minutes later.

PAULA	¿Vienes con nosotros, Diego?		Are you coming with us, Diego?
DIEGO	No, espero a mi hermana. Ella busca a su amiga Susana.		No, I am waiting for my sister. She is looking for her friend Susana.
NICOLÁS	¡Ahí están! Vamos, el concierto va a empezar.		There they are! Let's go, the concert is going to start.

9 ¡BUEN PROVECHO!

ENJOY YOUR MEAL!

A1 ¿Qué comemos hoy?

Los señores Álvarez escriben sobre los restaurantes de San Antonio para una guía turística. ¿Qué van a comer hoy? ¿Comida española, tex-mex, del Caribe, pizza o hamburguesas?

What do we eat today?

Mr. and Mrs. Álvarez write about the restaurants of San Antonio for a tourist guide. What are they going to eat today? Spanish, Tex-Mex, Caribbean food, pizza or hamburgers?

CAMARERA	¿Desean ver el menú? El plato del día es pollo con cebolla y salsa de tomate.		Would you like to see the menu? The specialty of the day is chicken with onions and tomato sauce.
SR. ÁLVAREZ	A mí no me gustan las cebollas. ¿Hay sopa?		I don't like onions. Do you have soup?
SRA. ÁLVAREZ	Queremos probar algo típico tex-mex.		We want to try something typically Tex-Mex.
CAMARERA	¿Puede ser chile con carne?		Can it be chili con carne?
CAMARERO	¿A ustedes les gustan las enchiladas? Es una especialidad de la casa.		Do you like enchiladas? It's a specialty of the house.
SRA. ÁLVAREZ	Sí, me gustan mucho. Quiero dos de carne y una de queso.		Yes, I like them very much. I want two beef and one cheese, please.
CAMARERA	¿Y de postre, señores?		And for dessert?
SRA. ÁLVAREZ	Un helado de chocolate, por favor, y café con leche.		Chocolate ice-cream, please, and coffee with milk.
SR. ÁLVAREZ	Fruta y té con limón para mí. Estoy a dieta.		Fruit and tea with lemon for me. I'm on a diet.
SRA. ÁLVAREZ	¡Qué rápido cenamos aquí!		How quickly we eat here!
SR. ÁLVAREZ	Sí, voy a pagar la cuenta.		Yes, I'm going to pay the bill.
SRA. ÁLVAREZ	¿Cuánto dejamos de propina?		How much tip should we leave?
SR. ÁLVAREZ	¡No sé cuánto . . . ni dónde!		I don't know how much . . . or where!

¡A la mesa!

A6 Comemos por la mañana, al mediodía, por la tarde y por la noche. A la hora de la merienda, o entre comidas, lo mejor es un bocadillo y un vaso de leche o de jugo.

Por la mañana, en el desayuno, nos gusta tomar café con leche o chocolate, comer pan con mantequilla, jalea o mermelada.

Al mediodía, en el almuerzo, nos gusta un bistec o pescado, arroz, verduras, y un postre. Nuestro postre favorito es el flan. A nosotros nos gusta una comida completa.

To the table!

We eat in the morning, at noon, in the afternoon and at night. For an afternoon snack, or between meals, the best thing is a sandwich and a glass of milk or juice.

In the morning, for breakfast, we like to have coffee and milk or chocolate, eat bread with butter, jelly or marmalade.

At noon, for lunch, we like a steak or fish, rice, vegetables, and dessert. Our favorite dessert is baked custard. We like a complete meal.

En el almuerzo, a mí me gusta comer un bocadillo. Me gustan los bocadillos de jamón y queso, con lechuga, tomate y mayonesa. Las papas fritas me encantan.

Por la noche, para la cena, en casa les gusta una comida ligera: tomar sopa, comer una tortilla con ensalada, pan, queso y fruta.

B1 Un picnic

ELENA ¿Qué haces?

CARLOS Preparo una tortilla para el picnic.

ELENA ¡Estupendo! A todos nos gusta la tortilla. Es muy rica. ¿Te ayudo?

CARLOS ¿Por qué no cortas estas patatas y esas cebollas en trozos pequeños? Después voy a freír todo.

ELENA Bueno, a lo dicho, hecho. ¡Ay!

CARLOS ¿Por qué lloras, Elena?

ELENA ¡Son las cebollas por supuesto! Y ahora, ¿qué?

CARLOS Ahora bato los huevos, añado las patatas y las cebollas y cocino todo en esta misma sartén. Tiene que dorarse de los dos lados. ¡Y aquí está nuestra tortilla!

ELENA ¡Ay, qué hambre tengo!

B3 La comida para el picnic

Miguel compra las frutas. Va a aquella frutería grande de la esquina.

—¿A cuánto están estas uvas? ¡Parecen buenísimas!

—A 500 pesos el kilo.

Alicia hace bocadillos de jamón y queso, de pollo y de atún. ¡Qué sabrosos!

—¡Alicia, estos bocadillos son deliciosos!

Sofía compra pasteles en una pastelería muy buena.

—¡Es difícil decidir! ¿Llevo esta tarta de manzanas o ese bizcocho de chocolate? ¡Mira aquel pastel con fresas!

Manuel trae los refrescos.

—Tiene el jugo, las gaseosas y el agua mineral en el coche.

— . . . ¡Ah!, y también tiene su guitarra. ¡Este picnic va a ser estupendo!

C1 Y por fin, ¡el picnic!

MIGUEL La sal, por favor. ¡Esta tortilla está perfecta! Pero, ¿dónde está Manuel con los refrescos? Tengo mucha sed.

For lunch, I like to eat a sandwich. I like ham and cheese sandwiches, with lettuce, tomato and mayonnaise. I love French fries.

At night, for dinner, at home they like a light meal: have some soup, eat an omelette with salad, bread, cheese and fruit.

A picnic

What are you doing?

I am preparing a Spanish omelette for the picnic.

Great! We all like Spanish omelette. It's delicious. Can I help you?

Why don't you cut these potatoes and those onions in small pieces? Then I will fry everything.

Well, no sooner said than done. Ah!

Why are you crying, Elena?

It's the onions of course! And now, what?

Now I beat the eggs, I add the potatoes and the onions and cook everything in the same frying pan. It has to brown on both sides. And here is our Spanish omelette!

Oh, I'm so hungry!

The food for the picnic

Miguel buys the fruit. He goes to that big fruit store on the corner.

How much are these grapes? They look very good!

500 pesos per kilo.

Alicia makes sandwiches of ham and cheese, chicken and tuna. How delicious!

Alicia, these sandwiches are delicious!

Sofía buys pastries at a very good pastry shop.

It's so difficult to decide! Should I take that apple tart or that chocolate cake? Look at that strawberry pie!

Manuel brings the sodas.

He has the juice, the sodas, and the mineral water in the car.

. . . Ah!, and he also has his guitar. This picnic is going to be great!

And at last, the picnic!

The salt, please. This omelette is perfect! But, where is Manuel with the sodas? I'm very thirsty.

ELENA	¡Paciencia! Comes por tres, ¿sabes? ¡Ah, aquí viene!	*Patience! You eat for three, you know? Ah, here he comes!*
MANUEL	¡Hola! ¡Cuánto tráfico! ¿Pongo la mesa? ¿Dónde van los refrescos?	*Hi! What a lot of traffic! Should I set the table? Where do the sodas go?*
ELENA	La mesa ya está.	*The table is already set.*
MIGUEL	Los refrescos, aquí, por favor, a mi lado.	*The sodas, here, please, beside me.*
ELENA	No, a tu lado, no. Miguel, ¿por qué no pones los refrescos debajo de ese árbol?	*No, not beside you. Miguel, why don't you put the sodas under that tree?*
ALICIA	Debes tener hambre, Manuel. ¿Quieres un bocadillo? ¿De queso o de jamón?	*You must be hungry, Manuel. Do you want a sandwich? Cheese or ham?*
MANUEL	De jamón, por favor. . . . ¡Qué rico está! Gracias, Alicia.	*Ham, please. . . . It's delicious! Thank you, Alicia.*
CARLOS	Este picnic necesita música. Miguel, ¿por qué no pones este casete? ¿Quieres bailar, Alicia?	*This picnic needs music. Miguel, why don't you play this cassette? Do you want to dance, Alicia?*
ALICIA	¡Cómo no! Es mi canción favorita.	*Of course! It's my favorite song.*
MIGUEL	Buena idea. Vamos, Elena. Si bailas conmigo, no como más.	*Good idea. Let's go, Elena. If you dance with me, I won't eat anymore.*
ELENA	¡No hay más remedio! Vamos, Miguel.	*I guess there's no choice! Let's go, Miguel.*

C12 Ponemos la mesa

Para el desayuno pongo:

vaso para el jugo, platillo para el pan y la mantequilla

plato hondo para el cereal, cuchara y servilleta

taza con platillo, y cucharita para el azúcar

Para el almuerzo ponemos:
plato hondo para la sopa
platillo para el sandwich y servilleta
sal, pimienta, mostaza y catsup

Para la comida o para la cena ellos ponen:

platillo para la ensalada, plato llano para la comida
tenedor, cuchillo, dos cucharitas, servilleta, vaso para el agua y platillo para el postre

We set the table

For breakfast I set:

a glass for the juice, a small plate for the bread and the butter

a bowl for the cereal, a spoon and a napkin

a cup with a saucer, and a teaspoon for the sugar

For lunch we set:
a soup plate
a small plate for the sandwich and a napkin
salt, pepper, mustard and ketchup

For dinner or for supper they set:

a small plate for the salad, a dinner plate

a fork, a knife, two teaspoons, a napkin, a water glass, and a small plate for dessert

10 UN VIAJE ESTUPENDO

A WONDERFUL TRIP

A1 El diario de Pilar

Querido diario:

Ayer llegó carta de Marisol, mi prima de Madrid. Casi nunca canto, pero ayer canté y bailé de alegría. ¡No puedo creerlo! ¡Una invitación para pasar una semana en Madrid! Hablé con mamá. Tengo permiso. Llamé a Marisol por teléfono. Mamá habló con tía Inés. Planeamos el viaje. ¡Todo está arreglado!

Pilar's diary

Dear diary:

Yesterday a letter arrived from Marisol, my cousin from Madrid. I almost never sing, but yesterday I sang and danced for joy. I can't believe it! An invitation to spend a week in Madrid! I talked to mom. I have permission to go. I called Marisol on the phone. Mom talked with Aunt Inés. We planned the trip. Everything's arranged!

El sábado . . . ¡a Madrid! . . . excursiones, visitas y paseos. Billy, mi amigo de Chicago, también va. ¡Qué suerte!

¿Sabes? Él ya estudió casi todos los mapas y miró los folletos de turismo. Marcó todos los lugares que quiere visitar. ¡Es tan organizado! Estoy segura que ya compró los billetes . . . y preparó las maletas . . . ¡con una semana de anticipación!

Saturday . . . to Madrid! . . . Excursions, visits and sightseeing trips. Billy, my friend from Chicago, is also going. What luck!

You know what? He already studied all the maps and looked at all the tourist brochures. He marked all the places he wants to visit. He is so organized! I'm sure he bought the tickets already . . . and prepared the suitcases . . . with a week left to go!

A14 Conversación de dos minutos
Carlos llama por teléfono a Isabel en un mal momento. Isabel está a punto de salir para el aeropuerto.

Two-minute conversation
Carlos calls Isabel on the phone at a bad time. Isabel is just about to leave for the airport.

CARLOS ¡Hola, Isabel! ¿Cómo estás?
ISABEL ¡Apuradísima! No puedo hablar ahora. Salimos para el aeropuerto dentro de dos minutos. Vamos a Barcelona.

Hi, Isabel! How are you?
In a big hurry! I can't talk now. We are leaving for the airport in two minutes. We are going to Barcelona.

CARLOS ¿A Barcelona?
ISABEL Sí. Vamos a visitar a la abuela. Mamá reservó los billetes de avión la semana pasada. Papá y mamá llamaron a la abuela anoche. Papá regresó de la oficina hace una hora. El taxi ya llegó . . . y yo todavía tengo que hacer mi maleta. ¡Adiós!

To Barcelona?
Yes. We are going to visit Grandmother. Mom reserved the plane tickets last week. Last night Dad and Mom called Grandmother. Dad returned from the office an hour ago. The taxi has already arrived . . . and I still have to pack my suitcase.

Goodbye!

B1 Pilar llama desde Madrid
Pilar llama a su casa. Su hermana Socorro contesta el teléfono. Socorro quiere saber todo lo que pasa. Pregunta sin parar.

Pilar calls from Madrid
Pilar calls home. Her sister Socorro answers the phone. Socorro wants to know everything that's happening. She asks questions non-stop.

SOCORRO ¡Hola, Pilar! ¿Cómo estás? ¿Y Billy? ¿Cómo llegaron? ¿Les gusta Madrid?

Hi, Pilar! How are you! And Billy? How was your arrival? Do you like Madrid?

PILAR Estamos muy bien, Socorro. ¿Está mamá?

We are very well, Socorro. Is mom there?

SOCORRO Sí, ya viene, pero, antes, ¿qué tal el viaje? ¿Adónde fueron hoy? ¿Qué hicieron?

Yes, she is coming now, but, first, how about the trip? Where did you go today? What did you do?

PILAR Fuimos primero a casa de los tíos. Dejamos nuestras cosas allí. Hablamos mucho. Hicimos planes también.

We first went to our aunt's and our uncle's house. We left our things there. We talked a lot. We also made plans.

SOCORRO Ya sé, ya sé . . ., pero, ¿qué más hicieron?

I know, I know . . ., but, what else did you do?

PILAR Hicimos muchas cosas.
SOCORRO ¿Fueron a la Gran Vía?
PILAR No, fuimos en moto hasta la Puerta de Alcalá. Caminamos mucho. Después fuimos al Parque del Retiro. Remamos en el estanque. ¡Pasamos un día fantástico!

We did a lot of things.
Did you go to the Gran Vía?
No, we went by motorcycle to the Puerta de Alcalá. We walked a lot. Then we went to the Parque del Retiro. We went rowing in the pond. We had a fantastic day!

Socorro	¡Qué envidia! Aquí viene mamá. ¡Hasta mañana!	How I envy you! Here comes mom. Until tomorrow!
Pilar	¡Adiós, Socorro!	Goodbye, Socorro!

C1 Un viaje corto

La mamá de Socorro quiere saber si está todo listo para el viaje a Granada.

A short trip

Socorro's mom wants to know if everything's ready for the trip to Granada.

Mamá	Socorro, ¿tienes los billetes?	Socorro, do you have the tickets?
Socorro	Sí, mamá, los tengo aquí.	Yes, mom, I have them here.
Mamá	¿Hiciste las maletas?	Did you pack the suitcases?
Socorro	Sí, mamá, las preparé.	Yes, mom, I prepared them.
Mamá	¿Y los regalos?	And the gifts?
Socorro	Están todos.	They are all here.
Mamá	¿Te llamó tu hermano?	Did your brother call you?
Socorro	Sí, me llamó esta mañana.	Yes, he called me this morning.
Mamá	¿Llamaste al taxi?	Did you call the taxi?
Socorro	Sí, ya lo llamé.	Yes, I called one already.
Mamá	Bueno, ¿qué más? . . . ¿Tiene tu papá nuestro número de teléfono?	Well, what else? . . . Does your dad have our phone number?
Socorro	Sí, lo tiene. Mamá, ¡por favor!, ¡sólo vamos a Granada por dos días!	Yes, he has it. Mom, please!, we are only going to Granada for two days!

11 ¡VAMOS DE COMPRAS!

WE ARE GOING SHOPPING!

A1 ¿Lo compramos?

Should we buy it?

Señora	Señorita, por favor.	Miss, please.
Vendedora	¿Qué desea, señora?	What would you like, ma'am?
Señora	Ese plato de cerámica, por favor.	That ceramic plate, please.
Vendedora	¿Cuál, el pequeño o el grande?	Which, the small one or the big one?
Señora	Los dos . . . Este plato es más grande que ése, pero cuesta menos, ¿por qué?	Both, . . . This plate is bigger than that one, but costs less. Why?
Vendedora	El más pequeño está hecho a mano. El grande es una imitación. No es de cerámica, es de plástico.	The small one is handmade. The big one is an imitation. It's not ceramic, it's plastic.
Señora	¡Oh, no! Yo quiero uno de cerámica, pero más barato que éste. ¿Y ése de allá?	Oh, no! I want a ceramic one, but cheaper than this one. And that one over there?
Vendedora	Cuesta igual que el de cerámica.	It costs the same as the ceramic one.
Señora	¡Oh! ¿Valen lo mismo? Muchas gracias.	Oh! They cost the same? Thank you very much.
Emilio	¿Qué te parece, Diego? ¿Qué cinturón llevamos?	What do you think, Diego? Which belt do we take?
Diego	No sé, pero a mí me gusta más el oscuro. Es más largo y más bonito que el claro.	I don't know, but I like the darker one more. It's longer and prettier than the lighter one.
Emilio	El claro no me gusta nada. El oscuro está bien, ¿no?	I don't like the lighter one at all. The darker one is fine, right?
Diego	No está mal, pero es más caro que el otro.	It's not bad, but it's more expensive than the other one.

EMILIO	¡No importa! Es bien lindo y es de cuero.	*It doesn't matter. It's very pretty and it's leather.*
CLARA	¡Mira esta blusa! Es una preciosura. Es de algodón. Está bordada a mano. ¿La compro?	*Look at that blouse! It's a beauty. It's cotton. It's embroidered by hand. Should I buy it?*
MARIANA	¡Buena idea! Voy a preguntar el precio. Por favor, señorita, ¿cuánto vale esta blusa en dólares?	*Good idea! I'm going to ask the price. Please, miss, how much is this blouse in dollars?*
VENDEDORA	Veinte dólares, señorita.	*Twenty dollars, miss.*
CLARA	Bueno, está bien. ¿Puedo pagar con tarjeta de crédito?	*Well, that's fine. Can I pay with a credit card?*
VENDEDORA	Sí, cómo no. En la caja, por favor.	*Yes, of course. At the cashier, please.*

A8 ¿Qué ropa compramos?

What should we buy?

abrigo	sombrero
chaqueta de lana	zapatos
suéter	vestido de
calcetines	algodón
jeans	falda
corbata	pañuelo de seda
camisa	blusa de nilón
traje	traje de baño
saco	
pantalones	

coat	*hat*
wool jacket	*shoes*
sweater	*cotton dress*
socks	*skirt*
jeans	*silk handkerchief*
tie	*nylon blouse*
shirt	*bathing suit*
suit	
jacket	
pants	

B1 ¡Es una ganga!
Marisa y su mamá están de compras en La Lujosa, una tienda de barrio.

It's a bargain!
Marisa and her mother are shopping in La Lujosa, a neighborhood store.

MAMÁ	¿Le compras dos regalos a Linda, un suéter y una cartera?	*Are you buying two gifts for Linda, a sweater and a purse?*
MARISA	No, mamá. Compro el suéter para mí y le compro la cartera a Linda. Le mando la cartera por correo, ¿no? ¿Qué te parece? Así la recibe pronto.	*No, mom. I am buying the sweater for me and the purse for Linda. I can send her the purse by mail, right? What do you think? That way she will receive it soon.*
MAMÁ	¡Buena idea! Ese suéter te queda muy bien. La cartera es de muy buena calidad. ¿Sabes cuánto cuesta?	*Good idea! That sweater looks very nice on you. The purse is of very good quality. Do you know how much it costs?*
MARISA	No. ¿Le preguntamos a la vendedora?	*No. Should we ask the salesperson?*
VENDEDORA	¿En qué puedo servirle, señorita?	*How may I help you, miss?*
MAMÁ	¿Cuánto cuesta esta cartera?	*How much is this purse?*
VENDEDORA	325 pesos, señora, pero está rebajada a 280 por esta semana. Es una oferta especial. No va a encontrar otra más barata.	*325 pesos, ma'am, but it's reduced to 280 for this week. It's a special offer. You are not going to find a cheaper one.*
MAMÁ	¡280 pesos! Es demasiado cara. Esa cartera no vale tanto. Vamos a otra tienda, Marisa.	*280 pesos! It's too expensive. That purse isn't worth that much. Let's go to another store, Marisa.*
MARISA	Por favor, mamá, ¡es una ganga! A Linda le va a encantar.	*Please, mom, it's a bargain! Linda will be delighted.*

MAMÁ	No pago más de 200 pesos. (En voz baja.) Pero hijita, tú no sabes regatear. Vas a ver.		*I won't pay more than 200 pesos. (In a low voice.) But daughter, you don't know how to bargain. You'll see.*
VENDEDORA	Perdón, señora. Como a su hija le gusta tanto, le dejo la cartera en 200 pesos. Más barata no puedo.		*Excuse me, ma'am. Since your daughter likes it so much, I'll let the purse go for 200 pesos. I can't let it go any cheaper.*
MAMÁ	Entonces, la llevamos. ¿Le puedo pagar con un cheque?		*Then, we'll take it. Can I pay you with a check?*

B9 El estéreo nuevo

Raúl quiere un estéreo nuevo . . . pero, ¿cuándo lo va a poder comprar? ¡El estéreo cuesta más de mil pesos! Raúl hace cuentas.

Si ahorro veinticinco pesos por semana . . . son cien por mes . . . en un año puedo tener el estéreo . . . ¡No, un año es mucho tiempo! Vamos a ver . . . ahorro el doble: doscientos pesos por mes . . . en dos meses son cuatrocientos . . . sí, en cinco meses, me compro el estéreo! pero, ¿voy a poder ahorrar?

The new stereo

Raúl wants a new stereo . . . but, when is he going to be able to buy it? The stereo costs more than a thousand pesos! Raúl does calculations.

If I save twenty-five pesos a week . . . that is a hundred a month . . . in a year I can have the stereo . . . No, a year is too much time! Let's see . . . I save twice as much: two hundred pesos a month . . . in two months that is four hundred . . . yes, in five months, I'll buy the stereo, but, will I be able to save?

B11 Los números del 100 al 1,000
cien
ciento uno,-a
ciento treinta y cuatro
doscientos,-as
doscientos,-as veintitrés
trescientos,-as
cuatrocientos,-as
quinientos,-as
seiscientos,-as
setecientos,-as
ochocientos,-as
novecientos,-as
mil

The numbers from 100 to 1,000
one hundred
one hundred and one
one hundred thirty–four
two hundred
two hundred twenty–three
three hundred
four hundred
five hundred
six hundred
seven hundred
eight hundred
nine hundred
one thousand

C1 Sección de quejas y reclamos
El Sr. Gómez no recibió el estéreo que compró. Ahora está en la Sección de quejas y reclamos.

Customer Service Department
Mr. Gómez did not receive the stereo he bought. Now he is in the Customer Service Department.

EMPLEADA	¿Señor?		*Sir?*
SR. GÓMEZ	Sí, señorita. Aquí tengo el recibo. Ustedes me prometieron el estéreo para el día 15. Hoy es 25, . . . y no lo recibí.		*Yes, miss. Here I have the receipt. You promised me the stereo for the 15th. Today is the 25th, . . . and I have not received it.*
EMPLEADA	El recibo, por favor. Ah, señor, ¿escribió usted una carta de reclamación?		*The receipt, please. Ah, sir, did you write a letter with your claim?*
SR. GÓMEZ	¡Señorita, por favor! Llamé por teléfono veinte veces, escribí dos cartas la semana pasada . . . , finalmente, decidí venir en persona.		*Miss, please! I called on the phone twenty times, I wrote two letters last week . . . , finally, I decided to come in person.*

EMPLEADA	¿Subió usted a la oficina del piso cinco?
SR. GÓMEZ	Sí, ya fui, me mandaron aquí.
EMPLEADA	A ver . . . un momento . . . ¿y quién le vendió el estéreo? Este pedido ya salió . . . usted va a recibir el estéreo mañana, a primera hora.
SR. GÓMEZ	Pero, señorita . . . Mi hijo no cumple años mañana . . . ¡su cumpleaños es hoy! ¡Y yo le prometí el estéreo!

Did you go up to the office on the fifth floor?

Yes, I went; they sent me here.
Let's see . . . one moment . . . and who sold you the stereo? This order left already . . . you are going to receive the stereo tomorrow, as early as possible.

But, miss . . . My son's birthday is not tomorrow . . . his birthday is today! And I promised him the stereo!

SPANISH-ENGLISH VOCABULARY

This vocabulary includes all the words and expressions appearing in the text of **Nuevos amigos.** Exceptions are names of people and of most countries and places.

Nouns are listed with their definite articles. Nouns referring to persons are given in the masculine and feminine form if the English is the same for both (**el aficionado, la aficionada,** fan). If the English word is different (**el abuelo,** grandfather; **la abuela,** grandmother), the words are listed separately. Adjectives are listed in the masculine singular form with the feminine ending shown after each adjective. Verbs are listed in the infinitive form. Verb forms introduced as vocabulary items are listed in the form they appeared in the text.

The number after each definition refers to the unit in which the word or expression is introduced.

The following abbreviations are used in this list: *adj.* adjective; *adv.* adverb; *com.* command; *dir.* direct; *f.* feminine; *fam.* familiar; *ind.* indicative; *inf.* infinitive; *m.* masculine; *obj.* object; *pl.* plural; *pol.* polite; *prep.* preposition; *pron.* pronoun; *sing.* singular; *sub.* subjunctive.

A

a at, to, **2**
  a casa (to) home, **5**; **a la derecha** on the right, **5**; **a la izquierda** on the left, **5**; **a la mesa** to the table, **9**; **a la noche** tonight, **7**; **a la una** at one o'clock, **2**; **a las diez** at ten o'clock, **2**; **a lo dicho, hecho** no sooner said than done, **9**; **a menudo** often, **3**; **a pie** on foot, **2**; **a primera hora** as early as possible, **11**; **¿a qué hora?** at what time?, **2**; **a veces** sometimes, **3**; **estar a punto de** to be on the verge of, **10**; **frente a** across from, **6**
  a ver let's see, **11**
abajo below, **5**
abandonado, -a abandoned, **2**
abre opens, **2**
el **abrigo** coat, **11**
abril April, **3**
abrimos: ¿lo abrimos? do we open it?, **2**
abrir to open, **2**
la **abuela** grandmother, **6**
el **abuelo** grandfather, **6**
  los abuelos grandparents, **6**; grandfathers, **6**
aburrido, -a boring, **2**
acaba de: lo que acaba de ocurrir what just happened, **11**
acabado, -a finished, **6**
la **academia** academy, **7**
el **accesorio** accessory, **11**

el **aceite** oil, **9**
aceptar to accept, **7**
acerca(n): se acerca(n) (they) come close, near, **6**
el **ácido** acid, **2**
aclamado, -a acclaimed, **7**
acompañar to accompany, **10**
acompañará: lo acompañará (it) will accompany you, **10**
acostumbrado: estar acostumbrado, -a to be used to, **11**
la **actividad** activity, **2**
el **actor** actor, **1**
actuar to act, **11**
acuerdo: de acuerdo all right, **3**
  de acuerdo con according to, **7**
además besides, **5**
adentro inside, **11**
adiós goodbye, **1**
la **adivinanza** guessing game, **6**
adivinar: ¡a adivinar! guess!, **3**
el **admirador, la admiradora** admirer, **7**
¿adónde? (to) where? **5**
la **aduana** customs, **5**
el **aduanero, la aduanera** customs agent, **5**
la **aeromoza, la azafata** stewardess, **5**
el **aeropuerto** airport, **5**
el **aficionado, la aficionada** fan, **3**
afuera outside, **11**
la **agencia** agency, **10**
la **agenda** appointment book, **2**
el, la **agente** agent, **6**
agosto August, **3**

agrícola agricultural, **5**
el **agua** (*f.*): **el agua mineral** mineral water, **9**
ahí there, **2**
ahora now, **2**
ahorrar to save, **11**
al (a + el) to the, at the (contraction), **2**
  al contrario on the contrary, **2**; **al lado de** beside, next to, **5**
el **álbum** album, **6**
la **alegría** happiness, **10**
la **alfarería** pottery, **11**
el **álgebra** (*f.*) algebra, **2**
algo something, **5**
el **algodón** cotton, **11**
alguno, -a, -os, -as some, **2**
alimenticio, -a: la píldora alimenticia food capsule, **10**
el **almuerzo** lunch, **2**
¡aló! hello, **5**
alto, -a tall, **6**
allá (over) there, **11**
allí there, **5**
amable kind, **6**
amado, -a loved, **7**
amarillo, -a yellow, **3**
el **ambiente** atmosphere, **11**
americano, -a American, **1**
el **amigo, la amiga** friend, **3**
la **amistad** friendship, **10**
el **amor** love, **7**
amplio, -a ample, abundant, **10**
amueblado, -a furnished, **6**
amurallado, -a walled, **5**

anaranjado, -a orange, 3
el **ángel** angel, 1
animado, -a lively, 11
el dibujo animado animated cartoon, 7
el **animal** animal, 10
anoche last night, 10
antes before, 10
la **anticipación: con una semana de anticipación** a week ahead of time, 10
antiguo, -a old, 10
antipático, -a not nice, 6
el **anuncio** ad, 10
anunciaron (they) announced, 2
añadir to add, 9
año year, 3
¿cuántos años tiene? how old are you (is he/she)? 6; **cumplir años** to have a birthday, 11; **tener . . . años** to be . . . years old, 6
apaga turns off, 2
el **apartamento** apartment, 6
apoderarse: tratar de apoderarse de to try to seize, 11
apretar (ie) to press, 9
aprobado, -a passing, average, 2
aprovechado, -a above average, 2
apto. (abbreviation for *apartamento*) apt., 6
apuradísimo, -a in a big hurry, 10
aquel, aquella that, 9
aquél, aquélla that one, 11
aquellos, -as those, 9
aquéllos, -as those, 11
aquí here, 5
el **árbol** tree, 9
el árbol genealógico family tree, 6
el **archivo** file, 10
arder to burn, 10
la **arquitectura** architecture, 5
el **arte** art, 5
artístico, -a artistic, 2
la educación artística art class, 2
arreglado, -a arranged, 10
arriba up (there), 5
el **arroz** rice, 9
asesinar to murder, 6
así so, thus, 1
se dice así this is how to say it, 1; **no es así** it's not so, 1; that way, then, 11
el **asiento** seat, 5
la **asignatura** subject, 2
el **Atlántico** Atlantic, 2
el, la **atleta** athlete, 3
atlético, -a athletic, 3
el **átomo** atom, 2
el **atún** tuna, 9
el **auto** car, automobile, 2
en auto by car, 2
el **autobús** bus, 2
el autobús escolar school bus, 2; **en autobús** by bus, 2

autónomo, -a autonomous, 2
avanzado, -a advanced, 3
la **avenida** avenue, 10
la **aventura** adventure, 7
el **avión** airplane, 5
ayer yesterday, 10
ayudar to help, 9
el **azúcar** sugar, 9
azul blue, 3

B

el **bachillerato** secondary education program, 2
bailar to dance, 3
el **baile** dance, 7
bajar to get off, 7
bajo, -a short, 6; **en voz baja** in a low voice, 11
la **bala** bullet, 10
el **balón** ball (basketball, volleyball, soccer ball), 3
el **ballet** ballet, 2
el **banco** bank, 10
el **baño** bathroom, 5
el traje de baño bathing suit, 11
barato, -a cheap, 11
el **barrio** neighborhood, 11
basado, -a based, 7
básico, -a basic, 10
el **básquetbol** basketball, 3
¡basta de . . .! enough . . .! 7
bastante rather, 2; a lot, 7
el **bastón** (*pl.* **bastones**) pole, 3
(de esquiar) ski pole, 3
el **bate** bat, 3
batir to beat, 9
beber to drink, 5
el **béisbol** baseball, 3
la **bicicleta** bicycle, 2
en bicicleta by bicycle, 2; **montar en bicicleta** to ride a bicycle, 3
bien well, good, fine, 1; very, 6
quedar bien to look nice (on), 11
bienvenido, -a welcome, 6
el **billete** ticket, 10
la **billetera** wallet, 11
la **biología** biology, 2
el **bistec** beefsteak, 9
el **bizcocho** cake, 9
blanco, -a white, 3
la **blusa** blouse, 11
el **bocadillo** snack, sandwich, 9
la **boda: las bodas de plata** silver wedding anniversary, 7
el **boletín** report card, 2
el **bolígrafo** ballpoint pen, 2
el **bolsillo** pocket, 5
bonito, -a pretty, 6
¡qué cuarto tan bonito! what a pretty room! 6
bordado, -a embroidered, 11
bordo: a bordo on board, 5
las **botas** boots, 3; **(de esquiar)** ski boots, 3

el **botón** (*pl.* **botones**) button, 9
brindar to offer, 10
la **broma** joke, 2
buen: ¡buen provecho! hearty appetite! 9
hace (muy) buen tiempo it's (very) nice out, 3
bueno, -a good, 1
well, 1; **¿bueno?** hello 5; **buenas noches** good evening, good night, hello, 1; **buenas tardes** good afternoon, 1; **buenos días** good morning, 1
buenísimo, -a very good, 9
buscar to look for, 5
los busca is looking for them, 7

C

la **cabeza: el dolor de cabeza** headache, 2
cada each, 3
caer: se cae it falls, 11
el **café** coffeeshop, 7; coffee, 9
la **cafetería** cafeteria, 5
la **caja** cashier's desk, 11
el **calcetín** (*pl.* **calcetines**) sock, 11
la **calculadora** calculator, 2
calentar to heat, 9
la **calidad** quality, 11
caliente hot, 9
la **calificación** grade, 2
calmado, -a calmed down, 11
el **calor: hace (mucho) calor** it's (very) hot out, 3
la **calle** street, 3
la **cámara** camera, 5
la **camarera** waitress, 9
el **camarero** waiter, 9
cambiado, -a changed, 7
cambiar to cash, 5; **cambiar (de)** to change, 5
el **cambio: la casa de cambio** money exchange office, 5
caminar to walk, 10
el **camión** truck, 11
la **camisa** shirt, 11
la camisa de vestir dress shirt, 11
la **camiseta** T-shirt, 11
el **campeón, la campeona** champion, 3
el **campeonato: el Campeonato mundial de fútbol** World Cup Soccer Championships, 3
el **campo** country, 6
el **canal** channel, 2
la **canasta** basketball hoop, 3
la **canción** song, 9
la **cancha: la cancha de tenis** tennis court, 3
cansado, -a tired, 11
cantar to sing, 3
la **capital** capital, 1
el **carácter** character, 2
la **cárcel** jail, 7
el **Caribe** Caribbean, 9
cariñoso, -a affectionate, 6

la **carne** meat, **9**
    el chile con carne Mexican dish of beans, ground beef and chilies, **9**
  caro, -a expensive, **11**
la **carta** letter, **5**
la **cartera** schoolbag, **2**; purse, **5**
el **carro** cart, **5**
la **casa** house, **6**; home, **5**
  a casa (to) home, **5**; **la casa de cambio** money exchange office, **5**; **estás en tu casa** make yourself at home (*fam. sing.*), **6**
  casado, -a married, **6**
el **casete** cassette, **5**
casi almost, **2**
el **castellano** Castilian (language), **2**
  castigado, -a punished, **7**
el **catsup** ketchup, **9**
la **categoría** category, **3**
catorce fourteen, **2**
la **cebolla** onion, **9**
la **célula** cell, **2**
la **cena** dinner, supper, **9**
  cenar to have dinner, **9**
el **centro** center, **5**
la **cerámica** ceramic (material), **11**
cerca (de) near, **5**
el **cereal** cereal, **9**
la **cereza** cherry, **9**
cero zero, **2**
cien, ciento a hundred, **2**
la **ciencia** science, **2**
  la ciencia-ficción science fiction, **7**; **las ciencias naturales** natural science, **2**; **las ciencias sociales** social science, **2**
ciento a hundred, **11**
cierto, -a certain, correct, **2**
cinco five, **2**
cincuenta fifty, **2**
el **cine** movies, **7**; movie theater, **7**
el **cinturón** (*pl.* **cinturones**) belt, **3**
el **círculo** circle, **2**
la **ciudad** city, **2**
  cívico, -a: la formación social, moral y cívica civics, **2**
claro, -a light (in color), **11**
claro of course, **10**
la **clase** classroom, **1**; class, **2**; kind, **7**
clásico, -a classic, **2**
el, la **cliente** customer, **11**
el **club** club, **7**
la **cocina** kitchen, **6**; cooking, cuisine, **6**
cocinar to cook, **9**
el **coche** car, **5**
el **colador** colander, **9**
la **colección** collection, **10**
el **colegio** school, **1**
el **color** color, **3**
la **combinación** combination, **1**
la **comedia** comedy, **7**
el **comedor** dining room, **6**
comenzar (ie) to start, begin, **6**

comienza a sentir starts to feel, **6**
comer to eat, **5**
comercial commercial, **10**
cómico, -a comic, comical, **7**
la **comida** food, meal, dinner, **9**
como about, **2**; as, as if, like, **3**; since, **11**
¿cómo? how? **1**
  ¿cómo es? what's he (she, it) like? **6**; **¿cómo está?** how are you? (*pol. sing.*), **1**; **¿cómo estás?** how are you? (*fam. sing.*), **1**; **¿cómo se llama él (ella)?** what's his (her) name? **1**; **¿cómo te llamas tú?** what's your name? (*fam. sing.*), **1**; **cómo no** of course, **6**
cómodo, -a comfortable, **6**
compartir to share, **6**
el **compás** (*pl.* **compases**) compass, **2**
la **competencia** competition, **3**
complacido, -a pleased, **11**
completar to complete, **1**
completo, -a complete, **9**
el, la **cómplice** accomplice, **10**
la **composición** composition, **3**
el **compositor** composer, **2**
la **compra** shopping, **2**
  estar de compras to be shopping, **11**
comprar to buy, **5**
comprender to understand, **11**
la **comprensión** comprehension, **1**
la **computadora** computer, **2**
la **comunicación: ¡la comunicación se cortó!** we were cut off! **5**
con with, **2**
  con permiso excuse me, **6**; **con una semana de anticipación** a week ahead of time, **10**; **el chile con carne** Mexican dish of beans, ground beef and chilies, **9**; **de acuerdo con** according to, **7**
el **concierto** concert, **7**
la **condición** condition, **6**
el **conductor, la conductora** conductor, **10**
la **confusión** confusion, **2**
  ¡qué confusión! what a mixup! **5**
conmigo with me, **9**
conocer (zc) to know, meet, be acquainted with, **7**
la **conquista** conquest, **7**
conseguir to get, **6**
contado: al contado cash, **6**
contestar to answer, **5**
  no contestan there's no answer, **5**
contigo with you, **6**
continuar to continue, **5**
el **contrario: al contrario** on the contrary, **2**
el **control: el control de pasaportes** passport control, **5**

controlar to control, **3**
  controlarlo to control it, **3**
convenciste; me convenciste you convinced me, **10**
conversar to converse, talk, **6**
el **copiloto** copilot, **5**
la **corbata** tie, **11**
el **corredor, -a** runner, **3**
el **correo: correos** post office, **5**; **por correo** by mail, **11**
correr to run, **2**
la **corrida** bullfighting, **3**
corro I run, **2**
cortar to cut, **9**
  ¡la comunicación se cortó! we were cut off!, **5**; **cortarlas fino** to cut (them) in thin slices, **9**
las **Cortes** Spanish Parliament, **10**
corto, -a short, **10**
la **cosa** thing, **6**
la **costa** coast, **5**
la **costumbre** custom, **11**
el **crédito: la tarjeta de crédito** credit card, **11**
creer to think, believe, **5**; **creerlo** believe it, **10**
el **crimen** crime, **7**
el, la **criminal** criminal, **7**
el **crítico, la crítica** critic, **7**
cruzar to cross, **9**
el **cuaderno** notebook, **2**
¿cuál? what? which? **2**
cualquier any, **10**
cuando when, **6**
¿cuándo? when? **2**
¿cuántas veces? how many times? **7**
¿cuánto? how much? **2**
  ¿cuánto cuesta? how much does it cost? **2**; **¿cuánto cuestan?** how much do they cost? **2**; **¿cuánto vale?** how much does it cost? **11**
¡cuánto, -a!: ¡cuánta gente! what a lot of people! **7**
¿cuántos, -as? how many? **2**
  ¿cúantos años tiene? how old are you (is he/she)? **6**
cuarenta forty, **2**
cuarto quarter hour, **2**
cuarto, -a fourth, **5**
el **cuarto** room, **6**; (abbreviation ctos.), **6**
  ¡qué cuarto tan bonito! what a pretty room! **6**
cuatro four, **2**
cuatrocientos, -as four hundred, **11**
la **cuchara** spoon, **9**
la **cucharada** tablespoonful, **9**
la **cucharita** teaspoon, **9**
el **cuchillo** knife, **9**
la **cuenta** bill, check, **9 hacer cuentas** to do calculations, **11**
el **cuento** story, **7**
el **cuero** leather, **11**
cuesta: it costs, **2**; **¿cuánto cuesta?** how much does it cost? **2**

cuestan: ¿cuánto cuestan? how much do they cost? **2**
¡cuidado! be careful!, **10**
el **cumpleaños** birthday, **11**
cumplir: cumplir años to have a birthday, **11**

CH

chao so long, 'bye, **1**
la **chaqueta** jacket, **11**
la **charla** small talk, **1**
el **cheque: el cheque de viajero** traveler's check, **5**
la **chica** girl, **1**
el **chico** boy, **1**
el **chile: el chile con carne** dish of beans, ground beef and chilies, **9**
chocar to collide, **10**
el **chocolate** chocolate, **9**
los **churros** doughnut-like pastry, **9**

D

dar: dar una película to show a movie, **7**
dar una vuelta to go for a walk, **7**
de from, **1**; of, **2**; (made) of, **11**; **al lado de** beside, **5**; **de acuerdo** all right, **3**; **de acuerdo con** according to, **7**; **de Alice: la cartera de Alice** Alice's purse, **5**; **de compras** shopping, **11**; **¿de dónde?** from where?, **1**; **de él** his, **6**; **de ella** hers, **6**; **de ellas** theirs(f.), **6**; **de ellos** theirs (m.), **6**; **de la mañana** in the morning, A.M., **5**; **de la noche** at night, P.M., **5**; **de nada** you're welcome, **1**; **de nuevo** again, **6**; **de plástico** (made of) plastic, **11**; **de postre** for dessert, **9**; **de pronto** suddenly, **3**; **¿de qué es?** what's it made of? **11**; **de repente** suddenly, **10**; **de usted** yours (pol. sing.), **6**; **de ustedes** yours (pl.), **6**; **el (de)** the one (made of), **11**; **estar a punto de** to be on the verge of, **10**; **estar de compras** to be shopping, **11**; **más de . . .** more than . . . , **11**; **menos de . . .** less than . . . , **11**; **uno, -a (de)** one, **7**
debajo (de) under, **9**
debemos we ought to, **3**
deber should, ought to, **5**
¿debo . . .? should I . . .?, **5**
decidir to decide, **5**
decir to say, **7**
dejan: dejan de pensar en (they) stop thinking of, **3**
dejar to leave (behind), **9**; to allow, let, **11**
le dejo la cartera en . . . I'll let the purse go for . . ., **11**

del (de + el) of the, from the (contraction), **2**
delante (de) in front (of), **5**
delgado, -a thin, **6**
delicioso, -a delicious, **9**
demás: los demás the rest, **3**
demasiado, -a too (much), **11**
dentro (de) in, within, **5**
depender to depend, **11**
el **deporte: los deportes** sports, **2**
la **derecha: a la derecha** on the right, **5**
desaparecer disappear, **6**
el **desayuno** breakfast, **9**
desde from, **3**; **desde . . . hasta** from . . . to, **10**
desear to like, to want, **9**
desierto, -a deserted, **2**
desmaya: se desmaya faints, **6**
desp. abbreviation for después, **6**
despierto: me despierto I wake up, **2**
después then, **5**; **después de** after, **1**
el **destino** destiny, **10**
detenido, -a suspended, **7**; detained, **5**
detrás (de) behind, **5**
devolver (ue) to return, **11**
el **día** day, **1**
buenos días good morning, **1**; **el plato del día** specialty of the day, **9**; **los días de la semana** days of the week, **2**
el **diálogo** dialog, **1**
el **diario** diary, **10**
el **dibujo** drawing, **2**
el dibujo animado animated cartoon, **7**
el **diccionario** dictionary, **2**
dice: se dice así that's the way to say it, **1**
dice it says, **2**; **dice que . . .** he (she) says (that) . . ., **3**
diciembre December, **3**
el **dictado** dictation, **1**
dicho: a lo dicho, hecho no sooner said than done, **9**
diecinueve nineteen, **2**
dieciocho eighteen, **2**
dieciséis sixteen, **2**
diecisiete seventeen, **2**
diez ten, **2**
a las diez at ten o'clock, **2**
diferente different, **3**
difícil difficult, **2**
¡diga! hello? **5**
digo I mean, **6**
el **dinero** money, **2**
directamente straight, **7**
el **director, la directora** director, **1**
el **disco** record, **3**
la **discoteca** disco, **7**
distinguido, -a excellent, **2**
la **diversión** diversion, pastime, **7**
divertido, -a fun, **3**
doble: ahorrar el doble to save twice as much, **11**

doce twelve, **2**
el **doctor,** (m.) doctor; **la doctora** (f.) doctor, **1**
el **dólar** dollar, **2**
el **dolor: el dolor de cabeza** headache, **2**
el **domingo** Sunday, **2**
¿dónde? where?, **1**
¿de dónde? from where? **1**; **¿de dónde es ella?** where is she from?, **1**
dore: se dore to brown, **9**
dorm. abbreviation for dormitorio, **6**
dos two, **2**
los, las dos both, **1**; the two, **6**
doscientos, -as two hundred, **11**
dulce sweet, **9**; **hogar, dulce hogar** home, sweet home, **6**

E

echar: echarles to add to them, **9**
echó poured, **6**
la **educación: la educación artística** art class, **2**
la educación física physical education, **2**
EE.UU. (abbreviation for Estados Unidos) U.S., **1**
egoísta selfish, **6**
el **ejercicio: el traje de ejercicio** warm-up suit, **11**
el the, **1**; **el (de)** the one (made of), **11**
él he, **1**; him, **9**; **de él** his, **6**
eléctrico, -a electric, **3**
el **elefante** elephant, **10**
elegante elegant, **11**
ella she, **1**; her, it, **9**
de ella hers, **6**
ellas they, (f.) **1**; them, **9**; **de ellas** theirs, **6**
ellos they, (m.), **1**; them, **9**
de ellos theirs, **6**
el **embarque: la puerta de embarque** boarding gate, **5**
empezado: ha empezado it has begun, **7**
empezar (ie) to start, begin, **6**
el **empleado, la empleada** employee, **5**
la **emoción** emotion, **10**
en in, **1**; by, **2**; at, on, **5**
en auto by car, **2**; **en autobús** by bus, **2**; **en bicicleta** by bicycle, **2**; **en metro** by subway, **2**; **en persona** in person, **11**; **¿en qué puedo servirle?** how may I help you? (pol.), **11**; **en serio** seriously, **7**; **en todo momento** every time, **3**; **en venta** on sale, **2**; **en voz baja** in a low voice, **11**; **estás en tu casa** make yourself at home (fam. sing.), **6**; **le dejo la cartera en . . .** I'll let the purse go for . . ., **11**; **patinar en hielo** to ice skate, **3**

encantar to delight, 9; **me en-cantan** I love them, 9

encontrar (ue) to find, 11

la **encuesta** survey, 2

la **enchilada** Mexican dish—rolled tortilla filled with meat or cheese, 9

enero January, 3

enfadado, -a angry, 11

enfrente: enfrente de in front of, 10

enorme huge, 5

la **ensalada** salad, 9

la **entidad** entity, 2

entonces then, 5

la **entrada** entrance, 6; admission ticket, 7

entrar to enter, 5; **entro a** I go in(to), 2

entre between, 5

la **entrevista** interview, 1

el **entrevistador, la entrevistadora** interviewer, 2

entrevistar to interview, 7

entro a I go in(to), 2

la **envidia: ¡qué envidia!** what envy (I feel)!, what luck! 10

el **equipaje** baggage, 5

la **sección de equipaje** baggage claim, 5

el **equipo** team, 3

equivocado, -a: número equivocado wrong number, 5

el **error** error, 2

es: ¿cómo es? what's he (she, it) like? 6

¿de dónde es ella? where is she from? 1; **¿de qué es?** what's it made of? 11; **es la una** it's one o'clock, 2; **es un placer . . .** it's a pleasure . . ., 6; **es verdad** it's true, 3; **no es así** it's not so, 1; **¿qué hora es?** what time is it? 2

la **escala: hacer escala** to make a stop-over, 5

escapar to escape, 6

escoger: a escoger let's choose, 1

escolar: el autobús escolar school bus, 2

el **rendimiento escolar** scholastic progress, 2

escondido, -a hidden, 3

escríbenos write us, 6

escribir to write, 5

¡escucha! listen!, 2

escuchar to listen, 5

escuchaste you heard, 9

la **escuela** school, 1

la **escuela primaria** elementary school, 2; **la escuela secundaria** secondary school, 2

la **escultura** sculpture, 2

ese, -a that, 9

ése, -a that one, 11

esos, -as those, 9

ésos, -as those, 11

esencial essential, 1

espacial: el traje espacial space suit, 10

España Spain, 1

el **español** Spanish (language), 2

se habla español Spanish is spoken here, 1

español, española Spanish, 1

especial special, 9

la **especialidad** speciality, 9

la **especie** species, 10

el **espectáculo** show, 7

espera waits, 2

la **espera: la sala de espera** waiting room, 5

esperando waiting, 7

esperar to wait (for), 5

la **esposa** wife, 6

el **esposo** husband, 6

los **esposos** husband and wife, 6; husbands, 6

esquiar to ski, skiing, 3

los **bastones de esquiar** ski poles, 3; **las botas de esquiar** ski boots, 3

la **esquina** corner (street), 9

los **esquís** skis, 3

esta this, 9; **esta noche** tonight, 7

esta tarde this afternoon, 7

está: ¿cómo está? how are you? (*pol. sing.*), 1

está ocupado it's busy, 5; **ya está todo** everything's finished, 5

estar casado, -a to be married, 6

la **estación** season, 3; station, 10

el **estacionamiento** parking, 10

el **estadio** stadium, 3

los **Estados Unidos** (abbreviation EE.UU.) United States, 1

estamos we are, 3

el **estampado** print (in clothes), 11

están they are, 3

¿están ustedes? are you? (*pl.*), 1

el **estanque** pond, 10

estar to be, 5

¿cómo está? how are you? (*pol. sing.*), 1; **¿cómo estás?** how are you? (*fam. sing.*), 1; **está ocupado, -a** busy, 5; **estamos** we are, 3; **están** they are, 3; **¿cómo están ustedes?** how are you? (*pl.*), 1; **estar a punto de** to be on the verge of, 10; **estar acostumbrado, -a** to be used to, 11; **estar de compras** to be shopping, 11; **la sala de estar** family room, 6

estás: estás en tu casa make yourself at home (*fam. sing.*), 6

¿cómo estás? how are you? (*fam. sing.*), 1

el **este** east, 1; **al este** to the east, 1

este, -a this, 9

esta noche tonight, 7; **esta tarde** this afternoon, 7

éste, -a this one, 11

el **estéreo** stereo, 11

estos, -as these, 9

éstos, -as these, 11

estoy: estoy seguro I'm sure, 2

estrecho, -a narrow, 5

la **estrella** star, 2

el **estreno** premiere, 7

la **estructura** structure, 1

el, la **estudiante** student, 2

estudiar to study, 3

el **estudio** study, 2

estupendamente wonderfully, 11

estupendo, -a great, stupendous, 3

la **etiqueta** label, 2

Europa Europe, 1

la **evaluación** evaluation, 2

el **examen** exam, test, 7

exc. abbreviation for excelente, 6

excitante exciting, 7

la **exclamación** exclamation, 6

la **excursión** excursion, pleasure trip, 10

existir to exist, 7

exótico, -a exotic, 7

la **experiencia** experience, 10

experto, -a expert, 3

explicar to explain, 11

explorar to explore, 10

la **explosión** explosion, 10

exquisito, -a exquisite, 9

extracurricular extracurricular, 2

F

fácil easy, 2

la **falda** skirt, 11

faltar: falta algo something's missing, 1; to miss, 7

las **fallas** giant figures, 10

fam. abbreviation for *familia*, 6

la **fama** fame, 10

la **familia** family, 5

familiar familiar, 11

famoso, -a famous, 5

el **fanfarrón** braggart, 3

fantástico, -a fantastic, 7

fascinante fascinating, 7

el **favor: por favor** please, 1

favorito, -a favorite, 2, 3

febrero February, 3

feo, -a ugly, 6

la **feria** fair, 11

el **festival** festival, 11

festivo, -a festive, 10

la **fiesta** party, 7

fijo, -a fixed, 11

la **fila** line, 7

la **filosofía** philosophy, 2

el **fin: el fin de semana** weekend, 7

por fin finally, 2

final final, 2

finalmente finally, 11

fino: cortarlas fino to cut (them) in thin slices, 9

la **física** physics, 2

físico, -a: la educación física physical education, 2

flaco, -a skinny, 6

el **flan** baked custard, 9

la **flor** flower, **5**
el **folleto** brochure, **10**
la **formación: la formación social, moral y cívica** civics, **2**
la **foto** photo, **6**
la **fotografía** photography, **1** photograph, **6**; **tomar fotografías** to take photographs, **3**
fotográfico, -a photographic, **10**
el **fotógrafo, la fotógrafa** photographer, **1**
el **francés** French (language), **2**
Francia France, **1**
la **frase** sentence; phrase, **7**
freír to fry, **9**
frente a across from, **6**
la **fresa** strawberry, **9**
fresco, -a: hace fresco it's cool out, **3**
los **frijoles** beans, **9**
el **frío: hace (mucho) frío** it's (very) cold out, **3**
frito, -a fried, **9**
la **fruta** fruit, **9**
la **frutería** fruit store, **9**
fuerte heavy, **2**
la **función** function, **7**
funcionaba it functioned, **11**
funcionar to function, **11**
el **fútbol** soccer, **2**
 el Campeonato mundial de fútbol World Cup Soccer Championship, **3**
 futurista futuristic, **7**
el **futuro** future, **5**

G

galáctico, -a galactic, **10**
la **galaxia** galaxy, **10**
la **gana: tener ganas de** to feel like, **7**
el **ganador, la ganadora** winner, **2**
ganar to win, **3**
la **ganga** bargain, **11**
el **garaje** garage, **6**
la **gaseosa** soda, **9**
el **gato** cat, **7**
 genealógico, -a: el árbol genealógico family tree, **6**
generalmente generally, **11**
generoso, -a generous, **6**
el **genio** genius, **2**
la **gente** people, **7**
 ¡cuánta gente! what a lot of people! **7**
la **geografía** geography, **2**
la **geometría** geometry, **2**
gigante giant, **11**
la **gimnasia** gymnastics, **3**
el **gobernador, la gobernadora** governor, **1**
el **gol** goal, **3**
la **goma** eraser, **2**
gordo, -a fat, **6**
gracias thank you, **1**
 muchas gracias thank you

very much, **3**
gráfico, -a: el taller gráfico printing plant, **11**
el **gramo** gram (0.35 ounce), **9**
gran great, **5**
grande large, **6**
 más grande que bigger than, **11**
gritar to shout, **3**
el **grito: el último grito** the last word, **10**
el **grupo** group, **5**
el **guante** glove, mitt, **3**
guapo, -a handsome, **6**
 ¡qué guapo! how handsome! **6**
la **guía** guidebook, **9**; **el, la guía** guide, **10**
la **guitarra** guitar, **3**
gustar to like, to be pleasing to, **3**
le gusta you like (*pol. sing.*), he/she likes, **3**; **les gusta(n)** you (they) like, **9**; **me gusta** I like, **3**; **no me gusta nada** I don't like it at all, **11**; **nos gusta(n)** we like, **9**; **te gusta** you like (*fam. sing.*), **3**
el **gusto: mucho gusto** nice to meet you, **1**

H

habla: se habla español Spanish is spoken here, **1**
habla speaks, **2**
hablan (they) speak, **1**
hablar to speak, talk, **3**
 él habla (he's) speaking (on the phone), **5**
hable: ¡qué hable! speech!, **3**
hace: hace (muy) buen tiempo it's (very) nice out, **3**; **hace (mucho) calor** it's (very) hot out, **3**; **hace fresco** it's cool out, **3**; **hace (mucho) frío** it's (very) cold out, **3**; **hace (muy) mal tiempo** the weather is (very) bad, **3**; **hace (mucho) sol** it's (very) sunny, **3**; **hace una hora** an hour ago, **10**; **hace (mucho) viento** it's (very) windy, **3**
hacer to do, **5**
 to make **5**; **hacer cuentas** to do calculations, **11**; **hacer escala** to make a stopover, **5**; **hacer la maleta** to pack a suitcase, **10**; **¿qué puedo hacer?** what can I do? **2**; **se hace trizas** it smashes into pieces, **11**
hacia towards, **10**
el **hambre** (*f.*): **tener (mucha) hambre** to be (very) hungry, **5**
la **hamburguesa** hamburger, **1**
hasta as far as, **10**
 desde . . . hasta from . . . to, **10**; **hasta luego** see you later, **1**; **hasta mañana** see you tomorrow, **1**
hay there is, there are, **2**

no hay más remedio it can't be helped, **9**; **no hay ningún** there isn't any, **10**; **¿qué hay?** what's up? **1**
haz make (*com.*), **2**
hecho: a lo dicho, hecho no sooner said than done, **9**; **hecho, -a a mano** handmade, **11**
el **helado** ice cream, **7**
la **hermana** sister, **6**
el **hermano** brother, **6**
 el hermano menor younger brother, **1**; **los hermanos** brother(s) and sister(s), **6**; brothers, **6**
el **hielo** ice, **3**
 patinar en hielo to ice skate, **3**
el **hierro** iron, **11**
la **hija** daughter, **6**
el **hijo** son, **6**
los **hijos** children, **6**; sons, **6**
hipnotizado, -a hypnotized, **3**
la **historia** history, **2**; story, **7**
histórico, -a historic, historical, **5**
el **hogar: hogar, dulce hogar** home, sweet home, **6**
la **hoguera** bonfire, **10**
hola hello, **1**; hello? **5**
el **hombre** man, **6**
hondo, -a deep, **9**
el **honor** honor, **3**
la **hora** time, hour, **2**
 a primera hora as early as possible, **11**; **¿a qué hora?** at what time? **2**; **hace una hora** an hour ago, **10**; **¿qué hora es?** what time is it? **2**
el **horario** schedule, **2**
horrible horrible, **3**
hoy today, **2**
la **huerta** orchard, **5**
el **huevo** egg, **9**

I

la **idea** idea, **1**
ideal ideal, **3**
la **identificación** identification, **9**
igual (que) the same (as), **11**
igualmente likewise, **6**
la **imaginación** imagination, **1**
imaginario, -a imaginary, **3**
la **imitación** imitation, **11**
impecable impeccable, **6**
importante important, **6**
importar to matter, **11**
 ¡no importa! it doesn't matter! **11**
imposible impossible, **3**
la **inasistencia** absence, **2**
la **independencia** independence, **2**
indica (it) indicates, **2**
indicar to suggest, **5**
industrial industrial, **5**
la **información** information (booth), **5**
el **informe** report, **7**

el **ingeniero, la ingeniera** engineer, 1

el **inglés** English (language), 2

el **ingrediente** ingredient, 9

inmediatamente immediately, 10

inocente innocent, 7

inolvidable unforgettable, 10

la **instrucción** instruction, 7

inteligente intelligent, 6

intercambiar to exchange, 6

intercambian miradas (they) exchange glances, 6

el **intercambio** interchange, 11

interesante interesting, 2

interesar to interest, 11

no me interesa I don't care, 11

interior interior, 5

internacional international, 5

interplanetario, -a interplanetary, 10

el **invasor, la invasora** invader, 7

el **inventario** inventory, 2

el **invierno** winter, 3

la **invitación** invitation, 10

el **invitado, la invitada** guest, 6

invitar to invite, 6

ir to go, 5

¿si vamos . . .? what if we go . . .? 7; **¡vamos!** let's go! 6; **van** they go, 5

irme: tengo que irme I must go, 11

la **isla** island, 1

la **izquierda: a la izquierda** on the left, 5

J

la **jalea** jelly, 9

el **jamón** ham, 9

el **jardín** garden, 6

los **jeans** jeans, 11

el, la **joven** young man, woman 9

los **jóvenes** young people, 11

el **judo** judo, 3

el **juego** game, 3

los **Juegos Olímpicos** Olympic Games, 3

el **jueves** Thursday, 2

jugar (ue) to play, 3

el **jugo** juice, 9

julio July, 3

junio June, 3

Júpiter Jupiter, 10

la **juventud** youth, 7

K

el **kilo** kilogram (2.2 pounds), 9

el **kilómetro** kilometer (.62 miles), 5

L

la the, 1; you (*pol. sing.*), her, it (*obj. pron.*), 10

lácteo, -a: la Vía Láctea Milky Way, 10

el **lado** side, 9; **al lado de** beside, 5

la **lana** wool, 11

el **lápiz** (*pl.* **lápices**) pencil, 2

el **lapso** term, 2

largo, -a wide, 11

las the (*fem. pl.*), 2; you (*pl.*), them (*obj. pron.*), 10

la **lástima: ¡qué lástima!** what a shame! 7

lavar: lavarlas to wash (them), 9

le you (*pol. sing.*), him, her, (*indir. obj.*) 9

le gusta you like (*pol. sing.*), he/she likes, 3

la **lectura** reading, 1

la **leche** milk, 9

la **lechuga** lettuce, 9

leer to read, 1

las **legumbres** vegetables, 10

lejos (de) far (from), 5

les you (*pl.*), them (*obj. pron.*), 9

les gusta (n) you (they) like, 9

levanta: se levanta gets up (*sing.*), 6

libre free, 6

los ratos libres, 2; **el tiempo libre** free time, 6

el **libro** book, 2

ligero, -a light (meal), 9

el **limón** lemon, 9

lindo, -a pretty, 6

el **lío** complication, 7

la **lista** list, 11

listo, -a ready, 10

la **literatura** literature, 2

el **litro** liter (1.05 quarts), 9

lo you (*pol. sing.*), him, it (*dir. obj.*), 10

¿lo abrimos? do we open it?, 2; **lo mejor** the best (thing), 9; **lo mismo** the same thing, 7; **lo mismo (que)** the same (as), 11; **lo que** what, that, 7; **lo que pasa** what's happening, 10; **¿lo sabes?** do you know it? (*fam. sing.*) 1; **lo siento** I'm sorry, 7; **por lo menos** at least, 7

loco, -a crazy, 7

el **locutor, la locutora** announcer, 2; newscaster, 3

los the (*m. pl.*), 2; you (*pl.*), them, 10

luego: hasta luego see you later, 1

el **lugar** place, 5

lunar lunar, 10

el **lunes** Monday, 2

la **luz** (*pl.* **luces**) light, 10

LL

llamar to call, 5

¿cómo se llama él (ella)? what's his (her) name? 1; **¿cómo te llamas tú?** what's your name? (*fam. sing.*), 1

llano, -a flat, 9

la **llegada** arrival, 5

llegando: siguen llegando (they)

keep coming, 11

llegar to arrive, 5

llego I arrive, 2

llevar to take, 9

llorar to cry, 9

llueve it's raining, 3

M

la **madrastra** stepmother, 6

la **madre** mother, 6

magnífico, -a magnificent, 3

el **mago, la maga** wizard, 7

mal bad, 1

hace (muy) mal tiempo the weather is (very) bad, 3; **muy mal** awful, terrible, 1

la **maleta** suitcase, 5

hacer la maleta to pack a suitcase, 10

la **mamá** mom, 1

mandar to send, 11

la **manga** sleeve, 11

la **mano** hand, 11

la **mantequilla** butter, 9

las **manualidades** industrial arts, 2

la **manzana** apple, 9

mañana tomorrow, 3

hasta mañana see you tomorrow, 1

la **mañana** morning, 3

de la mañana in the morning, A.M., 5; **por la mañana** in the morning, 3

el **mapa** map, 5

el **mar** sea, 1

el Mar Mediterráneo Mediterranean Sea, 2

la **marca** brand, 11

el **marcador** felt-tip marker, 2

marcar to mark, 10

los **mariachis** Mexican band of strolling musicians, 9

los **mariscos** seafood, 10

Marte Mars, 7

el **martes** Tuesday, 2

marzo March, 3

marrón brown, 3

más more, else, 2

most, 6; **más de . . .** more than . . ., 11; **más grande que** bigger than, 11; **más o menos** so-so, 1; **más . . . que** more . . . than, 11; **más tarde** later, 7; **no hay más remedio** it can't be helped, 9; **¿qué más necesitas?** what else do you need? (*fam. sing.*), 2

las **matemáticas** mathematics, 2

la **materia** subject, 2

mayo May, 3

la **mayonesa** mayonnaise, 9

mayor older, 6

me me, 9, 10

me gusta I like, 3; **me llamo . . .** my name is . . ., 1; **no me gusta nada** I don't like it at all, 11

la **medalla de oro** gold medal, 3
la **medianoche** midnight, 10
las **medias** socks, 11
el **mediodía** noon, 9
mediterráneo, -a Mediterranean, 2
    el Mar Mediterráneo Mediterranean Sea, 2
mejor better, 7
    best, 7; **mejor . . .** it would be better to . . ., 7; **lo mejor** the best (thing), 9
el **melocotón** peach, 9
la **melodía** melody, 2
el **melón** melon, 9
menor younger, 1
    el hermano menor younger brother, 1
menos less, 1
    más o menos so-so, 1; **menos de . . .** less than . . ., 11; **por lo menos** at least, 7
el **mensaje** message, 9
el **menú** menu, 9
menudo: a menudo often, 3
el **mercado** market, 11
la **merienda** snack, light meal in the afternoon, 9
la **mermelada** marmalade, 9
el **mes** month, 3
la **mesa** table, 9
    a la mesa to the table, 9
    poner la mesa to set the table, 9
la **meta** finish line, 3
métrico, -a metric, 11
el **metro** subway, 2; **en metro** by subway, 2
mexicano, -a Mexican (*adj.*), 9
mexicano americanos Mexican Americans, 1
la **mezcla** mixture, 7
mi my, 2
mí me, 9
el **miércoles** Wednesday, 2
mil a thousand, 11
el **minuto** minute, 7
¡mira! look! (*com.*), 2
la **mirada** glance, look, 6
    intercambian miradas (they) exchange glances, 6
mirar to look at, watch, 3
    ¡mira! look! 2
    ¿me miras? are you looking at me? (*fam. sing.*), 3; **miran: se miran** (they) look at each other, 7
la **misión** mission, 7
mismo, -a same, 9
    lo mismo the same thing, 7; **lo mismo (que)** the same (as), 11
el **misterio** mystery, 3
moderado, -a moderate, 11
moderno, -a modern, 11
modesto, -a modest, 6
el **mole** spicy chocolate sauce, 9
el **momento** moment, 2
    en todo momento every time, 3;

un momento just a moment, 6
el **monstruo** monster, 10
montar to ride, 3
    montar en bicicleta to ride a bicycle, 3
el **Monte de Piedad** pawnshop in Mexico City, 11
moral: la formación social, moral y cívica civics, 2
moreno, -a dark (hair, complexion), 6
la **mostaza** mustard, 9
la **moto** motorcycle, 10
mover (ue) to move, 9; **moverlas** to move (*pl. f.*), 9
mucho a lot (*adv.*), 3
mucho, -a a lot (of), 2
    mucho gusto nice to meet you, 1; **mucho tiempo** a long time, 10
muchos, -as many, a lot (of), 2
    muchas gracias thank you very much, 3
la **mujer** woman, 10
mundial: el Campeonato mundial de fútbol World Cup Soccer Championship, 3
el **mundo** world, 3; **todo el mundo** everybody, 1
murió: se murió he's dead, 6
el **museo** museum, 10
la **música** music, 2
musical musical, 7
el **músico, la música** musician, 7
muy very, 1; **muy mal** awful, terrible, 1

N

nada nothing, 1
    de nada you're welcome, 1; **no me gusta nada** I don't like it at all, 11
nadar to swim, 3
nadie no one, nobody, 7
    nadie más nobody else, 2
la **naranja** orange, 9
la **natación** swimming, 3
natural: las ciencias naturales natural science, 2
la **nave** (space)ship, 10
necesitar to need, 9
    necesitas you need (*fam. sing.*), 2; **¿qué más necesitas?** what else do you need? (*fam. sing.*), 2
negro, -a black, 3
nervioso, -a nervous, 2
ni . . . ni neither . . . nor, 9
nieva it's snowing, 3
el **nilón** nylon, 11
ningún: no hay ningún there isn't any, 10
ninguna: en ninguna parte nowhere, 11
el **nitrógeno** nitrogen, 2
no no, 1; not, 2; **¿no?** right? 6
    no contestan there's no answer, 5; **no es así** it's not so, 1; **no hay más remedio** it can't be helped, 9; **¡no importa!** it doesn't matter! 11; **no me gusta nada** I don't like it at all, 11; **¿por qué no . . .?** why don't we . . .? 5; **yo no** not me, 5
la **noche** night, 3
    a la noche at night, 7; **buenas noches** good evening, good night, 1; **de la noche** at night, P.M., 5; **esta noche** tonight, 7; **por la noche** at night, 3
el **nombre** name, 3
el **norte** north, 5; **al norte** to the north, 1
norteamericano, -a North American, 6
nos us, 9; **nos gusta(n)** we like, 9
nosotras we (*f.*) 1; us (*f.*), 9
nosotros we (*m.* or *m. and f.*), 11; us (*m.* or *m. and f.*), 9; **de nosotros** about us, 6
notable very good, 2
las **noticias** news, 2
el **noticiero** newsreel, 7
novecientos, -as nine hundred, 11
noventa ninety, 2
la **novia** girlfriend, 3
noviembre November, 3
el **núcleo** nucleus, 2
nuestro, -a, -os, -as our, 6
nueve nine, 2
nuevo, -a new, 1
    de nuevo again, 6
el **número** number, 2
    size, 11; **número equivocado** wrong number, 5
nunca never, 3

O

o or, 2
el **objeto** object, 11
el **Océano Pacífico** Pacific Ocean, 2
octubre October, 3
ocupado, -a: está ocupado it's busy, 5
ocurrir: lo que acaba de ocurrir what just happened, 11
ochenta eighty, 2
ocho eight, 2
ochocientos, -as eight hundred, 11
odiar to hate, 3; **odio** I hate, 3
el **oeste** west, 5
    al oeste to the west, 1; **la película del oeste** Western (movie), 7
la **oferta** offer, 11
oficial official, 7
la **oficina** office, 10
ofrecer to offer, 11
olímpico, -a: los Juegos Olímpicos Olympic Games, 3
olvidar to forget, 10

no olvides don't forget, 10
once eleven, 2
la **opinión** opinion, 2
ordenar to put in order, 7
organizado, -a organized, 10
original original, 10
la **orilla** shore, 5
el **oro** gold, 3
   la **medalla de oro** gold medal, 3
os you (*fam. pl.*), 11
oscuro, -a dark, 11
el **otoño** fall, autumn, 3
otro, -a other, another, 2
   otra vez again, 5
el **oxígeno** oxygen, 2
¡oye! hey! 1; **se oye** one hears, 11

P

la **paciencia** patience, 9
el **padrastro** stepfather, 6
   los **padrastros** stepparents, 6; stepfathers, 6
el **padre** father, 6
   los **padres** parents, 6; fathers, 6
la **paella valenciana** hearty saffron-flavored dish of rice, meat, seafood and vegetables, 9
pagar to pay, 9
el **país** country, 1
la **palabra** word, 1
el **palacio** palace, 11
el **pan** bread, 9
Panamá Panama, 1
los **pantalones** pants, 11
el **pañuelo** handkerchief, 11
la **papa** potato **las papas fritas** french fries, 9
el **papá** dad, 6
el **paquete** package, parcel, 11
para to, in order to, for, 3
   ¿para qué? for what? what for? 5
la **parada** stop, 7
paralizado, -a paralyzed, 10
parar to stop, 10
parecer to seem; **¿qué te parece . . .?** what do you think of . . .? (*fam. sing.*), 6
el **parque** park, 7
la **parte** part, 1
   en ninguna parte nowhere, 11; **por todas partes** everywhere, 11
participar to participate, to take part, 3
   participar de to share in, 10
la **partícula** particle, 2
el **partido** game, match, 3
pasa: ¿qué pasa? what's happening, 1
   todo lo que pasa everything that's happening, 10
pasado, -a last, past, 10

la semana pasada last week, 10
el **pasado** past, 5
el **pasajero, la pasajera** passenger, 5
el **pasaporte** passport, 5
   el control de pasaportes passport control, 5
pasar to spend (time), 6
   to come in, 6; to happen, 9; to pass by, 9; **pasa** come in, 6; **pasar por** to pass through, 3
el **pasatiempo** pastime, 3
pasear to go for a walk, 7
el **paseo** stroll, walk, 1; sightseeing trip, 10
el **pasillo** hall, 6
el **paso** step, 3
el **pastel** pie, 9
la **pastelería** pastry, pastry shop, 9
la **patata** potato (Spain), 9
patear to kick, 3
patinar to skate, 3
   patinar en hielo to ice skate, 3
el **patio** inner courtyard, patio, 1
el **pedido** order, 11
   pedir (i) to ask (for something), order, 9
pegue: para que no se pegue so it doesn't stick, 9
pelar to peel, 9
la **película** film, movie, 7
   dar una película to show a movie, 7; **la película de terror** horror movie, 7; **la película del oeste** Western, 7; **la película policial** detective movie, 7
peligroso, -a dangerous, 3
pelirrojo, -a redheaded, 6
la **pelota** ball (baseball, tennis ball), 3
la **pena: ¡qué pena!** what a pity! 1
pensar (ie) to think, plan, 7
   dejan de pensar en they stop thinking of, 3
pequeño, -a small, little, 6
la **pera** pear, 9
la **perdición** doom, 7
   perdón excuse me, 2
perfecto, -a perfect, 9
el **periódico** newspaper, 5
el, la **periodista** journalist, 3
el **permiso** permission, 10
   con permiso excuse me, 6; **permiso** excuse me, 7
pero but, 2
persistir to continue, 11
la **persona** person, 11
   en persona in person, 11
Perú Peru, 1
el **pescado** fish, 9
la **peseta** monetary unit of Spain, 5
el **peso** monetary unit of Mexico, Colombia and Chile, 9
el **picnic** picnic, 9
el **pie** foot, 2
   a pie on foot, 2
la **piedad: el Monte de Piedad** pawnshop in Mexico City, 11

el, la **pijama** pajamas, 11
la **pila** battery, 2
la **píldora: la píldora alimenticia** food capsule, 10
el **piloto** pilot, 5
la **pimienta** pepper, 9
pintoresco, -a picturesque, 5
la **pintura** painting, 2
la **piña** pineapple, 9
la **piscina** pool, 7
el **piso** floor, story, 11
la **pizza** pizza, 9
el **placer** pleasure, 11
   es un placer . . . it's a pleasure . . ., 6
el **plan** plan, 10
   planear to plan, 10
el **planeta** planet, 10
el **plano** floor plan, 6
el **plástico** plastic, 11
   de plástico made of plastic, 11
la **plata** silver, 7
   las bodas de plata silver wedding anniversary, 7
el **plátano** banana, plantain, 9
el **platillo** saucer, small plate, 9
   el plato hondo soup dish, bowl, 9
el **plato** dish, plate, 9
   el plato del día specialty of the day, 9
la **playa** beach, 3
la **pluma** fountain pen, 2
pobre poor, 2
poco, -a little, 2
   poco tiempo a short time, 10
podemos: podemos ver we can see, 5
poder (ue) to be able, can, 7
   ¿en qué puedo servirle? how may I help you? (*pol.*), 11; **puedes** you can (*fam. sing.*), 6; **¿qué puedo hacer?** what can I do? 2
la **policía** police, 5
   policial: la película policial detective movie, 7
el **pollo** chicken, 9
poner to put, 9
   poner la mesa to set the table, 9
   por for, 2; along, 3; through, 5
   por correo by mail, 11; **por favor** please, 1; **por fin** finally, at last, 2; **por la mañana** in the morning, 3; **por la noche** at night, 3; **por la tarde** in the afternoon, 3; **por lo menos** at least, 7; **¿por qué?** why? 2; **¿por qué no . . .?** why don't we . . .? 5; **por semana** per week, 7; **¡por supuesto!** of course! 6; **por teléfono** on the telephone, 3
porque because, 2
portátil portable, 2
la **posición** position, 2
la **postal** postcard, 5

el **postre** dessert, 9
   de postre for dessert, 9
   practicar to practice, play, 3
el **precio** price, 2
   preciso, -a precise, 11
la **preciosura** thing of beauty, 11
   preferido, -a favorite, 2
la **pregunta** question, 3
   preguntar to ask, 10
el **premio** prize, 3
   prende turns on, 3
   prender to turn on (an appliance), 3
   preocupado, -a worried, 7
   preparar to prepare, 9
la **presentación** introduction, 1
el **presidente, la presidenta** president, 2
   previo, -a previous, last, 2
   primario, -a: la escuela primaria elementary school, 2
la **primavera** spring, 3
   primer, -o, -a first, 1
   a primera hora as early as possible, 11
   primero first, 5
el **primo, la prima** cousin, 3
   principal main, 9
el, la **principiante** beginner, 3
   probar to try, 9
el **producto** product, 11
el **profesor, la profesora** teacher, 1
el **programa** program, show, 7
   prohibido, -a forbidden, 6
   prometer to promise, 11
   pronto soon, 10
   de pronto suddenly, 3
el **pronto** down payment, 6
la **pronunciación** pronunciation, 1
la **propiedad: propiedades** real estate, 6
la **propina** tip, 9
el **provecho: ¡buen provecho!** hearty appetite! 9
   próximo, -a next, 7
el **proyecto** project, plan, 1
   puedes you can (*fam. sing.*), 6
   puedo: ¿en qué puedo servirle? how may I help you? (*pol.*), 11
   ¿qué puedo hacer? what can I do? 2
la **puerta** door, 6; gate, 5
   la Puerta del Sol famous plaza in Madrid, 9; **tocan a la puerta** (they) are knocking at the door, 1
el **puerto** port, 5
el **puesto** market booth, 11
el **punto** point, 10
   estar a punto de to be on the verge of, 10
   púrpura purple, 7

Q

   que that, 5
   dice que . . . he (she) says (that) . . ., 3; **igual (que)** the same (as), 11; **lo que** what,

that, 7; **lo mismo (que)** the same (as), 11; **más (grande) que** (bigger) than, 11; **más . . . que** more . . . than, 11; **tener que** to have to, 7
¿qué? what, 2
   ¿qué hay? what's up?, 1; **¿qué hora es?** what time is it?, 2; **¿qué más necesitas?** what else do you need? (*fam. sing.*), 2; **¿qué pasa?** what's happening?, 1; **¿qué tal?** how are things?, 1; **¿qué te parece . . .?** what do you think of . . .? (*fam. sing.*), 6; **¿qué tiempo hace?** what's the weather?, 3; **¿a qué hora?** at what time?, 2; **¿de qué es?** what's it made of?, 11; **¿en qué puedo servirle?** how may I help you? (*pol.*), 11; **¿para qué?** for what?, 5; **¿por qué?** why?, 2; **¿por qué no . . .?** why don't we . . .?, 5
¡qué . . . !: ¡qué confusión! what a mixup! 5
   ¡qué cuarto tan bonito! what a pretty room! 6; **¡qué envidia!** what envy (I feel)!, what luck! 10; **¡qué guapo!** how handsome! 6; **¡qué lástima!** what a shame! 7; **¡qué pena!** what a pity! 1; **¡qué suerte!** what luck! 5
¡que hable! speech! 3
quedar: quedar bien to look nice on (clothing), 11
la **queja** complaint, 11
   la sección de quejas y reclamos customer service department, 11
   quemar to burn, 10
   se queman they are burned, 10
   querer (ie) to want, 6
   quiere he wants, 5
   querido, -a dear, 10
el **queso** cheese, 9
   ¿quién? who? 1
   quiere he wants, 5
   quieto, -a quiet, 11
   quinto, -a fifth, 11
la **química** chemistry, 2
   quince fifteen, 2
   quinientos, -as five hundred, 11
   quitar to throw out, 9

R

el **radio** radio, 3
   rápido quickly, 2
la **raqueta** racquet, 3
el **Rastro** flea market in Madrid, 10
el **rato** short time, 2
   los ratos libres free time, 2
la **razón: tener razón** to be right, 5
la **reacción** reaction, 1
la **rebaja** discount, 2
   rebajado, -a reduced (in price), 11

   rebajar to lower the price, 11
   recibir to receive, 11
el **recibo** receipt, 11
   recitar to recite, 6
la **reclamación** claim, 11
el **reclamo** claim, 11
   la sección de quejas y reclamos customer service department, 11
   reconocer (zc) to recognize, 10
el **recreo** recess, 2
el **rectángulo** rectangle, 2
   recuerdos regards, 1
la **red** net, 3
la **referencia** reference, 6
el **refresco** soda, 6
el **refugio** refuge, 9
el **regalo** present, gift, 1
   regateando bargaining, 11
   regatear to bargain, 11
el **regateo** bargaining, 11
   regional regional, 3
la **regla** ruler, 2
   regresar to return, 10
   regular so-so, 1
el **rehén** (*pl.* **rehenes**) hostage, 5
la **religión** religion, 2
   remar to row, 10
el **remedio: no hay más remedio** it can't be helped, 9
el **remitente** sender, 2
el **rendimiento: el rendimiento escolar** scholastic progress, 2
   reparar to repair, 11
el **repaso** review, 4
   repente: de repente suddenly, 10
la **repetición** repetition, 2
el **reportero, la reportera** reporter, 3
la **reproducción** reproduction, 10
la **república** republic, 2
   reservar to reserve, 10
   resistir to resist, 7
la **respuesta** answer, 1
el **restaurante** restaurant, 9
la **revista** magazine, 2
   revuelto, -a scrambled, 9
el **rey** king, 10
   rico, -a tasty, delicious (food), 9
el **rincón** corner, 7
el **río** river, 5
el **robot** robot, 10
el **rock** rock (music), 7
   romano, -a Roman, 5
la **ropa** clothes, 11
   rosa pink, 9
la **rosa** rose, 1
   rubio, -a fair, blonde, 6
la **rueda** wheel, 10
el **ruido** noise, 7
la **ruta** route, 10
la **rutina** routine, 10

S

el **sábado** Saturday, 2
   saber to know (a fact), 5; (+ inf) to know how (+ inf), 7

Spanish-English Vocabulary   **379**

¿lo sabes? do you know it? (*fam. sing.*), **1**; **¿sabes que . . .?** do you know that . . .? (*fam. sing.*), **1**; **¡ya sé!** I know it! **6**; **yo no sé** I don't know, **2**

sabes: ¿lo sabes? do you know it? (*fam. sing.*) **1**

el **saco** jacket, **11**

la **sal** salt, **9**

la **sala** living room, **6**
    la sala de espera waiting area, **5**; **la sala de estar** family room, **6**

sale (he or she) goes out, leaves, **3**

salen (they) leave, **3**

salir to go out, leave, **7**

la **salsa** sauce, **9**

saludar to greet, **10**

saludos greetings, **1**

salvar to save, **10**
    le salvaron la vida they saved his life, **10**

la **sandía** watermelon, **9**

el **sandwich** sandwich, **9**

la **sartén** frying pan, **9**

se: se dice así this is how you say it, **1**;
    ¿cómo se llama él (ella)? what's his (her) name? **1**; **¡la comunicación se cortó!** we were cut off! **5**; **se habla español** Spanish is spoken here, **1**; **se llama . . .** his (her) name is . . ., **1**

sé: ¡ya sé! I know it! **6**

yo no sé I don't know, **2**

la **sección** department, **11**
    la sección de equipaje baggage claim, **5**; **la sección de quejas y reclamos** customer service department, **11**

secreto, -a secret, **7**

el **secuestro** hijacking, **5**

secundario, -a: la escuela secundaria secondary school, **2**

la **sed: tener (mucha) sed** to be (very) thirsty, **9**

la **seda** silk, **11**

seguimos: ¿la seguimos? do we follow her?, **10**

siguen (they) follow, **5**
    siguen llegando (they) keep coming, **11**

segundo, -a second, **8**

seguro, -a sure, **1**

seis six, **2**

seiscientos, -as six hundred, **11**

la **selección** selection, **11**

el **sello** stamp, **5**

la **semana** week, **2**
    con una semana de anticipación a week ahead of time, **10**; **el fin de semana** weekend, **7**; **por semana** per week, **7**; **la semana pasada** last week, **10**

sencillamente simply, **7**

sensacional sensational, **7**

sentado, -a (en) seated (at), **6**

sentir (ie) to feel, **6**
    comienza a sentir starts to feel, (*sing.*) **6**; **lo siento** I'm sorry, **7**

el **señor** (abbreviation Sr.) Mr., sir, **1**; man, **6**

la **señora** (abbreviation Sra.) Mrs., ma'am, **1**; woman, **6**

la **señorita** (abbreviation Srta.) Miss, **1**

septiembre September, **3**

ser to be, **1**
    ¿cómo es? what's he (she, it) like? **6**; **¿de dónde es ella?** where is she from? **1**; **¿de qué es?** what's it made of? **11**; **es la una** it's one o'clock, **2**; **es un placer . . .** it's a pleasure . . ., **6**; **es verdad** it's true, **3**; **¿qué hora es?** what time is it? **2**; **son las diez** it's ten o'clock, **2**

serio: en serio seriously, **7**

la **servilleta** napkin, **9**

servir (i) to serve, **11**
    ¿en qué puedo servirle? how may I help you? (*pol.*), **11**

sesenta sixty, **2**

setecientos, -as seven hundred, **11**

si if, **7**; **¿si vamos . . .?** what if we go . . .? **7**

sí yes, **1**; really, **3**

siempre always, **3**

siento: lo siento I'm sorry, **7**

siete seven, **2**

siguen (they) follow, **5**
    siguen llegando (they) keep coming, **11**

siguiente following, **7**

simpático, -a nice, **6**

sin without; **sin parar** without stopping, **10**

singular singular, **7**

la **situación** situation, **1**

sobre about, **9**

sobresaliente excellent, **2**

la **sobrina** niece, **6**

el **sobrino** nephew
    los sobrinos nephew(s) and niece(s), **6**; nephews, **6**

social: las ciencias sociales social science, **2**
    la formación social, moral y cívica civics, **2**

¡socorro! help!, **2**

el **sol: hace (mucho) sol** it's (very) sunny, **3**; sun, **4**
    la Puerta del Sol famous plaza in Madrid, **9**

sólo only, **1**

la **solución** solution, **2**

el **sombrero** hat, **11**

son: son las diez it's ten o'clock, **2**

el **sonido** sound, **7**

la **sopa** soup, **9**

la **sorpresa** surprise, **1**

el **sótano** basement, **6**

Sr. (abbreviation of *señor*) Mr., **1**

Sra. (abbreviation of *señora*) Mrs., Ma'am, **1**

Srta. (abbreviation of *señorita*) Miss, **1**

su(s) your (*pol. sing.*), his, her, its, **5**; their, **6**

subir to go up, **5**; **subir a** to get on, **5**; to get into, **10**

el **suburbio** suburb, **1**

suculento, -a succulent, **10**

Suramérica South America, **1**

el **sueño** dream, **7**

la **suerte: ¡qué suerte!** what luck! **5**

el **suéter** sweater, **11**

super super, **11**

supuesto, -a: ¡por supuesto! of course! **6**

el **sur** south, **1**; **al sur** to the south, **1**

el **suroeste** southwest, **1**
    al suroeste to the southwest, **1**

surtidos, -as assorted, **11**

suspenso suspended, below average, **2**

sustituir to substitute, **5**

T

el **taco** Mexican dish—folded tortilla filled with ground beef, tomatoes, lettuce, etc., **9**

tal: ¿qué tal? how are things? **1**; **tal vez** perhaps, **9**

el **talento** talent, **2**

la **talla** size, **11**

el **taller: el taller gráfico** printing plant, **11**

el **tamaño** size, **11**
    también also, too, **3**
    tan so, **6**; **¡qué cuarto tan bonito!** what a pretty room! **6**

tanto, -a so (as, that) much, **2**

las **tapas** appetizer, **9**

tarde late, **2**
    más tarde later, **7**

la **tarde** afternoon, **3**
    buenas tardes good afternoon, **1**; **esta tarde** this afternoon, **7**; **por la tarde** in the afternoon, **3**

la **tarea** homework, **2**

la **tarjeta** card, **1**
    la tarjeta de crédito credit card, **11**

la **tarta** tart, pastry, **9**

el **taxi** taxi, **5**

la **taza** cup, **9**
    te you (*fam. sing.*), **9**
    ¿cómo te llamas tú? what's your name? (*fam. sing.*), **1**; **te gusta** you like (*fam. sing.*), **3**

el **té** tea, **9**

el **teatro** theater, **7**

telefónico, -a telephone, **5**

el **teléfono** telephone, **3**
    por teléfono on the telephone, **3**

la **televisión** television, 2
el **televisor** television set, 2
el **templo** temple, 7
temprano early, 2
el **tenedor** fork, 9
tener to have, 2
¿**cuántos años tiene?** how old are you (is he/she)? 6; **tener . . . años** to be . . . years old, 6; **tener ganas de** to feel like, 7; **tener (mucha) hambre** to be (very) hungry, 5; **tener que** to have to, 7; **tener razón** to be right, 5; **tener (mucha) sed** to be (very) thirsty, 9; **tiene** it has, 2
tengo: tengo que irme I must go, 11
el **tenis** tennis, 3
la cancha de tenis tennis court, 3; **los zapatos de tenis** tennis shoes, 3
la **tentación** temptation, 7
tercer, -o, -a third, 12
termina it's over, 2
terminan they finish, 3
terminar to finish, 3
el **terror: la película de terror** horror movie, 7
el **testimonio** testimony, 5
texano, -a Texan, 9
ti you (*fam. sing.*), 9
la **tía** aunt, 6
el **tiempo** weather, 3
time, 6; **hace (muy) buen tiempo** it's (very) nice out, 3; **hace (muy) mal tiempo** the weather is (very) bad, 3; **mucho tiempo** a long time, 10; **poco tiempo** a short time, 10; **¿qué tiempo hace?** what's the weather? 3; **el tiempo libre** free time, 6; **todo el tiempo** all the time, 7
la **tienda** store, 2
tiene it has, 2
¿**cuántos años tiene?** how old is (he/she)? 6
el **tigre** tiger, 1
el **tío** uncle, 6
los tíos uncle(s) and aunt(s), 6; uncles, 6
típico, -a typical, 9
las **tiras cómicas** comic strips, 2
la **toalla** towel, 11
tocan: tocan a la puerta (they are) knocking at the door, 1
tocar to play (a musical instrument), 3
todavía still, 10
todo, -a all, 7; every, 3
whole, 6; **en todo momento** every time, 3; **todo el mundo** everybody, 1; **todo el tiempo** all the time, 7
todo everything, 3
ya está todo everything's finished, 5; **todo lo que pasa**

everything that's happening, 10
todos, -as all, every, 3; whole, 6
todos los días every day, 3
tomar to take, 3;
to have (to eat or drink), 7; **tomar fotografías** to take photographs, 7
tomo: lo tomo I take it, 2
el **tomate** tomato, 9
tonto, -a dumb, 6; fool, 1
la **tortilla** Mexican flat corn cake, 9; Spanish omelette, 9
el **total** total, 3
trabajar to work, 3
trabaje: que trabaje who works (*sub.*), 11
tradicional traditional, 11
trae brings, 9
el **tráfico** traffic, 9
la **tragedia** tragedy, 1
el **traje** suit, 11
el **traje de baño** bathing suit, 11; el **traje de ejercicio** warm-up suit, 11; el **traje espacial** space suit, 10
el **transbordador** carrier, 10
trasmitir to broadcast, 5
tratar de to try to, 11
tratar de apoderarse to try to seize, 11
trataron de they tried to, 11
trece thirteen, 2
treinta thirty, 2
tres three, 2
trescientos, -as three hundred, 11
el **triángulo** triangle, 2
triste sad, 11
trizas: se hace trizas it smashes into pieces, 11
el **trofeo** trophy, 3
el **trozo** piece, 9
tu(s) your (*fam. sing.*), 2
tú you (*fam. sing.*), 1
el **turismo** tourism, 10
el, la **turista** tourist, 12
turístico, -a: la guía turística tourist guidebook, 9

U

Ud. (abbreviation of *usted*) you (*pol. sing.*), 1
Uds. (abbreviation of *ustedes*) you (*pl.*), 1
último, -a: el último grito the last word, 10
un a, an, 2
un momento just a moment, 6
una a, an, 2
a la una at one o'clock, 2; **es la una** it's one o'clock, 2; **una vez** once, 7
la **unidad** unit, 1
uno one, 2
uno, -a (de) one (of), 7
unos, -as some, 2

usar to use, 6
usted (Ud.) you (*pol. sing.*), 1, 9
de usted your, 6
ustedes (Uds.) you (*pl.*), 1
de ustedes your, 6
la **uva** grape, 9

V

las **vacaciones** vacation, 6
vale it costs, 11
¿**cuánto vale?** how much does it cost? 11
valen they cost, 11
valenciano, -a from Valencia, 10
la **paella valenciana** hearty saffron-flavored dish of rice, meat, seafood and vegetables, 9
vamos let's go, 6
¿**si vamos . . .?** what if we go . . .? 7; **vamos a casa** let's go home, 3; **vamos a leer** let's read, 1; **vamos a ver** let's see, 2
van they go, 5
la **variedad** variety, 10
vario, -a various, 2
el **vaso** glass, 9
váyanse (*com.*) go away, 6
el **vecino, la vecina** neighbor, 1
el **vehículo** vehicle, 10
veinte twenty, 2
el **vendedor, la vendedora** salesperson, 2
vender to sell, 5
venir to come, 2
la **venta: en venta** on sale, 2
la **ventanilla** ticket window, 7
ver to see, 6
vamos a ver let's see, 2
el **verano** summer, 3
la **verdad: ¿verdad?** really? 2
right? 5; **es verdad** it's true, 3
verdadero, -a true, 7
verde green, 3
la **verdura** green vegetable, 9
el **vestido** dress, 11
vestir: la camisa de vestir dress shirt, 11
la **vez** (*pl.* **veces**) time, 7
a veces sometimes, 3; **dos veces** twice, 7; **otra vez** again, 5; **tal vez** perhaps, 9; **una vez** once, 7
la **vía: la Vía Láctea** Milky Way, 10
el **viaje** trip, 10
el **viajero: el cheque de viajero** traveler's check, 5
la **vida** life, 10
le salvaron la vida they saved his life, 10
el **viento: hace (mucho) viento** it's (very) windy, 3
el **viernes** Friday, 2
la **viñeta** vignette, 1
violeta violet, 10
la **visita** visit; visitor, 6
visitar to visit, 10
¡**viva!** long live!, 10

Spanish-English Vocabulary 381

vivir to live, **6**
vivo I live, **1**
el **vocabulario** vocabulary, **1**
el **volibol** volleyball, **3**
voltearla turn it over, **9**
volver (ue) to return, **7**
vosotras you (*f., fam. pl.*), **1**
vosotros you (*m., fam. pl.*), **1**
voy a I am going to (to indicate intention), **7**
la **voz: en voz baja** in a low voice, **11**

el **vuelo** flight, **5**
la **vuelta: dar una vuelta** to go for a walk, **7**
vuestro, -a, -os, -as your (*fam. pl.*), **6**

Y

y and, **1**
ya already, **2**; now, **10**; **ya está todo** everything's finished, **5**; **¡ya sé!** I know it! **6**; **ya viene** he (she) is coming, **10**
yo I, **1**
yo no not me, **5**; **yo no sé** I don't know, **2**

Z

el **zapato** shoe, **3**
los **zapatos de tenis** tennis shoes, **3**
la **zona** zone, **11**
el **zoológico** zoo, **10**

ENGLISH-SPANISH VOCABULARY

This vocabulary includes all the active words in the text of **Nuevos amigos.** These are the words listed in the vocabulary at the end of each unit. Spanish nouns are listed with the definite article. Spanish expressions are listed under the English words that the student would be most likely to look up.

The following abbreviations are used in this list: *adj.* adjective; *adv.* adverb; *com.* command; *dir.* direct; *f.* feminine; *fam.* familiar; *ind.* indicative; *inf.* infinitive; *m.* masculine; *obj.* object; *pl.* plural; *pol.* polite; *prep.* preposition; *pron.* pronoun; *sing.* singular; *sub.* subjunctive.

A

a un, una, **2**
above average (grade) aprovechado, -a, **2**
about como, **2**; sobre, **9**
academy la academia, **7**
accessory el accesorio, **11**
acquainted: be acquainted with conocer, **7**
across: across from frente a, **6**
activity la actividad, **1**
to **add** añadir, **9**
admission: admission ticket la entrada, **7**
advanced avanzado, -a, **3**
adventure la aventura, **7**
affectionate cariñoso, -a, **6**
after después de, **2**
afternoon la tarde, **3; good afternoon** buenas tardes, **1; in the afternoon** por la tarde, **3; this afternoon** esta tarde, **7**
again de nuevo, **6**
agent: customs agent el aduanero, **5**
ago: an hour ago hace una hora, **10**
ahead: a week ahead of time con una semana de anticipación, **10**
airplane el avión, **5**
airport el aeropuerto, **5**
algebra el álgebra (*f.*), **2**
all todos, **2**; todo, -a, -os, -as, **3, 7; all right** de acuerdo, **3; all the time** todo el tiempo, **7; I don't like it at all** no me gusta nada, **11**
to **allow** dejar, **11**
almost casi, **2**
already ya, **5**
also también, **3**
always siempre, **3**
A.M. de la mañana, **5**
American: North American norteamericano, -a, **6**
and y, **1**
angry enfadado, -a, **11**
animated: animated cartoon el dibujo animado, **7**

anniversary: silver wedding anniversary las bodas de plata, **7**
another otro, -a, -os, -as, **2, 3**
to **answer** contestar, **5; there's no answer** no contestan, **5**
apartment el apartamento, **6**
apple la manzana, **9**
April abril, **3**
arranged arreglado, -a, **10**
arrival la llegada, **5**
to **arrive** llegar, **5**
art: industrial arts las manualidades, **2**
as como, **3; as early as possible** a primera hora, **11; as far as** hasta, **10; as much** tanto, -a, **2; the same as** igual que, **11,** lo mismo que, **11**
to **ask** preguntar, **10**
at a, **2**; en, **5; at night** por la noche, **3,** de la noche, **5,** a la noche, **7; at one o'clock** a la una, **2; at ten o'clock** a las diez, **1; at the . . .** al (a + el), **2; at what time?** ¿a qué hora? **2**
athlete el, la atleta, **3**
August agosto, **3**
aunt la tía, **6; uncles and aunts** los tíos, **6**
automobile el auto, **2**
autonomous autónomo, -a, **2**
autumn el otoño, **3**
awful muy mal, **1**

B

bad mal, **1**
baggage el equipaje, **5; baggage claim** la sección de equipaje, **5**
ball el balón (basketball, volleyball, soccer ball), **3;** la pelota (baseball, tennis ball), **3**
ballet el ballet, **2**
ballpoint: ballpoint pen el bolígrafo, **2**
banana el plátano, **9**
bargain la ganga, **11**
to **bargain** regatear, **11**

baseball el béisbol, **3;** (the ball) la pelota, **3**
basketball el básquetbol, **3;** (the ball) el balón, **3; basketball hoop** la canasta, **3**
bat el bate, **3**
bathing: bathing suit el traje de baño, **11**
bathroom el baño, **5**
to **be** ser, **1**; estar, **5; be able** poder (ue), **7; be (very) hungry** tener (mucha) hambre, **5; be on the verge of** estar a punto de, **10; be pleasing to** gustar, **3; be shopping** estar de compras, **11; be . . . years old** tener . . . años, **6; be (very) thirsty** tener (mucha) sed, **9; be married** estar casado, **6**
beach la playa, **3**
beans los frijoles, **9**
to **beat** batir, **9**
beauty: thing of beauty la preciosura, **11**
because porque, **2**
beefsteak el bistec, **9**
before antes, **10**
beginner el, la principiante, **3**
behind detrás de, **5**
below abajo, **5; below average (grade)** suspenso, **2**
belt el cinturón (*pl.* cinturones), **3**
beside al lado de, **5**
best mejor, **7; the best (thing)** lo mejor, **9**
better mejor, **7; it would be better to . . .** mejor . . . , **7**
between entre, **5**
bicycle la bicicleta, **2; by bicycle** en bicicleta, **2; to ride a bicycle** montar en bicicleta, **3**
bigger: bigger than más grande que, **11**
bill la cuenta, **9**
biology la biología, **2**
birthday el cumpleaños, **11; to have a birthday** cumplir años, **11**
black negro, -a, **3**
blonde rubio, -a, **6**

blouse la blusa, 11
blue azul, 3
book el libro, 2
boot la bota, 3; **ski boots** las botas de esquiar, 3
booth: information booth la información, 5
boring aburrido, -a, 2
boy el chico, 1
braggart el fanfarrón, 3
bread el pan, 9
breakfast el desayuno, 9
brings trae, 9
brochure el folleto, 10
brother el hermano, 6; **brother(s) and sister(s)** los hermanos, 6
brown marrón, 3
to brown dorar, 9
bus el autobús, 2; **by bus** en autobús, 2; **school bus** el autobús escolar, 2
busy: it's busy está ocupado, 5
but pero, 2
butter la mantequilla, 9
to buy comprar, 5
by en, 2; **by bicycle** en bicicleta, 2; **by bus** en autobús, 2; **by car** en auto, 2; **by mail** por correo, 11; **by subway** en metro, 2
'bye chao, 1

C

café el café, 7
cafeteria la cafetería, 5
cake el bizcocho, 9
calculation: to do calculations hacer cuentas, 11
calculator la calculadora, 2
to call llamar, 5
camera la cámara, 5
can poder (ue), 7
car el auto, 2; el coche, 5; **by car** en auto, 2
card la tarjeta, 11; **credit card** la tarjeta de crédito, 11
Caribbean el Caribe, 9
cart el carro, 5
cartoon el dibujo animado, 7
to cash cambiar, 5
cashier: cashier's desk la caja, 11
cassette el casete, 9
category la categoría, 3
ceramics la cerámica (art), 2; (material), 11
cereal el cereal, 9
champion el campeón, la campeona, 3
to change cambiar de, 5
character carácter, 2
cheap barato, -a, 11
check la cuenta, 9; **traveler's check** el cheque de viajero, 5
cheese el queso, 9
chemistry la química, 2
cherry la cereza, 9
chicken el pollo, 9
children los hijos, 6

chocolate el chocolate, 9
to choose: let's choose a escoger, 1
city la ciudad, 2
claim el reclamo, 11; **baggage claim** la sección de equipaje, 5
class la clase, 2
classroom la clase, 1
clothes la ropa, 11
club el club, 7
coat el abrigo, 11
coffee el café, 9
coffeeshop el café, 7
cold: it's (very) cold out hace (mucho) frío, 3
color el color, 3
to come venir, 2; **to come in** pasar, 6
comfortable cómodo, -a, 6
comic(al) cómico, -a, 7
comic strips las tiras cómicas, 2
compass el compás (pl. compases), 2
complaint la queja, 11
complete completo, -a, 9
complication el lío, 7
computer la computadora, 2
concert el concierto, 7
contrary: on the contrary al contrario, 2
to cook cocinar, 9
cooking la cocina, 9
cool: it's cool out hace fresco, 3
corner la esquina, 9
cost: how much do they cost? ¿cuánto cuestan? 2; **how much does it cost?** ¿cuánto cuesta? 2, ¿cuánto vale?, 11; **it costs** cuesta, 2, vale, 11; **they cost** cuestan, 2, valen, 11
cotton el algodón, 11
course: of course! ¡por supuesto! 6; ¡cómo no! 11
court: tennis court la cancha de tenis, 3
courtyard: inner courtyard el patio, 1
crazy loco, -a, 7
credit: credit card la tarjeta de crédito, 11
crime el crimen, 7
to cry llorar, 9
cuisine la cocina, 9
cup la taza, 9
custard (baked) el flan, 9
customer el, la cliente, 11; **customer service department** la sección de quejas y reclamos, 11
customs la aduana, 5; **customs agent** el aduanero, 5
to cut cortar, 9

D

dad el papá, 6
dance el baile, 7
to dance bailar, 3
dark oscuro, -a, 11; **dark hair, complexion** moreno, -a, 6
daughter la hija, 6

day el día, 1; **every day** todos los días, 3; **specialty of the day** el plato del día, 9
dear querido, -a, 10
December diciembre, 3
to decide decidir, 5
deep hondo, -a, 9
delicious delicioso, -a, 9; rico, -a, 9; sabroso, -a, 9
to delight encantar, 11
department la sección, 11; **customer service department** la sección de quejas y reclamos, 11
desk: cashier's desk la caja, 11
dessert el postre, 9; **for dessert** de postre, 9
detective: detective movie la película policial, 7
diary el diario, 10
dictionary el diccionario, 2
diet la dieta, 9
difference la diferencia, 2
different diferente, 3
difficult difícil, 2
dining: dining room el comedor, 6
dinner la cena, 9; la comida, 9; **to have dinner** cenar, 9
disco la discoteca, 7
discount la rebaja, 2
dish el plato, 9
to do hacer, 5, 9; **do calculations** hacer cuentas, 11
door la puerta, 6
dollar el dólar, 2
double doble, 11
drawing el dibujo, 2
dress el vestido, 11
to drink beber, 5
dumb tonto, -a, 6

E

each cada, 3
early temprano, 2; **as early as possible** a primera hora, 11
easy fácil, 2
to eat comer, 5
education: physical education la educación física, 2
egg el huevo, 9
eight ocho, 2; **eight hundred** ochocientos, -as, 11
eighteen dieciocho, 2
eighty ochenta, 2
else más, 2; **what else?** ¿qué más? 2
embroidered bordado, -a, 11
employee el empleado, la empleada,
English (language) el inglés, 2
enough bastante, 2
to enter entrar, 5
entrance la entrada, 6
envy la envidia, 10; **what envy (I feel)!** ¡qué envidia! 10
eraser la goma, 2
evaluation la evaluación, 2

evening: good evening buenas noches, 1

every todo, -a, -os, as, 3; **every day** todos los días, 3; **every time** en todo momento, 3

everything todo, 3; **everything's finished** ya está todo, 5

exam el examen, 7

excellent excelente, so-bre-sa-lien-te, 2

exchange: money exchange la casa de cambio, 5

excursion la excursión, 10

excuse: excuse me perdón, 2; con permiso, 6; permiso, 7

expensive caro, -a, 11

extracurricular extracurricular, 2

F

fair la feria, 11

fall el otoño, 3

family la familia, 6; **family room** la sala de estar, 6

fantastic fantástico, -a, 3

far: far from lejos de, 5; **as far as** hasta, 10

fat gordo, -a, 6

father el padre, 6

favorite favorito, -a, 2, 3; preferido, -a, 2

February febrero, 3

to feel: feel like tener ganas de, 7

fifteen quince, 2

fifth quinto, -a (*adj.*), 11

fifty cincuenta, 2

film la película, 7

finally por fin, 2; finalmente, 11

to find encontrar (ue), 11

fine bien, 1

to finish terminar, 10

first primero, 5; primero, -o, -a, 11

fish el pescado, 9

five cinco, 2; **five hundred** quinientos, -as, 11

flat llano, -a, 9

flight el vuelo, 5

floor el piso, 11

food la comida, 9

foot el pie, 2; **on foot** a pie, 2

for por, 2; para, 3; **for what?** ¿para qué? 5

fork el tenedor, 9

forty cuarenta, 2

four cuatro, 2; **four hundred** cuatrocientos, -as, 11

fourteen catorce, 2

free: free time el tiempo libre, 6

French (language) el francés, 2; **french fries** papas fritas, 9

Friday el viernes, 2

friend el amigo, la amiga, 3

from de, 1; desde, 10

front: in front (of) delante (de), 5

fruit la fruta, 9; **fruit store** la frutería, 9

to fry freír, 9

frying pan la sartén, 9

fun divertido, -a, 3

funny gracioso, -a, 9

G

game el juego, 3; el partido, 3; **Olympic Games** los Juegos Olímpicos, 3

garage el garaje, 6

garden el jardín, 6

gate la puerta, 6

generally generalmente, 11

generous generoso, -a, 6

genius el genio, 2

geography la geografía, 2

geometry la geometría, 2

to get: get off bajar, 7

girl la chica, 1

glass el vaso, 9

glove el guante, 3

to go ir, 5; **go for a walk** dar una vuelta, 7; pasear, 7; **go out** salir, 7; **go up** subir, 5

gold el oro, 3; **gold medal** la medalla de oro, 3

good bueno, -a, 1; bien, 1; **good afternoon** buenas tardes, 1; **good evening** buenas noches, 1; **good morning** buenos días, 1; **good night** buenas noches, 1; **very good** buenísimo, -a, 9

goodbye adiós, 1

grandfather el abuelo, 6

grandmother la abuela, 6

grandparents los abuelos, 6

grape la uva, 9

great estupendo, -a, 3

green verde, 3; **green vegetable** la verdura, 9

group el grupo, 5

to guess: guess! ¡a adivinar! 3

guidebook la guía, 9

guitar la guitarra, 3

gymnastics la gimnasia, 3

H

hall el pasillo, 6

ham el jamón, 9

hamburger la hamburguesa, 9

hand la mano, 11

handkerchief el pañuelo, 11

handmade hecho, -a a mano, 11

handsome guapo, -a, 6

happiness la alegría, 10

hard difícil, 2

hat sombrero, 11

hate: I hate odio, 3

to have tener, 2; **(to eat or drink)** tomar, 7; **have a birthday** cumplir años, 11; **have dinner** cenar, 9; **have to** tener que, 7

he él, 1

heavy fuerte, 2

hello hola, 1; **hello? (on the phone)** ¡aló!, ¿bueno?, ¡diga!, ¿hola? 5

to help ayudar, 9; **help!** ¡socorro!, 2; **how may I help you?** ¿en qué puedo servirle? (*pol. sing.*), 11; **it can't be helped** no hay más remedio, 9

her (*poss.*) su(s), 5; de ella, 6

her le (*indir. obj.*), 9; ella (*obj. of prep.*), 9; (*dir. obj.*) la, 10

here aquí, 5

hey! ¡oye! 1

him él (*obj. of prep.*), 9; le (*indir. obj.*), 9; lo (*dir. obj.*), 10

his su(s), 5; de él, 6

history la historia, 2

home la casa, 6; **(to) home** a casa, 5; **make yourself at home** estás en tu casa (*fam. sing.*), 6

homework la tarea, 2

hoop: basketball hoop la canasta, 3

horrible horrible, 3

horror: horror movie la película de terror, 7

hot: it's (very) hot out hace (mucho) calor, 3

hour la hora, 2; **an hour ago** hace una hora, 10

house la casa, 6

how? ¿cómo? 1; **how are things?** ¿qué tal? 1; **how are you?** ¿cómo está? (*pol. sing.*), 1, ¿cómo estás? (*fam. sing.*), 1; **how old is (he/she)?** ¿cuántos años tiene? 6

how!: how handsome! ¡qué guapo! 6

how: how many? ¿cuántos, -as? 2; **how many times?** ¿cuántas veces?, 7

how: how much? ¿cuánto? 2; **how much do they cost?** ¿cuánto cuestan? 2; **how much does it cost?** ¿cuánto cuesta? 2, ¿cuánto vale? 11

hundred cien, 2, ciento, 11; **eight hundred** ochocientos, -as, 11; **five hundred** quinientos, -as, 11; **nine hundred** novecientos, -as, 11; **seven hundred** setecientos, -as, 11; **six hundred** seiscientos, -as, 11; **three hundred** trescientos, -as, 11; **two hundred** doscientos, -as, 11

hungry: to be (very) hungry tener (mucha) hambre, 2

hurry: in a big hurry apuradísimo, -a, 10

husband el esposo, 6; **husband and wife** los esposos, 6

I

I yo, 1

ice el hielo, 3

ice cream el helado, 7

to ice skate patinar en hielo, 3

idea la idea, 9

ideal ideal, 3

if si, 7; **what if we go . . .?** ¿si vamos . . .? 7

important importante, 6

in en, 1; **in front of** delante de, 5; **in order to** para, 3; **in person** en persona, 11

information: information booth la información, 5

intelligent inteligente, 6

interesting interesante, 2

international internacional, 5

to **interview** entrevistar, 7

invitation la invitación, 10

to **invite** invitar, 6

it (*obj. of prep.*) él, ella, 9; (*indir. obj.*) le, 9; (*dir. obj.*) lo, la, 10

item el artículo, 11

its su(s), 5

J

jacket la chaqueta, el saco, 11

January enero, 3

jeans los jeans, 11

jelly la jalea, 9

to **jog** correr, 3

judo el judo, 3

juice el jugo, 9

July julio, 3

June junio, 3

K

ketchup el catsup, 9

kilo(gram) el kilo (2.2 pounds), 9

kind amable, 6; la clase, 7

kitchen la cocina, 6

knife el cuchillo, 9

to **know** conocer, 7; **know a fact** saber, 7; **know how** (+ inf) saber (+ inf), 7; **I don't know** yo no sé, 2; **I know it!** ¡ya sé! 6

L

large grande, 11

last pasado, -a, 10; **last night** anoche, 10; **last week** la semana pasada, 11

late tarde, 2

later más tarde, 7; **see you later** hasta luego, 1

leather el cuero, 11

to **leave (behind)** dejar, 9

left: on the left a la izquierda, 5

lemon el limón, 9

less menos, 11; **less than . . .** menos de . . ., 11

let dejar, 11; **I'll let the purse go for . . .** le dejo la cartera en . . ., 11

let's: let's go! ¡vamos! (*com.*), 6; **let's see** a ver, 11

letter la carta, 5

lettuce la lechuga, 9

light (in color) claro, -a, 11; **(meal)** ligero, -a, 9

like como, 3

to **like** gustar, 3; **he (she) likes** le gusta, 3; **I don't like it at all** no me gusta nada, 11; **I like** me gusta, 3; **they like** les gusta(n), 9; **we like** nos gusta(n), 9; **you like** te gusta (*fam. sing.*), 3, le gusta (*pol. sing.*), 3, les gusta (*pl.*), 9

likewise igualmente, 6

limit: off limits prohibido, -a, 6

line la fila, 7

list la lista, 11

to **listen (to)** escuchar, 3

little pequeño, -a, 6; **a little** poca, 2

to **live** vivir, 6

living room la sala, 6

long: a long time mucho tiempo, 10

to **look: look at** mirar, 3; **look!** ¡mira! (*com.*), 2; **look for** buscar, 5; **look nice on** quedar bien, 11

lot: a lot mucho, 3

lot: a lot (of) mucho, -a, -os, -as, 2

love el amor, 7

luck: what luck! ¡qué suerte!, 5; ¡qué envidia! 10

lunch el almuerzo, 2

M

ma'am la señora, 1

made: made of de, 11; **made of plastic** de plástico, 11; **what's it made of?** ¿de qué es?, 11

magazine la revista, 2

magnificent magnífico, -a, 3

mail: by mail por correo, 11

main principal, 9

to **make** hacer, 5, 9; **make yourself at home** estás en tu casa (*fam. sing.*), 6

man el hombre, 2; el señor, 6

many muchos, -as, 2; **how many?** ¿cuántos, -as? 2

map el mapa, 5

March marzo, 3

to **mark** marcar, 10

marker el marcador, 2

market el mercado, 11

marmalade la mermelada, 9

married casado, -a, 6

match el partido, 3

mathematics las matemáticas, 2

matter: it doesn't matter! ¡no importa! 11

May mayo, 3

mayonnaise la mayonesa, 9

me mí (*obj. of prep.*), 9; me (*indir. obj.*), 9; me (*dir. obj.*), 10; **not me** yo no, 5; **with me** conmigo, 9

meal la comida, 9

meat la carne, 9

medal la medalla, 3; **gold medal** la medalla de oro, 3

to **meet** conocer, 7; **nice to meet you** mucho gusto, 1

melon el melón, 9

menu el menú, 9

Mexican mexicano, -a, 1

Mexican Americans mexicano americanos, 1

Mexico México, 5

milk la leche, 9

minute el minuto, 7

Miss la señorita, 1

mitt el guante, 3

mixup: what a mixup! ¡qué confusión! 5

mom la mamá, 5

moment: just a moment un momento, 6

Monday el lunes, 2

money el dinero, 2; **money exchange** la casa de cambio, 5

month el mes, 3

more más, 6; **more . . . than** más . . . que, 11; **more than . . .** más de . . ., 11

morning la mañana, 3; **good morning** buenos días, 1; **in the morning** por la mañana, 3, de la mañana, 5

most más, 6

mother la madre, 6

motorcycle la moto, 10

movie la película, 7; **detective movie** la película policial, 7; **horror movie** la película de terror, 7; **to show a movie** dar una película, 7; **Western** la película del oeste, 7

movies el cine, 7

Mr. (abbreviation of *señor*), 1

Mrs. (abbreviation of *señora*), 1

much: as much tanto, -a, 2; **how much** ¿cuánto?, 2; **how much do they cost?** ¿cuánto cuestan?, 2; **how much does it cost?** ¿cuánto cuesta? 2, ¿cuánto vale? 11; **so much** tanto, -a, 2; **that much** tanto, -a, 2

musical película musical, 7

music la música, 2

mustard la mostaza, 9

my mi, 2

N

name: his (her) name is . . . se llama . . ., 1; **my name is . . .** me llamo, 1; **what's his (her) name?** ¿cómo se llama él (ella)? 1

napkin la servilleta, 9

near cerca (de), 5

to **need** necesitar, 3

neighborhood el barrio, 11

neither ni, 9

net la red, 3

never nunca, 3

new nuevo, -a, 1

newspaper el periódico, 5

next próximo, -a, 7

nice simpático, -a, 7; it's (very) nice out hace (muy) buen tiempo, 3; to look nice on (clothing) quedar bien, 11; nice to meet you mucho gusto, 1; not nice antipático, -a, 6
night la noche, 3; at night por la noche, 3; de la noche, 5; a la noche, 7; good night buenas noches, 1; last night anoche, 10
nine nueve, 2; nine hundred novecientos, -as, 11
nineteen diecinueve, 2
ninety noventa, 2
no no, 1
noise el ruido, 7
noon el mediodía, 9
nor ni, 9
North American norteamericano, -a, 6
not no, 2; not me yo no, 5
notebook el cuaderno, 2
November noviembre, 3
now ahora, 2
number el número, 2; wrong number el número equivocado, 5
nylon el nilón, 11

O

o'clock: at one o'clock a la una, 2; at ten o'clock a las diez, 2; it's one o'clock es la una, 2; it's ten o'clock son las diez, 2
October octubre, 3
of de, 2; of the del (de+el), 2; of course! ¡por supuesto! 6
off: get off bajar, 7; off limits prohibido, -a, 6
offer la oferta, 11
office la oficina, 10
official oficial, 7
often a menudo, 3
old: to be . . . years old tener . . . años, 6; how old are you (is he/she)? ¿cuántos años tiene? 6
Olympic: Olympic Games los Juegos Olímpicos, 3
on en, 5; on foot a pie, 2; on sale en venta, 2; on the contrary al contrario, 2; on the left a la izquierda, 5; on the right a la derecha, 5; on the telephone por teléfono, 3
once una vez, 7
one un, una, 2
one uno, -a (de), 2, 7; that one ése, -a, 11; aquél, aquélla, 11; the one (made of) el (de), 11; this one éste, -a, 11
onion la cebolla, 9
only sólo (adv.), 1
opinion la opinión, 2
or o, 7
orange (color) anaranjado, -a, 3
orange la naranja, 9

orchard la huerta, 5
order el pedido, 11; in order to para, 3
organized organizado, -a, 10
other otro, -a, -os, -as, 2, 3
our nuestro, -a, -os, -as, 6
over: over there allá, 11

P

pack (a suitcase) hacer la maleta, 10
painting la pintura, 2
pan: frying pan la sartén, 9
Panama Panamá, 1
pants los pantalones, 11
parents los padres, 6
park el parque, 7
part la parte, 2
to participate participar, 3
party la fiesta, 7
passing (grade) aprobado, -a, 2
passport el pasaporte, 5
pastime el pasatiempo, 3
pastry la pastelería, la tarta, 9; pastry shop la pastelería, 9
patience la paciencia, 9
to pay pagar, 9
peach el melocotón, 9
pear la pera, 9
pen: ballpoint pen el bolígrafo, 2; fountain pen la pluma, 2
pencil el lápiz (pl. lápices), 2
people la gente, 7
pepper la pimienta, 9
per: per week por semana, 7
perfect perfecto, -a, 9
permission el permiso, 10
person: in person en persona, 11
Peru Perú, 1
philosophy la filosofía, 2
photo la foto, 6
photograph la fotografía, 6; take photographs tomar fotografías, 3
photography la fotografía, 2
physical: physical education la educación física, 2
physics la física, 2
picnic el picnic, 9
pie el pastel, 9
piece el trozo, 9
pineapple la piña, 9
pink rosa, 9
pity: what a pity! ¡qué pena! 1; ¡qué lástima! 7
pizza la pizza, 9
place el lugar, 5
plantain el plátano, 9
plan el plan, 10
to plan pensar (ie), 7; planear, 10
plastic el plástico, 11; made of plastic de plástico, 11
plate el plato, 9; small plate el platillo, 9
to play jugar (ue), 3; (a sport) practicar, 3; (a musical instrument) tocar, 9
please por favor, 1

pleasing: to be pleasing to gustar, 3
pleasure el placer, 11; it's a pleasure es un placer, 6
P.M. de la noche, 5
pocket el bolsillo, 5
pole el bastón, 3; ski poles los bastones de esquiar, 3
pond el estanque, 10
pool la piscina, 7
possible: as early as possible a primera hora, 11
post office correos, 5
postcard la postal, 5
potato la patata (Spain), 9
to practice practicar, 3
to prepare preparar, 9
present el regalo, 10
pretty bonito, -a, 6; lindo, -a, 6
price el precio, 2
prize el premio, 3
problem el problema, 2
program el programa, 7
to promise prometer, 11
Puerto Rico Puerto Rico, 1
purse la cartera, 5
to put poner, 9

Q

quality la calidad, 11
question la pregunta, 3
quickly rápido, 2

R

racquet la raqueta, 3
to rain: it's raining llueve, 2
rather bastante, 2
ready listo, -a, 10
really? ¿verdad? 2
receipt el recibo, 11
to receive recibir, 11
recess el recreo, 2
record el disco, 3
redheaded pelirrojo, -a, 6
reduced (in price) rebajado, -a, 11
to reserve reservar, 10
rest: the rest los demás, 3
restaurant el restaurante, 9
to return volver (ue), 7; regresar, 10
rice el arroz, 9
to ride: ride a bicycle montar en bicicleta, 3
right: all right de acuerdo, 3; on the right a la derecha, 5
right? ¿verdad? 5; ¿no? 5
rock (music) el rock, 7
room el cuarto, 6; dining room el comedor, 6; family room la sala de estar, 6; living room la sala, 6; waiting room la sala de espera, 5
to row remar, 10
ruler la regla, 2
to run correr, 3

English-Spanish Vocabulary   387

388   **For Reference**

there allí, 5; **over there** allá, 11
there: there is, there are hay, 2
these estos, -as, 9; éstos, -as, 11
they ellos, ellas, 1
thin delgado, -a, 6
thing la cosa, 6
to **think** creer, 5; pensar (ie), 7; **what do you think of . . .?** ¿qué te parece. . .? (*fam. sing.*), 6
thirsty: to be (very) thirsty tener (mucha) sed, 9
thirteen trece, 2
thirty treinta, 2
this este, -a, 9; **this afternoon** esta tarde, 7; **this one** éste, -a, 11
those esos, -as, 9; aquellos, -as, 9
thousand mil, 11
three tres, 2; **three hundred** trescientos, -as, 11
through por, 5
Thursday el jueves, 2
ticket el billete, 10; **ticket window** la ventanilla, 7
tie la corbata, 11
time la hora, 2; el tiempo, 6; la vez (*pl.* veces), 7; **a long time** mucho tiempo, 10; **a short time** poco tiempo, 10; **all the time** todo el tiempo, 7; **a week ahead of time** con una semana de anticipación, 10; **at what time?** ¿a qué hora? 2; **free time** el tiempo libre, 6; **to spend time** pasar, 6; **what time is it?** ¿qué hora es? 2
tip la propina, 9
tired cansado, -a, 11
to a, 2; para, 3; **to the** al (a + el), 2; **to where?** ¿adónde? 5
today hoy, 2
tomato el tomate, 9
tomorrow mañana, 3; **see you tomorrow** hasta mañana, 1
tonight esta noche, 7
too también, 3; **too much** demasiado -a, 11
total el total, 3
tourism el turismo, 10
tourist el, la turista, 11; turístico, -a, 9
traffic el tráfico, 9
traveler: traveler's check el cheque de viajero, 5
tree el árbol, 9
trip el viaje, 10; **pleasure trip** la excursión, 10
trophy el trofeo, 3
true: it's true es verdad, 3
to **try** probar, 9
Tuesday el martes, 2
tuna el atún, 9
twelve doce, 2
twenty veinte, 2
twice dos veces, 7
two dos, 2; **the two** los, las dos, 6; **two hundred** doscientos, -as, 11
typical típico, -a, 9

U

ugly feo, -a, 6
uncle el tío, 6; **uncles and aunts** los tíos, 6
under debajo (de), 9
United States los Estados Unidos (abbreviation EE.UU.), 1
up (there) arriba, 5
us nos, 9; nosotros, nosotras, 9
to **use** usar, 6

V

vacation las vacaciones, 6
very muy, 1; bien, 6; **very good** buenísimo, -a, 9; **very good (grade)** notable, 2
vegetable: green vegetable la verdura, 9
verge: to be on the verge of estar a punto de, 10
vignette la viñeta, 1
visit la visita, 6
visitor la visita, 6
voice: in a low voice en voz baja, 11
volleyball el volibol, 3; **(the ball)** el balón, 3

W

to **wait (for)** esperar, 5
waiter el camarero, 9
waiting: waiting area la sala de espera, 5
waitress la camarera, 9
to **walk** caminar, 10
to **want** querer (ie), 6
to **watch** mirar, 3
water el agua (*f.*), 9
watermelon la sandía, 9
we nosotros, nosotras, 1
weather el tiempo, 3; **the weather is very bad** hace muy mal tiempo, 3; **what's the weather?** ¿qué tiempo hace? 3
wedding: silver wedding anniversary las bodas de plata, 7
Wednesday el miércoles, 2
week la semana, 2; **last week** la semana pasada, 10; **per week** por semana, 7
weekend el fin de semana, 7
welcome bienvenido, -a, 6; **you're welcome** de nada, 1
well bueno, -a, 1; bien, 1
Western (movie) la película del oeste, 7
what lo que, 7
what? ¿cuál? 2; ¿qué? 2; **at what time?** ¿a qué hora? 2; **what else?** ¿qué más? 2; **what for?** ¿para qué? 5; **what if we go . . .?** ¿si vamos . . .? 7; **what's his (her) name?** ¿cómo se llama él (ella)? 1; **what's the weather?** ¿qué tiempo hace? 3
what!: what a lot of people! ¡cuánta gente! 7; **what a mixup!**

¡qué confusión! 5; **what a pity!** ¡qué pena! 1, ¡qué lástima! 7; **what a pretty room!** ¡qué cuarto tan bonito! 6; **what a shame!** ¡qué lástima! 7; **what envy I feel!** ¡qué envidia! 10; **what luck!** ¡qué suerte! 5, ¡qué envidia! 10
when cuando, 6
when? ¿cuándo? 2
where? ¿dónde? 1; **to where?** ¿adónde? 5
white blanco, -a, 3
who? ¿quién? 1
whole todo, -a, -os, -as, 6
why? ¿por qué? 2; **why don't we . . .?** ¿por qué no . . .? 5
wide largo, -a, 11
wife la esposa, 6; **husband and wife** los esposos, 6
to **win** ganar, 3
window: ticket window la ventanilla, 7
windy: it's (very) windy hace (mucho) viento, 3
winter el invierno, 3
to **wish** desear, 11
with con, 2; **with me** conmigo, 9
without sin, 10
woman la señora, 6
wool la lana, 11
to **work** trabajar, 3
to **write** escribir, 5
wrong: wrong number el número equivocado, 5

Y

year el año, 3
yellow amarillo, -a, 3
yes sí, 1
yesterday ayer, 10
you (*subj.*) tú (*fam. sing.*), 1; usted (*pol. sing.*) (abbreviation Ud.), 1; vosotros, vosotras (*fam. pl.*); ustedes (*pl.*) (abbreviation Uds.), 1
you (*dir. obj.*) te (*fam. sing.*), 10; lo, la (*pol. sing.*), 10; los, las (*pl.*), 10; os (*fam. pl.*), 11
you (*indir. obj.*) te (*fam. sing.*), 9; le (*pol. sing.*), 9; les (*pl.*), 9; os (*fam. pl,*), 11
you (*obj. of prep.*) ti (*fam. sing.*), 9; usted (*pol. sing.*), 9; ustedes (*pl..*), 9
young: young people los jóvenes, 11
your(s) tu(s) (*fam. sing.*), 2; su(s) (*pol. sing. and pl.*), 5; vuestro, -a, -os, -as (*fam. pl.*), 6; de usted (*pol. sing,*), 6; de ustedes (*pol. pl.*), 6
youth la juventud, 7

Z

zero cero, 2

INDEX

The numbers and letters after each entry refer to the unit and section where the entry first appears.

UNIT 3, 90, HBJ Photo; 91(tl), HBJ Photo/Daniel Aubry; 91(tr), HBJ Photo/Peter Menzel; 91(b), HBJ Photo/David Phillips; 92(tl, bl, br), HBJ Photo; 92(tr) Tony Freeman/Photo-Edit; 94, Peter Menzel/Stock, Boston; 96(all), HBJ Photo/Earl Kogler; 98(both), HBJ Photo/Daniel Aubry; 102(tl), HBJ Photo; 102(tc), Stuart Cohen; 102(tr), HBJ Photo/ Daniel Aubry; 102(cl), HBJ Photo; 102(c), HBJ Photo/Sam Joosten; 102(cr), HBJ Photo/ Daniel Aubry; 102(b), Duomo Photography; 106(l), HBJ Photo; 106(r), HBJ Photo/Mark Antman; 108(l), Stuart Cohen; 108(c), HBJ Photo; 108(r), HBJ Photo; 109(tl), HBJ Photo/ Daniel Aubry; 109(r), HBJ Photo/David Phillips; 109(bl), Jeff Persons/New England Stock; 111(tl), John Elk III/Wheeler Pictures; 111(r), M. Reichenthal/The Stock Market; (bl) Albertson/Stock, Boston; 111(inset), Craig Aurness/Woodfin Camp & Assoc.; 112(tl), Stuart Cohen; 112(tr), Stuart Cohen; 112(tlc), HBJ Photo/Stephanie Maze; 112(trc), Stuart Cohen; 112(cl), Stuart Cohen; 112(cr), Stuart Cohen; 112(blc), HBJ Photo/ Stephanie Maze; 112(brc), HBJ Photo/Gerhard Gscheidle; 112(bl), HBJ Photo; 112(br), Stuart Cohen

UNIT 4, 120, Luis Villota/The Stock Market; 121(tl), Joe Viesti; 121(tr), Luis Villota/The Stock Market; 121(bl), Joe Viesti; 121(br), Luis Villota/The Stock Market; 125(tl), Marc Dubin/Wheeler Pictures; 125(tr), Marc Dubin/Wheeler Pictures; 125(bl), Peter Menzel/ Wheeler Pictures; 125(br), Joe Viesti; 126(tl), Peter Menzel/Wheeler Pictures; 126(tr), Frank Fournier/Contact/Woodfin Camp & Assoc.; 126(cr), Marc Dublin/Wheeler Pictures; 126(bl), Peter Menzel/Wheeler Pictures; 126(br), M. Reichenthal/The Stock Market; 127(tl), Dan Budnick/Woodfin Camp & Assoc.; 127(tr), Luis Villota/The Stock Market; 127(bl), Lawrence Migdale/Photo Researchers; 127(br), Gerhard Gscheidle/The Image Bank; 128(t), Kal Muller/Woodfin Camp & Assoc.; 128(cr), Joe Viesti; 128(bl), Joe Viesti; 128(c), Lee Boltin; 128(bc), Joe Viesti; 128(br), Joe Viesti; 129(t), Joe Viesti; 129(c), Richard Steedman/The Stock Market; 129(bl), Luis Villota/The Stock Market; 129(br), Joe Viesti; 130(t), Luis Villota; 130(c), Victor Engelbert/Photo Researchers; 130(b), HBJ Photo/Peter Menzel; 131(t), Enrique Shore/Woodfin Camp & Assoc.; 131(l), HBJ Photo/ Peter Menzel; 131(r), HBJ Photo/Peter Menzel; 131(b), HBJ Photo/Peter Menzel; 132(t), Earl Dibble/Photo Researchers; 132(l), Anthony Edgeworth/The Stock Market; 132(r), HBJ Photo/David Phillips; 132(b), John Mason/The Stock Market; 133(t), Jim Rudnick/ The Stock Market; 133(c), HBJ Photo/Stephanie Maze; 133(b), HBJ Photo/David Phillips;

UNIT 5, 134, Jim Rudnick/The Stock Market; 135(all), HBJ Photo/Daniel Aubry; 136(all), HBJ Photo/Daniel Aubry; 138, HBJ Photo/Daniel Aubry; 139(t), HBJ Photo/Daniel Aubry; 139(b), Miguel/The Image Bank; 140, HBJ Photo/Daniel Aubry; 144, HBJ Photo/ Daniel Aubry; 146(both), HBJ Photo/Daniel Aubry; 147, Jim Cartier/Photo Researchers; 149(both), HBJ Photo/Daniel Aubry; 150(both), A. G. E. Fotostock/Wheeler Pictures; 153, HBJ Photo/Daniel Aubry; 154, HBJ Photo/Daniel Aubry; 155(both), HBJ Photo/ Daniel Aubry; 158(all), Joe Viesti; 159(tl), Luis Giner/The Stock Market; 159(r), Joe Viesti; 159(bl), Owen Franken/Stock, Boston

UNIT 6, 162, HBJ Photo/Stephanie Maze; 163(all), HBJ Photo/Stephanie Maze; 164(both), HBJ Photo/Stephanie Maze; 165, HBJ Photo/Stephanie Maze; 168(all), HBJ Photo/Stephanie Maze; 170, HBJ Photo/Stephanie Maze; 171, HBJ Photo/Stephanie Maze; 172(all), HBJ Photo/Stephanie Maze; 173, HBJ Photo/Stephanie Maze; 177(all), HBJ Photo/Stephanie Maze; 181, Stephen McBrady/PhotoEdit; 183, HBJ Photo/Stephanie Maze; 184(tl), HBJ Photo/Stephanie Maze; 184(tcl), HBJ Photo/Stephanie Maze; 184(tcr), HBJ Photo/Stephanie Maze; 184(tr), HBJ Photo/Stephanie Maze; 184(cl), Stuart Cohen; 184(clc), HBJ Photo/Stephanie Maze; 184(c), HBJ Photo/Stephanie Maze; 184(crc), HBJ Photo/Stephanie Maze; 184(cr), HBJ Photo/Stephanie Maze; 184(bl), HBJ Photo/Stepha-nie Maze; 184(bcl), HBJ Photo/Stephanie Maze; 184(bc), HBJ Photo/Stephanie Maze; 184(bcr), HBJ Photo/Stephanie Maze; 184(br), HBJ Photo/Stephanie Maze

UNIT 7, 192, HBJ Photo/David Phillips; 193(all), HBJ Photo/David Phillips; 194(both), HBJ Photo/David Phillips; 196(tl), HBJ Photo; 196(tr), HBJ Photo/David Phillips; 196(bl), Stuart Cohen; 196(bc), Stuart Cohen; 196(br), HBJ Photo; 198(both), HBJ Photo/David Phillips; 199(both), HBJ Photo/David Phillips; 204, HBJ Photo/David Phillips; 207, HBJ Photo; 208(both), HBJ Photo/David Phillips; 209(all), HBJ Photo/David Phillips; 213, HBJ Photo; 214(tl), HBJ Photo/Oscar Buitrago; 214(tr), HBJ Photo/David Phillips; 214(bl), HBJ Photo/David Phillips; 214(br), HBJ Photo/David Phillips

UNIT 8, 222, HBJ Photo/Daniel Aubry; 223(both), HBJ Photo/Daniel Aubry; 225(all), HBJ Photo/Daniel Aubry; 227(t), Joe Viesti; 227(c), Stephanie Maze/Woodfin Camp & Assoc.; 227(b), Owen Franken/Stock, Boston; 228(t), Albertson/Stock, Boston; 228(l), Robert Frerck/Woodfin Camp & Assoc.; 228(r), Frank Fournier/Contact/Woodfin Camp & Assoc.; 229(tl), Michelle Burgess/The Stock Market; 229(tr), H. Wendler/The Image Bank; 229(bl), Joe Viesti; 229(br), Porterfield/Chickering/Photo Researchers; 230(t), Richard Steedman/The Stock Market; 230(c), Martha Cooper/Peter Arnold, Inc.; 230(b), Lee Boltin; 231(t), Joe Viesti; 231(cl), John Mason/The Stock Market; 231(cr), Claudia Parks/The Stock Market; 231(b), Howard Millard; 232(tl), HBJ Photo/Peter Menzel; 232(tr), Loren McIntyre/Woodfin Camp & Assoc.; 232(cl), Joe Viesti; 232(cr), Joe Viesti; 232(b), Viviane Holbrooke/The Stock Market; 233(t), HBJ Photo/Peter Menzel; 233(cl), Loren McIntyre/Woodfin Camp & Assoc.; 233(cr), Loren McIntyre/Woodfin Camp &

Assoc.; 233(bl), Ian Strange/Photo Researchers; 233(br), Jacques Jangoux/Peter Arnold, Inc.; 234(t), F. Gohier/Photo Researchers; 234(cl), Joe Viesti; 234(cr), Peter Menzel; 234(b), F. Gohier/Photo Researchers; 235(t), HBJ Photo/Daniel Aubry; 235(c), HBJ Photo/Daniel Aubry; 235(b), HBJ Photo/Peter Menzel

UNIT 9, 236, HBJ Photo/Daniel Aubry; 237(tl), HBJ Photo; 237(tr), HBJ Photo/Oscar Buitrago; 237(b), HBJ Photo/Daniel Aubry; 239(t), HBJ Photo/Bob Daemmrich; 239(b), HBJ Photo; 244(all), HBJ Photo/Earl Kogler; 246(both), HBJ Photo/Daniel Aubry; 250, HBJ Photo/Rodney Jones; 252(both), HBJ Photo; 258, HBJ Photo/Mark Antman; 259, HBJ Photo/Daniel Aubry; 261(tl), HBJ Photo/Stephanie Maze; 261(tr), Stuart Cohen; 261(bl), HBJ Photo/Mark Antman; 261(br), Anne Heimann/The Stock Market; 264, HBJ Photo; 265, HBJ Photo

UNIT 10, 268, HBJ Photo/Daniel Aubry; 269(all), HBJ Photo/Daniel Aubry; 270, HBJ Photo/Rodney Jones; 271(both), A. G. E. Fotostock/Wheeler Pictures; 274(both), HBJ Photo/Daniel Aubry; 275(both), Joe Viesti; 277(t), Bruce Hayes/Photo Researchers; 277(cl), Luis Villota/The Stock Market; 244(c), A. G. E. Fotostock/Wheeler Pictures; 277(cr), Stephanie Maze/Woodfin Camp & Assoc.; 277(b), HBJ Photo; 278(all), HBJ Photo/Rodney Jones; 279, Robert Frerck/Woodfin Camp & Assoc.; 282(l), Joe Viesti; 282(lc), Peter Menzel/Wheeler Pictures; 282(rc), Stephanie Maze; 282(r), Joe Viesti; 284(all), HBJ Photo/Daniel Aubry; 285(all), A. G. E. Fotostock/Wheeler Pictures; 288(t), HBJ Photo; 288(b), A. G. E. Fotostock/Wheeler Pictures; 290(l), Joe Viesti; 290(r), HBJ Photo; 294(l), A. G. E. Fotostock/Wheeler Pictures; 294(r), Claudia Parks/The Stock Market; 295, Dr. Jean Lorre/Photo Researchers

UNIT 11, 298, HBJ Photo/Peter Menzel; 299(tl), HBJ Photo; 299(tr), HBJ Photo; 299(b), HBJ Photo/Stephanie Maze; 300(t), HBJ Photo/Stephanie Maze; 300(c), HBJ Photo/Arturo Salinas; 300(b), HBJ Photo/Stephanie Maze; 306(all), HBJ Photo/Stephanie Maze; 307, HBJ Photo/Stephanie Maze; 308, HBJ Photo/Stephanie Maze; 309, HBJ Photo/Stephanie Maze; 312, HBJ Photo/Stephanie Maze; 313(l), Benn Mitchell; 313(r), HBJ Photo/Stephanie Maze; 314, HBJ Photo/Stephanie Maze; 319, HBJ Photo/Stephanie Maze; 321, HBJ Photo/Stephanie Maze; 325(l), Jules Bucher/Photo Researchers; 325(r), Benn Mitchell

UNIT 12, 328, HBJ Photo/Gerhard Gscheidle; 329(both), Benn Mitchell; 330, Stuart Cohen/The Stock Market; 331(l), G. Schiff/Photo Researchers; 331(r), Benn Mitchell; 331(b), Benn Mitchell; 332, Stuart Cohen; 333(t), Joe Viesti; 333(cl), Luis Castañeda/The Image Bank; 333(cr), Luis Castañeda/The Image Bank; 333(b), Craig Aurness/Woodfin Camp & Assoc.; 334(tl), Luis Castañeda/The Image Bank; 334(tr), Joe Viesti; 334(bl), Luis Castañeda/The Image Bank; 334(br), Robert Frerck/The Stock Market; 335(tl), Luis Castañeda/The Image Bank; 335(tr), Luis Castañeda/The Image Bank; 335(cl), Jonathan Blair/Woodfin Camp & Assoc.; 335(cr), Joe Viesti; 335(b), Joe Viesti; 336(tl), Joe Viesti; 336(tr), Joe Viesti; 336(cl), Joe Viesti; 336(cr), Luis Villota/The Stock Market; 336(b), Claudia Parks/The Stock Market; 337(tl), M. C. Magruder/The Image Bank; 337(tr), David Hiser/The Image Bank; 337(cl), John Lewis Stage/The Image Bank; 337(cr), Gary Cralle/The Image Bank; 337(b), Harvey Lloyd/Peter Arnold, Inc.; 338(tl), Paolo Gori/The Image Bank; 338(tr), David Hiser/The Image Bank; 338(cl), John Dominis/Wheeler Pictures; 338(cr), Gerhard Gscheidle/Peter Arnold, Inc.; 338(b), John Dominis/Wheeler Pictures; 339(all), Joe Viesti; 340(tl), Enrique Shore/Woodfin Camp & Assoc.; 340(tr), Luis Villota/The Stock Market; 340(cl), Joe Viesti; 340(cr), Joe Viesti; 340(b), Joe Viesti

ART CREDITS   Agustín Fernández: 16, 32, 33, 37, 38, 40, 42, 62, 64, 67, 81(b), 95(b), 96, 97, 99, 100, 107, 124, 137, 147, 174, 202, 210, 238, 245, 247, 249, 257, 306 and 320
Manuel García: 56, 57, 88, 89, 116, 117, 118, 119, 160, 162, 188, 190, 191, 220, 221, 266, 267, 296, 297 and 327
Len Ebert: 17, 73, 74, 76, 77, 81(c), 101, 240, 253, 255, 303 and 311
Anita Lovitt: 106, 270, 283 and 324
Susan Dietrich: 142, 179 and 182
Kathi Branson: 123, 143, 205